The anthropological romance of Bali 1597–1972

Cambridge Studies in Cultural Systems

Clifford Geertz, editor

1 The anthropological romance of Bali 1597–1972: Dynamic perspectives in marriage and caste, politics and religion
James A. Boon

2 Sherpas through their rituals
Sherry B. Ortner

Illustration of 'A King from the Island Bally or Galle' in the seventeenth-century German voyage literature edited by L. Hulsius (1620). See Chapter I. (Photographed by Division of Rare Books, Firestone Library, Princeton University).

The anthropological romance of Bali 1597–1972

Dynamic perspectives in marriage and caste, politics and religion

JAMES A. BOON

Associate Professor of Anthropology
Cornell University

CAMBRIDGE UNIVERSITY PRESS

Cambridge
London New York Melbourne

Published by the Syndics of the Cambridge University Press
The Pitt Building, Trumpington Street, Cambridge CB2 1RP
Bentley House, 200 Euston Road, London NW1 2DB
32 East 57th Street, New York, NY 10022, USA
296 Beaconsfield Parade, Middle Park, Melbourne 3206, Australia

First published 1977

Printed in the United States of America

Library of Congress Cataloging in Publication Data

Boon, James A

The anthropological romance of Bali, 1597–1972

(Cambridge studies in cultural systems; 1)

Bibliography: p.

1. Ethnology – Indonesia – Bali (Island) 2. Bali (Island) – Social life and customs. I. Title.
II. Series.
GN635.I65B66 301.29′598′6 76-19626
ISBN 0 521 21398 3

Contents

Thanks to Olivian

Della menatapnya sejenak, lalu tersenyum. Ada sesuatu yang ke-ibu2an dalam pandangan serta senyumnya itu. 'Apakah semua klient anda tidak bersalah?'

'Begitulah kata para juri. Dan memang merekalah yang bertugas mengadili.'

Della menghela napas panjang dan mengangkat bahu. 'Anda menang,' ujarnya . . .

(Ind. Gardner: 74)

'Mang, 'Dek, Balik, ajak Tili, 'Mang!

Preface

Because of the special nature of anthropological-historical research, often more individuals and institutions deserve thanks for their assistance than the actual results seem to warrant. In light of this fact, I hesitate to confess that the following acknowledgements should in fairness be even more extensive.

An initial study-trip to Indonesia (May–July, 1971) was made as Ford Foundation Consultant to assist Clifford Geertz in a survey of social science work in Java and Bali. Thanks are due Jack Bresnan and everyone then in the Jakarta Ford office for their help, especially Ted Smith who provided generous aid with procedural matters on this and a later trip. Sol Tax and Sam Stanley at the time kindly arranged for my leave from the Center for the Study of Man, Smithsonian Institute.

The fieldwork proper was funded by an N.I.M.H. Combination Research Fellowship (1971–73) which enabled my wife and daughter and myself to reside in southwest Bali January–November, 1972. I express gratitude to Professor Koentjaraningrat for his recommendation of the research as suitable for Indonesian sponsorship by the Lembaga Ilmu Pengetahuan Indonesia.

Among the many informative Balinese who provided the living substance of this study, a special part was played by (*almarhum*) I Gde Ktut Buwana who tirelessly responded to my awkward queries. Bapak Alit Bajra and his wife and family opened their home to us, and I Gde Made Ardika brought pleasure to work with his lively powers of observation and much-needed sense of humor. Thanks also to I Gusti Ngurah Rai Mirsa and I Gde Astawa for their time and to I Gusti Ngurah Bagus of Bali Museum and I Made Widyana and others at the Fakultas Hukum, Universitas Udayana, Den Pasar for their cooperation.

That my wife and I were suffering a serious tropical disease that eventually precluded fieldwork in northern Bali explains (along with the island's demographic density) our occasional sense of identification with the bird in the haiku:

> An exhausted sparrow
> in the midst
> Of a crowd of children

Yet the men within the masses – our friends and neighbors – received us warmly, a fact perhaps attributable more to our toddler's gregarious charms than to any professional skills of our own. Moreover, in 1957 Clifford and Hildred Geertz had left behind in southwest Bali something that augmented the pleasure (and, I like to hope, the scholarly value) of my family's subsequent stay in Tabanan: fond memories among informants, passed on to their children, of relating to anthropologists and, consequently, high hopes on confronting another one. A fieldworker could ask nothing more important of his predecessors.

At the University of Chicago David Schneider, Milton Singer, and Paul Friedrich provided advice in planning and executing fieldwork and in writing a doctoral dissertation based on its results. Portions of the present study that figured in that dissertation have benefited from the influence of these three teacher-scholars. In particular D. Schneider's insistence on cultural models and M. Singer's emphasis on traditional bases of innovation pervade this account.

The archival and historical sections were completed at the Institute for Advanced Study, Princeton, New Jersey. Here Carl Kaysen and many members and visitors in social sciences and historical studies facilitated interdisciplinary research. Continuous discussions with Clifford and Hildred Geertz enriched the time at Princeton. Also, a summer grant-in-aid from the Wenner-Gren Foundation for Anthropological Research and funding from Duke University for proofing the final manuscript are acknowleged with appreciation.

Several Indonesianists and scholars of social theory provided forums for discussing material with colleagues and students. Conferences organized by Alton Becker and Aram Yengoyan at the University of Michigan, by Benedict R. O'G. Anderson at the Indonesian Literature Conference, University of Wisconsin, and by Bruce Lawrence and Richard Fox at Duke University were very important for my own work, and they evidenced the exciting current state of Indonesian and Southeast Asian studies and of cross-cultural work on Asian religions. Clifford Geertz at the Institute for Advanced Study, James Siegel at Cornell University, and Milton Singer at the University of Chicago arranged for me to test ideas on various discerning audiences. Other colleagues and students who have been helpful either through extensive conversations or in passing comments include in particular James Peacock, and also Mahadev Apte, Ed Boer, Robert Conkling, James Fox, Ernestine Friedl, Steve Lansing, Mark Leone, Harry Levy, Philip McKean, Mark and Angela Hobart, Sherry Ortner, Lawrence Rosen, Jean Taylor, W.O. Wolters, and Hervé Varenne.

Thanks also to Walter Lippincott and to Jennifer Stevens, Kathy Barnes, Amy Jackson, Dina Smith and to my wife's and my own parents for invaluable practical help.

All research was conducted in Indonesian supplemented with Balinese; no interpreters were used. The area of investigation (principally Tabanan District) is heavily bilingual, and virtually any male the least analytically inclined is fluent in Indonesian – the language of the schools – as well as commoner Balinese. Some are adept in courtly, Sanskritized Balinese as well. All translations from sources listed with Dutch or Indonesian titles in the bibliography are my own. In accordance with N.I.M.H. provisions I have altered the names of actual persons who appear in this and other publications based on fieldwork.

Spelling of Balinese terms follows that used in the excellent Dutch-English translation series listed in the bibliography under *Bali Studies* . . . (1960, 1969) except that 'Ksatriya' is spelled 'Satria' and 'Wesya' is 'Wesia'; for simplicity's sake diacritical marks are omitted. Indonesian terms are spelled according to the 1972 orthographic reform. For both Balinese and Indonesian, letters are pronounced approximately as in English; however, Balinese final vowels are lengthened and stressed, and in Indonesian words English 'ch' is spelled'c.' We indicate Indonesian as opposed to Balinese by 'Ind;' Dutch terms should be self-evident. The complex matter of low, middle, and high levels in Balinese is discussed briefly in Kersten's introductory grammar (1948: 7–14); yet the sociolinguistics of the island has barely begun. The persistent confusion of spelling standards for Balinese, Kawi, and Archipelago Sanskrit remains a handicap in philological studies of Bali's many-languaged textual materials (cf. Hooykaas 1964c: 13–14). In investigations of living social systems, however, this particular problem is less crippling, since articulate informants are often as amused by a misspelled term as a mispronounced one; and they consider neither an insurmountable obstacle to communication.

The different parts of this study have been organized integrally. The playful chapter titles of Part I are meant to suggest the development from casual curiosity to sophisticated analysis in the history of cross-cultural encounters in Bali. I feel this analytic review of dated source materials is crucial in understanding current developments in Balinese religion and politics or lasting patterns in marriage and caste. Nevertheless, for the reader interested solely in the 'ethnographic crunch', who doubts the relevance of any history of ideas, I have begun Part II with a summary recapitulation of basic Balinese society and culture. The interrelation of our 'temporal perspective' with modern social and cultural processes is particularly clear in Chapter 4, in which I try to show how an indigenous Balinese sense of history supports options in social organization, and in Chapter 9, in which enduring literary and religious images are related to the ebb and flow of time in society. The significance of the latter discussion would be lost, I think, to the artistic or philological enthusiast who refused to traverse the sociological and political thicket of Chapters 7 and 8 beforehand.

This study risks alienating several parties. In a sense it asks questions of social customs that philologists and historians often ask of texts and documents, and it asks questions of texts that anthropologists often ask of social customs. Put most argumentatively, we are concerned with the ritual of subsistence and politics and the needs of status and belief. We hope to show how Balinese rules and values of imaginative expressions mesh with rules and values of strict behavior, and more generally how ideas and actions interpenetrate.

Two portions of this study have appeared in somewhat different form as journal articles: much of Chapter 4 as 'The Progress of the Ancestors in a Balinese Temple

Group, pre-1906–1972,' reproduced from *The Journal of Asian Studies* XXXIV: 7–25, 1974; part of Chapter 6 as 'The Balinese Marriage Predicament – Individual, Strategical, Cultural,' reproduced from the *American Ethnologist* 3: 191–214, 1976.

One might think of 'Bali' as anthropology's 'Shakespeare.' An author might do so somewhat defensively to justify yet another book about Bali. Look how far we must go, he can muse, to overtake publications on the 'Bali' of world literature. Such musings are not to imply that Bali is worthier than other tidy islands with two-million-plus inhabitants. But for particular reasons to be discussed, the corpus of its Indo-Pacific social and cultural forms was richly textured by native authors, has been concordanced and interpreted by a distinguished line of cross-cultural readers, and provides continuing challenges to understanding. In the massive library of world ethnography, Bali, both comic and tragic, would seem to represent something analogous to a few all-encompassing folios of varying patterns of meaning.

J.A.B.

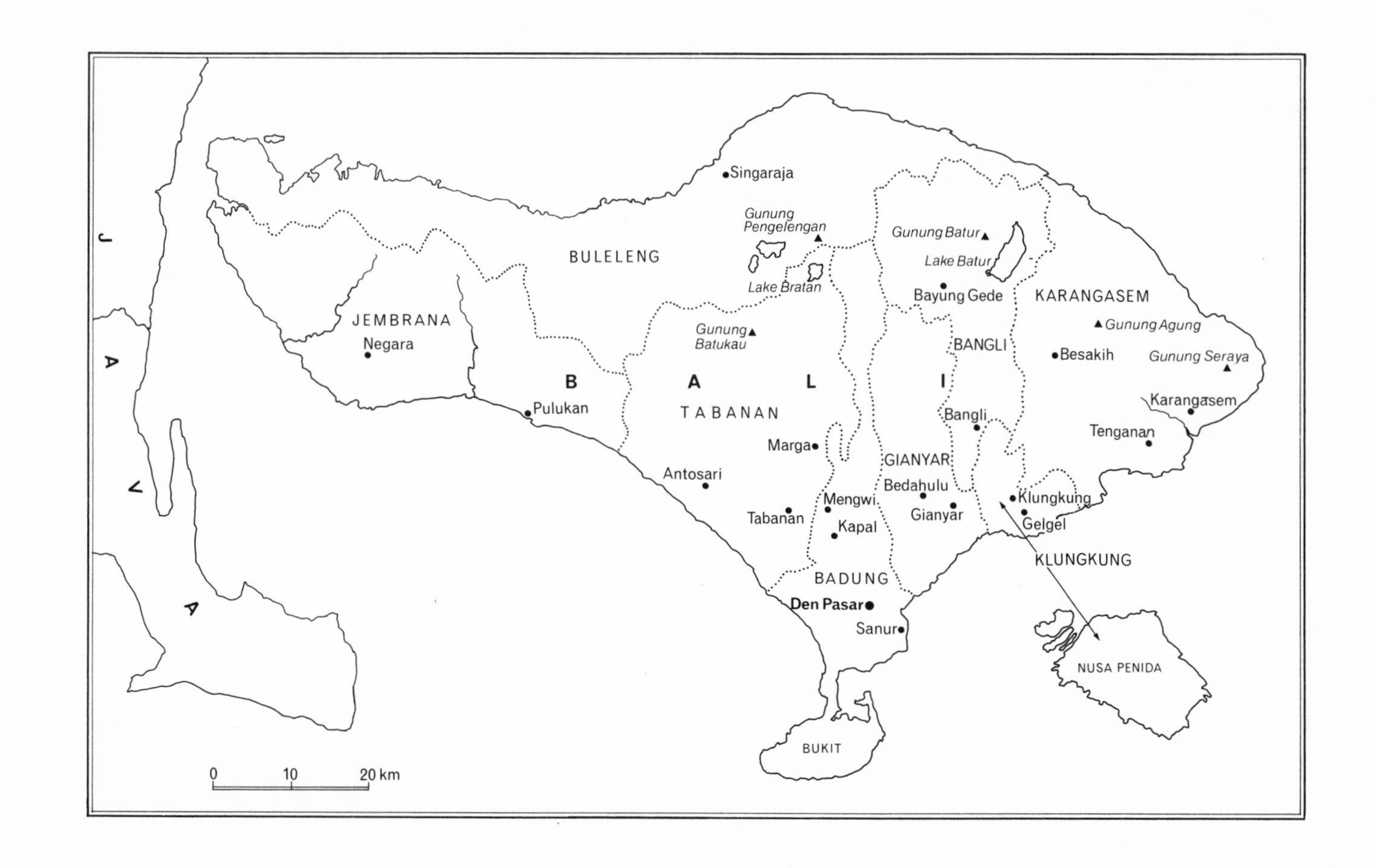

JAVA
BALI
Singaraja
Gunung Pengelengan
BULELENG
Lake Bratan
Gunung Batur
Lake Batur
Bayung Gede
KARANGASEM
Gunung Agung
Besakih
Gunung Seraya
Karangasem
Tenganan
JEMBRANA
Negara
Gunung Batukau
BANGLI
Pulukan
TABANAN
Bangli
Marga
GIANYAR
Antosari
Bedahulu
Mengwi
Tabanan
Kapal
Gianyar
Klungkung
Gelgel
KLUNGKUNG
BADUNG
Den Pasar
Sanur
NUSA PENIDA
BUKIT
0
10
20 km

Introduction
Beyond epic

On maps with a transverse mercator projection, Bali – in the very center of the Indonesian archipelago, which comprises the largest and most populous nation of Southeast Asia – lies about half as far from India as Hawaii. The same might be said of its Indo-Pacific culture.

This study combines fieldwork analysis, archival research, and the application of comparativist schemes of social institutions. It introduces Balinese studies to the nonspecialist by reviewing the history and direction of anthropological views of the island, and it interprets the interrelation of ideas and actions involving subsistence, marriage, caste, and the religious and political qualities of space. We are in search of more adequate holistic images of Balinese culture than those conveyed in the labels ordinarily applied: 'Third World' by planners, 'Hindu' by the Indonesian religious establishments, 'paradise' by sixteenth-century sailors as well as their twentieth-century bohemian successors, 'pork-eating, noncircumcising heterodoxy' by surrounding ardent Muslims, 'marriers of father's brother's daughter' by standard anthropological kinship theory, and many more.

Simple factual specifications on Bali are intriguing but ultimately unenlightening. In the Southeast Asian scheme of things, the island harbors one of those 'miniature outposts of plains civilization' (Burling 1964: 8) which benefits from monsoonal rains and whose dramatic irrigated terraces have yielded rich harvests of rice since at least the ninth century A.D. It is possibly the courts of Bali that are described by emissaries in the sixth-century Chinese *History of the Liang Dynasty*. Bali next appears in inscriptions as the seat of the tenth-century, South-Asian-style Varmadeva dynasty whose Sanskrit titles 'indicate that the rulers considered themselves to be scions of the Satria family' (Sarkar 1970: 46). It seems that subsequently Indo-Javanese culture was introduced by Udayana, whose sons (including Erlangga) continued until 1077. Little else can be guessed until 1343:

In the first part of the 13th century, Bali passed under Javanese hegemony again, because, according to the testimony of Chau Ju-kua, Bali was among the fifteen vassal States of Java. After the fall of Kadiri in 1222 A.D., she seems to have snapped the bond of yoke, because Paramesvara Sri Hyang ning hyang Adilancana bore a title signifying political independence. But this spell of independence was of short duration, as king Krtanagara of Java sent a military expedition to Bali in 1284 A.D. and imprisoned the king. The death of Krtanagara in 1292, however, signalized

> the reassertion of Balinese independence, but this was again quenched in blood in the Javanese military expedition of 1343 A.D., in which Gajah Mada distinguished himself. According to tradition preserved in the *Pamancangah*, the first capital was set up at Samprangan (about modern Gianyar) but *Usana Java* described the place to be Gelgel. These were the greatest days of Majapahitan imperialism; it ensured rapid transformation of Bali under the impact of Indo-Javanese influences which had started infiltrating into Bali since the 11th century. Indeed, it is clear from the decrees of 1394 and 1398 that Bali was still a dependency at the close of the 14th century A.D. If we now look back upon the History of Bali during the fourteenth century, we can say that the year 1343 was a turning point in the History of Bali, as it ensured a period of full Indo-Javanese-Balinese cultural synthesis and thereby provided a matrix for a refugee civilization from Java after the Muslim conquest (Sarkar 1970: 47–8).

As we shall see later, the ultimate significance of this turning point and the nature of this 'refugee civilization' are still being determined.

Bali's estimated current population is around 2.2 million, with an additional 0.2 million Bali-Hindus in the western part of neighboring Lombok, possibly subjected by Bali's eastern kingdom Karangasem as early as the eighteenth century (cf. Crawford 1820: 136). These millions are compressed on Bali into less than 6,000 square kilometers (including nearby Nusa Penida), less than 20 percent of it suitable for double-irrigated rice harvests and over 30 percent comprised of unproductive wasteland and critical forest reserves (cf. Raka 1955). Population has soared throughout this century. In 1921 Lekkerkerker records it as 859,400; the total for the colonial census of 1930 was 1,101,393. The Indonesian national census of 1961 was 1,782,529, and the election registration figure of 1971 was 2,106,264 (Hanna 1972a: 2). None of these figures is reliable but the broad trend is obvious. Since the 1960s the old favored varieties of rice have been replaced by the less delectable high-yield strains (now mechanically hulled) associated with Asia's 'Green Revolution', but production still falls short of the island's needs (Ravenholt 1973, Hanna 1972c). Moreover, in Bali as in Java a priority government program is the transmigration of village groups to the Outer Islands where they can establish outposts of wet-rice technology. In Bali, however, the indisputably top-priority program is tourism, the impact of which is concentrated in a small triangle of south-southeast Bali stretching between the airport on the island's sandspit, the capital Den Pasar, and several artisan and beachside communities eastward (McKean and Bagus 1971, Hanna 1972b).

Everyone has heard of Bali, if not in touristic lore saluting this supposed tropical Shangri-la, then in news dispatches concerning either the devastating volcano eruption in 1963 that obliterated lives, villages, temples, and precious paddy, or the massacres during 1965–6 that eliminated tens of thousands of suspected Communist party sympathizers. In Bali as elsewhere in Indonesia this aftermath (as much over land as politics) to the attempted coup in Jakarta appears to have marked the end of a luxuriant proliferation of partisan organizations since independence in 1948.

These topical specifications suggest many epithets for Bali other than 'land of a thousand temples:' overpopulated, underfed, intensely politicized, ecologically perilous, violent. Taken together and in the island's superficially serene context, what do they mean? In this study such isolated facts of history, subsistence, population pressure, and political tragedy will be related to complex patterns of values and actions in Balinese culture. Certain areas neglected in earlier research receive special attention: the connections among distant localities, apart from the defunct political and military organization of precolonial states; the process of title and status mobility in a changing society; and the complementarity in Bali between principles of caste and principles of marriage. We move across the history of ideas of Bali to analyze flexibilities in basic social, political, and economic institutions and profound religious, ritual, and literary concerns. To lend the whole a thematic coherence, we develop along the way an extended analogy between Bali's dynamic, lustrous culture and Indo-European principles of 'romance.'

Whatever Epic may mean, it implies some weight and solidity; Romance means nothing, if it does not convey some notion of mystery and fantasy (Ker 1957:4).

'Romance' – no frivolous epithet this, but a highly charged concept from comparative world literature and the history of ideas concerning the relation between social rules, literary images of historical change, and the beliefs and practices of different components of a political and religious hierarchy. In its abstract sense as a view of society and history, romance emerges out of epic. Epic posits constant, consistently principled, heroic familial aristocracies whose leaders establish the lawful and the just at the expense of the enemies of right. Romance portrays vulnerable, disguised protagonists, partial social misfits who sense surpassing ideals and must prove the ultimate feasibility of actualizing those ideals often against magical odds. In principle, epic legitimates a ruling elite, explains the sacred underpinnings of its authority, and portrays the expansion of its system of culture and law. Romance qualifies such solid, stolid, architectonic achievements in the blood line; it envisions sacred forces less limited to, controlled by, and correlated with temporal authority. Romance detects tears in the hierarchical fabric, and its task is to stitch them in time. While the distinction between epic and romance is usually applied to literature, it can reflect on cultures as well.[1]

Of course, the labels themselves are only relative. Every epic – whether expressed in cultural forms or literary texts or, as usual, both – contains seeds of romance; and every romance harbors souvenirs of epic. In general, epic forms project the more grave image of aristocratic heroics. Romance properly concerns champions rather than heroes; they are, sociologically speaking, unsuitable candidates for sacred elevation, but they are surrounded by signs and tokens of semimiraculous birth, prone to mystical insights, and acquainted with the natural and rustic orders more intimately than their privileged aristocratic counterparts.

Epic is a monumentalization of the ruling authority, the highborn singing their own achievements to themselves. Romance is a popularization that embraces vernacular concerns, a compromise between courtly standards and the surrounding sub-literate world. Romance studiously incorporates local native lore into the imagery of the political and religious elite. Thus, for example, the great Arthurian romances of twelfth-century Europe hearken wistfully back to the epic days of King Arthur but themselves deal with post-heroic episodes of fallible adventurers who encounter the Druidic magic of forests, the sacralia of Christ, and the new-found wonders of romantic epiphanies of love.

The two strains of Western literature often isolated as 'first epic' (for example, *Song of Roland*), 'then romance' (for example, *Yvain*) are consolidated in Hindu literary genres. Yet throughout Indo-European traditions the epic attitude stresses birthright, propitiation of the gods, clashes of good and evil, and the eventual victory of legitimate political and religious authority; it is weighty. Romance reveals more personalized individuals, earthy champions in mystic contact with divine protectors as they engage the complex world; it is fantastic. The romance strain of South Asian literary materials possibly developed after the epic strain. But the two are intimately intertwined in those tales and legends collected and recorded as the *Ramayana* and the *Mahabharata*, this 'library of opera' dating from 400 B.C. to 400 A.D. in India (Van Buitenen 1973: xxv), and still presented in courtly Javanese arts and performed everywhere in Bali. For us the essential point is that the romance characteristics of these South Asian sources have been highlighted in Bali and indeed augmented in its social life. While the pre-Islamic Javanese social and religious context possibly echoed the epic aspects of Hindu texts, the Balinese social and religious context that perpetuated and elaborated these same sources after Java became Islamized came to reflect their romance aspects in its marriage rules, its concepts of mystical powers, its theories of individual love, and much more.

The same point can be put more boldly. If, for example, the *Mahabharata* is composed according to both a 'baronial tradition' and a 'newer and less baronial imagination' (Van Buitenen 1973: xix), then Java, we can conjecture, accentuated the former and Bali, we are sure, accentuated the latter. The South Asian literary cycles contain many implicit models for sociocosmological systems; consider, for example, 'the tangle of the Adiparan, which begins, one might say, with folktale, moves into myth then romance and dynastic legend intermingled with something like hagiography, and only then, never abandoning these threads, winds them into the fabric of a gradually emerging epic' (Hiltebeitel 1974: 230). Whereas Hindu-Javanese courts styled themselves after the implicit dynastic-epic dimensions, or appear to have done so from the records that remain, Hindu-Bali grew increasingly to reflect the dimensions of romance. Particularly when seen from a comparativist perspective, the workings of Balinese marriage, caste-status, and political authority today conform more to principles of romance than to principles of epic. Such dynamics lend Bali the air of a social, and literary, romance in action.

Balinese literature and ritual often evoke an ideal golden age of harmonious hierarchical order in a well tuned cosmos. This age is identified with Java and with the elite perpetuators of Javanese courts who supposedly conveyed heightened civilization to Bali. While we do not know whether the civilization of Majapahit Java was in actuality epical, the important point is that many Balinese think it was. The ritual manuals of Brahmana priests in Bali try to emulate such a Brahmanical age where 'the baronage is in league with brahmindom, and brahmindom is allied with the baronage' in directing the ultimate rites of religious and political life. On this epic image as well, the Netherlands modeled its colonial administration. But other portions of Balinese literature, ritual, and social rules place value on the recurring interruptions in this hierarchical order and on the incursion of mystic revelation at certain times and places for certain individuals. These elements of Balinese culture highlight social change, romantic adventure, and shifts and tensions in the religious and political hierarchy. Moreover, in both Java and Bali the Hindu literary and dramatic view of life ebbs and flows above a satirical, sometimes farcical, undercurrent. The fool-like Indonesian clowns – beloved of the people and the god-kings alike – who persistently reflect and reject courtly comportment, attitudes, and obsessions, without ever overthrowing them, are like a persistent promise of romance even where the epic vision seems to have won out. Even in the more stately dramatic and literary images of royal Java, the clowns execute pratfalls amidst the perfected hierarchies between gods and men and between rulers and subjects. The clowns suggest the ever present impending necessity to dismantle, to adapt, to humanize, even to vulgarize courtly schemes, at least temporarily, in order to survive. Bali, then, is the macrohistorical realization of this promise of the clowns. It is the latest – or last? – adaptation, vernacularization, and reorientation of the hierarchies of Hindu-Buddhist Indonesia.

The traditional pliability of the Balinese social order was long neglected by outside observers for historical and sometimes for political reasons. Early philologists discerned in large part the rigid epic side of Balinese life and history, presumably in continuity with Java, because they relied on the literary texts of Brahmana priests and ruling courts which are the mainstay of a static view of religion and society. But at other levels of the social order, exceptions to the hierarchy have always been crucial. And many developments in modern Bali concerning caste, marriage, religion, and politics can be explained only in reference to the traditional means of understanding adjustments in the status quo.

This then is part of the romance of Bali: an alternate outlook on society and history implicit in social rules, ritual, and literature. This dynamic view typically characterizes not the epical, and apical, ranks of the hierarchy, nor the bottom ranks whose members often revere the apex as mortals revere gods, but the active middling families and locales as they seek to gain advantage from new contexts – for example, in the context of modern Bali. Yet even modern Bali is not precisely a 'new' context since it conforms to articulate patterns in old Balinese ideas of historical and cultural flux.

A holistic concept of Bali as romance might appear a throwback to anyone familiar with earlier Dutch views on the island. Bali was first perceived and repeatedly described as 'feudal.' The label evoked certain prerogatives of its overlords and priestly castes, in particular their enhanced religious worth and favored treatment under law for criminal offenses. The Dutch could thus justify liberating Balinese peasants from a vestigial Dark Age. But proclaiming Bali feudal obscured crucial aspects of landownership, subsistence production, and the nature of the bonds joining one Balinese to another, whether his equal, superior, or subordinate.[2]

The question thus becomes: if not feudal, what? And the preliminary answers are best shrouded in syllogisms. One such syllogism, perhaps useful in providing bearings for the non-Asianist, is this: If pre-Islamic Java were Renaissancelike in its elaborate schemes, certainly rivaling Plotinus or Plato, of the interrelation of cosmos, art, and society, then Bali was and is more loosely mannerist. The supposedly powerful and centralized courts of Hindu-Buddhist Java recorded their control of vast stretches of fertile plains. History tells us that Bali then served as a repository for the grandiose schemes of divine monarchy, caste divisions, religious purity, and stratified political authority, many of whose proponents apparently abandoned Java upon the advent of Islam. But ethnography reveals that this stately apparatus was somewhat top-heavy for such an islet. Bits and pieces of Majapahit Java's majestic florescence were squeezed into the few small plains and many ravines of a probably underpopulated mountainous acreage the size of Delaware. If this process had involved merely a few formal migrations, it would have been rather like condensing the whole of Versailles – values, ideas, pageants, authority, literature, and architecture – onto the Isle St. Louis or packing the belief system of the Vatican and its supporting Italian states off to a shrunken Sardinia. As we shall see, it is more likely that Balinese hierarchy emerged less abruptly during a centuries-long give and take with East Java and other sources of Hindu-Buddhist traditions. While Bali's court centers continued to manifest intransigence and distance, the hierarchical patterns they embodied doubtless filtered downward. Although actual rajas were few, most commoners could be sufficiently acquainted with high-caste practices to assume rajalike airs vis-à-vis their younger brothers, sons or nephews, and they could demand honorifics and general forms of respect to express this relationship. The courts, of course, remained exclusive and they kept tight control on access to certain privileges and kinds of expertise. Yet, we can surmise that, as many expressions of status were in a relative sense popularized, policies of irrigation control, principles of marriage, and other social and political correlates of the symbolic schemes, along with the schemes themselves, were adjusted and refined to engage the more properly Balinese conditions, with the elaborate scope and scale of the earlier Javanese infrastructure now gone.

At the close of the sixteenth century, a few Dutch sailors stumbled into this complex situation, thus initiating the long adventure of trying to understand the process from outside, even as new events were continually altering it. The often overlooked flexibility of Bali has grown particularly conspicuous during the postcolonial era, especially since 1965. And regardless of how Bali evolved from pre-Islamic Java, it is certain that within Bali today the dynamics of romance recur.

By reiterating the notion of romance, I hope to create a field of associations between Balinese social, religious, and literary patterns. After reading this study, it should seem appropriate that, for example: (1) South Asian motifs have been incorporated into Panji tales which, however, articulate a distinctly Balinese marriage system and a perhaps Oceanic value on individual love; and (2) although Balinese rice bins are filled with a regularity that suggests social stability, the continual shifts and realignments in actual residence, status relations, and political forces – often conceptualized as caste bonds and divisions among temple congregations – allow baronial ambitions to rise and fall, ebb and flow, ricocheting through diverse sectors of society, including communist ones, even occasionally to surge out of the lower echelons in the form of mystic quests to sacred fonts of divine authority according to ideals that are as much political as religious.

Balinese culture is, then, a romance of ideas and actions which, like any romance, implicitly plays against an alternative self-image. Within Balinese traditions this image of fixed order, which we would call an alter-epic, is called in stratificational terms *warna* or caste, in political terms 'divine kingship,' and in historical terms 'Majapahit Java.' This implicit epic is the set of social and cultural ideas Bali persistently wanes from and waxes to but has probably never quite embodied and perhaps never conceivably could. Yet more often than not it is this alter-epic that has been proffered by outside observers as the simplified essence of Bali, thus obscuring the far more alluring romance.

Part I
Temporal perspectives

> Every perspective requires a metaphor, implicit or explicit, for its organizational base.
>
> (Burke 1957: 132)

The case could be argued that, by itself, the favored anthropological endeavor called fieldwork rarely if ever provides an original holistic theory of a particular culture. In the broad task of conceptualizing the very nature of a body of ethnographic data – in the properly ethnological task – fieldwork merely confirms past assumptions while adding a few details hitherto overlooked. Of course ethnographic descriptions rely on field data, but they derive from an ethnological tradition as well; and this fact is worth stressing, even celebrating. It points up the side of anthropology that is a cumulative, humanistic discipline at times incorporating, to borrow a recent felicitous phrase from Margaret Mead, 'echoes and analogies from four centuries and many minds' (1974: 908). Indeed, anthropology is more a cumulative discipline than the portable, ruggedly individual laboratory it often tries to appear. Accordingly, before broaching any ethnography, one does well to consider how the general frameworks and approaches it relies on ever materialized. The following chapters attempt not to explain the history of Balinese ethnology, but to suggest it as a set of intriguing problems – in intellectual and social history, as well as in anthropology – each worth more elaborate study in its own right.

1. Bali-tje: a discursive history of the earlier ethnology (post-1597)

The first images of Balinese culture were happily inscribed on Western consciousness following a stop there in 1597 by Cornelis de Houtman's renowned *eerste schipvaart* to the East Indies. Evidence exists that Magellan's expedition had sighted so-called Java Minor some eighty years earlier, that the Portuguese had contacted Bali in midcentury, and that Sir Francis Drake and Thomas Cavendish predated Houtman's arrival by a few years (Hanna 1971a: 1–2). The island's name was known from a list of the Lesser Sundas obtained in 1521 by Magellan's scribe Pigafetta (Lach 1965: 2). But the initial representations of Balinese customs to enter the Western record were fruits of Houtman's final, perhaps least productive, and definitely most appealing stop.

Hindu spectacles

Most twentieth-century commentators on the history of Dutch-Balinese relations draw pleasure from the fact that they began not with a shot, but a seduction:

> The island had nothing to offer in the form of trade, but there were other attractions – a carefree way of life and comely women . . . Two young men found these charms irresistible, and the fleet sailed without them (Masselman 1963: 96).

Covarrubias exaggerates this point in relating that Houtman and his men 'fell in love with the island' and 'after a long sojourn . . . [they actually stayed less than a month] returned to Holland to report the discovery of the new "paradise"; others refused to leave Bali' (1937: 29).

We have no clear idea why these sailors abandoned their shipmates. The official report on Bali was not quite ecstatic, merely relatively positive in light of difficulties experienced by the beleaguered expedition in establishing trade agreements in Java. To the weary explorers, Bali became a pause for recuperation before returning home. Their favorable accounts of their experience produced the original image of what we might appropriately deem 'dear little Bali' (Bali-*tje*).

From the anecdotal to the sensational

Maps and reports of Bali were completed and published by 1598. Its size and mountainous profile lent themselves well to sixteenth-century guides to navigation; Bali's different volcanoes are identifiable from the first drawings. In 1598 a map appeared which illustrated the rajas and battling armies mentioned in a verbal account.[1] This chart is called 'crude and sloppy' in a modern commentary, but it is better appreciated as a different sort of illustration, a visual caption to communicate that the name 'Baly' stood for a mountainous, many rivered, war-waging island. Moreover, this conceptual portrait accurately situates the sacred mountain Gunung Agung and reveals the complex river drainage through the southern plains.

In 1625, the first thorough-going English summary of Dutch impressions of Bali (which does not forget to mention British claims of prior contact) is included by the Jacobean Samuel Purchas in his edited collection of the discovery literature left unpublished at the death of Richard Hakluyt:

> . . . Baly they called Hollandiola, for the fertilitie; there they watered.
>
> They sent to the King, who accompanied the Messenger to the shoare in a Chariot drawne with Buffals, holding the Whip in his owne hands, having three hundred followers, some with flame-formed Crises and long Speares, Bowes of Canes with poysoned Arrowes. Hee was feasted in Dishes of solid Gold. The Land is an equall and fertile plaine to the West, watered with many little Rivers (some made by hand) and so peopled that the King is able to bring into the field three hundred thousand foot, and one hundred thousand horsemen. Their horse are little like Islanders, their men blacke and using little Merchandize, but with Cotton Cloth in Prawes. The Iland is in compasse about twelve Germane miles. Their Religion is Ethnike, ordered by the Brachmanes or Bramenes, in whose Disciplines the King is trayned up. They have also Banianes which weare about their neckes a stone as bigge as an Egge with a hole in it, whence hang forth three threds; they call it Tambarene, and thinke the Deitie thereby represented: they abstaine from flesh and fish, but not (as the Java Pythagoreans) from Marriage. Once they may marry, and when they dye their Wives are buried quicke with them. Every seventh day they keepe holy, and many other Holidayes in the yeare besides with solemne Ceremonies. Their Wives burne with their dead Husbands. Here they heard of Captaine Drakes being there eighteene yeares before, and called one Strait by his name. The King observeth state, is spoken to with hands folded, by the best. The Quillon hath power there as the Chancellor in Poland. Two of their companie forsooke them and stayed on the Iland. And of the two hundred fortie nine there were now left but ninetie. In February they began their returne (Purchas 1625).

Purchas distilled his overview from the more lengthy Dutch logs and journals, taking several accompanying plates as guides to the primary features of Balinese life. These early descriptions include William Lodewyckszoon's log of the expedition, which appeared in 1598, Steerman Jacob Janszoon Kackerlack's supplementary journal of the same year, and the diary of midshipman Aernout Lintgenszoon, although the availability of the latter's account to the seventeenth-century reading public remains obscure (Rouffaer and Ijzerman 1915, 1925, 1929).

The most noticeable stylization in Purchas's account is that the several test stops and hesitating contacts along the Balinese coast described by Lodewycks are condensed into a single grandiose arrival. In Purchas's version it appears as if the Balinese king and his entourage had been awaiting the advent of the worthy West, when actually through the week diverse islanders were leading a depleted crew to water here, an anchorage there, later asking the sailors if they hailed from the Moluccas.[2] Purchas's sensationalism aimed at evoking a sense of splendiferous trade in commodities, in order to revitalize the mercantile endeavor under James I and then Charles I. By 1625 it was Holland rather than Spain that had to be challenged; accordingly Purchas highlighted the glory of Dutch cross-cultural contacts, a glory that by implication could as easily belong to Britain's monarch.

Lodewycks' original lacked such theatrics. For example, to commemorate the initial arrival of Balinese on board a Dutch vessel, he mustered nothing dramatic, merely the simple note that 'many inhabitants boarded us' (Rouffaer and Ijzerman 1915: 197). This 'first connected description of the island of Bali from the European viewpoint' (1915: 197n) is relatively straightforward, methodical, and even-handed. The merchandise-minded sailor mentions the weaving skills of Bali's western province Jembrana. He itemizes fauna, fruit and metals, describes weapons, and assesses Balinese military strength, and he makes notes on the lack of spices and the availability of drugs. Finally we are told that Balinese engage in little or no sea trade and that Chinese come here to exchange swords and porcelain for cloth.

Such pedestrian details aside, Lodewycks' more general views of Bali were limited by the typologies at his disposal. His label of Balinese as 'black' may have stemmed from his observation of the Papuan slaves who often boarded the ship Mauritius, or it may simply reflect a residual category not directly related to phenotype. Lodewycks knew at least that Balinese were not 'Moors'; in fact he alludes to the islanders' religion by deeming them 'Heathens' who 'pray to whatever they first meet in the morning.'[3] As the modern commentary explains, 'Heathen' here means non-Mohammedan, which is the most pertinent observation Lodewycks could have made about Balinese religion, arriving there from coastal Java. Yet his remarks entered the historical record to be repeated, nearly verbatim, a century later in an Englishman's report on Bali: '[the Balinese] are exceeding Brutish People and the Simplest of Heathens. Their God is whatever they first cast their Eye on in the Morning . . . (Frick and Schweitzer 1700: 109). Following a century of Protestant reformism, heathen has come to imply 'simplest.' The same remark that began as a distinction in sectarian types – Christian/Mohammedan/Heathen – has become a protoevolutionary index of backwardness. Such is the crooked path of progress in ethnology.

Kings, not chiefs

Like his colleagues, Lodewycks found most impressive the office of 'king,' as observed when the ship's emissaries were conducted to Gelgel. He is most interested in the indigenous royal monopolies in external trade and in policies against the export of rice, to insure that the surplus would be consumed yearly in elaborate feasts by the innumerable inhabitants. Apart from this, Lodewycks provides the first simplified, vividly distorted portrait of Bali as an authoritarian maharajadom:

Besides the King is a governor that they call Quillor. He rules over the island as does the great chancellor in Poland. And beneath these stand many other lords, each governing his quarter in the name of the king, which occurs in great harmony (*eendrachticheyt*) . . . (1915: 201).

Finally, Lodewycks rounds things off with a paraphrase of a royal Balinese chronicle (*babad*), which relates how some years earlier the king's close blood-relatives had attempted a conspiracy against him and were subsequently banished to a neighboring island. As we shall see, this native text receives much less attention than the regal splendor of the apparently legitimate king atop his sedan chair, although the chronicle of bloodshed would have served as a more appropriate blazon of Balinese royalty. Only centuries later, after Berg's work (1929) on the sixteenth-century *Pamancangah* texts from Gelgel, did it become completely clear that these first Dutch visitors had stumbled not into a stable realm of an unchallenged divine monarch, but into a generation-long battle between brothers and uncles and nephews for control of the Gelgel palace, marked by the disastrous participation in a war in Java:

When early in 1597 the first Dutchmen arrived at the coast of Blangbangan, the savage war (*woesteoorlog*) between Pasuruhan and Blangbangan was in full swing (Rouffaer and Ijzerman 1929: xlvi).

But even as this was recognized, Dutch scholars tended to assume this state of affairs was only a temporary lapse in a normal stabilized and centralized golden age (*glorietijdperk*) rather than the general conditions and mechanics of statehood in the Balinese system. The Dutch had skirted in and out and round about a perpetual civil war, only to gain the impression of stability from the ritual surfaces of timeless central authority.

Kackerlack's much briefer piece (1598) goes on explicitly to designate the island of Baly a kingdom (*Conickrijk*). The regal trappings, complete with scribes and priests, prevented these observers from conceptualizing Bali as tribal chiefdoms such as those known from North America. (Later, however, a chiefly level [*hoofden*] had to be added to handle certain local complexities in the chain of political authority.) Kackerlack dwells on the generosity of the islanders who brought hogs, ducks, and many fruits and foodstuffs to the sailors; the Dutch in turn, reciprocated with gifts for the king – coral drinking glasses, shoes, mirrors, and so forth (1925: 169–71). And Kackerlack distinguishes what he heard about, such as a king on a buffalo cart, from what he actually observed, such as the lay of rice fields.

Aernout Lintgens' story is by contrast a thorough-going narrative, complete with vivid scenic details and artfully postponed surprises. He relates his week-long adventire (February 9–16, 1597) in establishing contact with the king's ministers, in instigating correspondence with the Dutch captain, and in arranging for the delivery of the latter's gifts before his own reception at the royal palace in Gelgel. With the help of Jan the Portuguese, apparently coming from Mataram and serving as translator, Lintgens amasses much information that can only be called ethnographic, and more often than not it arose from questions posed by the king of Bali. Here is the West's first report on Balinese marriage:

Then the King asked us how old we were; I answered 'around twenty-five, and Roedenborrich around twenty-three,' then if we were all married; to this I answered 'no,' then I told how in our land the men were not married before twenty years of age, then in great surprise did he communicate that in the island of Baelle the manner was for youths to marry at twelve years and that daughters are betrothed at nine years of age (1929: 77).

Lintgens describes the mode of paying the king homage, the deformed courtiers, a royal procession, the outlying palaces; we learn of the ministers' wives and concubines and impressive material wealth. He obtains a list of important 'cities' and assessments of strength of arms and overall population. We also hear of a Balinese view as to why the Dutch-Bali relations are certain to be unusually friendly:

. . . the minister (*kijlloer*) . . . said that we and they are totally alike, for they saw that we eat pork meat, while no Turks or Moors do this, and that moreover we eat meat also on Friday and Saturday, while no Spaniards or Portuguese do . . . (p. 81).

(Of special note are the structuralist systematics of this indigenous Balinese theory of cultural variation. It employs three oppositions: meat/not meat, pork/other meat, and sometimes/always; and it combines them differently to articulate three categories of mankind.)

The most practical information provides additional details of Bali's commercial isolationism: whenever foreigners arrived from outside to purchase cotton goods, they were not permitted to travel inland and could only stay as long as their business required, 'so that they would not know anything about the Balinese treasures' (p. 87). Lintgens discloses how he exaggerated Dutch military strength to the king's aide and, showing him a map of Europe, claimed Holland was larger than China and included Germany, Scandinavia, and a portion of Russia (p. 90). There follows a sixteenth-century version of *The King and I* in which an astounded monarch, after viewing himself in the triptych mirror decorated with the image of a Dutch ship, first hears tell of northern winters and ice, and then suffers a geopolitical Copernican revolution – seeing that by European maps extending to the Philippines, *Baelle* is neither the center of the universe nor even very significant (p. 93). That at least is what Lintgens thought the king suffered.

Lintgens' story then tells how the Dutch emissaries at last arrive at the royal seat in Gelgel. There are brief but vivid descriptions of religious processions and ceremonies – 'some praying to the sun, some the moon, and some an ox' (p. 86) – of pleasure gardens graced with turtledoves and many other birds, and finally of the palace itself, with its steps, distinct sections, and slave quarters. At last, among the nobles (*edelliede*) in attendance at the court, Lintgens is dumbfounded to encounter a Portuguese-speaking Moluccan who inquired whether the monarch of Portugal were well and had been received in friendship by his counterpart in England. Bali was truly a culture of kings.

In short, Lintgens fully commends to his readers this Balinese court without understanding the nature of the rivalry among the island's many royal and noble houses, and, to judge by later evidence, insurgent commoners as well. Moreover, none of these briefs by sixteenth-century, partially educated sailors displays that puritanical, Calvinistic reaction to Indonesian customs evident in later reports. Indeed, a generation would lapse before the official attitude of the Dutch East India Company was consolidated – that 'proud burgher's revulsion of the ostentation and royal arbitrariness evident in Indonesia [which] speaks from many of the earlier records in the Company era' (Van der Kroef 1963: 7). However misunderstood, Bali's royal trappings were initially admired as such. For complex historical reasons, empathy antedated disdain.[4]

Like a polder *chez nous*

Apart from his delight over the island's benevolent royalty, Lintgens sensed in Bali a familiar quality, most evident from his descriptions of the village domestic quarters and the irrigation works that assure a 'surabundance of eatables.' It is all proclaimed a *jonck Hollandt* with its little towns and cities so cut across by water that it is 'amazing to see' (p. 85). This feeling of familiarity was transformed at one point into a delusion of identity, when in closing Lintgens described a massive fortified wall along a section of Bali's southern coast. His text was the source of a mystification that confused maps for generations to come. With no firm evidence, it has been attributed either to intoxication or to a mirage brought on by Lintgens' homesickness for the physically similar inner-wall that stood in Amsterdam in the late sixteenth century (Rouffaer and Ijzerman 1929: vlvii, 1).

Regardless, the kernel of truth behind the delusion is Lintgens' reassured sense of *gemakkelijkheid* amidst his Balinese surroundings. We wonder today what reinforced this cross-cultural coziness and a totally speculative answer beckons. That barren North Sea bog called in the *Odyssey* 'a land of fog and gloom where there is no sun' had devised a delicate ecological balance somewhat remindful of the one found in this tropical land of volcanic fertility where the danger was paddies parched from too much sun. In the Netherlands 'diking produced its own code of law. When a break occurred, drums sounded for all men to pick up their spades and rush to the scene' (Masselman 1963: 3–5). The windmills, network of canals, and continuous repair-work and silting duties related to the Dutch landscape were very much like the river dams, irrigation channels and tunnels, and their requisite labor related to the Balinese landscape where irrigation likewise produced its own code of law. One subsistance technology protected fertile fields from an intrusive sea, the other protected unlikely rice paddies from the ever threatening failure of the water tapped up in the mountains to ripple through lands of hostile antagonists, eventually to irrigate one's own fields before flowing on. Both ecosystems have the quality of meticulous surplus-yielding games of survival in the face of pending disaster. At least a James Michener might assume this was why the descendants of commoner Frisian-Viking dog lovers (the legendary founders of Amsterdam), who made profits in spite of the fog and gloom, felt a harmony with descendants of Javanese ancestral gods (the founders of Hindu-Bali) who worshipped the tropical sun. It is difficult to surmise a better reason. While we shall, alas, probably never know exactly why the Dutch and the Balinese saw eye to eye, it is safe to say that in terms of domestic scale and elaborate hydrotechnology, they were made for each other. And even in 1921, Lekkerkerker was still insisting in his sweeping portrait of *De Baliërs*, and in particular of their irrigation unit: 'a *subak* is somewhat comparable to a plot of reclaimed land at home' [*Een subak is eenigszins te vergelijken met een polder ten onzent*. . . (1921: 149)].

Pictorial emblems

While Lintgens' work is a tantalizing narrative of an original attraction between different worlds, the visual record from the Houtman expedition better suggests the nature of Balinese ethnology, and perhaps of any ethnology. Three illustrations were printed with the log in 1598: (1) slaves (*slaven*) shouldering a noble's (*Edelluyd*) palanquin, (2) a king being drawn by white buffalos (*witte Buffels*) in a cart, sheltered by an umbrella, and (3) a wife following her husband into his cremation flames to the accompaniment of several musicians. There are accurate aspects in the sedan-chair, but the cart is a Dutch *bolderwagen*, the instrumentalists are Indian, and no one in the expedition had witnessed a cremation.[5] In fact, the musical accompaniment is a near copy of an illustration of cremations in Portuguese Goa that appeared in the remarkably influential *Itenerario [Voyage or Passage by Jan Huyghen van Linschoten to East or Portugal's India (1579–1592)]* by the seasoned traveler Linschoten and the collector Paludamus. A copy of this major impetus to Dutch investment in exploration accompanied the Houtman expedition. Its illustrations were presumed adequate to depict things Balinese, since, according to sixteenth-century concepts of cultural geography passed down from medieval cosmographies and the great Iberian chronicles, Bali was an extension of India:

With Goa as its focal point (according to the Itinerary) India stretched westward as far as Prester John's Land (Ethiopia). It included all of Southeast Asia, and it was only grudgingly admitted that China (Cathay) and Japan might have to be excluded. All of the East India archipelago fell within its boundaries: Sumatra, Java, and the Spice Islands (Masselman 1963: 71–2).

Contrary to the view of some twentieth-century commentators, it was not 'fantasy' to use an engraving of Goa-widow-burning to represent a reputed Balinese custom; it was simply applying the nearest known equivalent. In Western eyes there was never a Bali *per se*, but only a Bali derived. The original ethnological idea of Bali sprang full-grown from the records of Portuguese Goa, as in some ways it should have.

The three engravings in the Houtman account were subsequently redrawn into a composite emblem of 'A King on the Island Bally' published with a summary of the Dutch reports in the famous translations of travel literature by Levin Hulsius. (See Frontispiece.) The Dutch *bolderwagen* remains the vehicle of an umbrella-shaded king, but the suttee scene has been reduced to a background embellishment in miniature along with a sun worshiper and another *Ethnike Brahmane*, here praying before a cow. The illustration of regal Bali as including practices of Surya (the sun) worship, abstention from eating beef, and the ceremonial suicide of widows has improved for the wrong reasons. By reducing the size of the suttee scene, the musical instruments have been obscured so that they cannot be recognized as Indian, Balinese, or anything else. But this was less for the sake of ethnographic accuracy, than to produce a pleasing, balanced illustration to adorn this first cocktail table book (cf. Dutch *prachtwerk*) on Bali. The Dutch published exhaustive travel literature to compile practical information for navigation and commercial strategies; the Elizabethan-Jacobean British followed suit to stimulate interest in entering the world trade system at all. But the more compendious German collection of voyages begun in the late sixteenth century 'were primarily designed as entertaining and eye-catching examples of literature' in order to 'appeal to the popular taste for the remote and exotic' (Lach 1965, I: 215, 217). Thus, the first popularized portrait of Bali was in some ways less misleading than the first efforts at reportage, and the Hulsius emblem remained the most elaborate overview of Balinese practices for the next two centuries.[6]

The original engravings from Bali are worth considering in light of E.H. Gombrich's notion of 'adapted stereotypes' (1969: 71). It so happens that these first Western visual images were adapted from India, but this would be what Gombrich calls a 'pathological representation' only if the aim were to carefully distinguish South Asian practices from Balinese ones. More than two-hundred years were to pass before Westerners would attempt this. For the purposes of the sixteenth to eighteenth centuries, this pictorial record adequately emblazoned Bali as sun worshiping, woman immolating, and king honoring. Little matter to the pre-Baconian of 1597 that the musical instruments were not quite that way; little matter the particular circumstances in which women were really burned, the sun (if ever) really bowed to, and so on. A major interest in the art of ethnology is to convey a sense of the whole society, to typify it in some vivid, compelling manner. Like any essentially metaphorical procedure, ethnology thus resembles the arts of visual illusion, if one realizes there is no such thing as simple 'realism' and no possible one-to-one correspondence between that which is 'illusioned to' and the perceptual or conceptual apparatus by which the illusion is perpetrated. Rather in both visual representation and ethnology, here distinguished explicitly from ethnography insofar as ethnology hopes to 'capture the whole':

> Copying . . . proceeds through the rhythms of schema and correction. The schema is not the product of a process of 'abstraction,' of a tendency to 'simplify'; it represents the first approximate, loose category which is gradually tightened to fit the form it is to reproduce (Gombrich 1969: 74).

The first South Asianized loose images of Bali sufficiently distinguished its culture from Holland or Portugal or anything else Western European readers were likely to measure it against. The representations were tightened only when they became ambiguous, when they appeared to confuse two forms – Bali and Hindu India – that according to newly emerging criteria were eventually conceived as distinct.

This process of gradually tightening inadequate stereotypes continues. Nor are the stereotypes applied to a constant referent, but to an ever changing social life that has itself meanwhile been altered by incorporating new stereotypes. For example, Bali had been rearranging its death rites according to its own images of Indian cremation, which Balinese literati probably understood no better than Western literati later understood Balinese cremation. The West's first caption of Balinese cremation was a visual stereotype of a sociritual stereotype, whether the latter was actually brought to Bali from India or modeled on texts, or both. And Balinese ethnology – like all ethnology – continues to compound stereotypes, eventually producing, hopefully, tighter captions, but inevitably to the exclusion of certain cultural and social data perceived as critical from other vantage points.

Thus, from the very start Bali appeared South Asian, kingly and stable. Subsequently, little comparative study was made of continuities between Balinese social and ecological forms and those of less Hinduized islands in the Lesser Sundas, and almost no attention has been paid to the distinctly Oceanic quality of its culture. Yet, as we shall see, outside its Hinduized rites and Sanskritic texts, Bali can appear as much Polynesian as Indic. And while its wet-rice irrigation recalls Southeast Asia, its utilization of surplus production and its fine status gradations even within family lines suggest points further east as well. Indeed, it is provocative to reflect that, coming from the other direction, Houtman's voyagers might have emphasized not the Indic umbrella of Bali's 'kings,' but the physical elevation of its 'chiefs,' not the Brahmana legists, but the conspicuous expenditure in mass rites of an untradeable surplus, and not the worship of cows, but the tournamentlike competition among leaders to maintain devoted subjects – all traits of the Pacific. If those first ethnologists had arrived in Bali two centuries later, bringing their adaptable stereotypes not from Goa but from the hierarchies of the Maori or even Hawaii, what a different picture could have resulted!

Nineteenth-century interests

Although the initial Hindu stereotypes of *Baelle* were popularized in the West, during the seventeenth and eighteenth centuries the glories of Balinese royalty pass little noticed in the records of the Netherlands East India Company (V.O.C.). There are reports on occasional efforts to stabilize a trading post, on the going price of slaves conveyed to Batavia and the Moluccas, and on the availability of Balinese forces to aid the V.O.C. in its wars in Java (Nielsen 1928: 48–9). Significantly, Swellengrebel's brief discussion of Western literature on Bali (1960: 13–15) mentions nothing between Lintgenszoon's 1597 account and Sir S. Raffles' follow-up report from his visit in 1815. Nielson summarizes the unstable situation over these two centuries:

The Dutch trade company had in these days contracts with the kings (*Vorsten*) concerning the delivery of slaves, but vast trading posts had not yet been established on the island. As the Hollanders mastered the surrounding stretch, the Balinese kings withdrew themselves more, when they began to sense the danger that their independence was threatened. The friendly tone diminished and at the same time the English made the move to get a firm foothold on the island, so excellently suited as a base for their commerce in these waters (1928: 49).[7]

Indeed, Britain had long been eyeing Bali as a possible base of operations in the East Indies. In 1745, Thomas Astley includes the island in his collection of *Voyages and Travels* 'comprehending everything remarkable in its kind, in Europe, Asia, Africa and America.' But the main significance of the brief entry is that spices receive no mention:

Bali is an island to the eastwards of Makassar on eight degrees and a half South. It yields great store of rice, cotton-yarn, slaves, and coarse white cloth, which is in good request at *Bantam*. The Commodities for this place are the smallest sort of blue and white beads, iron, and coarse porcelain (Astley 1745: 505).

The relative dearth of commodities remained the problem from these first British and Dutch precolonial surveys through the Dutch colonial economic reports, up to and including the 1924 *Handbook*. The latter summary of the economic and administrative infrastructure of the Dutch East Indies mentions Bali only for its sugar industry, its pawnship system, opium control stations, salt monopolies, and, of course, schools. Dutch liberals could point with pride to such services provided for a resourceless island, especially in the light of the special labor policy:

For all the different provinces of the outer district special coolie-ordinances are enacted, except for Bali, Lombok, and Timor, where the importation of contract labor is not allowed (Handbook 1924: 133).

Bali lacked lands suitable for extensive plantation crops which might have warranted importing labor. There were no commodities of trade for colonial enterprises; tourism alone promised to yield significant profits.

Java Minor

> . . . the chief interest in Bali is archaeological and resides in the character of the inhabitants and their obstinate attachment to Hinduism after the lapse of centuries (Cabaton 1911: 361).

The Napoleonic wars first turned the attention of British and then Dutch officials toward Bali. Bali's strategic proximity to Java caused the new British administrators to seek stabilized relations with the island and to inaugurate serious study of its culture. The nature of British interests in the East Indies had become evident: 'The Archipelago was . . . important to Britain commercially as a market for Indian products, as a source of spices, and, much more, as a means of supplementing the trade with China' (Tarling 1962: 4). Meanwhile, the basis of Dutch commercial policy had radically altered, when insurmountable difficulties in monopolizing spice supplies throughout the vast archipelago led the V.O.C. to introduce plantation crops wherever feasible.

> More and more (the Dutch) concentrated on Java where especially from the 1720s, they developed the cultivation of coffee upon such terms as to enable them to compete in European markets with other sources of supply, and throughout the century their sovereignty was spreading over that populous island (Tarling 1962: 4).

The expansion of plantation cultivation had a profound impact on local social organization in many areas of Java; as one scholar has recently summarized this complex situation:

> Daendals, Raffles, and their successors strove mightily to transform the native social hierarchy into the rational bureaucracy and society of French Napoleonic and British Liberal ideals. In twenty years the new governor-generals of Java reduced the regents' retinues to a tenth of their former size; they stripped them of ranks, titles, and the parasols that had served as their symbols of authority. They prohibited the feasts that invited the people to participate in the regents' magnificence at circumcision, marriage, and promotion. They denied the regents' hereditary succession, and instead of allowing the regents to collect their customary tribute in labor and produce, they paid them salaries. Finally, Raffles initiated a 'land rent' system. Under that arrangement, the peasant would cease to pay tribute in kind to the regent, but would pay instead a tax in cash. It was expected that this requirement would encourage the peasant to raise his production so that he could market enough to pay his tax, fill his needs, and still reap a profit (Peacock 1973: 43).

And there was little Bali just next door.

From 1810–1817 Sir Stamford Raffles, the British lieutenant-governor-general of Batavia during Napoleon's occupation of the Netherlands, placed great importance on relations with Balinese rajas. Bali was a key factor in Raffles' plan permanently to refute Dutch claims of general sovereignty in the Indies:

Before the conquest of Java, he had regarded Bali as a state friendly to the British, and, as the island had never been conquered by the Dutch, he considered that any treaties entered into with the Balinese rulers were likely to survive any arrangements which might be the consequence of a peace in Europe (Bastin 1961: 133).

But the values and interests of the Balinese rajas caused difficulties in implementing the plan. By 1814, the raja of Buleleng turned against the governor-general who had cut into his profits by outlawing slavery and attempting to regulate opium sales. After the Dutch regained ascendancy in the Indies, they tried, following Raffles' example, to formalize relations with Bali. But until 1846 such efforts remained futile:

The rajas were interested in occasional military aid against Lombok, Mataram, and one another; the Dutch wanted to assert sovereignty and in doing so to devise political and commercial contracts valid in perpetuity. Neither side quite knew what the other was driving at, save that it was inacceptable (Hanna 1971a: 4).

Our main interest in Raffles is not that he gauged the political significance of Bali, somewhat in spite of itself, but that he revivified interest in the customs and conventions of its social life. His importance in the history of Balinese ethnology arises from a view of the relationship between Bali and its more prominent neighbor. This pronouncement became the cornerstone of Balinese studies:

The present state of *Bali* may be considered therefore, as a kind of commentary on the ancient condition of the natives of Java. Hinduism has here severed society into castes; it has introduced its divinities; it has extended its ceremonies into most of the transactions of life; it has enjoined or recommended some of its severest sacrifices, such as the burning of a widow on the funeral pyre of her husband; but yet the individual retains all the native manliness of his character and all the fire of the savage state (1817, Vol. II: ccxxxvi).

The finesse and finality of his assertion notwithstanding, Raffles acknowledged certain difficulties in considering Bali a remnant of pre-Mohammedan Java. For example, in his sensitive comments on paddy ownership he notes:

The tenure by which land is held differs widely from that which exists at present in the native provinces of Java. The sovereign is not here considered the universal landlord; on the contrary, the soil is almost invariably considered as the private property of the subject, in whatever manner it is cultivated or divided. It may be sold, let, pledged, devised, or otherwise disposed of, at the option of the proprietor, and without any reference to the will of the superior. The divisions of this property are generally very minute . . . (p. ccxxxiv).

This observation is vaguely inaccurate, because hamlet councils sometimes restrict how the individual proprietor-members can sell their land. Nevertheless, Raffles provides here an important qualification to the view dating from 1597 of the absolute power of Bali's despots. In general, however, the similitudes between these neighbors were constantly emphasized, rather than their equally remarkable divergences – for example, kinship and marriage. Without Raffles' concept of Bali as a literal Java Minor to sustain the interest of the English and their Dutch successors, the island's culture would have remained in obscurity even longer.

Otherwise, the report on Raffles' reconnaissance mission in 1815 contains little general insight into Balinese mores. His description of caste, for example, is inferior to the one by his less famous rival, John Crawfurd; Raffles is mistaken on point one when he assumes the princes are Brahmanas. However, Raffles correctly notes the existence of the optional marriage (*sentana*) in which a son-in-law resides in the house of his wife's father, and he gleans from Crawfurd two particularly anomalous customs:

The bodies of the dead are burnt, except in the case of children before they have shed their teeth, and of all persons dying of the smallpox (p. ccxxxvii).

Yet there is no effort to understand these variations in cremation practices.

A contemporary of Raffles, John Crawfurd, wrote a chapter 'On the Existence of the Hindu Religion in the Island of Bali' (1820) after his study trip in 1814. Like later nineteenth-century observers of Balinese religion, he was primarily concerned with its Hindu-Javanese components. And like their sixteenth-century forerunners, both Crawfurd and Raffles 'saw many things that struck them as being anything but Hindu, but they saw such things through Hindu spectacles, and so had a distorted view' (Swellengrebel, 1960: 25). Crawfurd provides the link between the initial 1597 characterization of Bali-Hinduism as a product of South Asia and the first definitive study in 1849 by the Sanskritist R. Friederich. Moreover, his *Descriptive Dictionary of the Indian Islands* (1856) presents a blend of practical information and anthropological observations which is sensitive to complexities in the diffusion of customs across cultures. Contrary to the received stereotypes, the dictionary even hints at possible flexibilities in the Balinese caste system:

A Waisya [Wesia] prince may even happen to take a fancy for the daughter of a Bramin [Brahmana], when it becomes expedient that he should be gratified. Mr. Zollinger, in his interesting account of Lomboc, gives an example. The young raja of Mataram in that island, A Balinese, fell in love with the daughter of the chief dewa. In order to possess her a friendly legal ceremony became necessary. The Bramin went through the form of expelling his daughter from his house, denouncing her as 'a wicked daughter.' By this she lost her rank as the daughter of a Bramin; but received into the raja's house, she became a Waisya, but at the same time a princess (Crawfurd 1856: 30).

Yet, Crawfurd's account of Bali-Hindu religion cannot escape the limits of its age; it adopts as representative the uppercrust. In Buleleng, Crawfurd interviewed 'Brahmens,' in particular Brahmana Siwa priests, whose sect 'may indeed be denominated the national religion.' He thus recounts the *pedanda* Siwa slant on religious life: their disdain for *pedanda boda* in Karangasem kingdom; the origins of the four *warnas* from the body parts of Brahma; the existence of so-called outcastes or

Chandala – potters, dyers, distillers, and leather dealers who are confined to the outskirts of villages. Accordingly, Crawfurd illustrates his ***History of the Indian Archipelago*** with two drawings made in Bali, one a Brahmana priest, the other a remarkably foreshortened portrait of a raja and his female attendant, both captured in that supreme state of lapsed psychological focus so characteristic of Balinese attending rituals and ceremonies.

Crawfurd's documentation of the cherished prerogatives of Brahmanas is enriched by direct comparisons with India. He gives detailed examples of contrast between Balinese and Indic food regulations: in Bali only the Brahmanas refused to eat with the inferior classes, and the raja drank tea prepared and handed to him by his attendants who were generally Sudras (1820: 6). And he alludes to a central paradox in Balinese marriage customs, lacking only the theoretical apparatus to elaborate it:

> The superior classes may take concubines from the inferior; but the opposite practice is strictly interdicted. The offspring of such unions, as in continental India. forms a variety of new castes. A legal marriage, however, can be contracted only between persons of equal rank, so that the four great classes are in this manner preserved distinct (1820: 4).

(With some concept of ideal/actual to better characterize these values, and, with a graduated scale between concubine/legitimate spouse, Crawfurd might have appreciated some of the particular properties of Balinese marriage values.) Suttee, cremation, the role of Brahmanas in state justice, deities and festivals are all compared and contrasted in a statement or two to corresponding traditions of India. The report concentrates on Kawi language, systems of chronology, legends of the migration of caste to Bali, tales from Indian epics, and other favorite topics of Brahmana literati. Finally, a few lines comprise the first tentative view of the relation of the state system of administration to local social and economic organization:

> Each village forms a little municipal community complete in itself, having its chief, a deputy, a village priest, etc., each entitled to some small remuneration from the funds of the village.
>
> The principle on which the land is assessed on Bali is peculiar . . . , reconciling and assimilating the interests of the sovereign and subject. The raja is, by a sort of fiction, considered the proprietor of all the water of irrigation, and to him are entrusted what in these countries may strictly be termed the important functions of managing and directing it. Each proprietor pays a tax proportionate to the supply he receives and the revenue of the prince is in the ratio of the quantity he supplies. It is his interest therefore, to keep the water courses in repair, to construct new canals and to extend the cultivation (Crawfurd 1820: 23).

To discern that a raja's power had more to do with water than with land was a provocative result of a few handicapped sessions with the Brahmanas of Buleleng in 1814.

Thus by 1820, Bali was classified as an atavism of old Java with a genuinely Hindu religion and state administration. These two holistic concepts of Balinese culture guided the major studies prior to the defeat of Buleleng in 1846 and influenced much of the subsequent research by long-term resident scholars. A heavily opinionated article in the *Singapore Chronicle* expressed puritanical contempt of many Balinese practices, yet it managed a few descriptive details concerning, for example, rites to ward off pestilence, especially cholera:

> They caused large representations of the most abominable lingum to be made, about 6 or 8 feet long, painted and carved to resemble that shameful emblem as much as possible, to frighten the pestilential devil, by something more impure and revolting than they supposed the soft genius of the cholera to be (Short acct. 1830: 25).

Another vivid instance of the clash of values that lets a little ethnography through is the disdain of practices surrounding twin births:

> They have also a singular idea, when a women is brought to bed of twins, that is an unlucky omen, and immediately on its being known, the woman with her husband and children are obliged to go and live on the seashore, or among the tombs, for the space of a month to purify themselves, after which they may return into the village upon a suitable sacrifice being made. Thus an evidence of fertility is considered by them unfortunate, and the poor woman and her new-born babes, are exposed to all the inclemency of the weather out of doors, just at the time when they need the most attention (p. 26).

The major advance over Raffles and Crawfurd comes with information on sources of royal revenue, in particular:

> the land-tax, which is about 2 rupees [*rupiahs*] per acre annually, for cultivated rice-fields, nothing being charged on fields cultivated with other products, and this tax, being levied only on the score of the water necessary for irrigation, which is supposed to be the property of the sovereign (p. 5).

The report mentions payments by Chinese for their control of imports and exports, and income accruing from the marriages of subjects: following a marriage by capture, 20 percent of the compensation money, paid by the husband's group to his wife's group to legitimize the union, goes to the king. Finally, when marriage or descent breaks down (that is, by divorce or a sonless widow), the afflicted women and their property are appropriated by the court for its pleasure, to serve as concubines, or profitable tradeswomen, or prostitutes. Also, male criminals, cast out of their domestic locales, were sheltered by the court for its use.

By 1830, Balinese royalty appeared to be kings of the water surrounded by the dregs of society, and no one knew by what authority.

The limited image of despots

In 1817 after Britain relinquished the Indies, a Dutch commissioner, H.A. Van den Broek, visited Bali. In 1835, he published his profile of the island's kingdoms and a general description of Balinese social usages. Van den Broek at last considers anew the continual hostility among these 'very religious' kings (1835: 24) first glimpsed in Lodewycks' previously mentioned 1597 paraphrase of the royal chronicle. He documents the seesawing royal authority in Karangasem, Lombok, and Buleleng. Moreover, he alludes to marriages among royal houses of different kingdoms in noting 'the most important wife of the King (*vorst*) of Klungkung is usually a princess of Karangasem' (p. 164); and he mentions the bonds of friendship and marriage alliance uniting Badung, Tabanan, Gianyar and Mengwi against Karangasem, Klungkung, and Buleleng (p. 175). Tabanan, 'one of the greatest and mightiest kingdoms of Bali' with its extra-bountiful rice-fields, is contrasted with the smaller, less fruitful, yet more densely populated Klungkung. Yet, ironically, the king of Klungkung enjoys a privileged status over the other ruling houses:

> The king is named Dewa-agung, which means great god or highest godhead; all the other kings have unlimited and idolizing (*onbepaalden enafgodischen*) reverence for the King of Klungkung . . . Also, he never has to fear any invasion into his land, and is never enveloped in wars, unless he himself chooses one or another party, in which case the opponent does not fear, for purposes of defense, to move against him (p. 182).

His portrait of kingdoms includes Karangasem and Jembrana as well, with notes on the Islamic Sasak and Buginese populations within these areas. There is already an implicit assumption that these flanking kingdoms are a diminution from the Klungkung ideal. Van den Broek appreciates Tabanan kingdom's economic advantages, yet his Hindu spectacles prevent viewing the different regions as different adaptations to variable land and climate, defense needs, trade opportunities, and so forth. The flexibility of Balinese courtly institutions, especially where they face out on non-Hindu populations, should have been given a weight equal to their capacity to perpetuate and to replicate a Hindu-Javanese sacred ideal. Yet Van den Broek's successors also stressed the Javanese timelessness of Balinese culture and made minimal comparisons eastward. In particular, when V.E. Korn came to explain the divergent village-area of Tenganan (1933), he conceptualized it predominantly as pre-Bali-Hindu rather than as part of the culture-area stretching on to Lombok, Sumbawa, and beyond.

Van den Broek follows his profile of kings and kingdoms with a provocative report on Balinese customs. He documents the prejudices of the priests and kings against the original inhabitants of Bali and presents a theory of caste which, more than a list of the four *warna*-categories, correlates *warna* with varieties of death rites:

> . . . they have even as the Hindus four castes; the first is the Priestly, the second the Royal (*Vorstelijke*), the third the Middlecaste, and the fourth the Low or common caste. The corpses of the first two named are burned with great pomp, even as takes place among Brahmanas, those of the middlecaste are buried, and those of the lower caste are left above ground by the side of the road, a prey to weather and scavengers (p. 186–7).

This composite scheme foreshadows later classifications of Balinese into corpse-exposing, casteless mountain-peoples (*Bali Aga*) and the Hinduized population with its differential cremation rights, stretching from immediate burning for kings to eventual cremation after disinterment for ordinary commoners. Thus, according to later views, Van den Broek had confused Sudras with Bali Aga; but the intimate connection between death and public status was already obvious in 1835.

Van den Broek, if read carefully, represents a quantum leap over his predecessors. Although he perpetuates clichés of the absolute monarchy coupled with the 'blind trust' of the king in his priests (p. 194), he lets provocative exceptions to this supposed slave-based absolutism filter through; for example:

> After the cremation of the [prince's] corpse, both slaves were given their freedom and married to each other . . . and given household goods, two buffalos and rice-fields (p. 188).

Such passing comments highlight lengthy descriptions of rites, processions, and feastdays with their puppet theatre, dance performances, cock and cricket fights, and gambling. Included is a knowledgeable allusion to marriage ranks:

> Polygamy (*veelwijwerij*) is generally allowed; they can have as many wives as wealth permits; however, an ordinary Balinese seldom has more than one. Chiefs (*Hoofden*) usually have three, four or five, according to their rank and income, while the rajas commonly keep from eighty to a hundred or more wives, all of whom are considered legitimate (*echtevrowen*), although they occupy different ranks in accordance with the descent (*afkomst*) of each. The children also are all considered legitimate, and bear the title Gusti (which signifies Prince or Nobleman). They are classified according to the rank of their mother. A portion of these wives are fit for the public ceremony of the raja and accompany him in public, carrying his *betel* supplies, writing tools, toilet articles, mirrors, fans and so forth (p. 200).

Later we shall trace the implications of this pattern in modern Bali well beyond the province of royalty.

Apart from its ethnographic content, Van den Broek's report is patently politically minded. He concludes that a European administration could only improve and expand the island's culture and that the rajas, while impressed with Dutch superiority in matters of war, still regard Europeans as monsters and continue to oppress a worthy populace:

> These folk, once having been brought under the authority of Netherlands' rule, should obey her command as willingly as they have respected their rajas, especially when they discover that their lot will be thereby remarkably improved (pp. 225–36).

Van den Broek later stoops to strategy: 'If the Netherlands should come to war with Bali, Jembrana would be the best landing place' (p. 234). Most remarkably, he pauses to project what a commoner must really think about his overlord; this supposed flow of Balinese consciousness is set in quotation marks:

> I am an insignificant creature (*nietig wezen*), of no consequence. The raja has the disposal of all my possessions, my person, my wife, and children. If I sink beneath

the burden of duties which he had imposed on me . . . I exist only before him, and all the good I enjoy descends from my raja, whose slave and property I am (p. 206).

With this unlikely confessional, stylistically psalmlike, the rajas are defamed as external oppressors of the native Balinese *bevolking*. Yet, prior to his concluding crescendo of excerptable slogans to justify any future occupation of Bali, Van den Broek offers a convincing general description of the state administration which stresses not helpless victimage but the limits of the raja's power.[8]

The scattered account of the state administration commences characteristically with a sweeping generalization, soon belied by Van den Broek's own data:

The manner of government is absolutely despotic or arbitrary; the raja (*vorst*) decides all affairs, whether criminal or civil, although for external matters he is assisted by a council of important chiefs and by a priest. In affairs of state he consults with the lesser Gustis, usually his brothers, half-brothers, or cousins (p. 212).

He captures some of the flavor of repeated court models down through the administrative apparatus without ever clearly distinguishing 'Maha raja' (that is, the Dewa of Klungkung) from rajas of the other kingdoms, from their politically powerful kin, from village-area notables, from administrative aides to the courts (*Perbekels*), and so on:

The small subordinate rajas (*vorstjes*) in their own dominions are as arbitrary despots as the higher rajas (*Hoofdvorsten*), and assume no further responsibility to the latter than to lead the chief warriors when asked (p. 213).

Lesser lords had to deliver materials or produce from lands to support building projects:

These lesser rajas are usually brothers, uncles, or other near relatives of the upper raja. In the capital city [court center] itself there are always as well some of the rajas kinsmen who have a certain number of people immediately under them and at their disposal . . . Such people are independently governed without the interference of the upper raja . . . (213).

In the conquered lands, as was the case in Jembrana, these rajas are taxable (*cijns baar*) and must deliver a portion of income to their superior raja. The lesser Gustis, such as the cousins of the raja, make up most of the latter, and occupy one or another position at court . . .

Some of them are chiefs (*Hoofden*) of sections and have a specific number of neighborhoods (*Kampongs*) under their management, where they are concerned with the raja's policy and collection of his income . . . These same functions are also filled by chiefs who are not of royal descent, and these bear the title *Perbukkel* . . . (214).

Van den Broek does not sort out all these functionaries. He recognizes that direct control of local areas by rajas is highly variable. For the peripheral kingdoms of Jembrana and Buleleng, he lists courtly replicas down the status gradations from *Hoofdvorsten* (whoever they may be) to *voorsten*, to *voorstjes* (Gustis?), to *Hoofden* – each official boasting an assorted entourage.

Van den Broek is clearest on the differentiation by status of high crimes and punishments (*delictenrecht*) – always the easiest information to obtain on Bali, since it was the speciality of Brahmana literati. But his most enlightening insight concerns the compartmentalized impact of the raja's state system on the island's subsistence economy, on the collection of taxes, and on the waging of war.

The revenues of the rajas consist of a kind of land-tax, which every farmer who has rice fields must bring in, amounting to ten *dubbeltjes* for each landed proprietor, whether farming many or few fields. The *vorst* was paid a specific tribute for marriages. In Badung this amounts to four Spanish piastres for each marriage. In case of indigence this tax is fulfilled in installments. [We shall see later that such provisions varied among different overlords and kingdoms.] There is also a toll levied on bazaars or markets, which are tolerably extensive; moreover on cockfights, besides other gambling games, and on holding opium dens (*afioenkitten*). In kingdoms with harbors the raja leases the import and export duties to Chinese or even to Balinese, although this seldom yields much profit . . .

The rajas have their own rice fields, and it is figured they produce sufficiently for their consumption; these are worked by their subjects in regular turns, for which they receive a portion of the crop, I think a quarter share [this also varies greatly] which is distributed on equal terms to all who perform this work. In the event of crop failure, it is calculated how much the raja would thereby be short, and this amount is made up by a proportionate contribution over all the farmers. In this way, the rajas assure that they and those who belong to their courts are never exposed to shortage (*aan gebrek zijn bloot gesteld*).

The exclusive right to hold puppet theatre (*wayangs*) and *Ronggings* are the rajas', and this provides them considerable revenue. They also have all extensive manufacture of silk and other fabrics . . . also many fruiting and flowering trees, the produce of which they have sold in the markets and along the road. All this was cared for by their wives whose major occupation consisted of weaving . . .

Opium, iron, and all necessary foreign articles are purchased by the rajas and on their behalf are resold on a small scale to their subjects with great usury. If the folk perform a service for them, to pay for it, however, on the following day they hold shadow puppet plays or cockfights in their palace, and are thus sure that the farthing expended would within twenty-four hours be back in their coffers. I have already mentioned that the slave trade made up one of the most important sources of the rajas' income . . . (219–21).

The rajas always had ample opportunity to procure the desired number of slaves as when pardoning to that end criminals condemned to death . . .

. . . All orphans who have no father or mother belong to the raja, as do all wives who, owing to discord, were repudiated. Forbidding this trade is naturally a thorn in the side, and the rajas' income is thereby notably reduced.

Their method of war is most ridiculous and can be considered more as a childhood game than as a serious affair. Every Balinese [this is certainly exaggerated] from fourteen to fifty years old is a soldier and must at his raja's command immediately repair to arms, consisting of a pike furnished him by the raja and of a Kris, his own. The Gustis and chiefs (*Hoofden*) are the commanders, for there exists no separation between the civil (*burgerlijke*) and military function (*vak*); the rank which a chief bears in the former is likewise awarded him in the latter . . . Every neighborhood leader (*kampongshoofd*) commands his men and brings them to the chief of the division . . . A division usually consists of four or five neighborhoods amounting to fifteen hundred to two thousand able-bodied men. A Gusti commands the entire army, under the superior command of the raja . . .

. . . The offensive army attempts to penetrate the line of demarcation, where on both sides there are always deep ditches and high ramparts of earth. In the middle is only a passage around fifteen feet wide. Between the batteries of the two parties is a plain of around half a mile square that is considered as neutral territory, and serves as thoroughfare to the battlefield.

. . . Several champions . . . come on this intervening space, and challenge their opponents, whereupon at last the two armies rush at each other with pointed spears. As soon as either of the two armies has ten or twelve dead, it hastily flees . . .

Prisoners are never spared, but killed on the spot; the supposition that they are apt to be sold as slaves is totally groundless, although during wartime rajas do send poaching squads to distant neighborhoods in the enemy's territory, to carry off the peaceful and defenseless inhabitants; they make these slaves or sell them to be transported overseas, as soon as the opportunity arises.

. . . When a Balinese army processes, the raja is always well in the rearguard, so far that he is totally out of range. He sits on a palanquin surrounded by a crowd of his wives who must be witnesses to his heroic exploits . . . (p. 224).

More sacred icon than commander-in-chief, the raja in battle appears absolute. It is this ritual stereotype of power which, in spite of the notable limits on state influence in taxation, production, and (more than likely) conscription, stands out most vividly in Van den Broek's account. The image of a many wived king on his palanquin, safely removed from harm, sponsor of the recent slave trade, allows the Dutch still to brand Bali a despotic regime – local landownership and subsistence economics notwithstanding.

Van den Broek calls war here a children's game; he might more accurately have deemed it a life or death ritual, where antagonists strike blows at their enemies within the purview of other-worldly rulers – a basic scene in Javanese-Balinese drama and shadow-puppet theater. Indeed, many Balinese traditions portray the ideal raja and his allied Brahmana priests as such epical semidivinities, only provisionally earth-bound, who dispatch their military heroes – the *patihs* of Hindu-Javanese statecraft – to perform legendary tasks.[9] Yet these epical aspects are only half the story. There are also those Balinese traditions which value what happens when the epic falters, when the rigid social code symbolized by caste divisions and the purity of the high born kingship repeatedly succumbs, only to be reconstituted. This other half of Bali occurs in the local-commoner aftermath of the aristocratic mass suicides (*puputan*), in the alternative, extra-birthright mystic modes of legitimacy, in the rearticulation of hierarchical values at lower levels of the society, in the adaptation of esoteric court-literature into the vernacular, and in the tardy hotbed of political activity (1965) seventeen years after the revolutionary demise of a pro-upper-caste colonial regime. After the epic-ending deluge, the romance.

In short, the glare from Van den Broek's lingering image of divine power at the top prevented many subsequent observers of Bali from perceiving those alternative traditional values it is our intention to stress. To emphasize the courtly epic of politico-religious expansion is to deemphasize the visionary romance of refurbishing authority when the court inevitably crumbles. Again, epic projects an aristocracy's conception of its own achievements; romance allows commoner champions, local social and religious organizations, and other elements beyond the control of the ruling elite to be celebrated as contributing forces to society. Though romance is not a revolutionary inverse vantage from the bottom up, it at least allows for institutional flexibility so as to reconstitute values and patterns prone to repeated upheaval. The systematic basis of what one can, by stretching the point, call Bali's romance phase can only be appreciated by observing how Hindu caste and religious ideals penetrate ordinary localities, how hierarchical concerns can characterize an acephalous political structure as easily as one with its crown intact, and how, upon the introduction of new institutional frameworks such as political parties and commercial enterprises, the alternative conceptions of power, legitimacy, and society can be revived.

In the century following Van den Broek, ethnographers amassed much information on commoners, on Sudra groups, and so forth. But the holistic ethnological overview of Bali continued to stress the epic courtly qualities of Bali-Hindu traditions throughout the colonial period. The Bali of Indonesian independence, especially since Sukarno's own elitist policies – favoring the traditional bureaucratic elite or *pamong praja* – began to falter in the early 1960s, has experienced extreme challenges to courtly traditions of rigid social divisions and authority by birthright. In this latter context, it is the social romance, also traditional, that has flourished.

Northern sketches

. . . *het 'land van den Orang-utan en den Paradjis-vogel,' gelijk Wallace het noemt, voor vetteweg het weinigmeer dan terra incognita is* (van Eck 1879: 102).

Northern Bali was forced to recognize Dutch suzerainty in 1849; in 1882 a direct Netherlands East Indies government was established. These two events opened the island's language, literature, religious customs, and agriculture to regular research by Westerners. In 1849 the German Sanskritist R. Friederich published his seminal field studies on Balinese legal writings, Brahmana Siwa worship, castes, and calendars. Together with H.N. van der Tuuk's Kawi-Balinese-Dutch dictionary (1897–1912), this investigation remains the foundation for subsequent philological work. Indeed, 'with Friederich the scholarly study of Balinese culture by Westerners had begun' (Swellengrebel 1960: 14).[10]

Besides perfecting tools for translating the rich textual materials of profoundly literate Hindu-Bali, field researchers turned as well to those other nineteenth-century romantic concerns: local color and the lot of the common man. The Dutch civil servant P.L. van Bloemen Waanders and an early Protestant missionary, R. van Eck, tirelessly recorded notes and sketches of diverse customs. Their work reflected the new respect generated by European romanticism for the humble and even unseemly usages. Together with F.A. Liefrinck's documents on irrigation in northern Bali and western Lombok, these compilations corrected earlier exaggerations of the role played by royal courts in integrating Balinese society. As Swellengrebel has indicated, this post-1849 research perhaps succeeded too well:

They developed an eye for the special significance of the *desa* community and its culture, so different from that of the court sphere. The emerging picture of Bali became more varied and variegated than before, and richer in details – so much so that scholars sometimes threatened to be drowned in particulars and variants. Writers became more and more cautious with generalization (1960: 15).

What began as a reaction against too much emphasis on the court sphere, ended as an over isolation and a reification of the *desa* community.

Before reviewing how the twentieth century catalogued this prescientism ethnography, we should at least sample its engaging descriptions. Most studies remained literally sketches, to illustrate varied aspects of Balinese life: daily routines, cures and diseases, black magic, cremation, and so forth. We can take as a convenient example of these rambling accounts R. van Eck's study of the cockfight.

Liefrinck had pinpointed a practical aspect of Bali's favorite pastime in details on harvest festivals at irrigation temples:

Each *sawah* owner must provide a certain number of cocks proportionate to the size of his holding. Those who fail to do so, the owners of cocks that refuse to fight are fined half a guilder per cock. The fine and the proceeds of the percentage levy on the stake money are used to defray the costs of the festival (1969: 37).

In 1879 van Eck provides a fuller description. He deems cockfights the Indian passion; he feels the Balinese case should serve to illustrate its importance among Javanese (before it was outlawed) and Buginese, Makassarese, and Malay peoples in general. This 'life and death battle' of cocks at temple gates is an expiatory offering (*zoen offers*) for the players. It is a 'national institution' of varying scope. There are two-month contests with high stakes, supported by rajas for the population at large, excepting priests, on specific holidays. There are also shorter contests at lower stakes and local fights either for the members of a village-area (*tetajen desa*) or an irrigation society (*tetajen subak*) after harvest (p. 106). Van Eck notes the high costs of betting, the role of moneylenders, and the fervent desire of every Balinese to possess a winning cock, which no offer would cause him to give up: 'He'd sooner sell you his wife!' (p. 107). The gambling addict, 'if necessary, would bet his costly Kris, his hard-earned paddy, yes, even his wife and children.' The latter remark is 'no exaggeration'; and van Eck cites cases of men who lost their families on a cockfight. Debtors are jailed; only the moneylenders get rich. Finally after the tally of social costs, 'it is time that we witness something of such a cockfight.' Van Eck describes the open tent over a stepped-down ampitheater with its quarters for audience, players, and referees, and the innermost area where 'the bloody battle is waged.' Then he evokes the entire scene with stylistic verve:

The courtyard is already filled with players. Most have one or two feathered heroes (*gevederde helden*) next to them in a wooden or bamboo-woven cage. Others, from the treasure of Chinese coin (*Kepeng*) placed before them, furnish proof that they intend being anything but idle onlookers. Yonder in the vicinity of the *vorst*, one also sees a seated priest, who properly ought not be here, but whose Balinese nature, in the event of a cockfight, runs contrary to dogma.

Everyone impatiently awaits the moment when the *juru Kemong* will give the signal. Who is this? I should almost say the main figure in the ring. Look, he is sitting over there on the southside of the courtyard (p. 109).

Van Eck mentions the drum, the sinking coconut shell used by this official to time the matches, and the other referees that assure fair play. Finally,

There goes the drum! The first pair of players steps out, each with his cock in hand, there is some to-do over who will take the east side, who the west. At last they are agreed. Now, first the *Ebenburtigkeit* of both fighting cocks is tested out (already properly proved at home), and their 'hero's blood' is by various devices brought toward the boiling point (p. 109).

He explains how the cocks' relative strengths are assessed and describes the critical procedure of attaching the spurs (*tajen*).

Allons donc! . . . The spectators grow lively. Each bets a larger or smaller sum on the cock that appears to him most valiant (p. 110).

He evokes the uproar of bets and counterbets and then equates the state of the owners with that of their animals:

The players themselves do not call out. Deadly calm and without speaking a word . . . each awaits the moment when he can attack his opponent, whom he [perhaps] never before saw, but who in these few minutes has already become his mortal enemy (p. 110).

Thereupon van Eck portrays in vividly colloquial snatches of phrases and quotations the climax to what is essentially, as Geertz has expressed it, 'a chicken hacking another mindlessly to bits' (1972c: 27).

This 'typical match' decided, van Eck concludes with a Dutch translation of the forty-five written provisions that carefully prescribe appropriate measures for any foreseeable controversy. The articles cover everything: how to decide especially close contests; how to maintain tranquility in the village area; punishments for failing to pay off bets; requisite offerings; proper behavior among contestants; and so forth. Such provisions long helped insure another characteristic also noted by Geertz in recent Balinese cockfights: the relative absence of any altercation.

To better appreciate the aims and achievements of so much of these nineteenth-century sketches, it is worth measuring van Eck's 1879 description against C. Geertz's (1972c) detailed interpretation of the same kind of event, as observed during 1957–8. Van Eck's study was advanced for its day. Of course, he expressed the standard missionary's dismay over the strains gambling puts on harmonious family life, and he recorded in full the formal legal underpinnings that prospective colonial administrators would need to know in order to formulate a policy on cockfights. But such duties accomplished, he manages to enter into the drama of emotions in combat and to suggest their intensity with a series of verbal montages, close-ups, and fade-outs. The reader is left with less a sense of pity for the wives and children than a strong desire to experience for himself this bit of exotica.

Van Eck possesses both the prose style and the sensibilities to capture the event itself. But the depth of his evocation is limited by his scientific will to generalize and the requirements he thought this entailed. Van Eck wanted this match to represent not just all Balinese cockfights, but the same 'passion' throughout the Indies and Malaysia. To this end it was necessary to empty his description of any contextual data specific to Bali. According to his standards, to generalize about all Malayo-Indies cockfights, he could safely stress only feathered furies backed by betting addicts, since this is all that is common across the variants. Here was that nineteenth-century predicament: a romantic attraction to local color but the lingering neoclassical suspicion that local color was superficial and that underneath lay the universal abstract form itself.[11]

Geertz's treatment brings a fresh range of perspectives to Balinese cockfights, including a Weberian one, in the sense that:

> Weber's social science focused on understanding individual events and historically located entities, conceived in their uniquely given individuality, rather than searching for universal generalizations about classes of units or events . . . it was a comparative method that was to proceed with the use of 'ideal types,' that focused on extreme cases rather than on the average case . . . (Gouldner 1974: 99).

In this view, it is pointless to seek average cases of complex cultural forms. This is most clearly the case where the forms vary as widely as cockfights in different areas of Indonesia. But even in relatively homogeneous regions – for example, Hindu-Bali – this comparativist approach eschews the average and embraces the extreme. Geertz does not survey the range of Balinese cockfights; rather he telescopes repeated observations into an ideal-typical description of a choice elaboration of the form in one village-area. Here the cockfight is capable of clarifying, satisfying, and intensifying its participants' innermost social being, a profound status drive. By carefully plotting each match against the social factions in this community of hotly competitive iron-smith ancestor groups, Geertz reveals the cockfight as a public stage for Bali-Hindu social action. This is not necessarily what the cockfight averages out to be but what it, apparently, strains to become. Indeed, elsewhere in progressive Balinese towns of greater ethnic diversity, we find cockfights which, rather than being the center ring of status competition, are literally sideshows. Tabanan town, for example, sports a large cockpit, but the regular players are only a small minority of the population. And the real addicts include two *Hajis* from the Islamic quarter and several Chinese who – it is suggested by proud, condescending, and poorer Balinese – have nothing better to do with their time or money.

Geertz conclusively demonstrates the potential of cockfights to register with raw intensity Balinese status concerns. But if they did this equally always and everywhere, cockfights, it could be argued, would be superfluous, unremoved from reality and thus useless as significant commentary on experience. If social life matched perfectly its depiction in rites, there would be little sense in ritual refresher courses. This is the major problem with a functionalist theory of ritual and myth as social charter. Functionalists tried to surmount the nineteenth-century difficulty in combining local color with adequate generalization by meshing too closely the gears of social organization and cultural expression. Any cultural performances – rites, games, dramas – must be distorted from their presumed actual reference if they are to have any impact, if they are to say something. And it is precisely when the cockfight is bigger than life that this ritual verges on art; this is the point of Geertz's study of 'metasocial commentary' (p. 26). Finally, cockfights can be at least secondarily vitalized in Bali by the awareness that what is everyone's outspoken passion in one village is the deviant's marginal obsession in a psychologically distant town. The same form that becomes life and death drama in Geertz's account serves as tragicomedy in Tabanan, 1972.

The rich sociological dimensions of ritual and art escaped Van Eck and his contemporaries because they restricted their sketches to averageable aspects of local color. By divesting cultural events of their particularities, early observers obscured a critical feature of the rites and customs they were among the first to admire: the capacity to persist over highly variable social contexts, yet to be fine-tuned to harmonize with them. Nevertheless, our romantic masters of the ethnographic sketch developed empathy not only for hacking chickens, but for magical curing practices, demonic dances, and many of the daily routines of Bali. Their achievement is all the more notable, since it was not always in the professional interests of these missionaries and civil servants to empathize at all.[12]

2. Balipedia: concerted documentation (1880s–1920s)

The engaging sketches by erstwhile fieldworkers were handicapped by being restricted to the northern areas of Bali. It was obvious that the broad southern plains contained a fuller elaboration of Hindu courtly ideals of power and law that stood in uncertain relationship with reputedly self-governing local communities. The northern rice-producing area is smaller, steeper, and poorer. To this day the region seems somehow less Balinese, with its conspicuous heterogeneous quarters of Chinese and Buginese traders and other Bali-Islam groups. One entered the kingdom of Buleleng through a gate of 'foreign' culture, never witnessing the full panoply of Bali-Hindu architecture, temple networks, and ritual processions until passing beyond the central mountains. Yet this relative impoverishment of Hindu state elaborations perhaps helped the irrigation technology in the north stand out more conspicuously. The southern areas were opened for continuous research only after the tragic collapse of their warring kingdoms during 1906–8, marked by the sensational suicides in the royal courts. Meanwhile, working out of Buleleng and the Balinese portion of neighboring Lombok, F.A. Liefrinck had established new scholarly standards for Balinese studies.

Maximizing rice

By recent calculations, the contented Balinese is one who consumes 500 grams of rice daily (Hanna 1972c: 1). Irrigation technology has been traced by epigraphers to 800–900 A.D., and it remains the most orderly and admirable feature of Bali's occasionally quaking, very damp and hilly landscape, this constant challenge to native engineers. F.A. Liefrinck, *Resident* of Bali and Lombok from 1896 to 1901, spent part of his long career in the civil service describing irrigation works and the local customs and policies surrounding them. His detailed writings began in the 1880s; they remained the solid foundation for later studies by C.G. Grader and other reports on irrigation (for example, Raka 1955) and interpretations of the Balinese rice cult (for example, Wirz, 1929),

Grassroots control

Liefrinck discovered that the *subak* system worked upwards from the grass roots, that it was fundamentally local and in principle democratically controlled. The role of the rajas appeared to be distinctly marginal, as he describes in the following passage:

> While land was sometimes opened up by order of the rulers for their own advantage, in general they refrained from taking any initiative as regards large-scale land clearage or the digging of new irrigation conduits, for they had to reckon with the independent spirit of their subjects (1969: 4).

Nearly every aspect of the elaborate irrigation process remained under local initiative: terracing ravines; developing the intricate plans of dams, channels, culverlets, and so on that conveyed water in equity to the maximum number of paddy fields along a given watershed; planting, cultivating, maintaining, and protecting irrigated plots; and harvesting, storing, and distributing their product. Yet, in a way still not perfectly understood, the raja personified what this delicate system made possible: equal access to water.

> Ownership of the water in the river and the wells [sources of the irrigation supply] is vested in the ruler and the ruler may dispose of it as he wishes. This concept differs from the principle applying in the same connection in other countries. In Java and Italy, for example, where water is no less essential for group cultivation, well water is regarded as being the property of the owner of the land on which the well is located. In Java, ownership of the river water is not encompassed by any definitive ruling. There is much to commend the concept of absolute rights of ownership vested in the ruler providing the ruler exercises these rights judiciously for the well-being of all his subjects. It is a means of obviating the arbitrary assumption of control over river water by occupants of ground along the upper reaches of the streams who are otherwise inclined to ignore the consequences for the crops on lower-lying ground (1969: 44).

In Buleleng Liefrinck records a literal control of water by the rajas:

> The right to permanent use of this water is ceded by the ruler and in return the applicants are required to pay a yearly levy (p. 45).

Subsequent investigators have questioned whether the ruler's control over water was actually so direct throughout Hindu-Balinese history (Van Stein Callenfels 1947: 104); it was more likely symbolic than jural. The rajas were symbols that water, versus land, was a translocal commodity and the viability of their court centers depended on assuring that water remained translocal. Their courts achieved this end by elaborating legal and ritual systems that increased both the feasibility and the appeal of a reliable rice surplus.

The *subak* system differentiated the complex process of watering paddies from all other areas of domestic and political, but not religious, life. Building on Liefrinck's work, Geertz has summarized this 'sociological defining feature of the Balinese irrigation system.'

> . . . it is organized into a separate independent, completely autonomous social form, called the *subak* . . .
> This membership is completely independent of any other social characteristic – residence (all [or most] *subaks* have people from various villages, and any one individual with much land at all will belong to several *subaks*), caste, kinship position, and so on (1972a: 27).

This institution is insulated, at least *de jure*, from matters of kinship: one's *subak* interests can conflict with those of a brother or a son. Or nowadays subsistence is on a different sociological axis from politics or anything else: one's own interests can conflict with those of a member of the same party, a colleague or boss, and so on. How much this is so should become clear later. Perhaps even more important, rice irrigation is insulated from other components of the subsistence system as well:

> . . . It must also be stressed that the *subak* is in no sense a collective farm. On his own land (which he can sell, rent, tenant, or whatever, as he wishes), within the regulation set by the *subak*, the individual peasant is his own master working in his own way, consuming (or selling) his own produce. The *subak* never engages in the actual process of cultivation as such nor, as I say of marketing; it regulates irrigation and that's all it does (1972a: 29).

Over the centuries institutions surrounding Balinese irrigation have been constantly refined to insure the maximum production – however irregular the distribution – of one highly regarded commodity and to prevent any conceivable advantage from accruing to the failure to achieve maximum production, given the water conditions. Diminished production hurts only oneself, or rather one's immediate hearth – those persons, usually husband, wife and children, eating from the same rice pot.

This is, baldly stated, what Liefrinck discerned, although he never analyzed it in a very schematic fashion. He detailed the procedures of council organization and the functioning of the irrigation temples that give Balinese agriculture an air more of ritual action than of subsistence behavior. The basic principle is simple:

> Those members with the same allocation of water are all obligated to participate to the same extent in the work that is collectively performed (Liefrinck 1969: 17).

Of course in reality there were and are many provisions for sharecropping, for purchasing exemptions, and for delegating tasks. High-caste landowners can persistently eschew physical labor as beneath them. But the responsibility, and council vote, of each *subak* member has traditionally been equal, regardless of rank.

Avoiding conflicts and markets

The complex rules, rights, and regulations are as meticulous in the water control of *subaks* as in the religious affairs of village areas and in the funeral and cremation tasks of hamlets. A sense of the delicate, surprisingly egalitarian basis of the system first noted by Liefrinck is quickly glimpsed from Grader's later study in Jembrana. We recall how in Bali water flows naturally in deep river gorges that descend from center-volcano-high to peripheral-ocean-low. The slopes of the gorges are terraced and, the higher on the slope the paddy is situated, the further back upstream the water must be diverted from the river and channeled to reach it. But water distribution is constructed in a way so as to preclude antagonism between two directly proximate paddy-owners in the same *subak*. As Grader explains in discussing the fiscal unit of the *subak*, 'Just as in the *banjar* (hamlet), the fiscal unit is the *paon* (hearth), in the *subak* it is the *pengalapan*, the water inlet of a *kesit*' (1960a: 273). Moreover:

> By *pengalapan* is meant the water inlet through which one *kesit* of *sawahs* is irrigated from the conduit. A *kesit* consists of a series of *sawah* plots lying one behind the other and belonging to the same person. If behind a *kesit* there is another belonging to some one else, the latter never receives the excess irrigation water from the *kesit* lying upstream, as in the case for the *sawahs* of one *kesit*; instead, a special branch conduit is constructed from the main conduit along the *sawah* dikes of the upstream *kesit* to the other *kesit*. The holders of the sawah plots beside this conduit for whom the water is not intended may not appropriate any water from it without running the risk of being punished by the *subak* for water theft (Grader 1960a: 270).

All the members draw water from the conduit. But in principle within the *subak* one man's water does not flow directly from another man's paddy. Rather direct antagonism can only arise between *subaks*. And this is precisely where the incorporated councils arbitrate any disputes. Moreover, cases could be appealed to the raja's council. This procedure was adopted to minimize interference with actual production.

Nevertheless, wet-rice agriculture was hardly a tranquil enterprise; witness the hostilities of the 1880s:

> Where the rivers in Bali traverse the territories of different principalities, disputes often arise over the use of the water. Moreover, it is customary in the frequent wars between the various principalities for the rulers of the higher inland regions to divert the rivers supplying the rice fields nearer the coast or to block the streams at the given point and then release a flow of water that destroys all the dams on the river below that point. Incalculable damage has been caused by these strategems (Liefrinck 1969: 43).

We can surmise that as population increased, and as cross-cutting civic, religious, economic, political, and status affiliations grew more intertwined – especially after the Dutch undercut the rajas' influence first in the North, then the South – there was little chance of restricting the effects of interfering with the water supply to a specific enemy. As it became more difficult to find several individuals with *subak* interests just alike, it must have been impossible to find a *subak* unit, all of whose members one wanted to harm. Yet hostilities recur. A great backlog of antagonisms, many of them involving water rights, was vented in the political turmoil of 1965. And during the severe drought of 1972, when cattle dropped dead at pasture and exroyal politicians in progressive districts were borne to the fields in raja fashion to ask the gods for water, conditions were like the ones described by Liefrinck in the 1880s:

> In those *subaks* where the supply of water is limited, it is the practice to have the conduit patrolled day and night whenever the water-level of the river becomes low. These patrols . . . keep constant watch to guard against any likely cause of damage and to prevent any attempts to fish in the conduit, but primarily to hinder the theft of water by owners of lower-lying *sawahs*. Such vigilance is understandable, as water theft is sometimes systematically contrived by tunnelling (Liefrinck 1969: 22).

We shall return to religious and ritual aspects of rice production later. For now we should note that Liefrinck appreciated that along with the actual technology, the rice-cult ritual itself was an index of the carefully regulated, cooperative control of water. For example, he summarizes the successive rites during stages of the growth cycle, culminating in the harvest festival as follows:

> The main offerings are prepared by the family of the *usaba* [irrigation temple] priest, the *pemangku* [either compensated in kind or exempted from *subak* service]. But every housewife in the *subak* community has been busy for days making simpler offerings for which the finest flowers and the best fruits are used. Additional items required for the *usaba* ceremonies and for the festival meals eaten at the temple – rice, meat, fruit, sweets, and so on – must be supplied by the members of the *sekaha subak* in proportion to the area of the *sawah* holdings and in accordance with a permanent list stipulating which items each member has to contribute for this and other occasions (Liefrinck 1969: 33–4).

Subsequent observers should have heeded Liefrinck's account of these careful calculations of responsibilities in the rice cult, which echo in ritual similar calculations in actual labor required, depending on the amount of paddy owned and, thus, water received. His successors might then have tended less to imagine that Bali reflected a vague spirit of generous cooperation, usually labeled with the famous Indonesian slogan *gotong-royang*. Rather they might have appreciated more the skillful capacity of these agriculturalists to balance and control individual interests in rigorous fair-share procedures that rival any bureaucratic process yet devised in the Indonesian nation. (For an analogous point regarding Java, see the important study by Koentjaraningrat, 1967b.) In Bali the ritual component is as critical as the labor component. And it is the ritual component, which the Balinese themselves view as indispensable, that lends a cottage-industry quality to wet-rice production. Even where women still do not work in the fields, the entire membership of a kitchen – men, women, children – must contribute to the successful agricultural cycle. The time consumed by the preparation of religious offerings probably approaches that consumed by manual labor, once terracing has been completed.

Finally, it is important to note that Balinese avoid as far as possible relying on market redistribution networks to stock their rice granaries. It remains remarkably true today that Balinese, even the most privileged and progressive, refuse to dissociate themselves completely from the subsistence production-system. The path of rice from the paddy to storage in the houseyard *lubang* should not be mediated by a market connection; this, I think, comes near being a religious value. In bygone times even rajas, while they would not labor in the fields, had to own sufficient lands to stock their own granaries; the public tax went largely for mass rituals. In the eyes of Balinese there is a slight stigma attached to anyone who must purchase rice from the market system that was extended under the colonial regime and then under the Indonesian nation. This factor still vividly distinguishes Bali's economy from that of Java. Even urbane Balinese white-collar elites and merchants refuse to become totally alienated from wet-rice subsistence. They remain attached to village-area localities where the tie between households and irrigation councils remains approximately as Liefrinck described it.[1]

In conclusion, without expressing the matter precisely in this way, Liefrinck revealed how rice production could be elaborately controlled yet still remain outside the otherwise elaborate market system. Moreover, he and his successors stressed the relative autonomy of local irrigation councils – as long as no one jeopardized the water supply – whose members' interests coincide only because they draw water from the same source but explicitly not from one another. In a sense, Liefrinck's achievement was to appreciate how much of his description and analysis was prefabricated in the very apparatus of Balinese irrigation. To guide him he had both the conspicuous technology of the island and the elaborate temples and shrines that flag each critical juncture in water control. He wedded a straightforward empirical method to Bali's irrigation apparatus which, without being constrained by any theoretical model, affords a ready made flow-chart. The major omission in Liefrinck was how the isolable institution called *subak* relates to other customs and practices in Bali, and the always changing answers to this question remain problems for current research. But his studies opened the way to integrated theories of Balinese society and culture and posed the implicit challenge to other observers to live up to his example.

Encyclopedic scope

Prolonged exposure to the more elaborate Bali-Hindu culture in the South enriched the portrait of Bali in the influential *Encyclopaedie van Nederlandsch-Indië* (1917). This 'highly intelligent folk' inhabited, in terms of prosperity and scenery, 'one of the most important islands of the East-India archipelago' (de Bruyn-Kops 1917: 107). From their cozy, reasonable canals to their romantic suicides during the colonial conquest, the Balinese appealed strongly to a Dutch public. No other part of the East Indies displayed such familiar poles of values and experience in so exotic a setting. Bali had seemed commodious to Lintgens in 1597; it seemed this and more to Rouffaer in his introduction to Nieuwenkamp's (1906–10) stunning *prachtwerk* on the island's creative life and art:

> What character, what style, what power of artistic ability in all the Balinese productions of architecture, sculpture, painting and drawing, metalwork, textiles, carving, pottery . . . Art lives in Bali! Here folk life and folk religion and folk art is still a beautiful totality (*Geheel*), as in Gothic Europe especially or in Renaissance times as well (Rouffaer 1906: vii).

But what was the nature of the society that created this world of art?

Native institutions

The *Encyclopedia* does not completely escape outright subjectivity: 'If the body is more robust, so does the spirit of the Balinese appear more energetic than that of the Javanese' (1917: 116). It worries over a few standard traits: topless women, floral grooming, and, more important, hair – dark black worn long by all men and women, save princes who cut it short, and priests who bind it. Yet its serious account of the island's history and society provides a summary of nineteenth-century findings which affected basic assumptions about Bali throughout the colonial period.

The caste system (*kastenstelsel*) appears to be the primary institutional framework. There is little notion that this elitist theory of Balinese society might vary with the informant's status. Nor do investigators suspect that caste codes could merely be more accessible to foreign interrogators, rather than representative of the whole society. Caste is taken largely as fact rather than ideology:

> Along with Hinduism the caste system – the division of the people into strata (*lagen*) or statuses (*standen*) – was brought to Bali and Lombok and is being maintained to this day. The four statuses are in order: 1) Brahmanas, 2) Satrias, 3) Wesias, and 4) Sudras. The connection between the practice of specific occupations and services and the castes that must have originally existed in *voor-Indië* (Brahmana-clergy, Satria-knighthood, Wesia-commerce, Sudra-servitude) has been completely forgotten among Balinese, and probably never existed. Thus among other things, people of all castes take part in agriculture and stand as each other's equals in rights and duties pertaining to it (de Bruyn-Kops 1917: 117).

While as great a proportion of Brahmanas might farm fields as Sudras, only Brahmanas have the right to become *pedanda* priests:

> Although there are four statuses, in speaking of 'someone of caste' one means a person from one of the three first-mentioned categories, the *triwangsa* or the nobility (*adel*). These are the 'twice-borns,' *dwijati*, in contrast to the once-born (*ekajati*), the lowfolk . . .[2]
>
> In Bali the Brahmana caste falls into two main groups, Siwa and Buda, the former is further split into five subdivisions – Kemenuh, Keniten, Mas, Manuba and Petapan. The two major groups show a difference in religious views; the subdividing of the Siwa group is the result of an inferior progeny (*minderwaardig nakomelingschap*) from the marriages between Brahmana men and women from a lower caste.

Still such offspring . . . , provided they are legitimate children – remain members of the father's caste (p. 117).

The actual mechanism for this maintenance of father's caste, in spite of any inferiority implied by his mother's rank or his own birth position, remained obscure. Future Dutch ethnographers worked on the problem but neglected the intimately related marriage system. Moreover, they regarded this subdivision of Brahmana Siwa as literal, historical fact, and they sought confirmation in the royal chronicles. Observers overlooked how such schemes might be rhetorically loaded to accentuate the status of Brahmana Siwa at the expense of Brahmana Boda.

The *Encyclopedia* article notes the Brahmana male-title (*Ida*) and female-title (*Idoyo*) and the special role of priests:

From Brahmanas come pedanda priests, who stand in a very high regard and are considered more or less as saints. Also persons belonging to the Satria or Wesia caste – in Lombok at least – could acquire priesthood; although in practice such a thing does not occur (pp. 117–18).

Yet there is little sense that the Balinese of Lombok might be seeking to legitimate their own status in a way expressly to out rival their land of origin, although this possibility had earlier been alluded to by Friederich:

. . . the Balinese of Lombok, and especially their prince, are much richer than those of Bali . . . ; and secondly, the Balinese of Lombok, and particularly the present prince, are looked down upon, and said to be ignorant in their religion and their customs, by the Balinese of Bali, and especially by the Dewa Agung, whom the people of Lombok do not acknowledge. Now to refute these unfavorable opinions, they show themselves to be much more precise in the performance of their religious duties than the majority of the Balinese in Bali (1849: 98).

Such aloofness by inhabitants of Klungkung and Gianyar remains proverbial even today.

The relation between a *pedanda* priest and a novice is documented, by the *Encyclopedia*, along with the oft-itemized ideal ascetic-comportment of priests: never lie, avoid wicked passions, abstain from pork (Bali's prized dish), maintain ritual purity and a sacred life, so to achieve divinity after death. Finally, the perpetual dilemma concerning priests and marriage arises:

Women also can work their way up to the clergy and are titled *pedanda-istri*; the wives of *pedandas* must in all events be consecrated in the learning of their spouses. Although it is considered very seemly for a *pedanda* to have only one wife, many *pedandas* have more wives, and from lower statuses as well. At the highest degree of holiness stands the priest who upon his consecration makes a vow to have no relationship with any women during his life (p. 117).

The image of the *pedanda* still harbors conflicting ideals in modern Bali. South Asian texts depict him as a celibate, pure renouncer. Bali-Hindu ritual requires him to possess a consort who helps in sacred ceremonies, and native chronicles of caste project an arch polygynist whose different wives produced the ranked subdivisions of all Brahmanas. *Pedanda* roles were perhaps the first inherent conflict to be documented in Balinese culture, but the priestly image was insufficiently appreciated as a perpetual generator of argument.

In 1917, doctrine about the twice-borns – the Satrias and especially the Wesias – remained obscure:

The caste of Satria's is subdivided into 1) Satria dalem – including the people of the princely families of Klungkung, Bangli, and Gianyar, 2) Satria Predewa, 3) Satria Presangiang, 4) Satria Pungakan, 5) Satria Bagus. Title: Dewa for the man and Desak for the woman. The third caste, Wesia, includes a major group, the Aryas . . . divided into Arya Sentong, Beleteng, Waringin, Kapakisan, Belog and Benchulu. Title: Gusti for the man and Gusti-Ayu for the woman. In Karangasem and Lombok the Aryas were titled I Gusti. In Lombok, one recognizes also the Wargis, with the title Gusti or Dane, as the lowest class of Wesias; while in Jembrana and Tabanan a specific category of people from the Wesia caste bears the noble title: Salit (p. 117).

Such hints of regional variation later grew into Korn's monumental *Het Adatrecht van Bali* (1932), which records, for example, how *aryas* varied in title, rights, history, and power across locales and kingdoms. Already in the *Encyclopedia* the definition of *wargi* (lower women taken by superior males, that is, hypergamy) and the notion of *aryas* as a special group of the Wesia caste strains against the feudal analogy where *aryas* were envisioned as landed nobility. Difficulties with this *arya* scheme are most conspicuous in efforts to sort out the actual ruling houses by caste, with the obvious slippage between *warna* label and title indexes of status:

The rajas (*vorsten*) of Bali and Lombok belonged to the Satria and Wesia caste. Satrias (*Dewa*) were those from Klungkung, with the high title of Dewa Agung, and those from Bangli and Gianyar. The rest were Gustis. Although of lower caste, the princes as such stood above their Brahmana subjects (*onderdanen*) [yet they could not take a Brahmana wife]. They saw themselves willingly regarded as the earthly representative of the godhead, and this exalted position accords with the fact that their decisions or pronouncements (*paswaras*) were more powerful than the law codes (p. 118).

Special provisions that allow a prince to wed a Brahmana women to save his line from extinction here go unrecorded.

Earlier accounts had sensationalized the rajas' oppression of a worthy, democratic folk. Now that the colonial regime was stabilized, retrospects of the Balinese state were moderated. It was perhaps out of a high regard for the achievements in irrigation supported by the rajas that the *Encyclopedia* limits its tally of despotic excesses to these:

Naturally, under the raja administration the Triwangsa people had many privileges above commoner folk. They were only lightly punished for the same errors; the higher the status the less the penalty, with the understanding however that servants and slaves to some extent shared the same level of privilege as their masters. Such things were rendered metaphorically with the words *Kahaubaning waringin*, which means 'enjoyed from the shadow of the banyan tree.' . . . For a pendanda the defilement from touching a corpse lasts only five days, for a Brahmana, Satria, and

Wesia, ten, fifteen, and twenty days, respectively, and for a Sudra twenty-five. The corpse of a Brahman who dies of leprosy must remain buried ten years before it can be cremated, while that of a Sudra who succumbs of this illness must wait twenty-five years before it may be subjected to the process of cremation (purification and liberation of the soul) (p. 118).

An Indian optic focused the Brahmanas – at least their specialist priests, marriage excepted – and leading Satrias. However, it distorted the Wesias and *aryas* and completely blurred the Sudras. The latter seemed simply to be relatively prosperous agriculturalists, far better off than their Indic namesakes. Moreover, Bali was praised for lacking true pariahs:

The Sudras or Kaulas, although impure following the old Hindu opinion, were not despised in Bali and Lombok. Following Balinese conceptions those who deal in certain impurity-producing circumstances are definitely unclean, as for example, people who have drawn water where a corpse has been washed . . . , or over whose heads excrement has been poured . . . ; people from the *triwangsa* who have humbled themselves before Sudras, etc. There is a graduated difference in the duration of the impurity.

The lowest status in Balinese society (the Kaulas) naturally have no titles; as in Java, those who have children are called in daily life 'father of' (*Pan* or *Nang*) 'mother of' . . . (then follows the name of their eldest child). Apart from this in all statuses men were indicated with I and women with Ni, while between these prefixes and the proper names . . .

A general rule for all statuses obtains that men can marry women of lower birth (noblemen, even Sudra women) while women can only take as spouses men of the same or higher status. The wife who belongs to a lower status than her husband is called *penawing* in contrast with *bechik* or *padmi*, the wife of the same caste.

The children of *penawings* and *bechik* are also distinguished with the same names (p. 118).

Sudras were perceived in counter distinction to *triwangsas*. The unimportance of urbanized market-systems and the general lack of the urban/rural dichotomy so conspicuous in Islamized Java prevented the Dutch from conceptualizing Bali's mass of commoners – sometimes said to be sheltered, sometimes oppressed by the Hindu courts – as what we would today call a peasantry. In 1917 Sudras appeared to be mainly what their betters were not, which did not always work to their disadvantage, especially in the more sensational areas of courtly custom:

Sudras could not be followed into death by their wives; *triwangsas* could. If a widow withdrew after having declared herself ready to be sacrificed, she fell into the category of despicable creature (*verachte wezens*). On the other hand, the wife could achieve death either by stabbing herself with a Kris or having herself stabbed, '*mabela*' (she then received the honorific *bela*), after which her body was laid on the pyre; or she could jump living into the sea of fire, '*mesatia*' (then she received the honorific *satya*). From the moment the wife revealed her intention to follow her husband in death, she was regarded and treated as sacred (*heilige*) (p. 118).

That all this was denied to Sudra women, at least those who married Sudras, suggests the serious difficulties of any simple exploitation theory for traditional Balinese caste.

The *Encyclopedia* documents such privileges of status and mentions the titles that graduate the twice-born/Sudra distinction in the event of offspring from legitimate cross-category marriages (that is, upper male, lower female). But when it comes to generalizing about caste, it retreats to a simplistic importation scheme and pronounces the *triwangsa*/Sudra distinction absolute:

> As a last consideration of the *Kastenwezen*, it can be mentioned that non-Hindus, following Balinese understanding, were so far equated with Sudras that they never could be regarded as belonging to the *Triwangsa* (p. 118).

This conclusion overlooks the critical fact that, unlike 'non-Hindus,' Sudras are eventually cremated. At least in death they achieve pale echoes of Hindu courtly examples. How true this is in life as well should become evident in later chapters.

After caste, the second main rubric for characterizing Balinese life was religion. Three of the major liberal achievements the Dutch claimed for the administration were its prohibition of *suttee*, its elimination of slavery, and its exemplary religious tolerance. By religion is intended Hinduism as conveyed by Sanskritic and *Kawi* texts and activated in rites at the temples and shrines throughout the island. As for the Hinduism of Bali:

> After first mixing itself with another cult in Java, in Bali it absorbed various aspects of the Polynesian-animistic worship of the original inhabitants. Siwa is worshipped as Supreme God, while Brahma and Wisnu are considered not so much as particular gods but more as divine powers of Siwa (pp. 118–19).

The article reviews flexibilities in the complicated Balinese world view, with its parallel deistic and demonic incarnations of every cosmological attribute, not to mention its *desa* and family gods. Balinese religion is declared 'a pantheism in the broadest sense of the word':

> Religion saturates the whole life of a Balinese; the gods as well as the evil spirits (*butas*) are ubiquitous and their influence on the fate of men is always felt.
>
> Balinese life is one uninterrupted effort to befriend the gods and to placate or to drive out enemy spirits . . . (p. 119).

Somewhat surprising for a population so devoted to ceremonies and offerings to keep the gods and evil spirits in balance is the tolerance of Balinese for those who profess Islamic, Chinese, and Christian faiths. Less surprising is their refusal to embrace any of these themselves. Most notably:

> Christianity at present numbers no Balinese among its adherents. The sole Balinese who had been won over to the new doctrine, whether out of remorse of insanity, murdered the missionary Vroom (1881) (p. 119).

The discussion of religion emphasizes Bali's innumerable temples and shrines (*offerplaatsen*). In this area extensive philological and archaeological work had produced rich results. Four types of village temples are listed: (1) *pura desa* – for various general and localized gods; (2) *pura dalem* – the death temples consecrated to goddess Durga at cemetaries and cremation sites; (3) *pura segara* – on beaches for ocean gods; and (4) *pura bukit* – on hills and mountains for mountain gods. Moreover, in each irrigation society there is a *pura subak* dedicated to Sri, goddess of irrigated fields. The article cites one version of the list of six, or seven, holy temples that relate imperfectly to the division of the island into kingdom-districts (p. 122). But who worships where remains unclear, as does the interrelation of congregations. In Dutch scholarship the archaeology and theology of the temple system progressed far faster than the sociology.

Finally, brief mention is made of the commoner custodial-priests (*pemangkus*) in charge of temples, these walled-in sacred courtyards reserved for entertaining the gods during their periodic visitations from, according to Hindu conceptions, mountainward abodes. The article discusses religious aspects of the calendar, cycles of holidays and *lontar* manuscripts. It describes the pleasing rectilinear motifs of household and temple architecture, the pavilionlike chambers and shrines, and the organization of space according to its sacred/profane function and the purity/pollution entailed.

Everything else and law

Under the catch-all tag of 'customs and usages' (*zeden en gebruiken*) we find assembled any cross-culturally striking aspect of Bali that does not relate explicitly to 'caste,' 'religion,' 'agriculture and industry,' or the formal 'administration of justice' (*rechtspraak*). *Zeden en gebruiken* covers what ethnographers would later catalogue as social organization, family and marriage, ritual and magic, the arts, and, since this is Bali, a long entry on cremation. Included here are several ethnological themes important throughout the colonial period.

First, two types of village organization (*desa vereenigingen*) are distinguished. Membership in the old-style villages is limited to the families whose ancestors originally established the *desa*; they are governed by a council of elders with exclusive rights to houseland. Membership in the newer type *desa* includes outsiders (*vreemdelingen*). Thus the 'bond is no longer so heartfelt' (*innig*), and all heads of families are on the council and have property rights (p. 121). This theme of old kingroup *desas* versus newer composite *desas* was elaborated and historicized in future work. Its companion theme was the democratic operation of local councils for both village-area affairs and irrigation-society control.

> The equality in rights and duties in both categories of councils was extended so far that there was no question of any privileges for one or another caste or even for one or another quality of man.
>
> As members of a desa or subak council, a Brahmana stands as equal to a Sudra, a district leader (*punggawa*) stands as equal to the most lowly villager (p. 121).

This phrasing of the issue overlooks the fact that high castes tend to eschew *desa* affairs altogether; they have little practical interest in the council, since they boast independent ancestral temples, and their residential property is counted among lands alienated from localities by rajas. Also, traditionally such lines were relatively independent of irrigation societies, because royal and noble houses kept them supplied with a rice staple. Nevertheless, this independence was most likely never total, and the egalitarian provisions must certainly have limited local influence of twice-borns.

The *Encyclopedia*'s significant shift in emphasis to the local, commoner level of political and social organization reflected the important qualifications to earlier views of Balinese royalty that emerged from late nineteenth-century research. Subsequent colonial and post-war research confirmed this fact. H. Geertz has recently summarized the particularities of the typical traditional bonds between ordinary Balinese and their superiors:

> Commoners were 'owned' [i.e., specific services by them were 'owned'] by the various lesser lords as well as directly by the paramount prince in each region, and they could be 'bestowed' on others as gifts or seized from them as a result of military conquest . . . Some commoners paid only taxes to a lord, some were obliged to contribute goods and services for massive ceremonial festivals, while others worked for the lord as retainers or sharecroppers. Each individual commoner typically had several different lords 'owning' [various services of] various of their inhabitants. However, the governing of the village community itself was not the prerogative of the gentry, nor did the lords have much of importance to do with the irrigation societies. They served only as courts of last appeal for commoner disputes that could not be settled through their own councils. The main functions of the lords and princes, from the point of view of the village communities, were symbolic and ritualistic in that the ceremonies that the lords held periodically directly involved all the local population (1972: 64).

A major theme in Indonesian studies was woman's lot, one of the favored areas, along with prohibiting gambling, for proving the benefits of colonialism. Accordingly, the *Encyclopedia* proclaimed:

> As one of the good results of the expansion of our involvement in things Balinese must certainly be included the assuagement of the lot of women (p. 122).

Dutch observers considered family bonds in Bali strong and noted the clear sexual division of labor, with men laboring in the fields and women performing the constant household chores. Part of woman's 'very subordinate place' was thought to be most conspicuous in Balinese marriage practices. The *Encyclopedia* lists four types of marriage: (1) the father or guardian of the young man directs the proposal to the nearest male relations of the girl (*mepadik*); (2) abduction with mutual approval (*merangkat*); (3) violent abduction (*malangandang*) wherein the girl submits; and (4) the father or guardian of the girl makes the proposal to the elders of the youth (*sentana*).

Colonial officials showed concern for the individual female's will. They hoped to enforce traditional sanctions against violent abduction; the girl's outrage, if not always her family's, was to be sham only. The article notes special *sentana* marriages in which a son-in-law becomes legal heir; it documents customs concerning adultery and illegitimate offspring and records interesting taboos involving 'spiritual kinship' (*geestelijke verwantschap*) which forbid marriage with a house priest's or a *guru*'s daughter. But the general account of marriage restrictions mistakes a generational kinship terminology for a prohibition on near-kin marriage, and it assumes that relatives called by the same terms used for immediate family could not be spouses:

> Marriage prohibition because of blood or affinal relations goes further for a Balinese than for us, because for him all the relatives of the same generation were placed under the same category . . . Thus, he considered . . . the child of his brother as his child (p. 123).

Here the *Encyclopedia* was in factual error; a terminological 'brother-sister' are, under certain circumstances, preferred spouses. While in 1917 theories of caste were simplified and falsely historicized, theories of marriage were virtually lacking. The systematics of marriage remained invisible, partly because terms for kinsmen were not distinguished from marriage rules. Marriage was considered detrimental to those individuals, especially women, married against their will. We should note that while prohibiting a given marriage may oppress a particular woman's or, for that matter, man's will, it can also articulate an important social or cultural scheme. Colonial officials eventually enforced hypergamy among the upper ranks of the society; but they never learned to appreciate the significant play in cultural categories marriage necessarily entailed. They never wondered what all the marriage rites and different options and taboos might mean, what sort of social drama they might sustain.

The *Encyclopedia*'s treatment of agriculture and industry is accurate but necessarily brief; it commends the indigenous irrigation system:

> This exceptionally satisfactory organization is not of Hindu but of pure Balinese origin (p. 124).

Then the crafts are itemized and their quality assessed: apart from the performing arts there is architecture, stonecarving, woodcarving, metal-working, plaiting and weaving; gold, silver, and iron smiths; copperwork, fired earthenware, salt, palm-wine, lime, bricks, and so on. But, the complex social configurations and religious conceptions and taboos surrounding many of these arts and industries receive little mention.

This impressive 1917 summary concludes with *rechtspraak*, the most critical issue in colonial Bali, since this island of dubious economic importance could serve mainly as a proving ground for enlightened *zelfbestuur*. The article cites the precedence of royal ordinances (*paswaras*) over any conflicting legal codes from the Hindu law books. Then the complex Balinese legal institutions are compressed into a paragraph. It is this system of local and pan-Balinese jurisprudence that the Dutch, whenever their conscience would permit, tried to leave intact:

> The administration of justice of the *Raden van Kertas* [The 'college of Brahmanas' supported by each raja] is based on the *paswaras* in addition to the old codes (*wetboeken*) of which a great number, certainly more than ten, exist, the most important being Agama and Adigama. The Agama law code is rich with provisions taken directly from Hindu codes, besides which appear others of Javanese or Balinese origin. In contrast with the village and irrigation society regulations – following which all members, regardless of their caste, are fully equal in laws and obligations – in the law codes and *paswaras* the caste system appears strongly in the foreground. Following the *wetboeken*, the fact that someone committed some offence against another of higher caste produced aggravating circumstances, while in the opposite case extenuating circumstances were assumed. A Sudra who seriously offended a Brahmana was condemned to death; a Brahmana who offended a Sudra was merely required to pay a fine worth a few dimes. If an inferior does bodily harm to a superior there results punishment by mutilation, such as cutting off hands or feet . . . (pp. 126–7).

These harsh punishments and, perhaps even more, the prejudicial scale of penalties, dismayed Western observers. They hoped to purge such injustice, while preserving the legal spheres for irrigation and local custom and the old royal courts of appeals.

Thus, Balinese legal traditions created dilemmas for the Dutch administrators of the island. The indigenous system was found in many ways to be rational, in that laws were recorded, decisions were justified by precedent, and distinct spheres of jurisprudence were a long-lived institution. Moreover, in their local affairs indigenes adhered to principles of equality that abstracted individual legal rights and responsibilities from other social, economic, and religious attributes. Yet, elsewhere in the system certain strata of the society were set above the more severe penal code. Moreover, by reading between the lines of post-1849 reports, it is obvious that no simple explanation of blind oppression could explain commoner support of such differences. The lower strata actually seemed to believe their betters merited milder penalties for ostensibly the same offence.

Dutch administrators in Bali might have been able to accept radical hierarchy in title, learning, residence, property, religious merit, and so forth, but never in legal, especially, criminal, proceedings. In the conflict of the two legal systems we can best sense the poignance of that storied meeting, and mutual failure to comprehend, between the Ancient East and the New West. In modern Western traditions it was precisely in these instances in which the suspected wrongdoer confronted the state that theories of individual equality had been most fully realized – in principle equality under law had been achieved. Wherever the colonial record describes the efforts to reform beliefs in radical qualitative differences among strata of human society – expressed most vividly in differential criminal accountability – the history of ethnology becomes legitimately sensational: Western observers seem to have felt they were confronting Europe's own past before the Age of Reason. In terms of graded punishment whereby a superior's ritual purity mitigated the pollution of his offense, if in little else, the Balinese were 'feudal,' and the Dutch considered it their legal mission to enlighten them.

3. Baliology: twentieth-century systems (1920s–1950s)

Het mag trouwens betwijfeld worden of de inrichting der Balische samenleven wel ooit geheel verklaard zal kunnen worden.

(Korn 1932: 136)[1]

Balinese studies came of age only as the laissez-faire liberal period of the Dutch East Indies gave way to the post-1901 ethical era, with its governmental economic controls and programs in education and welfare. Bali's proximity to Java continued to facilitate extensive research well beyond anything warranted by the island's political and economic importance. Next door the heated dialectic of colonial politics, so crucial in the administration of Java since the culture system, continued:

> Thus by the end of the colonial era in Indonesia the Conservative and Liberal positions had altered almost 180° from their outlook a century or so before: The Conservative who in 1840 strongly defended the central role of government in economic life, and who looked askance at the demands of private capital to freely enter and develop the country, by 1940 had become the principal spokesman for that capital and saw himself usually aligned against the Neo-Liberalism of the government policies of the day (van der Kroef 1963: 30).

Issues of government control and supervision were less acute in Bali where little land was suitable for plantation crops. After 1908 scholars tended toward the neo-liberal persuasion which stressed 'a particularist view of Indonesian land rights in the context of humanitarian policy and its universalist correlates' (van der Kroef 1963: 55). Moreover, in Bali both the courtly traditions and the integrity of local customary usages were commended by colonial officials.

To understand how Balinese scholars could be both pro-*desa* and pro-court, we must recall several fundamental contrasts with Java. Bali's upper caste houses never endured the series of challenges to their authority suffered by the Javanese Hindu-Buddhist elites (the *priyayi*). Javanese *priyayi* jockeyed for spheres of influence throughout the nineteenth century as much of Java grew more intensely Islamic. Moreover, both of the two major successive colonial policies in Java drastically altered the *priyayi* role in society:

> The forced cultivation of export crops under the so-called Culture System (1830–1870) marked the beginnings of the disintegrative process. Though it strengthened

the authoritarian control of the *priyayi*-elite by turning the Regents into a hereditary class with an economic stake in the governmental produce monopoly, at the same time it started a progressive alienation between *priyayi* and the exploited peasantry, which came to regard the Regent as the tool of foreign rulers.

In 1870, the Liberal Era replaced the Culture System, opening Indonesia to the penetration of private capitalism . . . The new policy makers . . . tended to relegate these representatives of a 'backward' and 'feudal' system [the Regents] to political impotence. The resulting decline in *priyayi* prestige was furthered by the fact that Dutch private enterprise, in search of land leases and labor, tended to establish direct contacts with village heads, by-passing the Regents (Benda 1958: 33; cf. Walker and Tinker 1974: 62 ff).

Bali had escaped this radical alienation between court and commoner. Although several royal overlords committed suicide or were banished during Dutch take-over during 1906–8, and, although the nature of the complex bonds between subject and lord was soon reduced to simpler forms of taxation, the pervasive influence of the Balinese cultural elite continued unabated. Consequently, colonial administrators sought to preserve both the rich courtly traditions and the local *adat* spheres.

Finally, scholars in Bali tended to favor German *kulturkreise* or 'culture waves' frameworks over the protostructuralist approaches to society and cosmology that were being tested in Java, most notably by W.H. Rassers (1960). The early view of Bali as a stagnant pool left over from a Hindu wave out of pre-Mohammedan Java insured persistent historicization of any new findings.

Adat classification and variation

About when the *Encyclopedia* appeared, the systematic foundation for future studies of customary law (*adat*) was published by C. van Vollenhoven. The major classification of Indonesian populations in the 1860s, J.J. Hollander's racial scheme, was composed almost entirely of residual classes (cf. Avé 1970). Apart from the Negroid races of New Guinea, the Arab and Chinese foreigners, and the so-called mixed races, there was only one main division, the Batta race versus the Malay race. Balinese were consigned to the former, Javanese to the latter.

Van Vollenhoven's classification of 1918 drew on the ethnographic sketches briefly sampled above to posit nineteen law-areas (*rechtskringen*). As J.B. Avé observes, 'this classification proved to be the basis for the study of customary law in Indonesia until the Second World War' (1970: 96). Indeed, Van Vollenhoven was credited as:

> the creator of a new and typically Dutch form of science, whose sound and lasting foundation he laid for all time. Other nations have [as of WW II] hardly started the systematic investigation of the traditional legal forms among the populations of their overseas territories . . . (Korn 1948: 161).

The classification subdivides into four major types of communities: (1) genealogical groups, as in Borneo and New Guinea; (2) territorial communities with corporate genealogical groups, as in the Minangkabau of Sumatra; (3) territorial communities, as in the principalities of Java; and (4) areas which include all of the above plus voluntary associations (Avé 1970: 96). Since Bali fell into the fourth, residual category, *adat* scholars there had a complex task of documentation before them.

Local integrity

V.E. Korn tackled the task to become dean of Balinese *adat* studies. He recognized Liefrinck's formidable work as the 'foundation of every description of Balinese *adat* law.' But he recalled as well van Vollenhoven's observation that Liefrinck had restricted himself to practical accounts of three central factors: indigenous land rights (*grondenrecht*), royal rents (*landrente*), and local institutions (*dorpsinrichting*). Moreover, Liefrinck's account of organization within and between village-areas was inadequate (Korn 1932: 71, 75). The task for future scholarship was clear: to extend detailed compilations of native custom into more obscure areas, such as hereditary law.

The pervasive pseudohistorical scheme of Korn's work – indigenous Balinese, then Hindu – can easily be mistaken in retrospect as a naive 'conjectural history' of culture waves. Yet it is more accurately understood as reflecting a critical issue of the colonial administration. The insistence on the separation even in current life between original indigenous Balinese aspects and later Hindu importations arose from a famous earlier demonstration of the non-derivative, indigenous integrity of local Indonesian culture:

> Snouck Hurgronje, who coined the term 'adat law,' clearly showed to what a small extent Muhammedan law accounts for the content of adat law. The same argument in relation to Hindu law was elaborated by Lekkerkerker in his *Hindurecht in Indonesie* (1918) (Korn 1948: 164).

Hurgronje had convincingly argued that an adequate understanding of custom and law in Acheh is not forthcoming from philological expertise in Koranic materials (cf. Benda 1958: 20–31). This remained the position of the profieldwork faction of scholars over and against armchair anthropology. Lekkerkerker asserted the same point regarding Bali and its Sanskritic-Hindu overlay. Korn and his colleagues spent two decades confirming his assertion.

Korn's massive *Het Adatrecht van Bali* (1932) was an exemplary product of the 'new and typically Dutch form of science.' Seven-hundred pages are packed with most of the social rules and varying customary usages known in Bali. The tome divides everything according to Western legal divisions relevant to particular beliefs or customs: family law, inheritance law, property law, criminal law, and so forth. Yet the pervading theme is not standardization, but local variation. Korn did not try to force a Western legal apparatus onto a more subtle Balinese ritual and social life. Rather, knowing that the colonial administration had to promote Western concepts of human rights, he tried to plot the way best to preserve the rich variations of Balinese culture from a roughshod application of Dutch legal standards. If his work exaggerated the autonomy of each local *dorps republik*, it was partly to defend all locales from being reduced to average cases:

> It is the great sorrow of the foremost scholar on Bali, V.E. Korn . . . that the Netherlands authority, because of its tendency toward centralization, bypassed too rashly the *adat* and the freedoms of the different villages with their very diverse regulations, and that it greatly overestimated the Hinduization of Bali (Last 1950: 20).

The strength of Korn's *Het Adatrecht van Bali* – unrelenting insistence on variation from village-area to village-area or court to court – is its weakness as well. This sea of detail can be fished for bits of insight but provides few overall conclusions. Even current Dutch fieldworkers bemoan its tenebrous density and the heady specifics which undermine many a generalization about things Balinese. To a large extent, ethnography here lost sight of ethnology's task of epitomizing the whole, but for a once-understandable cause. Yet in its day, Korn's study appeared less desultory, since it imposed relative order on the rambling data then available, for example, the deeds, legal formulas, proverbs, village regulations, native descriptions of customary law, royal edicts, and so on documented in the *Adatrechtbundels*. A single illustration from this literature should convey its own unwieldy detail. This legal report on a case contesting an adoption procedure appeared in *Indische Gids* in 1922 and in Balinese and English in *Adatrechtbundels*, 1930:

> Deed of adoption of a female *sentana* (family continuator), not being the daughter of the adopting man himself; abridged. – Tabanan, Bali, 1890.
>
> Probation document for Pan Sukarja living in the village of Mambang and being under the authority of the *pamekel* I Gdē Dēwi who lives in the quarter Tegal, village Tabanan; these I Gdē Dēwi and Pan Sukarja being both subject to the Prince.
>
> The said Pan Sukarja has asked permission to yield his own daughter Ni Reganti, whereas she has been asked for by Pan Sukarni living in the village of Mambang and being under the authority of the pamekel Nang Mirit who lives in the quarter Grogak Kanginan village Tabanan; these Nang Mirit and Pan Sukarni being both subject to the Prince.
>
> . . . The Prince did already grant his assent.
>
> Further, the reason why Pan Sukarni has asked for the said Ni Reganti is in order to use her as a sentana.
>
> In case afterwards a villager from any of the four castes, within the jurisdiction of the same balē agung, happens to elope with Ni Reganti and is willing to be taken up in Pan Sukarni's house as a sentana, there will be no objection against this elopement. If, however, he is not disposed to be taken up in Pan Sukarni's house as a sentana, then the elopement with Ni Reganti will be unlawful: the maiden and the youngster must be separated immediately, the youngster moreover paying a fine of 24.500 kēpēngs; this fine is to be proffered to the Lord under whose jurisdiction the woman is.
>
> . . . The village chief and the quarter chief have already accepted Pan Sukarni's communication as related above.

> The aim of this probation document is this that its content cannot be contested in court (*Adatrechtbundels* 1930).

Such detail is not altogether useless for a more general ethnology. As Swellengrebel demonstrated in a later book (1948), the court records yield valuable insights into conflicts in native systems of classification and action. His analysis of a family dispute (1969) from the colonial period emphasizes stress, strategies, and competing interests and thus has a very modern ring to it. Korn, however, had ploughed these sources not for patterns of conflict, but for fine-grained details of variation.

Occasional Hinduization

Later our view on Balinese caste should illustrate the drawbacks of Korn's particularism. For now, we must note his important expansion of the old-fashioned/newfangled village-area theme. Korn called his theory of the variable penetration of royal authority and Hinduism into indigenous village republics the apanage system. Ideally it worked this way:

> The raja (*vorst*) chose as his own representative the *Pasek*, guardian founder (*grondvoogd*), the man in whom all *desa* powers were united . . . when establishing royal power over a *desa*, the monarch vested the *Pasek* with control, with the agreement that he was responsible for raising specified levies.
>
> The Hinduization (*verhindoesching*) of the *desa* administration signifies . . . that the *Pasek* and the *Bandesa* . . . [originally representatives of the two halves of the *desa* council] were later tinged Siwaic (p. 195).

Supporting this scheme with his own work in old-fashioned village-areas, especially the strikingly divergent Tenganan, Korn assumes that there inevitably were one or two such clearcut individual authority figures. Later he adds the complicating factor of the *pachatu* system:

> This apanage territory divides into two zones: Klungkung, Bangli and Gianyar and Mengwi, where the *pachatu* system was introduced; and Badung with Tabanan, forming the zone where the descendants of Aryo Damar won control and where free indigenous landed property was the general rule. In spite of this difference, in both areas (with *pachatus* and with indigenous ownership) the arrangement of the village is much the same. Now what do we mean by *pachatus*? *Pachatus* were originally village lands whose users the *rajas* made liable to palace service (*pangayah kadalem*). They were required to keep up the royal residence and to provide materials necessary for this maintenance, while these conscripts moreover had to bring to the raja or his representative a rural levy of rice or gold . . . Royal claims gradually alienated the *pachatu* land from the village (pp. 227–8).

This view of the apanage-*pachatu* system was seriously flawed: it obscured how the process could happen the other way around; how, for example, factious village-areas might seek attachments to courts – or might even fabricate their own courts? – to gain the upperhand on rival neighbors. Korn made it appear that the system inevitably worked from the top down and only to the advantage of the rajas; he underestimated any real appeal of courtly culture. Moreover, an exaggerated apanage theory forestalled understanding another mode of interlocal relations that was strikingly revealed in a 1937 article by Gregory Bateson. Here we learn that even after the colonial administration had partially undermined the *pachatu* networks of 'service localities' for royal properties, the so-called *dorps republick* themselves – not content with autonomy at least in religious matters – continued linking, with myths and ritual, local pockets of homeowners to distant religious shrines. This case is all the more interesting because the rapidly Hinduizing village-area of Kayubihi is becoming involved with a group which styles itself as non-Hindu (for example, it is antipolygyny):

> Bayung, like Tenganan [see Korn, 1933] has a satellite village outside its boundaries and this is called Peludu. People from Bayung who do not obey the local rules [*adat*] – for example, men who have two wives – go to live in Peludu and people from other communities who acquire land in Bayung (generally by lending money) come to live in Peludu to work the land while gradually they become citizens of Bayung. Peludu is a community which had grown enormously within native memory . . . Three kilometers down the road . . . is another new village called Katung. This is a colony from Kayubihi, an important village on the Bangli-Kintamani road . . .
>
> These three communities form the setting in which the old temple and the scrap of new myth . . . found their place as links between the three communities . . . The myth which they constructed contains no reference to the past; it is a bare skeleton of relationships in the present (Bateson 1970: 113, 134).

Bateson's study reflects the ample evidence in the 1930s that Hinduization was not necessarily imposed by an authoritarian ruler. The process of the give and take of Hinduization (and de-Hinduization!) in Bali is far more complex, one might say dialectic, than Korn's apanage theory conveys.[2] Rather than monarch regally bestowing favors on local populations, it might sometimes have been more a matter of commoners evolving their own lord, a master of their water to help them compete with other locales. Of course, it would never look this way in legendary retrospects. Korn's mistake came in implying his apanage model as a unified evolutionary scheme, rather than as a system of values applied differently under different circumstances and always projected retrospectively.

Current developments in Bali reinforce our suspicion that what appeared a new-Hinduized village-area in 1930 might have even looked old-fashioned by 1940. Many long enduring remote enclaves of Bali Aga notwithstanding, this possibility can be inferred from Bateson's article, although it is not stated explicitly. Moreover, Korn himself realized that an old-fashioned village might be touched by a Hindu court without totally succumbing to its influence. For example:

> Villages like Bayung Gede, Kayubihi, and many others in North Bali thus knew how to maintain their old-fashioned character, in spite of the introduction of palace service (1932: 229).

One might say, then, that time does not simply pass old-fashioned villages by; rather, in many ways they choose strategically to ignore it.

Thus, Korn underrated the fluidity between more and less courtly modes of expression and action. He shared with his predecessors the conservative status quo view of Balinese society and authority which sees the adoption of Hindu-caste values as a permanent and qualitative shift into a fuller state of culture. A vantage from the East-Central elaborate court centers understandably confirms this notion. But to gain a proper appreciation of social and cultural processes on the island, it must be recognized that the dichotomy between old-fashioned pre-Hindu versus Hindu-caste is neither exact nor necessarily serial. There are variable ways of conforming to bits and pieces of Hinduized beliefs and practices; reversals are frequent and not inevitably regarded by Balinese as failures. It is the positive values which prize the ebb out of – as a necessary prelude to a subsequently renewed flow into – the courtly version of social life we call the 'romance of Bali.'

Finally, Korn's strict division of Bali into the Central-East with *pachatu* lands and Badung and Tabanan without them was doubtless exaggerated. If Tabanan did not have royal service groups alienated from local village-areas prior to 1932, this did not prevent it from manifesting memories of such a system forty years later. Current local lore and practice echo *pachatu* traditions to a degree which makes it doubtful they are a total fabrication. In sum, Korn's apanage theory was an overstatement, but it must be admired as an important improvement on the earlier simple dichotomy summarized in the *Encyclopedia* between original hillsmen and Hindus of the plains.

As noted, Bateson's work (1937) alluded to central issues in the interrelation of social and cultural forms. Many of his contemporaries (outside the Dutch administration) prudently avoided documenting the workings of social organization and concentrated on the arts and the psyche instead (Belo 1970). The major exception was Jane Belo's work prior to her interest in the culture and personality school. She published several ethnographic analyses that were admired by Dutch *adat*-scholars. Most notably, her study of a Balinese family (1936) was favorably reviewed by Dutch scholars in the journal *Djawa* (Goris 1937a, Brandts Buys 1937); it was the first effort to assess the importance of father's-brother's-daughter's marriage (that is, patrilateral-parallel cousin).

Here was something whose significance had been grossly underestimated. This type of union had not even been mentioned in the *Encyclopedia*'s review of marriage. Korn, drawing on Kat Angelino's analysis (1920), later alludes to it in discussing legends of royal prerogatives and divine unions (1932). But Belo first stressed the possible frequency of such unions within a given group and, through her familiarity with recent anthropological kinship and marriage theory, attempted to analyze the significance of this preference in Balinese family structure. She misjudged the typicality of her case study, calling ordinary what must have been an ascendant group, and she failed to consider patriparallel-cousin marriage in light of other types. But that she found such a striking example of a favored anthropological trait (that is, taboo against or preference for marrying patriparallel cousins) which generally failed to be stressed or even reported in the ethnographic literature, poses an interesting problem in the history of Balinese studies. We shall return to this notable omission in an otherwise thorough-going Dutch record. For now, it is enough to note that the surest way to overlook the significance of strategical father's-brother's-daughter's marriage in Bali is to consider social ranks rigid and to read the system exclusively from the top down. From this centuries-old vantage point of foreign observers, a father's-brother's-daughter's marriage is likely to be taken merely as another caste-endogamous union, resulting from negative restrictions against highborn women wedding inferior males rather than from the positive preference to wed near kinsmen. It requires a view from the bottom up to grasp the cultural and social significance of repeated patriparallel-cousin unions. Belo's work relied less heavily on the traditional Dutch division of Bali into (1) endogamous Triwangsa, versus (2) commoners with marriage by capture. Her family study also helped fill another gap in the Dutch colonial record, 'where one will look long and hard to find any concrete individual or social group interacting with any other concrete individual or social group within the context of these [Balinese] statuses and institutions' (C. Geertz 1961: 500). Belo's fresh treatment paved the way for more careful studies of social dynamics and the values and norms of ambitious Balinese groups outside the chronicles of royalty.

By the start of WW II, there was undeniable, exhaustive, conclusive and irreproachable proof that it is the very nature of Balinese customary law to vary. Every hamlet, temple group, or voluntary club methodically distinguishes certain details of its beliefs, practices and regulations from what it knows of those in other such organizations. Almost by definition, neighboring *adats* must diverge; this is true whether the *adats* characterize two irrigation-societies, two hamlets, two principalities, two gamelon orchestras or two sets of coconut-squirrel exterminators. It is the limits of and sense to the variation that are difficult to discern. The legacy of Korn and many of his contemporaries is a richly detailed assortment of sociocultural traits: (1) A highly developed caste-system, inspired by India, obtained largely through the intermediary of pre-Mohammedan Java, whereby Balinese society was divided into four *warnas*: Brahmana, Satria, Wesia, and Sudra, the latter presumed to comprise over ninety percent of the population. (2) A maharaja in Klungkung kingdom and variable grades of overlords throughout each realm. (3) Named, hereditary 'guild-caste membership' (Belo 1949: 1) antedating conquest by Java. (4) Old-fashioned, pre-caste Bali Aga hill-peoples with ranked classes (Korn 1933). (5) Apparently distinct customs of nomenclature, inheritance, and so forth differentiating nobles and commoners. (6) Self-consciously divergent *adat*-practices from village-area to village-area and kingdom to kingdom: for example, one kingdom's commoners might be stereotyped as practicing primogeniture; their neighbors, ultimogeniture. (7) Variable agricultural and residential landowning patterns: for example, primary claims on productive lands by first settlers versus virtually equal claims by all; or residence owned communally versus individually. (8) Somehow optional, presumably patrilineal, groups with no exogamous clans, rather preferentially patriparallel-cousin marriage. (9) Bilateral generational kinship terms, complicated by an array of titular and status designations (cf. Geertz 1966). (10) Total incorporation of women into their husbands' lines (and traditionally, widow burning by rajas). (11) In the intensely Hinduized plains, an elaboration of death rites and subsequent cremation, whereby even the lowliest commoners participated in the elite ancestor-focused caste-ideology. These are just to name a few; it was a provocative list, but one with little sense of interrelationship.

The other major enterprise of scholars in South Bali was the cumulative archaeological and philological research on the continually renewed Balinese religious edifices and sacred texts, all critical to any serious ethnological interpretation. Moreover, I Wayan Bhadra and other Balinese scholars trained in Dutch methods made studies of their own society.[3] And a more pragmatic brand of research growing out of the *adatrechbundels* continued until the collapse of the colonial administration. J.B. Bakker (1937), for example, described consumption patterns and itemized family incomes and expenditures. Finally. J. Hunger amassed material on ordinary aspects of everyday religious life in Bali. Since those first sketches of the nineteenth-century, observers had detailed the particulars of every religious ritual. Hunger (1937) tallied the three levels of actual cost; how much the average Balinese must pay for the impressive series of transition rites in the life cycle, marked by: pregnancy, birth, afterbirth (*ari-ari*), loss of umbilical cord, twelfth day, forty-second day, third month, sixth month, first teeth, every sixth month (*oton*), first haircut, first menstruation, tooth filing, marriage, becoming a religious expert (*mewinten*), burial, cremation, twelfth day after cremation, forty-second day after cremation, and conclusive rite for the peace of the soul. He converted such ceremony prices, average festival-days expenditures, and temple-maintenance expenses into *guldens* to demonstrate their costliness. The Balinese mystique was obviously wearing thin. Who knows what policies an economically minded colonial administration might have applied to Balinese ritual traditions, whose nemesis in many ways is reformed frugality, had it endured!

Not Africa

In an earlier study, J. Hunger charted the lack of coincidence between governmental local units and *adat* hamlets and village-areas. He mentions the exceptional but suggestive cases in which the council temple (*bale agung*) of a village-area (*desa*) lies outside the actual residential area of its members. Hunger's account of complexities in the relation of social units to spatial units commences with a telling anecdote:

> . . . take an arbitrary village in South Bali and ask several residents the name of where they come from; you might be answered: this is *desa* Kabakaba, or *desa* Tjepaka, *banjar* (hamlet) Tegal Kepuh, or also banjar Dangihuma, depending on the

villagers and the qualities of their residences that should be most distinctly in view (1932: 603).

These varieties of residential classification constitute part of the variation whose 'form' became the subject of research by Clifford and Hildred Geertz in the Bali of independent Indonesia. Their fieldwork during 1957–8 returned to the Balinese 'reservoir of organizational forms' (C. Geertz 1963: 139) documented in the colonial period. C. Geertz cited four axioms in Dutch *adat*-scholarship that he felt distorted generalizations about Balinese society and culture:

> . . . the closed village notion, the cake of custom approach, the search for an ur-society, and the assumption of an exact formal congruence between symbolic systems and social structures in primitive societies (1961: 105).

He argued that the assumptions produced artificially isolated and reified corporate-villages; they confused process with substance and overlooked the play between symbols and organization. To counteract such distortions, he proposed that the pigeonholes of custom be replaced with the matrixes of sociocultural interaction.

Interpenetrating modes

Geertz conceptualizes the common set of organizational themes of highly variable Balinese village structure as 'organizational planes of significance' (1959: 991 ff). Rather than planes, we might view this 'set of invariant fundamental ingredients' as cross-cutting modes of categorizing and grouping Balinese actors. Later, this should facilitate our discussion of the role of the qualities of space in lending content to these abstractions. Correlating this view with Geertz (1959) produces the following outline.

Mode 1: temple membership. Every Balinese is categorized according to the various temples he or she regularly attends to revere gods and ancestors. Temple memberships can cut across kitchens (*kuren*, usually nuclear-family units), since women alone support marketplace temples, although the domestic consumption units they represent remain kitchens (cf. Bakker 1936: 595). The most conspicuous public temples are those complex shrines consecrated to divinities of the village-area or *desa*; these temples relate congregations to the sacred well-being of specific locales. To understand the dazzling variety of temples, *desa* and otherwise, we must scan the other levels of society they help order.

Mode 2: hamlet membership. The customary hamlet (*banjar adat*) subjects Balinese to a meeting-house council that sets policies regarding some areas of customary law. This mode can cut across ancestor groups (see Mode 5), depending on *banjar* policies. Hamlets are not simply territorial, but they ordinarily do not divide members of the same kitchen. Geertz notes that 'nonterritorial hamlet organization is actually frequent in Bali' (1959: 1002). Indeed, it is vital to remember that hamlets are never conceptualized as territorial units. Korn as well (1932: 94–5) recorded that kitchens (*kuren*) are not legal communities (*rechts-gemeenschap*) and that *banjars* are often not territorial units; but he sought to historicize this dimension. The hamlet is in some ways 'the implementing organ of the *desa adat*' (Geertz and Geertz 1975). And often the *desa adat* restricts the customary usages of those hamlet councils that support it. But in other areas the hamlets go their own way, and on rare occasions they might even switch their *desa* affiliation. The essential point is that hamlets are not merely divisions of village-areas. In principle the *banjar* and the *desa* are independent sets of affiliations for different religious and civic (also religious) functions. The degree of control of *desa* councils by *banjar* councils is highly variable as is the composition of *desa* councils.

Mode 3: irrigation group. A Balinese rice-cultivator gains membership in an irrigation society (*subak*) according to the location of the paddy he owns. The major traditional restriction was that paddy must lie in one's own kingdom, where water rights were at least symbolically vested in the raja. Land reform has altered this pattern by limiting landownership and with certain exceptions forbidding it outside one's own subdistrict (*kecamatan*). But the basic principle remains; one's economic interests do not necessarily coincide with those of a neighbor, a hamlet or village-area associate, or even a brother. What is beneficial to the one might be detrimental to the other.

Mode 4: rank. All Balinese are classified by principles of rank and caste. This, again, is a many faceted organizational plane. An individual's rank is, though not always consistently, conveyed through his title, and his group's status is conditioned by its wealth and occupations, its marriage network, and its general convergence with courtly fashions of life and legend. The elaboration of the ancestor temple – or still in some areas, the rice bin – is the major architectural expression of status. In certain circumstances to be discussed, not all descendants in the same ancestor-group are ascribed the same rank. In principle, prestige is independent of wealth; the title system insures this. Finally, Mode 4 overlaps Mode 1, since a man's rank is ascertained in part by the actual temples he attends and sometimes by the kinds of temples he will not attend. (Brahmana-Siwa priests, for example, tend to eschew *desa* origin-temples which they associate with Wisnu, the princely deity). Finally, it can happen that an individual or group attempts to change caste-status ascription by contriving a change in temple affiliation.

Mode 5: kinship. Another many faceted plane is the kinship mode; it consists of various concrete codes to categorize men as kinsmen and/or affines. A houseyard or a set of related houseyards harbors agnatic kinsmen and their wives. Agnatic kinsmen are referred to with generational terms, as are, sometimes, the kinsmen of origin of a mother who has married in from an outside group in which relations are good. Many of these bilateral terms have variants that signal the hierarchical element in any kin or affine relationship. Moreover, by congregating at an ancestor temple, participants confirm their descent ties, which can affect their caste-status as well. Thus, in this convoluted social topology, Mode 1 not only intersects Mode 4, but in some ways bends into and coincides with it; and part of 4 is isomorphic with part of 1.

Mode 6: voluntary cooperatives (sekaha). Balinese are remarkably clubby. They form voluntary cooperatives (*sekaha*) for numerous ends: Balinese form artistic drama groups and orchestras, religious or literary reading clubs (*sekaha bebasan*), and profit-making local savings and loan associations. A Balinese thus associates with others through his *sekaha* memberships; these are in principle independent of the other modes.

Mode 7: administrative units. The seventh mode parcels every Balinese into an administrative system. This system was standardized and rationalized by the Dutch, but it had precolonial precedents in which, for example, the raja of Tabanan tried to have units of five-hundred family-heads under an administrator. Significantly, this system is not congruent with hamlet, village-area, or irrigation-society organization. The national political apparatus and the extensive primary and secondary educational system are all part of this administrative network, but they must also tie in with the other varieties of categorization. It is a telling sign of modern Bali that every school is as much a temple association as it is a student body.

These seven planes of organisation, reconsidered here as modes of categorization, have been abstracted in different ways. Modes 2, 3, 6, and 7 are exemplary planes, simple components of experience treated in four different frameworks: Hamlets (2) relate men as custom-abiding citizens to some of their nearby associates in distinctive *adat* practices, especially in the areas of burial, cremation, and civic responsibilities. Irrigation societies (3) relate men as rice growers to the other parties with practical and religious interests in the same water. Voluntary cooperatives (6) relate an individual to any *ad hoc* group for specific ends, and the bureaucracy (7) relates men to government in workable numbers for the convenience of the state. In Indonesia outside of Bali, Mode 2, Mode 7, and often Mode 3 are generally part of the same institutional apparatus. Especially when compared to neighboring Java, the Balinese case is striking. Every Balinese is touched by levels 2 and 7, everyone that desires by 6, and every paddy owner by 3.

Status (4) and kinship (5), however, are more complex; they involve diverse criteria for ascribing rank and categorizing kinsmen and affines. Moreover, as we shall see, the criteria lend themselves to contradictory interpretations. Thus, unlike his *banjar adat*, *subak*, *desa dinas*, or voluntary *sekaha*, a Balinese might figure his status or even his kinship in ways liable to be disputed by others. Finally, it is unwise to consider temples (1) as a plane in the same stack at all. Rather, temples code associations across various kinds of social categorization; they are a metamode to index the other modes. Many temples refer to distinct social functions other than worship. *Subak* temples imply mutual water needs and rights. Ancestor temples involve ideas of religious descent important in kinship options. There are even temples that refer exclusively to the national bureaucracy which have been reclassified as *pura funksionil*; they illustrate how older temples can be redefined to license new dimensions of Balinese officialdom.

We shall discuss this complexity further when we turn to space as a principle of social classification. For now it is sufficient to distinguish among Geertz's seven general levels of organization three distinct types:

Type I. This includes simple principles of affiliation to independent associations: (a) customary hamlets (*banjar adat*); (b) irrigation societies; (c) voluntary clubs; and (d) the national bureaucratic divisions. There is no ambiguity in such associations.

Type II. This category involves more complex, disputable principles which categorize a Balinese according to: (a) kinship, and (b) titled rank. Both are affected by the presence of an ancestor temple.

Type III. This is the temple system itself, not merely another plane of organization, but an organization of organization. Some of the most conspicuous temples delineate village-area (*desa*) congregations. But various temples and shrines mark *banjars*, irrigation societies, sometimes clubs, and even the bureaucratic divisions. Again, ancestor temples have important effects on both kinship and status.

The major thrust of all this talk of planes and matrixes and modes is to discourage the search for an ultimate social cell. Building blocks will not do as a metaphor for Balinese social organization. In the swirl of status concerns and particular interest groups, Western observers long sought some zone of group identity, a *gemeenschap* that anchored it all. Many ethnographers of the colonial era assumed what they were looking for was the *desa*, the village-area association supporting three local temples. Any deviations from this image were explained with Korn's over-generalized historical scheme: once *gemeenschap*-like groups supposedly had been eroded by imported Hindu-status values that exaggerated the simple native social differentiation used to regulate these communities. The *desa* – this basically unifunctional association for maintaining an area of Bali's religious landscape – was inflated into a multiinterest moral unity based on a 'sense of community' (*gemeenschapbesef*) and 'a feeling of solidarity' (*saamhoorigheidsgevoel* – Kersten 1947: 48). Observers avoided explaining how a supposed *gemeenschap* could be indirectly composed of hamlets (*banjar*) in which relations among members were more like reciprocal lessor-lessee obligations than spontaneous communalism. The typical *banjar adat* constitution (*awig-awig*), for example, stipulates exacting responsibilities for cremation services: if *banjar* associates help with a small ceremony, they receive cigarettes and *sirih* in return, and only relatives helping in the kitchen earn a meal; if a middle-sized ceremony is planned, non-kin *banjar* associates still do not help in the kitchen, but they receive a meal of rice padded with coconut; if it is a large ceremony, the associates help in the kitchen and receive a full rice meal, often enough to take some home. Also, *banjar* associates must provide the necessary extra utensils for these preparations, until the corpse has been placed in its bier; and any ill feeling against the deceased must be disguised. If hamlet relations were this rigorously calibrated and circumscribed, how could a larger village-area be presumed to rest upon communal sentiment or *saamhoorigheidsgevoel*?[4]

It is difficult to discern any horizontal bonds that fuse group memberships in Bali. Even associations supporting temples are more aggregations than congregations. To endure, groups must show that their members share vertical relations to the same religious source. As later chapters will demonstrate, this is true even of voluntary cooperatives and political parties, if they are to last. It is true of ancestor groups as well; and the sibling bond itself, even between twins, is ultimately regarded as two vertical links from the same sacred source, a filiational rather than a collateral tie. Yet even to allude to the vertical quality of Balinese social relations requires one hastily to distinguish it from the classic vertical model of modern ethnology, segmentary systems of tribal Africa.

Group option

In her 1936 article, Jane Belo stumbled onto a self-conscious ancestor group. But hedged in by analytic injunctions of her day to report only typical microcosmic 'Jonesvilles' of Balinese family life, she failed to generalize the principles of *dadia* formation or to appreciate the importance of their optional nature. Colonial officials acknowledged the existence of commoner ancestor-groups under the many titles they actually bear, but they viewed such groups as pale shadows of high-caste ruling houses whose intervention determined their inferiors' durability. In many Dutch accounts prestigious commoner title-groups appeared merely to ride the coattails of their lords.

Then during 1957–8 – at the very time the Dutch remaining in Indonesia were expelled by Sukarno – H. and C. Geertz did fieldwork on social organization in a region where intense rivalry between commoner *dadias* was central to local social organization; and this was quite irrespective of neighboring high-caste groups or the houses of the lords whom these commoners traditionally served. Every Balinese village-area is atypical in some way; the area in question was inordinately involved in the *pachatu* system, according to which specific groups are sponsored by rulers to provide services to the kingdom. The ancestor groups of Tihingan have long specialized in fabricating metal gongs for the gamelon orchestras essential in temple rituals and royal performances (C. Geertz 1967). According to Hindu-Javanese cosmology, metal workers in particular are surrounded by ritual taboos (cf. Van Mook 1958). Metal-worker groups (*pande*) continue to be viewed as sacred and dangerous; special marriage policies are made in regard to them throughout Bali. Tihingan retains even now an air of mystery for outsiders, and its traditional occupational speciality might account in part for the policies of local endogamy (in addition to preferences for ancestor-group endogamy) reported by H. and C. Geertz (1975).

But however atypical, the advantage to this locality is the sharp focus it brings to principles of ancestor-group formation and maintenance. The quasi-incorporation of households into a public status group – with elaborate ancestor temples and legends of origins, with preferred endogamy, and with internal ranks, role differentiation, and sometimes occupational specialization – is a central concern of the second part of the present study. As H. and C. Geertz argue, only by emphasizing this commoner option can the centuries-old view by outsiders of the disjunction between noble practices and commoner customs be bridged. Nevertheless, a particular locality in Bali might reveal little or no ancestor- group organization at all:

> The forces determining the formation of a *dadia* out of an undifferentiated mass of houseyards and houseyard clusters are various. Wealth, which makes larger temples and more elaborate ceremonies possible, is obviously one such factor . . . The accidents of birthrate in small groups . . . are also of importance. The strength of status strivings, which are in part a reflex of the caste (or 'title group') composition of the village plays a role as well. Villages containing only a few commoner castes of nearly equal rank seem especially liable, for example, to develop strong *dadia* organization, because the struggle for local eminence in such communities tends to be keen. The relative strength of non-kinship organization which can serve as corporate sub-groups within the hamlet is also relevant. In some villages, for example, the expression of status rivalry may appear in the form of competition between dance, drama, and music groups formed on a voluntary, achieved skill basis rather than in the form of kin-based *dadias*, and such voluntary groups may take on broadly social, political, economic, and even religious functions as well (H. and C. Geertz 1975: 101–2).

The critical point for modern ethnological theory of descent groups is the fundamentally optional quality of such incorporation in Bali; this is what distinguishes it vividly from African segmentary systems:

> We have called the process of *dadia* formation in Bali 'differentiation,' a concept standing in contrast to 'segmentation.' Just as segmentation refers both to the nature of the overall structure of the [African] system as well as to the process of internal subdivision of its units, so also differentiation can be seen at work not only in the relationship between *dadia* and community, but also in the emergency within the *dadia* of what we have termed 'sub-dadias.' . . . a sub-dadia is not in complementary opposition to any other subdivision of the *dadia*. It is merely a nucleus of *dadia* members which is more tightly organized than the others, and which may have more power or ritual responsibilities than they. The sub-dadia exists as figure against the ground of the *dadia*, just as the *dadia* is figure against the ground of the local community.
>
> The characteristics listed by Middleton and Tait [for African systems] – nesting, constant segmentation, complementary opposition – do not fully describe the structure of a segmentary lineage system. Its foundation is a specific type of cultural model, one based mainly on an image of a series of parallel genealogical pyramids. It is this image – of a father, a set of sons, and a series of sets of grandsons – which

locates the points where segmentation can take place . . . (H. and C. Geertz 1975: 104–5).

To this African segmentary ideology, the authors oppose the Balinese differentiation ideology which 'completely lacks any cultural image or assumption of long chains or lines of descent.' Balinese ideology of organizational forms concerns the sacred origin-point (*kawitan*) and its spatial, legendary, religious, and kinship properties. Their study analyzes the sociological effects of this ideology in its most concentrated state, an extreme case of *kawitan* entrenched in the ardently traditionalist East-Central area of the Bali-Hindu culture cradle.

In Part II we will detect *kawitan* ideology as it diffuses across the Balinese religious and political landscape. Our examples come from the peripheral kingdoms of precolonial Bali, and even from fringe areas that were just being settled and organized according to Bali-Hindu principles as the Dutch took control. Here groups had not been assigned *pachatu*-ritual duties by court centers before colonialism; but in their subsequent development, which continues today, they have persisted in referring to *pachatu* concepts and courtly models. Under the conditions reported from Tihingan, *dadia* options of in-marriage and ritual self-sufficiency among a group of supposed progeny serve to fold a community in on itself and to intensify local status competition. Thus where population is dense and all the riceland is under cultivation and water resources are exhausted, this ideology can sustain intense status competition at the expense of rivals. But where resources are still to be tapped, these same principles – in their social form the *dadia*, in their religious form, *kawitan* – reveal their dynamic potential. A sacred ancestral source is projected and ceremonialized by descendants who, as they propagate, tend both to marry back into the more direct lines of descent from the reputed ancestor and to tie other areas (along with their products, groups, and arts) to this same sacred source so to elevate its importance. There is an intensification of attachment to the ancestor temple, which then serves as a sort of religious anchor for the expanding associates and the resources they control that are converted into offerings at the appropriate festival dates.

Such dynamic potential in the *dadia-kawitan* principles represents, again, the romance of Bali. This expansive phase of Balinese institutions is the cultural counterpoint both to rigidly endogamous specialized locales once supported by courts (for example, Tihingan) and to powerful court centers themselves whose rulers stage Brahmana-backed rites asserting their own intransigence, so to deny the importance of their rivals and the significance of their inferiors. As we shall see, in groups excited about their own expansion and approximation of high-caste forms, group-endogamous marriage, rather than 'a very simple, subdued, almost wholly intramural affair' (H. and C. Geertz 1975: 184) occurs with public pomp and with rituals that stress the uniting of distinct collateral divisions. Moreover, a pattern which appears in semistable Tihingan as an odd case of mixed-title fusion in a particular ancestor-group denigrated by its purist rivals (C. Geertz 1967: 222) has become in Tabanan,

Buleleng, and Badung during the 1960s and 1970s more rife than rare. Yet, ancestor groups who have achieved recognition are still quick to disparage one on the make, and they studiously ignore how problematic their own claims to augmented status once must have seemed. Having traced thus far how the important ancestor-group options in Bali finally emerged out of cross-cultural perspectives, we will turn in subsequent chapters to current Balinese social organization and hierarchical concerns in politics and religion to depict the romance of *dadia-Kawitan* on the move.

Résumé

The would-be science of anthropology tends to underestimate its own hard-won achievements by insufficiently recalling the changing contexts, goals, and obstacles that characterize particular cross-cultural encounters through time. While many anthropologists value and employ historical source materials, few attempt carefully to review the history of the anthropology of the societies they study, unless it is to suggest their predecessors' inadequacies in light of current standards of method and theory. Fears linger that an appreciative history of cross-cultural research might appear as an apology for pernicious distortions of the past, for ideological commitments that can no longer be excused, and for slanted views science would do better to forget. But any history of the ideas that constitute an ethnological tradition need only presume that mistaken views were likely mistaken for interesting reasons. Moreover, earlier accounts might have asked an occasional crucial question that in the subsequent shifts of anthropology's quasiparadigms has been forgotten.

By succumbing to the tendencies of hard sciences to purge their own pasts and to avoid serious attention to dated concepts (cf. Kuhn 1962), anthropology risks undermining a major basis of its claim to respectability. Rigorous scientific verification of ethnological generalizations might be impossible to design. But such ambitions aside, it appears indisputable that, for example, Balinese culture and society is understood more adequately now than in 1597, 1817, 1879, 1932, or 1956. Our sense of Balinese complexity has in the long run, not without setbacks, advanced. There remains due cause for skepticism that studying the ethnological past guarantees avoiding the same mistakes; besides, past mistakes are possibly more desirable than some present ones. But inspecting the whole ethnological tradition can clarify the accomplishments and/or shortcomings of an updated ethnological overview that stands uncertainly balanced on its shoulders.

Cultures are not captured by simple reportage. A responsible historical perspective helps correct the unsophisticated assumption that ethnographies on cross-cultural behavior are pure products of data collected. Actually an ethnography necessarily relies on more or less systematic sets of *idées reçus*, some rechecked under differing circumstances in the activity called fieldwork, some accepted outright, and many perhaps (still!) dating back to centuries-old assumptions that might well be conceptualized otherwise. Keeping gauge of the history of ethnology can both heighten our sense of the richness and moment of particular ethnographic problems over time, and help us refine current frameworks, even if we are not perfectly persuaded that the culture itself is about to be grasped once and for all.

A typical anthropological account would start with the sort of ethnographic capsule we have reserved for a subsequent chapter and would hardly bother about its historical sources. Ethnographic results are casually attributed to fieldwork, a sort of *veni, vidi, comprehendi.*[5] Yet, by now we have seen that the broad sweep of Balinese ethnography and ethnology contains much that is commendable. There was an early strain of disinterested curiosity about the island, and Bali's commercial shortcomings perhaps facilitated something approaching pure research.

Nevertheless, in perusing this literature we must beware of three particularly seductive fallacies that occasionally crop up. For example, in 1700 Bali was characterized with a philosophical concept of promiscuous anarchy:

> [The Balinese] know nothing of Marrying amongst 'em; But as it is among Brutes, Men and Women are in common to each other, which makes the Country very Populous (Frick and Schweitzer 1700: 109).

The fallacy here is to imagine Bali as subsystematic, inadequately integrated. Although this prejudice was supported in 1700 with an accurate empirical point about population density, it was never very convincing. Too many features of Bali implied order. Another mainstay in the repertoire of ethnological attitudes was recently couched in a not altogether bad pun:

> The Balinese is a devout Hindu, but he is a Balinese in that he perpetuates little nonsense about caste or sacred cows of any breed or brand (Hanna 1972a: 7).

But any effort to stress Bali's agricultural expertise and commonsensical restraints on religiosity at the expense of pervasive status concerns, rituals of trance, or any other sacred cows leaves one in the uncomfortable position of omitting from what is explained the bulk of what is witnessed. Finally a third fallacy – and a more seductive one because it is supported by the island's repetitive, orderly surfaces – is conveyed in Margaret Mead's momentary fancy of an inborn Balinese birdie:

> The Balinese are unusually photogenic and tend to compose in groups so that half the work of photography is done for the photographer (1970: 259).

Rather than merely appreciating how the Balinese cluster in a way which complement her own preferences in composition – as the Nuer must do in the eyes of another photographer, or in the viewfinders of other equipment, or according to other standards of composition – the observer here implies a natural Balinese sense of group portraiture. This verges on the fallacy of inbuilt harmony, perfect integration, super systematics, and this is the ethnological pitfall that has most often distorted perspectives on Bali.

Yet to complain of an occasional subjective bias is not to claim ethnology can totally escape distortion. Any holistic ethnological image of a society is slanted, since it necessarily preselects certain features of the cross-cultural encounter for extra emphasis. To typify an entire culture according to images of its political authority (for example, 'a kingdom') or its subsistence (for example, 'a peasantry'), or to characterize it as a collection of village communities or as a set of abstract modes is often to omit aspects of the self-conceptions or the cross-cultural perceptions of the inhabitants themselves, or some sector of them – such as that absence of pork restrictions so dear to the sixteenth-century Balinese nobility we met earlier. Moreover, any ethnological blazon can lock in general perspectives on a culture which may confine the questions posed by informed visitors for centuries.

In Bali's case, the original cross-cultural captions – 'absolute monarchy,' 'happy irrigationists' – proved particularly indelible, and they long impeded investigations into the legitimacy of authority and the participation of commoners in caste categories. The 'Bali' that emerged, partly as a reflex of sixteenth-century expectations, endured; and it is still with us today. The longevity of this initial idea of Bali can be partially and indirectly attributed to the paucity of research over the next two centuries. Spiceless Bali lacked commodities, save those for a furtive slave trade – furtive at least from the vantage of European images of the East Indies, since slavery never entered as a component into Dutch emblems of and for Bali. Thus, the general idea of its culture as epitomized at the end of the sixteenth century went largely unrevised – although Bali became a main supplier of slaves – until the early nineteenth century, when Bali's proximity to Java assumed great importance for British occupiers of the East Indies. Observers began again to ask not merely how to handle Bali, but what it was. Finally, toward the end of the same century with the development of passenger steamers and the new overseas tourist industry, those most conspicuous productions of Bali – its splendid temples and pervasive religious ceremonies – themselves became commodities of sorts, now that the customers could be shipped to them. The whole culture was packaged. Lintgens' original vision of cozy domesticity got dusted off, and it has been successfully reinstated and propagated anew in popular descriptions after every notorious exception that has marred twentieth-century Balinese history: the mass court suicides of 1906–8, the continuing years of Balinese violence bemoaned by Sukarno after the Indonesian Revolution, and the terroristic insurrections and marauding murder squads of 1965. Bali remains today in tourist stereotypes Asia's happy isle of homey *joi de vivre* and day-to-day artistic self-fulfillment: an appealing part-truth.

But it was the other caption of Bali – 'Hindu kingship' – that distorted in particular scholarly work. As suggested earlier, sixteenth-century accounts influenced the questions asked by nineteenth-century observers, including Sanskritists. Subsequent researchers began to investigate irrigation techniques and commoner localities less involved in the court life of the plains. But when it came to holistic images of Balinese culture, prominence still fell to the Hindu-Javanese literate traditions and to what philologists could disclose of notions of rank, ritual, and the nature of society and cosmos. Korn and many colleagues tried to correct this distortion. Perhaps bending too far the other way, they left us with an unlikely polarization: on the one hand, voluntarism and democratic control of subsistence and domestic civic affairs; on the other hand extreme status pride in statecraft and religion, decorum, language, etiquette, and so forth.

The challenge that remains is to surmount the polarity by devising an ethnology of Balinese culture as an integration of flexible social institutions and ideological themes. This is essential if we are to determine what practices of patriparallel cousin marriage are doing in a so-called caste system, or if we are to view Bali in the context of East Indonesia, rather than considering it a mere vestige of Majapahit Java, or if we are to situate it more adequately between Hocart's (1950) India and Fiji, or to understand how a somewhat Polynesian social organization can be correlated with supposedly South Asian beliefs. The history of ethnology in Bali presents the problem of discerning some of that same style thought to grace its natives' being – that is, controls on the resplendant variation – for its rich list of institutions and customs that read like a roster of the celebrated 'strange but true' in anthropological catalogues.

This review has attempted to suggest the episodic drift in the history of general ideas of Bali. It has been highly selective and intentionally shaped; it has omitted much of importance in order to highlight aspects of marriage, rank, and the inbuilt vulnerability of authority to be treated later. We began in 1597 with false assumptions that, judging from death rituals and worship, Bali was India; we ended in 1975 with strong assertions that, judging from descent and the transmission of rights and duties, Bali contrasts sharply with tribal Africa. Decidedly, much of the progress in ethnological understanding is to delineate ever more precisely what a given culture is not.

4. Bali now: an indigenous retrospect (pre–1906 to post–1971)

> Distinguished birth is like a cipher: it has no power in itself like wealth, or talent, or personal excellence, but it tells with all the power of a cipher, when added to either of the others.
>
> J.F. Boyes

Having seen how history has taken Bali into account, it is time to appreciate how Bali takes history into account. Since 1597 changing interpretations of Balinese events and institutions by outsiders have been engaging flexible interpretations by insiders, and the ideals and images on both sides make Bali look more epic, more rigidly and permanently stratified, than it actually is. For example, what Schrieke says of Middle Java is still true of Bali today, at least in its more ambitious circles:

> Descent was the proof of legitimacy *par excellence*. The fewer the evidences of a right of succession on the ground of heredity, the greater the effort which had to be made to adduce supernatural proofs of the justice of claims. And when claims based on heredity were (to say the least) dubious, the historiographer made every effort to smooth out genealogical irregularities (1957: 13).

This smoothing-out process characterizes present-day native exegetes in Bali just as it did courtly scribes of yore. The history of outsiders' ideas of the island has probably shifted no more than the subjects of its concerns. Perhaps romance does not emerge out of epic, but epic represents an idealized and diluted retrospect to patch over the vagaries and conflicts of history, politics, and religion that are the mainstay of romance.

We call this chapter 'Bali Now' to emphasize this native tendency to update history and render past events pertinent to current circumstances. The chronicles of Hindu-Buddhist Indonesia possess properties which elsewhere would be called myth (cf. Lévi-Strauss 1963: ch X).[1] In fact, if we might inject a philosophical note, Bali illustrates clearly how culture as much controls events, or at least the perception of them, as it is controlled by events. In particular, Balinese ancestor worship is a ready means of reinterpreting, in fact reconstituting, so-called history. Finally, in Bali now it is certain that any seemingly archaic ideas or practices should be frequently reinvestigated to see what fresh and active sense they have come, sometimes unintentionally, to conceal.

Bali has long been reputed for its capacity to maintain a distinctive social and cultural 'Balineseness' in the face of sweeping change. One persistent component on anthropological lists of the island's institutions has been the ancestor cult, often presented as a static custom of principally theological significance. In this chapter we will examine some complexities in the formulation, maintenance, and recent intensification of ancestor lore in a particular group through time. Our subject is a large Sudra group in Tabanan district: how its members explain the origin of their house in the classical era, account for its trials and accomplishments during the Dutch colonial period, and, with little sense of discontinuity, justify its role in modern Balinese politics, from Indonesian independence through the national elections of 1971. We first detail legends, rituals, and stories – cultural forces in their own right – celebrating central ancestors and leaders from the group's classical, colonial, and modern history. We will then describe practical social, political, and economic matters indirectly involved in these traditions. Finally, we will draw general conclusions regarding the significance of ancestors in Balinese society, in which legends and rituals commemorating specific deceased leaders are no mere antiquarian escape from the present nor a pale reflection of more practical realities, but an active commentary on, and a contributing force to, a group's internal dynamics and self-esteem.

Relatively corporate ancestor-groups are optional in Balinese social structure and are actualized by building a high-level (supra-houseyard) temple, often complemented by making intratemple marriages – for example, father's-brother's daughter. As the congregation supporting an ancestor temple expands, genealogical connections become obscure: outsiders might even be admitted if costs and upkeep grow burdensome; traditions of an ideal descent line may, however, persist. Yet the social integration of the group rests more on its temple duties per se and marriages between its members. According to high-caste traditions the ideal conveyors of a group's identity and status are eldest sons of eldest sons, especially if they are born of a marriage with a near patrikinswoman. Emphasis on eldest lines is an optional aspect of Balinese descent. Rules for actual inheritance of house property range from primogeniture to ultimogeniture, and every son assumes particular ceremonial responsibilities for ancestral shrines according to the share of productive fields and other material wealth received after the father's death. It is in certain textual traditions – the special province of royal houses, but imitated by ascendant commoner groups – that emphasis falls on eldest sons. An eldest son in the eldest agnatic line who is also the offspring of a patricousin marriage is enhanced in and of his descent; from birth he would be expected to be individually meritorious in keeping with this auspicious genealogy. But occupants of the most highly regarded genealogical positions are not necessarily bearers of the most elaborate legends. Practical leadership of a group often falls to members not automatically qualified by descent. More pragmatic qualities take precedence, and the figures of actual leaders are then apt to be embellished, almost apologetically, with posthumous legends, stories, and anecdotes to show why it was – actual genealogical position notwithstanding – that they succeeded to leadership.

The sacred legends documented for royal houses in classical Hinduized-Java and still current in contemporary Balinese society proliferate where social structural norms have been contradicted. For example, when an incorporated house reputedly arises from the descendants of a raja's concubine, as in the present case, or originates matrilocally, or when a subhouse temporarily achieves a prominence rivaling that of the original larger group without actually breaking away, plentiful magical and religious reasons are adduced to explain these states of affairs. Yet our general argument is not that contradicted social norms cause compensatory other-worldly concerns, but only that contradictions can renew interest in dormant ritual and lore. Patent social structural principles are axiomatic and need no such obvious reinforcement. To take a specific example, ancestor legends in Bali do not clarify why a genealogically appropriate primary descendant failed to measure up in individual achievements to his birth – that is not the issue. The descent and marriage principles are strong enough to withstand refutation by this frequent 'exceptional' case. A thousand conspicuously average eldest sons born of patricousin spouses would not refute the high-caste cultural 'rightness' of a lone ascendant figure in this position. The issue addressed by the legends is rather why individuals not so qualified by birth should achieve prominence. Such legends tackle the easier contradiction while avoiding the other unsolvable problem (why the genealogically privileged individual actually failed) that would be less the province of scholastic legend and more that of doubting philosophy. Scholasticism still reigns in Bali.

The ancestor-group of over five-hundred members, to be described, has been a significant political force in modern Bali; its sense of corporate and political identity is more developed than that of many ancestor-temple congregations (*pemaksan*). Yet this group's current use of legends and redefined rites to adjust to heterogenetic, even revolutionary, social changes recalls traditional ways of legitimizing augmented status in Bali in light of new opportunities. The group's elders relate current political policies to classical statecraft and detect varied echoes across the rapid succession of Balinese epochs. They thread together supple traditions which simultaneously celebrate great traditional Hindu founders of a self-sustaining social unit, articulate folk anxieties over demonic influences in times of hardship, and confront the life and death politics of post-Sukarno Indonesia. From the details of their own legends and the social context sustaining them, one can appreciate the complexities in the operation of ancestor cults in Bali and perhaps in neighboring islands as well.

The legendary trek of Marketside East

In Bali any politically significant group, regardless of caste standing, embellishes the story of its origins. Although our case study lacks a sacred manuscript legitimizing its status (*kawi suda*), elders have formulated a piecemeal account, set in an authentic classical landscape:

The ancestors arose out of Klungkung, the culture cradle of classical times. Its maharaja was requested by his royal counterpart in the second most eminent kingdom (Gianyar) to provide him a capable administrator. So Klungkung dispatched the younger brother and sister of a powerful official with the rank of Pasek – an honorific title applied to low-caste overseers of various temple congregations. This brother and sister – the ancestors – eventually turned up in the service of the ruling house of the adjacent kingdom (Badung). Jealousy over the raja's favor toward these importunate parvenus led his kinsmen to plot their murder: sensing danger, the ancestors fled. They paused at a place called Buit (Mengwi), but fearing their master's forces, continued their formulaic trek to Sudimarna in Tabanan kingdom. In time a neighbor was appointed irrigation officer by the raja, and he employed the male ancestor to itemize a rice shipment bound for the palace. The quality of penmanship so impressed the ruler that he inquired after its scribe and had him indentured to the court. The ancestors moved to a quarter of Tabanan town downstream from the noble neighborhood. The sister won the raja's love, became his concubine, and bore his son. The boy was eventually received at the palace to be educated in courtly ways, and his cleverness won him the post of first secretary (*Penyarikan*) of the realm. Consequently his name, I Gde Arta, and his descendants entered the official chronicles of the Tabanan royal dynasty. He was domiciled in houselands known as Marketside East, exresidence of a reputedly noble line banished for misconduct. The new residents, the only commoners in the high-caste quarter, assumed this place-name as their own title. And during 1906–8 I Gde Arta's descendants were found there by the Dutch conquerors, whereupon the previous story was compiled so to make their official standing more convincing to the new European perpetuators of the old Balinese order.

This story of the rise to prominence of I Gde Arta is plausible but unverifiable. Standardized accounts of migrations from the sacred center of Bali to its wilder, western fringes of diminished courtly influence – with typical episodes of way-stations erected, tribulations endured, and subsequent civic accomplishments – serve to legitimate the status of many Balinese groups. Yet the tale is ritually corroborated by ceremonies at the distant temples regarded as way-stations of the migration. Marketside East's rights to commemorate its ancestors there are acknowledged by the local groups associated with the same temples. For the period between I Gde Arta's installment as first secretary and the Dutch conquest, the story of Marketside East is partly confirmed by the legends of other Tabanan dynasties. Yet these would likely dispute Marketside East's own self-aggrandizing interpretations and elaborations through time of its story, such as the following.

Arta, they say, had a single son, his successor, known simply as 'First Secretary.' It is difficult to know how many generations this standardized second generation actually represents, and Marketside East's members do not care. What matters to them is that First Secretary bore three sons, not actually remembered, but still commemorated in the layout of Marketside East. The eldest succeeded as secretary and dwelled in the oldest, central quarter; the second, supervisor of palace repairs, lived in the east quarter, and the third, overseer of royal ricelands, lived in the south quarter. This idealized third generation – with each brother passing a prestigious duty to his eldest son – signified that Marketside East was entrenched in the classical administration of Tabanan. Traditions then stress how many sons each brother bore and whether there were any patriparallel cousin-marriages, an auspicious union in a prospering group. The youngest of the three brothers fathered by First Secretary was sonless, and other Marketside East relatives settled in the south subhouse, but ideals of the descent-based ground plan persisted. Emphasis falls, however, on the eldest brother. He had two sons: the elder bore only one son, but the latter took ten wives (one a patriparallel cousin); the first six wives each begat one son. The third brother also advanced the group's demographic strength. He bore ten remembered sons – one of whom made Marketside East's first patricousin marriage – so many that he built a northern extension of the original central quarter. But by this time, elders note, the Dutch were conquering Tabanan. The last Marketside East first secretary died in 1908, but his descendants filled other important posts during the colonial administration. Furthermore, thanks to their fecundity, Marketside East's population surpassed five hundred by the early 1970s. But the population figure refers to one group only because enough power of internal diplomacy, and ancestral will, was marshalled to hold the successive generations practically and ideologically intact.

This imperfectly recalled, precolonial genealogy is important to modern Marketside East because of privileges these predecessors reputedly won from the raja in matters of sex, status, power, and death, nearly everything dear to the classical Balinese. These current visions of past glories suggest how commoner groups often assumed royal prerogatives – an important phenomenon in traditional Balinese society.

Proud elders recount that in sexual affairs Marketside East was licensed to maintain, raja-fashion, a haremlike assemblage of outsider candidate-wives known as *chichirinan*. In the raja's case these girls were the flawless pick of the kingdom and included specimens abducted from the subjects of his own collaterals. Picture, as informants did, the fathers of the realm nervously harboring their loveliest daughters, forbidding them to bear towering offerings to temple festivals, lest they be espied by a royal scout and hustled into the closely protected female quarters of the palace, where the eyes of male visitors were restricted to foot level. For there was slim chance a girl would become a legitimate low-caste wife (*penawing*) of the raja, thus placing her family in an ongoing, advantageous wife-giving relationship (*wargi*) to the court. More likely after affording a few years' licentious satisfaction, she would degenerate into a slavelike servant. Supposing she did ascent to *penawing*, the danger persisted that if the over enamored raja treated her in a fashion suitable only for same-caste wives (*padmi*), she might incur the jealousy of the lesser royal families and not live to become even slavelike – or so recalled current informants from the tales of their fathers and grandfathers. They say that a wealthy father whose child had fallen into royal hands would often pay a bribe to retrieve her. Or rather than take a risk, a less wealthy father might perforate any desirable daughter's earlobe, and by this minor mutilation render her, by courtly standards, an unfit sexual partner for a semidivine king. But the father of an attractive commoner in kingdom times could seldom win, for a slightly mutilated (*chatat*) mate, if beneath the raja, was fair play for his first secretary and often ended up in Marketside East's seraglio. Such courtly privileges were complemented by restrictions on the royal houses of Tabanan against taking Marketside East's women as spouses. This decree helped sustain a higher incidence of endogamous unions in Marketside East which has continued until today.

In power as well this Sudra dynasty feels it rivaled the greatest houses of the land, with its own population of subjects – that is, slightly taxed audience for its rituals – extensive ricelands, and an entire quarter of subordinates (*parakans* to them as their ancestors had been to the raja) situated nearby who still assist loyally at Marketside East rites of passage. Most noteworthy, Marketside East claims to have counted as subjects a Satria group banished from its home kingdom for looting a temple and subsequently received by the Tabanan raja, established in a local area, and given to Marketside East. Elders boast that even a Brahmana household was their political subordinate. Such authority complemented Marketside East's enhanced status, manifest in the triple threshold then shielding it from the outside world; once inside not even Brahmanas failed to use the most respectful forms of address. So established, Marketside East men executed their privileged duties: witnessing dedications of new temples, managing shrines particularly sacred to the raja, and acting as military advisors. Current elders say Marketside East officials supervised royal medical services, oversaw maintenance of the palace, and even planted Tabanan's focal banyan tree, controlling access to its holy leaves, mandatory in certain ceremonies.

Finally, traditions persist concerning a classical Marketside East advantage in death as well – how the forebears were granted the high-caste right to employ multistoried towers (*tumpang*) on their cremation biers. They declined this prerogative, they now say, preferring the less ostentatious manner of signalling worth and status by adorning the Garuda (Wisnu's mount) inscribed on their biers with an exclusive symbolic thread of gold, whose significance could be grasped only by religious experts. This visible modesty of their forebears is now explained as a political stratagem to avoid provoking jealousy in form-conscious royal houses, jealousy which precipitated the downfall of many other ascendant groups. Yet stories of such ceremonial privileges enable current leaders to argue that in nearly everything but titles, and a higher one of these is likewise said to have been offered and refused, Marketside East consorted with kings and eventually outstripped them all.

Marketside East accrued more and more favors until the end of the reign of the penultimate raja in precolonial Tabanan. The latter's successor was imprisoned after 1906 by the Dutch conquerors of South Bali. Marketside East considers this an unsurprising end for a ruler who, displeased with his first secretary, had threatened to oust him and exile his whole house, as the predecessors of I Gde Arta had been ousted before Arta's coming. Only the personal charisma and influence of a Marketside East leader named Nyoman Madera preserved the integrity of the ancestor group. In 1908 he was appointed by the Dutch as leader of a western subdistrict. He obtained houseland in the area's administrative center, built an extension of Marketside East and, although a younger son, became as significant to the colonial traditions of the entire house as Arta is to the classical.

A magician of controversy recalled

After 1908, Madera constructed on this new houseland the first major extension temple of Marketside East. His reputation as prime mover of the branch group has in no way diminished thirty-five to forty years since his death.

Although the reasons for his early demise are seldom discussed, a probable diagnosis is offered by collateral Marketside East members ill disposed toward the newer branch: judging from his sexual habits (he attracted women by black magic) and his partly amputated left arm, he died of syphilis. The same people cite unusual provisions surrounding his death. He stipulated that he was to be buried not in a graveyard, but in his own isolated property, which required an arduous trek for his pallbearers. More bizarre still, it is told he proscribed his own cremation, willed he was never to have soul released from body, never to be ceremonially elevated to the rank of spiritualized ancestor. No more troublesome legacy could be imagined for a Balinese descendant. Some parties surmise that his scheme was to preserve his lands intact, since no one outside the ancestor-group would buy property sullied with a corpse and later deemed haunted, as evidenced by the repercussions when a kinsman tried to build a house nearby: his child was stricken mute; then he went blind temporarily and his wife went mad.

Yet Madera's strategy apparently overestimated the capacity of his own people to act contrary to their culture's primary values. In 1953, some twenty years after his death, his son sold a portion of the property to finance a fitting cremation. Members of the town house recall the standard ominous apparition – a classical script letter visible on the skull joint – seen when the skeleton was retrieved to be cleaned and reassembled. They assert that this exhumation marked the start of the subhouse's decline. Troubles, many attributed to Madera's ancestral ire, continued throughout the 1950s and 1960s, as relations with the town house worsened. The aloofness of Madera's son from Marketside East's general affairs while he was still prospering had aggravated problems. It is said that this self-interest and a series of poor judgments led to the depletion of his lands, the death of his first wife, and his ill health since remarrying.

Other troubles stemmed from yet another practical legacy by Nyoman Madera concerning an outsider wife. He left her a *chechatu*, a husband's provision for an outsider widow in case his family neglects her. When their daughter married her first cousin, her mother (Madera's widow) joined the cousin's household, rather than staying with her own son. Thus, management of the *chechatu* fell to this nephew, a member of the Marketside East's north quarter. When he and his wife moved to another location, they took the *chechatu* with them but not the mother. This left the son supporting his mother without her rightful income; consequently, the mother expressed the unthinkable intention of returning to her own family of origin to live. Such discord revolves around the fact that a member of north Marketside East refused to honor the bequest of Madera, whose direct descendants regard him as their sacred founder, but who appears to many town-based kinsfolk as merely a dead magician from a has-been offshoot of their ancestor-group.

Throughout the later colonial and earlier modern periods, the temple and houseyard founded by Madera fell into disrepair, and his legacy of paddy was depleted. The worst times coincided with the PKI (Communist Party of Indonesia) rise to power in the early 1960s, when property was reportedly swindled by PKI officials or simply taken over by sharecroppers, PKI sympathizers sheltered by such officials. Land reform confused the picture even more, but by then holdings had fallen below the new limits of the law. By 1972 Madera's sons and grandsons had instigated proceedings in the agrarian offices of Tabanan and Jakarta to regain lands now considered to have been acquired illegally. Like many Balinese under stress, Madera's son decided to seek advice from a seer (*balian*). He received a stock diagnosis that a redoubtable shade was responsible for the family's difficulties. Within the traditions of the subhouse, there was only one reasonable interpretation. Accordingly, long neglected ceremonial options were reactivated to atone for past remiss in the subhouse's religious ceremonies, so to propitiate ancestor Madera, who even in his lifetime, descendants reasoned, had possessed remarkable spiritual powers.

One option was to emphasize the birth anniversary of Madera himself, a perpetuation of his life-time celebrations now treated as a major temple festival (*odalan*), not for the origin day of the temple, but for the origin day of the principal ancestral spirit enshrined there. Other expenses included repairs on both the house temple and another shrine supported by the subhouse situated at a banyan tree growing on a barren knoll, parched in the dry season. Yet at the tree's base were two small fissures said to be filled perpetually with crystal clear water; here Madera had erected a simple shrine. In 1972, after twenty years of neglect, the temple was restored at considerable cost. Some kinsmen doubted the benefits of this investment in an old shrine isolated amidst unproductive coconut groves that would probably soon be sold.

Such were the varied fronts – economic, legal, ceremonial – on which Madera's descendants moved to regain past advantages. The legal measures enjoyed the support of the appropriate Marketside East professional resources: advice by an expert in the district and provincial bureaucracy, recommendations by an agricultural officer in Jakarta, and suggestions on court matters by a Tabanan judge – all kinsmen. In this respect then, it was a united ancestor-group effort. However, these procedures, especially the ceremonial elaborations, placed a strain on collateral relations by providing renewed occasions to think over past differences and breached loyalties.

Thus, the ancestor cult in Bali is not a simple ideological instrument for social integration; it can aggravate rifts as well as unify factions. Yet stories about a controversial ancestor help a group maintain cognizance of itself as a social entity in its own right. Traditions centering on even a partly malevolent ancestor constitute a concrete self-image for a group and its factions, in a context in which the array of organizational frameworks – civic hamlets, sacred-spatial *desa* congregations, separate irrigation societies, sundry voluntary clubs – can undermine the social necessity of any suprahousehold corporate organization at all. Moreover, even his detractors agree that Madera preserved Marketside East when it was threatened with dissolution; and, however controversial this ancestor eventually became, he constructively inspired a successor.

A political wizard on the threshold of ancestry

His mother had a perforated earlobe, his son a college education. Between the two worlds so tokened, Gde Anake, virtual successor to his father's younger brother and defender of his uncle Madera's memory, rose to prominence in post-colonial Marketside East. His father was an influential official reputed for powers to presage death and for a sexual appetite which drove him to his own early grave. Anake's outsider mother came from an important commoner line in an area near Madera's subhouse. She had brought a considerable dowry (*tat-tatan*) of riceland, stipulated by her family before the marriage to protect her rights and affirm her equal status. Gde Anake honored the affinal contract of his mother by facilitating further marriages with her group. And he is considered an apt successor to his father in one respect: of his four official wives (and 'who knows how many unofficial,' mused a favorite son) the last two produced descendants, three from the third and seven from the fourth. The latter wife was a patriparallel first cousin (*misan*) whom he married under family pressure. The insistence that Gde Anake take a family bride reflected the preeminence he enjoyed within Marketside East, in light of his professional accomplishment. He was – although the younger son, by an outsider mother, of a younger son – the most prominent resident in north Marketside East (the traditional first secretary elder line) and thus he merited a family spouse.

Anake liked to recall an episode early in his public career to suggest the traditional reliance of Tabanan royalty on Marketside East. In the latter 1920s the Dutch had not yet reestablished a member of the old royal house as ruler of Tabanan and bearer of the ultimate title *chokorda*. The principal claimant was, however, an important official. During his absence an assistant discovered that government funds had been taken for private use. Anake related how he hastened to warn the would-be successor to return home to conceal his crime. He complied, and a year later in colonial Tabanan a *chokorda* was once more heading the native administration. In Anake's view, however, the *chokorda* soon forgot the favor as he fell further under Dutch influence. Matters culminated one night when the raja and the local Dutch administrators summoned Anake and ordered him to support the proposed merger of Bali with Java, presumably part of a plan to place Bali's native administration under the more subjugated Javanese. Anake recalled with dramatic embellishment his momentous refusal: 'If not for Gde Anake you could not have become raja; now you've forsaken me.'

This now legendary episode represented to Anake in his old age the continual role of Marketside East in protecting the general welfare of Balinese citizenry and the legitimate status prerogatives of the royal house – all to the honor of Marketside East and its ancestors. He liked to recall a lifetime of such effort. To translate from his own list of accomplishments relating to Indonesian independence:

> In fact before being installed as subdistrict leader I was teacher in a government elementary school . . . , often instilling a nationalistic sentiment in my pupils and in my colleagues, until being switched to become irrigation chief . . . These events took place between 1916–28.
>
> At that time I obtained the office of subdistrict leader. By illegal but active means I opposed the colonial government and in 1928 joined in the proposal and establishment of a consumers' trade cooperative. Furthermore, I proposed and established educational institutions with nationalistic characteristics.

He was fired as subdistrict official because the Dutch disapproved activities reflecting obvious sympathies with the embryonic PNI (Nationalist Party of Indonesia). Committed to popular education, he established in 1939 a Parindra (Greater Indonesian Party) school for those excluded from Dutch schools. It was eventually closed down by the Japanese, but in 1949, during the Dutch NICA (Netherlands Indies Civil Administration) reoccupation, he founded another secondary school still important in Bali.

In the sequence of events surrounding Indonesia's bid for independence, populistic activism was discouraged. Under Japanese occupation, Gde Anake was imprisoned for a year in Den Pasar and his children deprived of an education. After Japan withdrew and the Netherlands returned, Anake remained in jail for the three years of the NICA regime. Following independence he was again imprisoned shortly before the 1955 elections by a police officer who feared his influence as a socialist. During one of these prison terms this radical populist learned from his fellow inmate, a Brahmana, the traditional significance of golden threads above Garuda birds on ostensibly commoner cremation biers and subsequently applied it to Marketside East's classical history, as noted previously.

Anake persisted in his political activism, with much of Marketside East behind him. He was a leader in organizing economic concerns in newly liberated Tabanan.[2] Disenchantment with corrupt colleagues in the Nationalist party led him to join the Socialist party. Anake served on Bali's provincial general assembly and acted briefly as its leader. In 1960, he became the governor's assistant in matters of religion, customary law, health, and education. Four years later in 1964, because of disagreement with Sukarno's NASAKOM (Unity of Nationalist, Religious People, and Communists) policy he withdrew into semiretirement. The latter proved, again, a decision of legendary proportions: within the year the Communist coup had aborted, Bali's governor had disappeared along with Sukarno, presumably into the latter's royal palace, and President Suharto's new military order was at hand.

Throughout Anake's career the base of his partisan activities was the Tabanan homestead, the entire population of which was consequently politicized. Marketside East's youth organization, once the sports champions of the district and always a strong competitor in traditional music and dance competitions, redirected its efforts to political campaigning, and, before any election, special ceremonies to propitiate the ancestors were performed by Marketside East's women. According to the current story, had the PKI been successful in the 20 September 1965 coup (Gerakan Tiga-pulu 'S' = GESTAPU), the whole of Marketside East – over five-hundred men, women and children – would have been exterminated. Anake's political persuasion dictated the group's position. Long antipathetic to the PNI, and not particularly promilitary, they were even more adverse to the PKI – a fact that was underscored when, after the anti-PKI mass murders following the 1965 attempted coup, not one Marketside East member and only a single affine in its extensive marriage network had disappeared.[3]

The elder's politics led his kinsmen to place great hopes in subsequent efforts by President Suharto's regime to simplify the party system, as it reorganized the national polity by replacing religious, nationalist, and ideological parties, administered from the top down, with supposedly realistic interest groups united from the grassroots up (work groups = *golongan karya* = GOLKAR). Marketside East's leaders found relatively acceptable a plan that sounded, if hardly democratic, at least populistic. With Gde Anake's blessings they helped the GOLKAR cause achieve its resounding success in Bali in the general elections of 1971, discussed in more detail later. Yet by mid-1972 Anake, retired and ailing, was ordering his recollections of Balinese politics from independence to the present as follows (loosely translated):

Yes, when the GESTAPU took place (1965) all the district heads of Bali were PNI (nationalist).

Maybe PSI (socialist) would have become more powerful if in 1955 before the general elections (pro-PNI) police had not entered and beaten people in the village areas. In those days PSI held PKI back; PKI (communist) couldn't do a thing. Then PNI became receptive to PKI and in 1960 PSI was outlawed. With PSI out of the picture, PNI was devoured by PKI. If there had been a general election then, PKI would definitely have won, because PNI promised more than it delivered, and there was too much corruption.

Now with GOLKAR there is still corruption, but at least the government is more stable. Yet people aren't content. GOLKAR promised to replace PNI, but PNI is still holding the good positions – Governor, secretaries, and so forth are still PNI. People are disappointed. Nearly all the government employees are old PNI. Many friends are stopping by here these days to talk and complain about GOLKAR pre-election, anti-PNI propaganda that duped them.

In June 1972, following a long illness, Gde Anake was hospitalized and diagnosed as suffering the contradictory effects of high blood pressure and low hemoglobin. Months later he suffered a relapse, marked by dizziness, fainting spells, and visions of his death and life hereafter. Disenchantment with modern medicine had led Marketside East's elders to seek help from netherly curers and mystic sages. One kinsman, himself a practicing mystic in East Java, concluded Anake's condition arose from improper practices of yoga: perhaps he had tried concentrating his body temperature down too low, without first atoning for an outstanding offense against the ancestors – whence the difficulty with his blood. While his more immediate family decided whether to send Anake to Java for more expert mystical advice, he had to be rehospitalized. Soon after he died; translated letters from his eldest son by his fourth wife convey the significance of this crisis in the life of the ancestor-group and suggest the initial stages of transforming an historical figure, indeed an inordinately worldly one, into a spiritual *bhatara*:

> Father departed us serenely . . . in the hospital precisely on the anniversary of his birthday. After he died a young doctor delivered the message, kept secret from us to avoid family panic, that Father had earlier left: 'I will return to the eternal (everlasting) world on my birthday.'
>
> The exemplary symbol of protection (*ibarat payung*) for our family in Marketside East is now no more.
>
> Long before he fell ill the dear departed requested of our family that when he passed away he be simply burned, not *honorably* cremated (*diaben*) – suffice it to use a little rice porridge and not more than twenty-five rupiah worth of offerings; only the materials for combustion should cost more. But the decision of our family could not reach this accord, because there remain other family members not yet *diaben* [i.e., they have been provisionally buried and await a suitable and financially feasible cremation date] ; some time all will be cremated together if possible. We came to accept this majority decision, but if it had been left to us, whatever the deceased requested would have been adhered to; we could do no more.
>
> We tried everything including netherly forces (a *balian*) as well as doctors, but could not help our father whom we loved. He has gone forever; will his grandchildren carry on the struggle for the ideals of the dear departed?
>
> Our eldest son arrived home on that day and was no longer able to control himself. Likewise our second and third sons lost their self control, as the atmosphere in our house became tumultuous with the echoing wails and cries of his 'grandchildren' and descendants-in-law. Some among them fell faint, no longer conscious of themselves, and we tried to overcome that state of sadness; but were carried along by the moaning current of tears from our family and relatives. Suddenly, inside a room crowded by friends, we in turn felt faint, as short-of-breath we perceived the crowds of men pressing into the forecourt of our ceremonial pavilion in Marketside East.

Long after Gde Anake's rich biography and specific political and legislative accomplishments are forgotten, his religiously significant prediction of an auspicious date of death will be retold. Although Anake is now temporarily relegated to that Balinese limbo of precremation burial, legends have already begun accruing to his life story which promise to make of him a significant ancestral shade, worthy successor to I Gde Arta.

Worldly achievements

The classical ancestor-group created and sustained by these ancestral figures has evolved with little break in tradition into a modern enterprise whose foundations are neither land nor business and industry but civic services – a decided advantage, given the political and economic vicissitudes since Indonesian independence. The group's continued success is most evident today from its residential, occupational and political achievements, all indirectly traced to the accomplishments of the ancestors.

Marketside East occupies a prestigious corner of old Tabanan. Its primary houseland is divided into four quarters: north with thirty-two family heads (married males), central with sixteen, south with five, and east with nine. Secondary town houseland with eleven family heads lies nearby. Ancestral accomplishments pertain principally to these houselands as they relate to one of Bali's modes of social organization, the *banjar adat* or 'customary hamlet.' Not exactly a territorial unit, it is better regarded more operationally: 'In most parts of Bali, the *banjar* may be rather simply defined as all those people subject to the decisions taken in one hamlet meeting house, or *bale banjar*:'

> Although it is not always exclusively territorial in membership, the hamlet council [*krama banjar*, composed of its family heads] has jurisdiction over most civil and domestic matters, such as marriage, divorce, inheritance and minor criminal acts . . . Many hamlet associations own all the houseland in the vicinity, and have full power to evict members for anti-social behavior. Each one has its own distinctive set of rules and regulations concerning membership qualifications, responsibilities, sanctions, etc . . . (Geertz 1959: 994; H. and C. Geertz 1964: 96).

As noted in Chapter 3, many such regulations concern mutual obligations for various grades of life crisis ceremonies. For apart from its civil functions the *banjar* serves as a task force for domestic rituals, especially burials and cremations.

Marketside East's houselands and loyalties slice across two *banjar adat* – we shall call them LB and SA – and this fact lends a peculiar sociological configuration to LB. The north, central, and south quarters of the primary houseblock and the extra northerly acquisition are in *banjar* LB, while the remaining east quarter and the secondary houseblock are subject to the decisions of SA's meeting house. Both of these court-town *banjars* have relatively limited social functions, serving mainly as ritual task forces. If, for example, a Marketside East resident of the east house dies, the ensuing rites – wake, corpse cleaning and homage by descendants (*mepegat*), burial, and later cremation – are performed both by representatives from the east-house's *banjar* (SA) and by that large portion of *banjar* LB comprised of his own ancestor-group. This situation arises merely from the fact that Marketside East overlies two *banjars*. More exceptionally, members from another section of houses in *banjar* LB known as 'north of the market' also assist in the rites of this east sub-house. This state of affairs stems from a virtual split in *banjar* LB. The major

Tabanan administrative office now lists LB as one governmental hamlet and two customary hamlets, North LB and South LB. The life-crisis rite responsibilities of North and South LB are the same, but their *adat* (eventually corrected by the official explaining this matter to 'their ideology') differs. This *banjar* split – the only semiofficial one in the history of modern Tabanan – occurred before the 1955 elections. LB was then dominated by descendants of its three noble houses who exerted pressure on their *banjar* associates to support the Nationalist party (PNI). Finally the Marketside East faction, strongly anti-PNI, formed a coalition under its own domination and began calling annual sessions of South LB in its own central quarter to handle customary affairs.

As one Marketside East informant reminisced: 'They (the nobility) were more numerous, feudal minded, and rich then; but they're poor now, and they've proved their lack of character by opportunistically forsaking their own Nationalist party to jump on the GOLKAR bandwagon.' (It should be noted that this informant is implicitly contrasting Marketside East's leaders who, although pro-GOLKAR now, abandoned the Socialist party only when it was banned by Sukarno or left IPKI, the League of Upholders of Indonesian Independence, only after its leadership dissolved). The split thus created North (mountainward) LB including a high-caste house (as far south as Marketside East), an area of its exservants, and the two other noble houses along with the many commoner courtyards they influence and South (seaward) LB including, besides its Marketside East houses, parts of 'north of the market,' half a dozen family heads across the street, and a few individual families, all north of the high-caste house which was under the ideological sway of Marketside East.

This tortuous division of *banjar* LB illustrates what has been called 'the paradox of Balinese politics,' wherein 'seemingly modern competition is in actuality not one of ideologies, but one of traditional factions, of ancient grudges and time-honored alliances' (H. Geertz 1959: 23). More concretely, however, the episode explains why people from 'north of the market' in *banjar* LB attend an arduous wake at Marketside East's east quarter in *banjar* SA – political and family loyalties taking precedence over the formal lines of *banjar* burial associations. And these complications would never have developed if long ago Marketside East's high-caste predecessors had not been exiled for a trivial indiscretion against their raja, thus making residential room for I Gde Arta, who founded this upstart commoner house which not only edged into aristocratic territory but, eventually, thanks to Madera and Anake, edged the aristocracy out of half of its own hamlet – or so goes the story.

Another factor in this group's solidarity – somewhat exceptional in the general Balinese context of gnawing factionalism – is the set of careful marriage policies backed by its elders. Clandestine elopement with outsider women is discouraged. Moreover, for a sonless father to take an outsider as son-in-law to succeed him (*nyentana*) is forbidden. Otherwise, prearranged advantageous outside marriages are encouraged, and endogamy within Marketside East is strongly advocated.

The group's current strength stems largely from the network of modern occupations held by its members, enabling them to function effectively in matters of the Indonesian nation state. The professional success results from the administrative role won from the Dutch by their predecessors, especially Madera. Marketside East's members thus early-on gained expertise in modern bureaucratic skills. And while the royal houses of old Tabanan contrived to protect their traditional privileges, and an occasional one to convert its past landed wealth and network of personal loyalties into a basis of economic power, Marketside East went to school. Elders explain that this was only natural, since the nearest colonial equivalent to their forefathers' classical duties was education.

Six brothers comprising the third generation of the newer houseyard in *banjar* SA epitomize Marketside East's achievements. The fourth brother became head of the new agricultural division of the school started in 1949 by his grandfather, demonstrated political acumen, and is said to be close to the governor of Bali. His brothers include a district government employee, a hotel assistant manager, a cook, a high school economics teacher, and a pharmacist in Surabaya. Six salaried, sufficiently prestigious positions for six brothers constitute a rare percentage of vocational security in contemporary Bali. But the main gauge of Marketside East's professional achievement is in the list of seven master's degrees, ten bachelor's (or the military school equivalents), and the suitably high positions attained by its post-independence generation. These include an agriculture department official in Jakarta, two district judges in Bali, a director-general of the Hindu-Buddhist religious organization in an East Java subdistrict, a pharmacist, a medical doctor, an information agency official, teachers, a transmigration official, and three military officers.

The extent of these accomplishments can be appreciated only by comparing this house to others in the district who had an opportunity to capitalize on Dutch favoritism – the high-caste houses that boast only an occasional teacher, engineer, military or police school graduate, or doctor. This includes a noble house of some four-hundred members, the second largest cohesive ancestor-group in Tabanan district. Marketside East thus represents a continuity in authority between the classical kingdoms and post-Sukarno Bali. And the tactic of lateral spread throughout the burgeoning civil service was no revolutionary program of a new generation, but a direct legacy of the ancestors, themselves good bureaucrats before there was a bureaucracy.

Marketside East's success was, however, limited. Compared to certain royal houses which remained in power in other kingdoms, Marketside East also succeeded in converting traditional advantages into a salaried professionalism, but not in controlling its district's politics and appointed offices. In fact during the period of fieldwork, Marketside East was basically opposed, politically and philosophically, to Tabanan's chief elected official. The group's long stand against the Nationalist party precluded any such hegemony. Even in post-1971 Tabanan under GOLKAR, a PNI stronghold continued to monopolize governmental offices, banks, and so forth, and to control the distribution of occupational favors. This fact explains the poorer showing by Marketside East in the professional life of Tabanan proper than its list of degree holders would have led one to expect.

Yet in actual elected offices after 1971, Marketside East led its district, with three seats in the Tabanan general assembly and two at the provincial level, all of them GOLKAR. Early in the GOLKAR developments, Marketside East moved concertedly to spread its members over as many district-level functional-groups as possible. Three of them were named candidates by the special screening committee in Den Pasar; they were placed high enough on the all GOLKAR candidate-list to be assigned three seats won by the nonparty in 1971.[4]

As of late 1972, just what the GOLKAR seats meant in terms of actual political power was unclear, but it was already obvious that in some ways they meant more and in some ways less than was first hoped by certain winners. GOLKAR representatives of Marketside East's persuasion – not aligned with the remaining PNI coalition – were alarmed by the central government's further measures after the 1971 elections to 'simplify' party politics: (1) the move to ban parties other than GOLKAR at the village and subdistrict levels, and (2) the subsequent proposal to have district chief-administrators appointed by Jakarta instead of elected by their district assembly. Both measures were justified at the organization's upper echelons as insurance against GOLKAR factiousness. Yet this tampering with the popular basis of governing officials began in 1972 to undermine what Marketside East considered itself to have represented throughout nineteenth- and twentieth-century Balinese politics, from its enlightened service under courtly rajas to its current influence in bureaucratic interest groups: the interests of the common people within the cultural framework of legitimized status.

Postscript

In spite of Marketside East's public political and occupational solidarity, recent events underscore the importance of visionary leaders in overcoming the factionalism inherent in Balinese ancestor-groups. We saw earlier that a mainstay of Marketside East's identity – ancestor Madera – was also a factor in its principle rift. Gde Anake, genuinely respectful of his predecessor, had avoided a final rupture between Madera's branch and the town group. Upon Anake's death (1972) persistent difficulties threatened to splinter the 520 descendants of I Gde Arta. Madera's eldest grandson had yet to visit the houseyard of Anake's son, and only recently had Madera's son again frequented north Marketside East, his own father's (Madera's) birthplace. This latter gesture reflected the most recent stratagem to improve relations: the first marriage between the town group and its extension. The theoretically ideal second-cousin (*mindon*) union in late 1971 joined Anake's daughter to Madera's grandson. Because of Anake's affection for this capable nephew, now son-in-law (considered a worthy successor of his grandfather), a complete rift was avoided.

Although Madera's grandson is now husband to his favorite nephew's daughter, tensions persist. The bride, for example, is reluctant to stay in her husband's subhouse, and a quarrel she had with her own eldest brother caused her husband's sister to stop associating with the brother's wife. Moreover, it is this north Market-side East brother who disrespectfully disclosed the previously mentioned syphilitic condition of Madera, and his wife who, in relating the tale of his exhumation and provisions for burial in his private property, quipped: 'Who would bother to bury him out there these days, now that the family is ruined!' Yet in spite of such occasional backbiting, sometimes in good-natured irony, the new marriage is the important fact, and, especially since the death of Anake, the already expected off-spring more important still. For it is really a new male descendant who, if anything could, would repair the schism, provided he displays the suitable legendary qualities of leadership.

The progress of ancestors

These recently enriched ancestral traditions of an important house in Southwest Bali illustrate a general development in current Indonesian religion and politics. In Central and East Java, in certain outer lands, and in various urban centers, there have been mass conversions to politically backed mystic sects and to both Christian and Hindu-Buddhist religious organizations. During the reactionary period following the failure in 1965 of the attempted communist coup many Indonesians quickly adopted a formal religion-cum-party to counteract any suspicions that they shared atheist-communist sentiments. Since then the effort by President Suharto's regime to phase out the political party system has aggravated this dislocation of social identities. In Bali there has been less evidence of subsequent religious conversion and more of a revitalization of traditional bases for legitimizing status. As party identity has diminished, caste identity has again begun to flourish. Later we shall see that throughout the island ordinary households have been rediscovering their rights to membership in various traditional islandwide temple congregations. Such groups tend to intensify ceremonial formats establishing their members as an extended ancestor-group, and they can even strive to become a voting bloc. Or, as in the previous pages, closeknit houses with traditional claims of superiority have, as party interests eclipse, been refurbishing indigenous Balinese schemes of rank as a potent political force.

Balinese culture affords a ready means of shifting back to the integrity of temple groups after a long preoccupation with national political parties, in that dispersed peoples sharing the same title can postulate mutual ancestors, enshrine them in temples, and recodify their common descent. This was traditionally one of the ways commoner houseyards styled themselves after aristocratic courts. Yet legends and rituals emphasizing spiritualized individuals – such as Arta, Madera, and doubtless soon Anake – run counter to other Balinese commoner usages producing a 'cultural veil which slips over the dead.' According to C. Geertz's interpretation, 'one is not defined, as in so many societies of the world, in terms of who produced one, . . .

some more or less grand founder of one's line . . . ' (Geertz 1966: 26). But whereas Geertz is emphasizing commoner terminologies and practices, Marketside East has long adopted more aristocratic means of commemorating godlike individual accomplishments in idealized stereotypes. Glorifying particular ancestral figures is a high-caste cultural option which was traditionally a factor in upward mobility, and which currently appears to be enjoying a new vogue as Balinese society adjusts to the post-Sukarno era.

Goris (1960a) generalizes as follows concerning what Grader called the 'various stages of deification' of Balinese ancestors:

> . . . we must point out a very important distinction which the Balinese make between two clearly separate groups of ancestors. The first of these groups consists of the dead who are not yet completely purified. This group is in turn subdivided in *pirata*, those not yet cremated, and *pitara*, those already cremated. The former are still completely impure . . . ; the latter have been purified, but are still considered as distinct, individual souls . . .
>
> The second group consists of the completely purified ancestors who are considered as divine . . .
>
> No contact is sought with the *pirata*, the dead who have not yet been cremated. On the contrary they are dangerous . . . Offerings must however be made for the redemption of their souls . . .
>
> The completely purified dead enjoy divine veneration . . . They are also transcendental, in the sense that they are no longer considered as separate individuals (like the *pitara*) but as 'the progenitor,' the soul of each ancestor being merged and coalesced with that of his forefathers as soon as he is no longer remembered as an individual (Bali, Studies . . . 1960: 84).

We have already seen plentiful exceptions in actual practice to this stock Balinese theology. In Marketside East the preeminent founder Arta is remembered as the offspring of a particular sister of a particularly legendary founder; Madera, twenty years after his transferral to purified *pitara*-status persists in his demonic influence; and the freshly buried Anake, a sullied *pirata*, is already imbued with sacrosanct qualities although his initial cremation is still perhaps a decade away. This modicum of social and political reality that influences the way ancestors are sublimated and affects the contents of their stages of deification should not be read as the breakdown of a traditional religious formula under the strains of modernization. Royal and noble houses in Bali have long celebrated specific forebears as gods or demons in order to argue their relative merits or to sanction their power.[5] The more mundane concerns of a struggling group and its constituent factions can qualify the way or the extent certain ancestors are – in and of their cultural forms – forgotten. Select ancestors may be festooned with high-Hindu religious or low-Balinese magical lore, especially if the ancestor-group factions or general policies they represent remain contentious.

In Bali the ancestor cult pertains to descent-defined quintessential founders and 'Big Man' pragmatic social-engineers at the same time. But these two aspects of ancestors – in anthropological stereotypes the African type versus the Melanesian –

are thought by Balinese to be complementary, intercorroborative. The greatest ancestors, such as I Gde Arta, were the Big Men of their time or are retrospectively construed as such. And the most politically savvy contemporary entrepreneur is endowed with divine attributes; moreover, he is urged to marry a cousin to enhance his own descent-line. On the one hand we find value placed on descent (for example, the ascendancy of Marketside East's elder line in the north quarter); on the other hand a plasticity in granting leadership roles to the more artful collateral members of a given house trying to maintain its corporate qualities under trying circumstances. Thus, Balinese descent values recall what have been termed 'status-lineages':

> The status lineage in Polynesia differs from the broader class of 'conventional' lineages in the lack of exogamy and in its lack of full commitment to either male or female descent lines (Goldman 1970: 422).

Yet in a sense Balinese ancestor-group options reverse traditional Polynesian lineality, such as the Maori *hapu* which is 'bilateral or endogamous in its lower ranks, preferentially patrilineal and patrilocal in its upper ranks' (Goldman 1970: 50). The fact that all deceased Balinese, elder and younger sons alike, are spiritualized and enshrined in the ancestral temple allows the exact lines of descent to be deemphasized, at least for purposes of legend and its revision. All properly cremated forebears are ancestors of the house; legends single out for glorification only the Big Men (cf. Sahlins 1963) whose acts reflect those capacities ideally handed down through eldest sons by group-endogamous wives, but more often actually not.

In Marketside East there is an idealized eldest descent-line, but the legendary ancestral spirit runs away from it: from Arta to Madera to Anake. This collateral divergence of the line of powerful influence (*sakti*) is explained by a repertory of legend about the long dead and by selective recall of the lives of recently deceased outstanding leaders. Moreover a particular ancestor, such as Madera, can be ritually accentuated by his direct descendants in order to challenge the dominance of the larger originating group by corroding its solidarity. A persistent tension in Balinese social life, heightened by the kind of lore here reviewed, is that any legendary protagonist who perpetuated a whole ancestor-group might eventually be reconstrued by his direct line as a sacred founder in his own right. In fact one might interpret that general Indonesian cultural emphasis on the founders of lines as compromising any descent principle from the very start. In the legends of Balinese social organization, it is as valued to initiate a new line as to perpetuate the old one. The incorporated houses of superior ancestor-groups are traced not to primeval first-humans, but to opportunistic, heroic clearers of locales who establish a source-temple for all who participate in its sanctity, however vague the actual descent-line grows.[6]

Theoretically all Balinese could live within strong ancestor-group organizations; actually they do not. In this context charismatic individuals, regardless of birth position, take on greater social significance; yet this fact does not preclude persistence of higher regard for senior descent-lines in groups following upper caste customs. Ancestor legends counteracting the simple theological 'stages of divine oblivion' applied to ordinary dead persons add an extra dimension to social life. But we should not see this mechanically as some higher evolutionary level of a larger scale political integration, as ancestor-focused, descent-based lineage organization above and beyond loosely associated agnatic-lines. It is true that an articulate ancestral tradition can help hold together lines which, if they remained unadorned agnatic relatives, would divide according to more pragmatic concerns. Yet such traditions can also subsequently divide the very groups that they, along with a superior temple and accompanying rituals plus inmarriage, initially help hold together. Rather than a clearcut instrument of more extensive social solidarity, a commemorated ancestry is better seen as an additional frame of discourse for articulating a group's legitimacy and status. The ancestor cult in Bali is less a patent advance in sociopolitical integration than a means of intensifying the social rhetoric, of enriching the argument that is the culture. It is uncertain if a Bali with legendary, unforgotten ancestors constitutes a better built, more solidary social machine than would a Bali without; but it definitely constitutes a better, at least a more intricate, story, a richer cultural argument.

Finally, such a cult does not necessarily impede social change or so-called modernization. The 'will of the ancestors' – interpreted by practitioners of trance and specialists in divine mysteries – is apt to be more responsive to new political and economic conditions than are the everyday concerns of more mundane actors. Judging from Marketside East and recent developments throughout the island, the ancestor cult is a living tradition, and the social factionalism uncertainly surmounted by gifted ancestors remains the legendary topic of Balinese culture and a central theme of its romance.

Yet ancestor worship is just one means, a particularly historicist one, available in Bali for implementing dynamic options in social life. Other such means in the areas of marriage, caste, politics, and ritual and religious organization are the subject of Part II.

Part II
Social and cultural dynamics

> . . . it is important, therefore, to ask first what problems are given by a particular culture, rather than assuming a priori that social action is oriented to the solution of general problems set by anthropological or sociological theory.
>
> (Schneider and Smith 1973: 6)

Although its terms are rarely quantified, Part II attempts to generalize about the approximately 2.2 million Balinese – a population larger than many isolates of routine anthropology yet smaller than its civilizations. We employ case studies and select ethnographic vignettes to point up parameters and dynamics of change. In this enterprise, numbers would often hinder more than help. For example, if one tries to count a given type of Balinese marriage in different locales, one ends by comparing hamlets to village-areas to bureaucratic subdistricts, finding sundry fragments of ancestor groups variably distributed over these units, sometimes wholly comprising them but usually not. Worse, one risks obscuring critical distinctions by counting father's-brother's-daughter marriages when 'family marriage,' variously construed, is the more relevant category both for understanding Balinese views and for purposes of comparison. Similar difficulties plague efforts to formulate a constant unit of caste. There has never been a reliable census of twice-born peoples in Bali, and below we discuss current flexibility and contention in Balinese status to suggest why castes cannot simply be tallied.

Lacking measurements, we study fragments of action and categories and we rely heavily on actors' ideas, but not indiscriminately. Following the anthropological school of structuralism, we consider obscure customs, such as native responses to the birth of twins, to be as important as vast sociological tendencies, such as 25 percent marriage type-X, in the analysis of implicit cultural categories. However, unlike certain structuralist works (for example, Lévi-Strauss 1969), we do not presume to be able to delimit the boundaries of a given type of social phenomena, such as kinship. Rather we trace out ideas of descent and marriage relations which, mythlike, open out into other areas of belief and value (cf. Boon and Schneider 1974).

This analytic strategy can appear more frivolous than serious monographs or more impressionistic than a hard study of supposedly real empirical institutions; but it is neither, for it must be broadly informed and must bear a host of cross-cultural concepts into the field, such as hypergamy, marriage cycles, *jajmani* systems of ritual division of labor, ritual communitas, and many more, in order to play Balinese expressions and responses against them. This approach to culture is fundamentally comparativist; as Dumont has expressed it:

> Following Mauss, we [take] 'cultural phenomena' to mean phenomena common to several societies in contact. For the sociologist, these are also of course social phenomena. Only, while social phenomena are internal to one society, phenomena called here 'cultural' are taken as external (to one society). Internal phenomena may be called social phenomena of the first order, and external or cultural phenomena may be called social phenomena of the second order. A somewhat narrow exegesis by Radcliffe-Brown of Durkheimian sociology may be responsible for the exclusive emphasis on the first order which, even in Africa, puts some obstacles in the way of comparison (Dumont 1970b: 6).

Finally, a study of cultural problems is not a siding with gossamer ideas and slippery symbols at the expense of firm and dependable praxis. It is rather a gamble that if culture makes sense, all significant aspects of social life must be put through systematic strainers to render them communicable both within and across groups (cf. Boon 1973b). In Part II we discuss the praxis of cousin marriage and status ambition and the hard realities of locality and politics, but we discuss them insofar as they are mediated by symbols and codes to instill in Balinese experience harmonies and contrasts which are both vivid and systematic and, partially at least, exportable.

5. The social matrix in place

From our discursive history of Balinese ethnology, we can formulate a synopsis of the island's culture designed to illuminate later on the systematic reliance of current events in Bali on traditional processes of flexibility, especially at the local level. In the next chapters we contextualize this ethnographic capsule by describing its elaboration in three important institutional cadres: space or locality, marriage, and caste status. To appreciate the sense of continuity in Balinese culture we must carefully explore the interpenetration of these three fundamental areas of native concern. They will add flesh to the following ethnographic skeleton, and suggest certain complexities implicit in these updated formulae.

Recapitulation to the present

Balinese are predominently wet-rice farmers; individuals own tiny plots of paddy, not necessarily near their residence, which they pass on to their sons. Inheritance customs vary greatly; ordinary commoners might bequeath paddy to all sons in equal shares and their houseland to either first-born, last-born or objectively selected sons, depending on the local *adat*. High-caste traditions, which are often imitated by successful commoner groups, emphasize the eldest-son line in matters of succession to specialized offices and of houseland inheritance as well. Regardless, any disparity in land inheritance among brothers is likely to be partially offset by heavier ritual obligations and costly temple maintenance duties for those who enjoy the advantage.

Owners of paddy plots watered by the same irrigation canal – who are not necessarily kinsmen or even neighbors – are organized into a cooperative (*subak*). A delicate system of rights and duties binds together all such irrigation cooperatives located along the same watershed area stretching from mountain lakes and springs to the densely settled oceanside plains. This elaborate system of water allocation requires ceremonies in specialized temples at the critical sluice points, which are controlled by councils and overseers chosen specifically for this purpose. A *subak* leader and his subordinates are elected by the members, and they have strictly delineated tasks:

The *klian subak* is not just a titular figure. He is responsible for the overall management of the *subak* district. In the area of finances he bears the responsibility for collection of all taxes, fees, levies, and fines from the *subak*'s members, as well as for accurate bookkeeping disbursements of *subak* funds (Birkelbach 1973: 160).

Ideally rice distribution is not mediated by the traditional market-networks that circulate local commodities and respond to shifting opportunities in export and import trades. In fact, the same social organization accommodates great fluctuations in the demands for marketable commodities, either within Bali or for export. There are different kinds of markets and each has a temple attended primarily by women:

Small village markets function for a few hours every morning; larger permanent markets are open daily but reach a peak every fifth day. There is also a weekly cattle market. This market network is very ancient. In the past, the finest luxury craft products were not sold in the market but were made on commission for the princes and gentry, who therefore had special patron relationships with certain craft-specialized villages. Today this function in regard to sponsoring the crafts has been taken over by private and governmental firms, which funnel the craft products into the tourist and export markets (H. Geertz 1972: 61).

Domestic and ancestral spheres of life are distinct and separate from the institutional frameworks for subsistence production and for marketing. A Balinese male inhabits a religio-domestic walled houseyard (*pekarangan*) with its origin temple and various practical and customary-ceremonial (*adat*) pavilions. The simplest form of houseyard social bonds consists of agnates plus dowryless outsider-wives who have been mock-captured (with or without subsequent payment of a bride-purchase compensation) and were consequently thrown away by their own houseyards of origin. Variations on this pattern are discussed later, but the important point is that any legitimate wife becomes a member of her husband's houseyard-temple (*sanggah*) group. There are two different traditional organizations of such houseyards. First, the hamlets (*banjar*) exist for purposes of reciprocal attendance at domestic life-crisis rites such as teeth filings and burials. Often hamlets have practical civic duties as well; their councils may control access to the houselands under their jurisdiction, stipulate other customary norms for members, and so forth. Second, the three-temple-cluster congregation (the village-area or *desa*) is responsible for maintaining the religious harmony of the sacred locale whose spirits are contacted in the appropriate three-temple-cluster (*kayangan tiga* = origin, maintenance, and death temples). The *desa* congregation is likewise distinguished by the particulars of its customary religious life, which are always in heightened contrast to neighboring *desa* congregations. Hamlet and village-area social units are not necessarily territorial groups in the sense of immediately proximate residents; the houseyards of members of one hamlet might be separated by the houseyards of members of other hamlets. Moreover, residents of the locale that is under the influence of a particular three-temple-cluster might even, somewhat exceptionally, pay homage to gods at a different three-temple-cluster, if they have traditions tracing their well-being to that locale. Thus, generally the village-area (*desa*) tends to include hamlets, but any simple taxonomic arrangement is an inadequate way of conceptualizing these two separate organizations of houseyards. Finally, one hamlet alone might support a three-temple-cluster, thus constituting a self-sufficient *desa*.

A given houseyard can be organized with other houseyards into a set of males reputedly descending from a single forebear; their families comprise the ancestor temple-group. This higher level ancestor temple-organization symbolizes the relationship of several houseyards just as the houseyard temple symbolizes the relationship of several brothers. The pattern is particularly characteristic of so-called high castes in Hindu Bali, but commoner houseyards can be organized in the same way. Often such a multiple-yard group – or, in the high-caste idiom, multiple-section 'house' – is flagged by a public temple. An ancestor group usually displays elaborate ritual and material manifestations of superior status, including prestigious titles and legends connecting it to other groups and locales involved in the past glories of the Balinese state.

According to caste ideology the three upper *warnas* – Brahmana, Satria, Wesia – are extensions of related yards and temples, each having branched out from origin points consecrated by Javanese heroes. Sudras are the rest, the 'outsiders' (*jaba*), but many Sudras also form groups which boast similar explanations for their relative elevation. The members of houseyards which are organized into more prestigious ancestor temple-groups, whether high caste or not, tend to deemphasize three-temple-cluster ceremonies (that is, *desa* ceremonies) under certain circumstances. If a locality contains just one ancestor temple-group and the rest are ordinary commoners, that ancestor group may remain aloof from *desa* rituals. However, where there are several ancestor groups, *desa* rituals might be converted into a stage for intense status competition among them, especially when their caste differences are obscure. Thus the pattern of exemplary ancestor groups is central in the dynamics of Balinese society and culture. The pattern reflects the ideology that defines caste relations throughout the small island, and it serves as a set of guidelines for any collection of houseyards trying to assert itself as a genuine, prestigious ancestor-group. The major optional components of a well formed group are: (1) a conspicuous ancestor-temple on a sacred plot; the temple members are relatively self-sufficient in various ritual and sociological matters to be discussed; (2) legends of a sacred forebear, whose qualities are remanifested in certain descendants, most auspiciously in the eldest agnatic-line; (3) a range of marriages, primarily near family marriages (first- or second-patriparallel cousin) together with favorable pre-arranged outside marriages; (4) graded ranks of descendants (at least implicitly) depending on the mother's rank – that is, lower descendants by lower mothers; and (5) a ritual occupational specialty; at the *warna* level Brahmanas specialize in the knowledge of sacred books, Satrias in ruling over subjects, Wesias not in trade but in administration (and both Satrias and Wesias ambiguously in warfare) and Sudras in agriculture. (Moreover, any ancestor-group might claim ritual occupational prerogatives, such as filling the post of custodian priest in a particular district temple.)

In a legal sense, divorce is easy; yet it has been reported as both frequent and unusual. The issue can be complicated by the type of marriage, the presence of dowered land, and the existence of offspring. A barren wife who was captured from outside is simply sent home, if her family will have her. The children of a divorced outsider-wife belong to the husband's group, but any such rule is subject to many qualifications which vary across local spheres of customary law. Divorce in a group-endogamous marriage would place great strain on the collateral bond; ordinarily, the husband continues supporting his family spouse and takes a second outsider-wife for his pleasure. Adoption, especially the 'borrowed son', is frequent in Bali as it is elsewhere in Indonesia.

Finally, temples – those ubiquitous walled-off sacred spaces reserved for periodic visitations by gods and spirits influencing particular aspects of social life – are by no means restricted to ancestor groups. Temples occur at each level of Balinese spatial organization, economic organization, and social organization. Individual houseyards, village-areas (*desa*), entire districts, and pan-Bali are all commemorated in temples. Every market, wet-rice irrigation cooperative, watershed division, and often profit-making voluntary club corresponds to the supporters of a given temple or shrine, and every Balinese has numerous temple affiliations for different purposes. C. Hooykaas here summarizes some of the non-Indic aspects of temple worship:

> There are nearly two million Hindus in Bali, but there is no temple for Siva or Visnu and no Brahman temple priests. We have thousands of temples here, but none of them *for* a god, but only for a worshipping community which worships there once in the year of 210 days, at the anniversary of the temple, its local and insular gods, admittedly beginning with Siva-Aditya, for whom the *padmasana* is destined. What I want to emphasize is that in India the focus is the God, *daily* worshipped by residents and non-residents; in Bali, villagers or sharers in an irrigation community, etc. once in 210 days gather to celebrate the temple anniversary; temple and anniversary or villagers are the focal point. Brahma-Visnu-Isvara may or may not have a place in such a temple (Hooykaas n.d.: 271; cf. Belo 1953: 7–8).

The eight districts of modern Bali correspond to the eight different spheres of royal houses delineated by colonial administrators following final Dutch conquest of the island during 1906–8. Earlier kingdoms were never rigid territories, but consisted of tenuous claims to the loyalties of subjects over and against rival claims by competing houses. In 1908, for example, the realm of Tabanan was recognized as including portions of Mengwi only vanquished in 1891. Moreover, within Tabanan's borders were included subkingdoms such as Krambitan and Marga that might themselves have eventually ceased to acknowledge the Tabanan raja's superiority, or they might even have tried to oust their superior, had not the Dutch frozen the system as they perceived it.

A raja in turn distributed his subjects among lesser administrators and warriors – often his collateral kinsmen. Political loyalties were expressed in contributions to the overlord's ceremonies, slight tax payments, and often performance of specialized tasks such as arts or warfare. In turn the raja was literally master of ceremonies for his peoples and the protector of the realm's religious rites of aspersion. In 1849 Friederich summarized the situation as follows:

> The primary feudal duty, as in the Middle Ages, is *service in war*; and further, the Punggawas [deputy overlords] and their subordinates have to furnish assistance in all *public works and festivals* of the prince, and the lower orders also have to carry out all the works of the Punggawas. The people, under the guidance of the Punggawas, have to build the princes' palaces and places of cremation, to repair the roads and besides this to contribute mostly in kind, towards the expenses of all offerings, family feasts, and cremations. The direct taxes are very unimportant; the common man pays a small tax on garden land, and a little more on sawahs [irrigated land]. The princes, therefore, cannot be rich, unless they possess considerable private means; they are powerful, however, so long as their names hold the Punggawas in subjection, and they can therefore celebrate their splendid feasts and cremations without cost to themselves, and sometimes even with advantage to their private treasuries, their faithful vassals zealously contributing to these ceremonies (p. 140).

Of course, such ceremonies served as models for rites and festivities throughout Balinese society, and subjects drew religious benefits from their lords' outsized productions, best illustrated in the tradition of mass commoner cremations of provisionally buried corpses to accompany a royal cremation.

Moreover, the paddy-owning peasants controlled their own irrigation cooperatives and their local councils assured the fair distribution of water as it flowed to the sea. The rajas and their courts could arbitrate disputes over resources and help plan expansion of irrigation facilities. In other words, the state organization facilitated growth of an intricate irrigation apparatus that was basically owned and operated locally. Wet-rice agriculture was thus a complex means of production that in practical terms of control and maintenance was not alienated from the masses. But the ultimate religious and political significance of the system's component cooperative-competitive *subak* organizations (ceremonialized in temple networks) was elaborated by exclusivistic, highly theatrical elites.

The court centers of precolonial times have become the sporadically bustling towns of today. Tabanan is typical of this transformation. Traditionally Tabanan was merely a village-area (*desa*) augmented by the royal palaces, the houses of various administrative and judiciary (Brahmana) lines, and a quarter of mercenaries, often Chinese, in league with the court. The town subsequently inherited the colonial and now the national bureaucratic apparatus for Tabanan district. In 1971 the district population was listed by the Kantor Kabupatan Tabanan as 331,614 – including 725 foreigners, mostly Chinese – distributed in 62,454 households (Ind. *rumah-tangga*). The district is divided into eight subdistricts (Ind. *kecamatan*) which correspond to traditional spheres of influence of lesser powerful lords: besides Tabanan we find Selemadeg, Penebel, Krambitan, Marga, Pupuan, Kediri, and Baturiti.

Certain recent developments have had far reaching consequences in Tabanan. National land reform under Sukarno that restricted holdings outside one's own subdistrict caused many large proprietors to sell lands or shift their residence. Relaxation of government restrictions, enforced in the 1950s, on the role of foreign-born residents in Indonesian business and commerce has allowed the Chinese to reassert themselves in the town's trade. Finally, Tabanan district has a reputation for excellent rice yields and intense politicization of both town and village areas. Communist party (PKI) activity thrived here in the early 1960s, and subsequently Tabanan suffered severely during the mass reaction to the attempted PKI coup in 1965. There are no reliable figures on the numbers killed, but district death estimates run as high as 10,000, and reports and rumors on the treatment of imprisoned communist suspects, especially women, are correspondingly gruesome. In 1972 the political situation in Tabanan as elsewhere in Bali was still very tentative:

> Land ownership is restricted by law [since the reform] to a maximum of 7.5 hectares of *sawah* or nine hectares of dry land. The large landowners, mainly the members of the traditional ruling families or of the Chinese business community, were divested of their properties on promise of what amounted to token compensation in swiftly inflating rupiahs – if, indeed any payment was made at all. These alleged reforms were carried out at a time when the Communist Party was achieving paramount influence in the Sukarno government. The Party leaders very shrewdly manipulated the law to penalize their political enemies and reward themselves and their adherents. As a result of these so-called reforms, large amounts of land changed hands . . . but no one seems willing even to risk an opinion as to how much the condition of the animosities over land often played a key role in the identification of potential victims of the 1966 massacres. Many peasants who had suddenly become landowners and Communists in recent years vanished from their homes, which were frequently burned, and nobody now inquires too closely about what disposition has since been made of their properties (Hanna 1972c: 7).

In spite of these sweeping events, Tabanan today reveals few signs of thoroughgoing change such as those visible in Den Pasar, the Balinese provincial capital and center of tourist trade. True, there are many repair garages behind the walls of traditional Tabanan houseyards. On the site of the old children's cemetery stand Chinese shops, and across the road a power plant sporadically transmits electricity to a few bulbs in nearby offices and houses. There is even a cemetery for national heroes on old lands of the exviceraja; these gravesites for veterans boast permanent tombstones which eventually will only mark where their occupants, exhumed and cremated, once reposed. Yet even then, in a peculiar Bali-Hindu accommodation to national militarist ideology, widows will persist in leaving offerings at these vacuous epitaphs. Such tokens of modernity, however, in themselves indicate little radical social change. In fact Tabanan in 1972 appeared less progressive than it had a decade or two earlier, since its current leader had neglected improving roads and hospitals for the sake of reconstructing and revitalizing the *desa*'s temple complexes.

Still, here and throughout Bali one senses persistent rumblings threatening more precipitous transformations of life and society, literally in the island's continued volcanic activity and possibly, too, in the rising tide of tourists that in 1972 were rapidly overspilling the confines recommended by international teams of planners

(Hanna 1972b). There is also the potential unrest of those who have been politically suppressed, including many Balinese who still go jobless for having affiliated with even a communist youth organization in their early years. But perhaps the most immediately ominous note is sounded in reports of government plans to interfere in local irrigation control, apparently, since the Dutch altered nearly everything else, a linchpin of the traditional Balinese social system.

Yet as of now there is a distinct continuity between old Bali and its most progressive contemporary areas. Even a foreign evangelistic wife of a Balinese Pentacostal convert – whose brothers, because they had abandoned Bali-Hindu, had been suspected of atheism and communism and were, thus, assassinated by their neighbors in a Tabanan District *desa* during the uprisings of 1965 – nevertheless observed that Tabanan remains 'a country town.'

The ritual landscape

Tot nu toe zijn er drie dingen waarover de meeste herrie en oneenigheid op Bali kan komen, dat zijn: grond, water en vrouen. Drie dingen die van groot belang zijn . . . Dan komt de religie . . . (Ravenswaay 1941).

By definition, Hindu-Bali contains no frontier. The historical process of converting forest into paddy to feed an increasing population is seen not as the advance of civilization into an obscure no-man's wilderness, but as the danger-laden conversion of demonic haunts into residences for men, into temples for gods, and into rice-fields for both. On the religious side there is godly, divine space and spooky, demonic space; on the practical side there is rice-production space and domestic space, and, secondarily, commercial zones. Whenever one variety of space is converted into another, elaborate rituals are performed so that the old, sacred/profane ritual attributes of the space do not conflict with the new. If forest becomes paddy, or paddy becomes houseland – the latter conceivable only under modern conditions of population pressure – or if a domestic portion of a houseyard is converted into a shrine, precise rituals are staged, always beginning with *dapdap* trees, a prime ingredient in sacralizing ordinary space. Moreover, to convert temple space into profane space is unthinkable.

Just as Balinese life-crisis rites represent the penetration of divine and demonic forces into the human career, so the ceremonial calendar can be seen as temporary intrusions of one kind of spatial attribute into another in the cycles of time. At every temple festival, divine-visitation space extends tentacularly (in sacred processions ritually insulated from the mundane surroundings by refined dancers) to demonic riversides for the bathing of the gods. In the famous Nyepi annual rite of stillness and ritual inversion, ordinary domestic and commercial space is infiltrated by demons. Moreover, the elaborate purity/pollution codes of Bali are fundamentally 'spatialized.' For example, traditional courts required widows and orphans (socially incomplete), dwarfs and deformed persons (physically incomplete), and an array of tabooed craft specialists to replicate in social forms the cosmological schemes the courts propounded. And all such varieties of polluted groups and individuals were assigned the appropriate spatial enclaves, either within the palace or somewhere in its apanage lands.

Qualitative properties of space are always conceived of as an inseparable set. Godly space implies demonic space implies domestic space implies rice space. This systematic interdependence is most apparent in the cosmographic schemes of the relations among the cardinal directions (cf. Swellengrebel 1960). But the same interdependence characterizes practical use of space as well. One must never convert all irrigable land into paddy because portions should remain dangerous forest and divine temples. Moreover, if pressed to define the central Indonesian notion of *adat* in its specifically Balinese context, one might say it is dharma attached to space. As in India, dharma in Bali refers to duty that is attentive to matters of religious purity/pollution (cf. *Upadeca* 1968). But in Bali people are attached to temples to perform the dharma of a certain space. Progeny perform the dharma of their sacred origin-point in ancestor temples. Congregations perform the dharma of village-area space in three-temple-clusters. In Bali, the Sanskritic concept of dharma pertains more to location than to individuals or groups, and it is the dharma of space that Balinese call *adat*.

Temple networks

Sociologically, a temple ties its congregation to a particular sacred space, and temple networks interrelate different sacred spaces, thus facilitating contacts between the respective congregations for varied ends. As we shall see, such a network might be a series of ancestor temples or merely different sorts of local temples whose mystic connections are described in legends or in religious documents stored in the temples.

Any Balinese temple can be read according to literate Hindu theology or according to folk magical beliefs.[1] But there is an inevitable sociopolitical dimension as well. To appreciate this aspect of all Balinese temples, we can consider a few shrines and sacred pedestals in the ancestor temples of the social group we discussed in Chapter 4. We recall that this group had adopted many high-caste patterns, but its temple network involves commoner groups and ordinary village-areas and irrigation societies in widespread locales. Its particular monuments include the following.

Two pedestals (*pelinggih*) enable the group to propitiate some spirits at distant temples, purportedly founded by its ancestors on their migration out of eastern Bali. The group still maintains shrines there and enjoys friendly relations with the local commoner groups that share them. Such distant shrines are known as *pesimpingan*.

One monument is reserved for visitations by the spirit of the raja who was their principal benefactor. Another marker commemorates relations with a lesser royal house, which received several of the group's women in marriage. Members of the royal lines occasionally bring offerings to these shrines.

There are thrones for the deities of health, economy, and agriculture; their Hindu names are known, but it is the functions themselves that are stressed, since they represent official classical duties which are still professional specializations.

Another pedestal refers to a northern irrigation-headwater temple, and two small thrones receive the spirits from forest shrines erected by the group's ancestors when searching for the spring this temple commemorates.

In some respects the ancestor temple represents the ideal unity of its congregation. Its principle structures – the orchestra pavilion and entrance threshold – are maintained by all the women of the group equally. No offshoot temple can be built with a taller entrance, which would imply that it outranked this sacred ancestral source of legitimate members of the group where all cyclical and life-crisis rites culminate. In other respects the temple represents the internal differentiation of the group. Each collateral division is responsible for repairing different shrines. If one of several brothers receives a larger paddy inheritance, he is likely to accrue heavier responsibilities for financing temple festivals. The ordinary adult male is concerned less with esoteric religious lore of the temples he supports than with his share of the upkeep and finances for ceremonies. Meticulous calculations to distribute fairly the practical monetary burden of maintaining an ancestor temple insure that a collateral division which claims higher prestige will have to pay for demonstrating it. The many thousand temples of 'the island of the gods' are not sustained by the fabled Balinese religiosity alone.

The temple also programs the group's participation in its immediate sacred surroundings. Holy water for its festivals must be collected at a nearby river shrine built by ancestors at the raja's bathing spot. On certain temple holy days, offerings for the ancestors must also be placed at another temple called *pura melanting*, the general designation for marketplace shrines. The significance of this temple is obscure; an ancestor from one of the collateral divisions outfitted this meditation site, which is connected with the spirits of another temple important in the migration legend of Tabanan's royal house. The ancestor's special mystic powers were apparently considered to affect economic prosperity. Thus the group still maintains his *pura melanting*, where many unrelated market women leave offerings.

The group's support of such shrines persists; leaders built the riverside shrine and *pura melanting* because of their active role in the power structure of Tabanan kingdom. Yet when the political basis abruptly disappeared during 1906–8, the temple duties survived. Such apparently hollow ceremonies and legends about past obligations can later facilitate renewing lapsed social bonds. A case in point concerns those shrines connected to an irrigation temple in the distant mountains, such as the northern irrigation-headwater temple mentioned previously. A government official, who belonged to the group and whose collateral division once supplied irrigation officers for the kingdom, had suffered a serious illness marked by tormented semiconsciousness. In 1971 he arose from his sickbed displaying untutored spiritual knowledge and a proclivity to enter trance; he determined to become a ritual specialist in acknowledgment of his cure. Legends credited his division's ancestors with once winning a competition, commissioned by the raja, among Brahmanas, Sengguhus (exorcist priests), and themselves to explore for new irrigation sources. After meditating in the forests, they discovered a spring and built a new temple there. Today this temple's festivals bring together leaders of all irrigation societies that receive water from its spring. To emphasize his group's traditional involvement, the trance-prone official promoted vigorous participation in the temple's harvest rites.

This renewed interest in a remote headwater temple cannot be explained by a single factor. Motivations range from doubtlessly genuine mystical convictions to the opportunism of astute politicians, for the ancestor group's success in the 1971 elections can be partly attributed to the strong support its candidates enjoyed throughout the area whose headwater temple they help support.

Thus, capitalizing on the social relations implicit in old shrines can be politically advantageous. Yet this case is only a vivid instance of a more general feature of Balinese temples and the locales they connect. Temples serve partially as catalogues of covert interlocal ties kept in ritual reserve until conditions warrant reactivating them for various advantages, sometimes political or economic. In particular *pesimpingan* pedestals enabled a group to maintain distant relations even under traditional conditions of warfare. The ritual-spatial connections persist when the social bonds are dormant. Because of such temple networks, new influences in Bali – whether fresh political movements or modern consumer goods – leapfrog from towns to remote settings, as innovators bypass similar temple congregations to concentrate activity at the particular sacred sites which harbor their ancestral interests. Just as real as the cosmological and ritual significance of temples are the political ambitions and status concerns they mediate. In Bali, temple networks amalgamate goal-specific strategies and religious-mystical beliefs into a single framework.

Village-area, land, and lore

The relation between the sociology of temples and space is most apparent in the famous *kayangan tiga*, the three-temple-clusters of the village-areas (*desa*). Balinese commoners, especially those not organized into ancestor groups, propitiate their originating Brahmanic forces (Dewa Penchipta) in an origin temple (*pura puseh*), which memorializes the founding of an *adat* territory. An origin temple is clustered with a death temple (*pura dalem*) for the propitiation of Sivaic forces (Dewa Pralina) and with a meeting-house temple (*pura bale agung*) for the Wisnuvaic forces (Dewa Pemilihara) of maintaining ritual order and purity.[2] Such village-area temples were supported by rajas to extend Hindu courtly patterns over the social landscape. Moreover, the *desa* temple-cluster implemented a kind of local organization which has been called uniquely Balinese:

> Bali is the only island in the archipelago where there has developed somewhat the idea of the incorporation of the municipality [or parish] (*rechtspersoonlijkheid der gemeente*) (Van Stein Callenfels 1947: 195).

Finally, legends appended to the territory under the influence of the deities of a particular desa temple-cluster often provide clues to local social dynamics.

Ideally, a *desa* membership is the congregation of this triumvirate of temples. But there are sociological complications in this religious architecture of local organization. The congregation that supports a three-temple-cluster can contain people other than the residents of the geographical area under its influence. Thus, it is misleading to view the *desa* as a confederation of hamlets (*banjar*). One *desa* territory might contain residential groups which are affiliated to another territory's three-temple-cluster. Or allegiances might even be divided between three-temple-clusters. Tabanan, for example, is among other things the name of a *desa* with a *kayangan tiga*. But there are members of *banjars* who acknowledge the Brahmanic forces of their lives in Tabanan's origin temple and the Sivaic forces in the death temple of a neighboring *desa*. One unusual *banjar* even has its own origin temple and uses Tabanan's death temple. Thus, to see the *kayangan tiga* even as a negatively defined 'legal community' (Geertz 1959: 1011), with distinctive purity/pollution rules and ritual detailing, although true in a broad sense, overlooks such cross-*desa* affiliations according to which persons attend three-temple-cluster ceremonies not as *banjar* members but as individual family heads with religious ties to that locality.

A further complication arises in the possible stratification of the *desa* membership itself. For example, Grader described a *ngarep/sampingan* contrast in North Bali:

> Comprising only thirty-five of the villagers, the members of the *desa ngarep* group together with the three highest officials of the village, constitute a distinct entity separate from the *sampingans*, the remainder of the inhabitants. The members of the *desa ngarep* group are the acknowledged *krama desa*, those who are descended directly from the founders of the village, and by reason of their status they incur more obligations than the *sampingans* (1969a: 162).

Belo correlated this status division with what she called 'the most usual pattern of land ownership:'

> The [village] fields are passed down by heredity in the male line but may not be alienated; they may not be bought by a foreigner or even by the member of an adjoining village . . . Only if there is a family line which comes to an end, an exceedingly rare occurence, do the village site and the portion of the fields worked by the family come up for sale to outsiders. Land so held is called *pachatu*. Two other types of holding are commonly spoken of, the *tetamian*, 'inheritance land,' and *labaan*, 'temple land.' *Tetamian* is the type customarily owned by members of the higher castes; it is generally passed on in the male line, too, but, in contrast to village

lands, can be sold or mortgaged. The third sort, *labaan*, is land held in common by members of a temple group for the support of the temple and its priest (Belo 1949: 7).

Bali does reveal scattered traditions of first-settlers' precedents familiar in Indonesia.[3] But Belo claimed too much for this pattern; the scheme she outlines supposes that virgin land is opened by commoner, locally oriented settlers. Where high-caste groups have initiated new settlements, or where many distinct *desas* grow out of factions in populous village-areas, the pattern of unalienable village fields is compromised from the outset. In modern Bali seldom does the sacred territory of *desa* temples correspond to the agricultural lands of its congregation, and seldom are any unalienable lands the property of an actual core group of original settlers.

Belo tried to identify religious space (the area of influence of *desa* deities) with agricultural space (the productive fields of *desa* members). Her contemporaries made the related mistake of identifying religious space with the sum of the residential space (*banjar*); this caused them to overlook complexities in community development. For example, Covarrubias summarized a standard view of social change:

> Most important of *banjar* property is a little communal temple (*pamaksan*). If the *banjar* grows beyond the function of village quarters, or 'ward,' its *pamaksan* temple may become a temple of 'origin'; then they will build their formal village temple (*pura desa*), their temple of the dead, out in the cemetery, and, having the three reglementary temples (*kayangan tiga*) that every complete community needs, they will ask for independence from the village and will become a full-fledged free *desa* (1937: 63).

Several difficulties arise: (1) A growing *banjar* might simply divide as another *banjar-adat* association and not incorporate itself as a separate *desa*. (2) Frequently in organizing a new *desa* three-temple-cluster, a set of *banjars* or factions first erects a death temple nearby; later they might take the more controversial and costly step of building the rest of the *kayangan tiga.*[4] (3) The process – rarely simply a matter of harmoniously amalgamating a 'full-fledged free *desa*' – can become politicized and provoke local factions. Moreover, new temples always require approval of officials who must also supervise dedication ceremonies, and a group must be legitimized to provide *desa* leaders and temple custodians as well.

In the ethnographic literature of this period, the process whereby temples mediate social groups and religious localities is indirectly discussed in analyses of the mother-daughter village pattern:

> Such a village[-area] is economically and politically independent of all others, except for a curious relation of blood. It often happens that various neighboring villages are united by a strong bond into an association of related villages which worship a common original ancestor and with a common temple of 'origin' located in the oldest village of the group, which they recognize as a 'head' or 'mother' village. From this it is supposed that the other villages sprung, and when they grew became independent. Such village associations cooperate with one another by sending offerings and representatives to the temple feasts of the other *desas* (Covarrubias 1937: 58).

But most observers assumed the process was slow and irreversible. Goris, for example, describing archaic Selat near the state temple Besakih, implied that the principle of mother-daughter villages anticipates formal 'village federations:'

In the course of time, however, a mother village can acquire the status of a principal village at the head of a village federation of former daughter villages which have become completely independent. It has still not been definitely established whether there are village federations which have not developed from the relationship mother village-daughter villages (Goris 1969c: 222).

Only Bateson's article (1937) suggested how quickly and opportunistically such interlocal ties could be fabricated, thanks to temple legends and trancers who express new strategic economic and political relationships 'as social ties between clubs, temples, or villages' (Bateson and Mead 1942: 259). What we saw earlier with regard to ancestor-temple networks is equally true of the mother-*desa* pattern: in the absence of genealogical connections and irrespective of actual historical events, mystic proclamations and ritual activations of presumably forgotten relations can involve residents of one locality in the affairs of another. The process relies on the way temples tie households vertically to a sacred space and join different spaces horizontally to each other.

Finally, we should note that spatial lore is an important concern even when not commemorated in a particular temple. The social reputation of individuals or groups is often meshed with the legendary attributes of their localities. In fact, one could include space as an eighth mode of social classification that combines with the seven previously viewed in Chapter 3. Consider again Tabanan town: site of the old royal palaces, district governmental headquarters, and commercial center for Chinese and Islamic merchants – but in purely Balinese terms, merely a very enlarged village-area (*desa*). As an official administrative unit, Tabanan includes sixteen governmental hamlets (*banjar dinas*). Many are coterminous with customary hamlets (*banjar adat*) whose members support the three-temple-cluster of *desa-adat* Tabanan. (And some of the hamlets with *adat* affiliations here also fall into neighboring administrative units.) However, some of these *banjar adat* include members from distinct localities with special place-names and lore. For example, the governmental hamlet Malkangin includes members of two *adat* hamlets, Malkangin and Pande; the latter named for its traditional metal smiths. But Malkangin includes as well a separate, isolated residential complex called Dangin Charik where the reputed descendants of the three Brahmana families who first settled there live. Dangin Charik is a unit not circumscribed by any of the seven formal modes in our social matrix. It is not usefully considered as a sub-*banjar-adat* unit, since not all *banjars* contain such units; nor do the Balinese consider it this way. Dangin Charik is rather a differentiated sacred spot – next to a supernatural forest – with a Brahmana *pedanda* much in demand as a ceremonial officiant. Other residents from here are viewed across the mystique of their locale.

Dangin Charik contains vestiges of the precolonial *pachatu* system; its Brahmana residents, once supported by a royal or noble line, possibly affiliated with *banjar*

Malkangin after its patrons lost their power. But not all special residential areas are simple archaisms of the courtly cosmography. Tabanan includes another hamlet with an area known popularly as Dalem, because it borders the death temple and town graveyard. Its residents have a reputation for black magical potency; it is a likely area for witchcraft. According to some informants, it is appropriate for communism as well, which explains why the PKI was centered here. But even before 1965, a person was thought of as being from Dalem rather than being from the *banjar adat* that includes it.

One final example should illustrate the full elaboration of this factor of legendary locality in Balinese social organization. There is a place called Pangkong Prabu. Its residents meet in the *adat* council-house of a Tabanan *banjar*, although their houseyards lie two kilometers away, separated by Tabanan's new special governmental *banjar* and a cemetery for national heroes. In matters of both customary law and governmental administration, the twenty-four family heads in Pangkong Prabu face west to Tabanan. However, their marriage network and their social relations based on an enhanced commoner rank of *Pasek* (to be discussed later) face eastwards toward nearby Sangolan, a single *adat*-hamlet that nevertheless supports its own *desa* temple-cluster which is part of a different government unit altogether. Thus, Pangkong Prabu reveals radical tortion in its social matrix, but its vivid identity stems from the sanctity of its location. As the name suggests, it straddles a small stream; and it is overshadowed by a lofty banyan where, once upon a time, a holy man achieved *moksa*. The number-two raja of Tabanan once constructed a royal shrine to confirm his house's participation in the site's auspiciousness. The family heads of Pangkong Prabu were limited to ten, all considered descendants of the holy man, and the eldest line became the source of successive extraordinarily pure *pemangkus*, custodians of the royal shrine. Today the old royal patrons barely maintain the shrine, but the significance of Pangkong Prabu has not diminished. To be a resident there is to dwell in a locale of holy danger. As the current *pemangku* recalls, once even a Madurese Muslim, son of a Haji, was attracted by the power of the spot to pay homage beneath the banyan tree to the spirits of this place.

Thus, the complicated principles of Balinese social organization based on diverse sets of affiliations for individual family heads, stretch over a landscape rich in symbols and lore of spatial identity. This tendency to assign religious attributes to localities was supported and harnessed by the rajas and their advisors. A space can be defined and coded by some sort of temple, and an individual or group participates in its nature.[5] The space might be named for an ideal aspect of the group occupying it, as in *Banjar Pande* (smiṭh's hamlet). Or the space may be intrinsically enchanted and its residents subject to 'contagion,' as in Dalem or Pangkong Prabu. Foreign enclaves – such as the Islamic 'Kampong Jawa' of Tabanan – are, in fact, viewed by Balinese as such legendary localities. Any new residential area is watched closely to see if it reveals signs of particular pure/impure qualities; if such signs are detected, a temple will likely be built to acknowledge them, and a group will be elevated to oversee the temple's proper maintenance.

Subsistence festivals of foresight

Just as ancestor worship and village-area rituals facilitate flexible social ties across locales, irrigation-temple rites implement adjustments to fluctuating environmental conditions affecting wet-rice agriculture. Balinese irrigation employs an elaborate system of shrines at every juncture of water distribution, where each phase of the growth cycle is complemented by rituals. The most obvious ecological strain on maximum rice production is, of course, drought. But the perhaps less obvious strain on the perpetuation of careful control of water allocation is an occasional over-abundance of water which could foster laxity in maintaining the apparatus of controls. The calendars of rituals within a watershed allow for staggering water supplies throughout the growing period. When and where water is plentiful enough, the rituals call for contemporaneous pan-watershed harvests, yet they preserve precise calendrical observations that would permit reinstating staggered harvests up and down the watershed slope, if water resources became overtaxed. This dynamic function of irrigation rituals demands closer inspection.

C. Geertz has summarized the cyclic rhythm of the Balinese rice cult (cf. Wirz 1927):

> it is conducted at every level of the *subak* from the individual terrace, through the various subsections of the *subak*, to the *subak* as a whole . . . These various ceremonies are symbolically linked to cultivation . . . to ensure intersubak coordination within a given drainage region – a region, say, ten to fifteen miles wide and thirty-five or so long, fanning out as you descend from mountain to sea. The cult consists of nine major named stages. These stages follow in a fixed order at a pace generally determined, *once the first stage is initiated*, by the intrinsic ecological rhythms of rice growing.
>
> *Subaks* at the top of the system begin the ceremonial cycle, and with it the cultivation sequence, in December; *subaks* at the bottom, near the coast, begin it in April; those in between topographically are in between temporally as well.
>
> When a higher *subak* is flooding its terrace preparatory to ploughing, a lower is clearing its. When a lower is flooding a higher is planting. When a lower is celebrating the yellowing of the rice and thus the promise about a month hence of harvest, the higher is already carrying the sheaves to the barns.
>
> Indeed, as water is the central limiting factor in the *subak* ecosystem, if *subak* cycles were not staggered, wet rice cultivation in Bali could never have attained, and could not maintain, a fraction of its actual extent . . . (C. Geertz 1972a: 30–1).

In this closely controlled timing of water allocation, overlords, by sponsoring adjudicating courts of appeal to expand the scope of the irrigation system beyond the mere cooperation of adjoining *subak* councils, perhaps had their greatest practical impact.

The previous description pictures irrigation under conditions of greatest natural strain, with smaller upland terraces flooded during a relatively drier month to reserve the wetter month for broader coastal fields. We should note, however, that the rituals that surround and help complement rice production also envision an ecological context in which such careful regulation is unnecessary. This is the alternate harvest ritual format considered most auspicious if all paddy has been harvested simultaneously and its bounty celebrated in unison. However, even when the staggered cycles of planting which maximize the efficient use of scarce water are not required, the cycles are still recognized in the rituals conducted at the irrigation temples. There is, in short, what we might call an archival aspect to the rice cult which allows for the reactivation of staggered cycles, choreographed, so to speak, according to the ritual calendar that continues apace regardless of actual water conditions. In a sense, the rituals store information that increases the irrigation system's adaptability in the complex process of continually expanding irrigated fields. A not-too-conjectural mainstay in the history of Balinese irrigation would run as follows: a new spring is tapped and the surrounding forest land converted into paddy; for a while water is ample, but as more lands are opened for cultivation, either water must be augmented or staggered cycles of usage commenced. Later, if several very wet seasons ensue, or particularly if new sources of water are discovered and channeled into the system, then the staggering can be gradually relaxed. And the impulse to return to simultaneous harvests will persist, since this practice releases everyone from the more arduous field chores to perform concerted harvest rituals, and other ceremonial works (*Karya*).

This capacity for switching between simultaneous harvesting and staggered harvesting, each of which responds to different practical exigencies and social preferences, reflects alternate expectations among Balinese concerning the water supply, expectations most systematically expressed in the contrast between harvest festivals called *ngebekin* and those called *ngusaba*. The contrast is outlined by Grader in his discussion of three varieties of Balinese irrigation shrines: (1) small, unwalled offering columns at sluice points or weirs (*chatu*), (2) headwater temples for one or more *subaks* (*pura ulun charik*) and (3) 'sanctuaries which were originally *desa* temples that one or more *subaks* helped to worship, after which in the course of time, all the expenses connected with the temple services and offering ceremonials have gradually fallen to the *subak* or *subaks*, though others may continue to participate in its services, either as a *desa* or as individuals (*pura penyungsungan subak*):'

For all the temples and other places of worship there are certain times when religious ceremonies are held, either periodically or as occasion demands. The periodical ceremonies are divided into *ngerainin* and *ngebekin* or *ngusaba*.

Ngerainin consists of making a flower offering in the *puras ulun charik* and *penyungsungan subak*; it takes place on certain favorable days (*rerainan*) such as full moon, new moon, Wednesday-Klion, Anggara Kasih (Tuesday-Klion), and the like, and is performed by the *pemangku* without the members of the subak being present. No *ngerainin* takes place at the chatus, which, since they are not *puras*, do not have *pemangkus*.

The harvest festival is celebrated in the last stage of the ripening of the rice, in alternate years as *ngebekin* and *ngusaba*. New moon is considered a favorable time for *ngebekin*, while *ngusaba* takes place at full moon. The former ceremony has the character of an offering to the demons; the latter, primarily a festival of thanksgiving to the deity, is more elaborate than *ngebekin* and is often accompanied by the placing of festive poles of bamboo (*penjor*) at each kesit. The *puras penyungsungan subak* follow a pattern similar to that of the *puras ulun charik*. There, too, *ngebekin* and *ngusaba* alternate every other year or every two hundred ten days, depending on whether the Hindu-Balinese or the Javanese-Balinese calendar is followed, with the festival being held on the anniversary (*odalan*) of the temple. *Ngebekin* is the 'little' festival; the *ngusaba* or the *pura penyungsungan subak* is also called *odalan* (Grader 1960a: 274, 276).

The *ngebekin/ngusaba* contrast thus involves ritual acknowledgment first of potential demonic interference with rice production and then of divine benevolence in bestowing abundant harvests. These ritual formats alternate mechanically regardless of the actual current harvest, but they can be more accentuated in certain environmental extremes. Consider, for example, the *ngebekin* harvest in 1972 of an extremely rich, heavily double-cropped watershed area in southwest Bali. Because water is in general abundant here – even more so after several recent very wet years – the *subaks* in this area had tended toward simultaneous harvests; throughout the season mile after mile of gradual slope revealed paddy of the same hue, first seedling green, later strapling chartreuse, finally golden ripe. In terms of actual yields the rites oriented against scarcity in this area recall the ideals of those celebrating plenty elsewhere; the small harvest ritual here would qualify as enormous in many other watersheds of Bali. This is especially true, since in these relatively unstaggered *subaks*, a festival celebrates an actual just completed harvest, whereas elsewhere staggered harvests mean that the new moon or full moon festival cannot actually apply to all the fields and cultivators but recognizes in part harvests past or ones to come. Yet in 1972 the peasants in southwest Bali who were acknowledging in a demonic register a bountiful wet-year harvest were also currently experiencing a severe drought which bade ill for the next crop. In this respect, then, the *ngebekin* ritual keyed with actuality insofar as the harvest festival served as the occasion for intense trance activity and demonic possessions by many interested parties, including about a dozen *pemangku* priests from all over the watershed area who warned of conflicts to come and prescribed measures of water allocation for warding them off. Here was a case of a demon-oriented festival, dictated by the permutational calendar, at the moment of a plentiful harvest projecting, however, an impending setback in productivity. At such times trancers can be expected to enunciate policies which could reinstate here and there staggered planting to help minimize the impact of the current drought.

This extreme case from 1972 helps us better appreciate the complex temporal dimensions of the rice cult whose rituals are active agents in precision water control. A given harvest festival invokes the immediate past by the actual bounty displayed. The festivals register the timeless qualities of the whole ecosystem by requiring alternate forms to pacify demons or to entertain gods, regardless of the current harvest. Yet the festivals cope with the immediate future by exchanging information, often in trance performances, concerning the coming season's inter-*subak* relations;

this information must as well be sensitive to any current environmental or political pressures. Finally, the whole ritual process looks to the distant future by requiring full productivity to enhance harvest celebrations, even when particularly favorable conditions might otherwise allow relaxation of the terse cooperative organization and the rigorous temporal calculations. Regardless of fluctuations in water supply or difficulties in inter-*subak* relations, and often in spite of new colonial and now national policies, both the work force and the calendrical calibrations are kept in gear in the event of an always anticipated water shortage. The system is implemented by a social organization of subsistence which pits groups against groups rather than individuals against individuals, but groups who realize that it is in the interest of all to maintain a flexible system of maximized water allocation.

We submit then, that the plenty/scarcity distinction in the Balinese rice cult is, among other things, part of the ritual foresight which requires a surplus to be harvested and in part consumed this year, not just to store in reserves, but to insure that the social apparatus of labor cooperation and interdigited growth cycles never be curtailed, even for a season. This, of course, is not to reduce the rice cult merely to a functional lubrication in case the social and calendrical machinery of subsistence grows rusty. Indeed, the content of rituals is constrained by many other values as well; for example, the Balinese reluctance, we noted earlier, to release rice into an anonymous and impersonal market system recalls the stigmas in South-Asian Hinduism attached to middleman operations in handling foodstuffs, as opposed to agriculturally preparing food for harvest in the field and domestically preparing food for consumption at the hearth.[6] However, while both Bali and South Asia tend to deny status and esteem to the merchant of subsistence crops, this value is put to opposite social uses. In Bali it reinforces the tendency for each household or ancestor group to stock its own rice bins from its own paddy – a sort of endo-subsistence. In South Asia the value helps implement the whole set of specialized ritual occupations in the hierarchical exchange system, here suggested in near biblical phrasing:

> High Status [in India] is symbolized by being able to take the rarest kinds of food from the fewest people. It is much better to give and have one's food taken than it is to receive. A Brahman theoretically can take only uncooked food from anyone of lower status than himself, at a feast, a Brahman should cook his own food (Cohn 1973: 131).

As we saw earlier, Bali's striking divergence from India in this respect was recorded even in the early nineteenth century. But since then the comparative study of subsistence values – such as differential uses of a stigma on marketing staples – has made little headway in the Indo-Pacific.

For our purposes the important point is the flexibility of Bali's subsistence system guaranteed partly by the ritual apparatus surrounding it, which can stagger water usage up and down a slope, or shift the whole periodicity of planting, growth and harvest depending on various factors. The government take-over of Balinese *subak*-organizations and planning that is often tested and constantly rumored might manage to increase yields for a time in certain sample areas, but it is doubtful if the national bureaucracy could work out a rationalized scheme as effective in fine tuning the entire rice-production system to the ever changing exigencies of fluctuating differential needs for each other's water.

Balinese irrigation has yet to be studied systematically as an active means of adaptation that is intrinsically dynamic and expansive, rather than in equilibrium. The system is receptive to new agricultural and trade endeavors (for example, frog 'husbandry' in the paddies) as long as they are not detrimental to rice production.[7] And other foodstuffs in Bali can become more significant than outside planners often allow. Corn, for example, is generally listed as a poor and unwanted substitute for rice (cf. Hanna 1972c). But merely observing that no Balinese prefers corn over rice obscures the fact that once such a substandard crop is introduced, and especially when it becomes required in ceremonial offerings, different qualities of strains are developed, different local areas become reputed for producing superior varieties, and some of the cultic meaning formerly ascribed most to rice begins to accrue. To fully understand the dynamics of Balinese subsistence a long-term study, preferably by Balinese, would have to assess its twofold vantage on water shortage versus abundance and document the strategies and results when one leads to the other. Moreover, a thorough study would stress the multitemporal perspectives and the readiness to support additional agricultural activities if new needs or markets or meanings arise.

Again the *ngebekin/ngusaba* contrast would, I think, be central in such an investigation, and it could lead to comparisons toward the east as well as the west. For, if Bali's omission of markets from the religious and ritual value placed on food provisioning appears somehow Indic, its showy celebrations of a frequent surplus can appear outright Oceanic. The relative insulation of wet-rice subsistence from Balinese caste compelled many observers to view the island's society as essentially communal, only stratified by an intrusion of foreign, Hindu decadence. But this same state of affairs might have easily suggested the Pacific. Balinese demonstrate an overriding concern with prestige and social ranks, but only on the foundation of a guaranteed surplus for which traditionally the apical social status is somehow held religiously, and litigiously, responsible. In this respect precolonial Bali resembled those intriguing Pacific societies which appear on the one hand tribelike, in that different social segments are equally assured basic subsistence, yet statelike in that elites gain the authority to manage the luxurious expenditure of a recurring surplus. Thus Bali is not, for example, unlike what can be guessed about ancient Polynesia:

> The democratic land tenure of [Polynesian] Traditional Societies may be explained therefore, by the concept of honor that does not involve high chiefs in the practical affairs of agriculture. Their honor is met when they receive first-fruits as token tribute and when the lands prosper generally (Goldman 1970: 556).

Substitute Archipelago Sanskrit *sakti* for Polynesian honor or *mana* and the passage could as well apply to Bali. Many technical terms have been suggested for these status systems – somehow supratribe yet still substate. Most of the terms are based on kinship lineage rules, and they seem inadequate since they omit the sense of holistic statehood that is vividly expressed during the ritual display and/or consumption of a surplus by the society's entire population or by some representative sample. The importance of this holistic self-image in such systems is particularly conspicuous in Bali because of its elaboration of a Hindu-*warna* scheme to articulate a native sense of totalized hierarchical universe atop a reliable and abundant rice harvest.

In the case of Bali, lacking an appropriate technical term, we might provisionally think of its subsistence/status configuration as one more dimension of the culture's 'romance.' Here we find agriculturalists ritually consuming a surplus staple in festivals where information can be conveyed to forestall any threatened shortage, and all to preclude the necessity to market the food staple that is the object and the subject of their island's principal cult. Clearly Balinese rice culture remains a challenging and fertile field for comprehensive comparative studies of subsistence values – from India, through the Lesser Sundas of Indonesia, to the Pacific.

Corporate location

Groups shift, change, fragment, expand, and migrate; space remains. Part of the indisputable reality behind outsiders' impressions of Bali's profound religiosity concerns the wedding of lore and topography. Balinese refuse to let the legends and stories they append to locales eclipse, in spite of the geographic mobility (epitomized in sacred trek legends) that has probably prevailed for centuries, especially as population has increased with new irrigable land available for settlement. Colonial health measures accelerated population growth, and the Dutch roads and dams enabled irrigation to be extended well beyond the areas cultivated under the traditional *subak*-technology. Later we shall review Dutch restrictions on caste mobility; here we should note that by territorializing both the spheres of influence of courts and the bonds between lords and subjects, the colonial administration doubtless inhibited traditional geographic mobility, especially across kingdoms. There is no reason not to assume that displacement was frequent in precolonial Bali. Rajas imported religious experts and artisans from other areas; they planted specialist groups wherever new shrines and temples were dedicated, and these groups in turn forged status bonds with the local population. Relocation likely resulted also from journeys to distant festivals at irrigation or state temples where relationships were consolidated far from home. If one can generalize at all from current events, status competition and pervasive antagonism in the home *banjar* must often have forced groups to migrate either to seek land or to escape punishment for infractions of local *adat*. While the rajas capitalized on such tendencies, the colonial administration discouraged them altogether; and we can speculate that for the period of

Dutch control Bali looked less geographically mobile than for the period immediately prior.

In one sense – especially in contrast to neighboring Islamized, mercantilized, and extensively urbanized Java – Bali reveals traditional localization:

> Even though Balinese society is densely populated, highly stratified, and complexly differentiated . . . , it is at the same time sharply localized. Nearly every relationship is both a personal one, in the sense that the actors have been fully acquainted . . . , and also a clearly defined one . . . (H. Geertz 1963: 57).

But there remains a peculiar aspect to Balinese localism which sets it apart from general stereotypes of traditional societies. Social units are tied to spatial units without being exactly territorialized. A long-time personal acquaintance is often a member of a distant temple congregation, to which one journeys on festival days. An individual or group is primarily localized in its houseyard or set of houseyards and secondarily localized in the *banjar* residential-complex and in the village-area religious zone. But such secondary locales can include far flung temples. Thus social groups in Bali are not in any simple sense territorialized, and a group's social identity can persist if it migrates, even (traditionally) across kingdoms.

This matter can be expressed another way: while corporate groups are merely optional, corporate locations are fundamental. Bali contains two primary types of practical space: walled-in yards for domestic life, and irrigated fields for rice production. Both are cleared from the dense tropical forest, ideally to remain for all time. The religious well-being of domestic space is assured through the civic, death, and cremation regulations of *banjar* organization. The religious well-being of paddy is assured through the ritual and practical regulations of *subak* organization. And the successful maintenance and balance of domestic life and agricultural life is celebrated in village-area temples that themselves assure the well-being of a territory. The spaces and the relations among them are fixed; groups that attend to the religious needs of spaces are flexible.

Within the walls

This basic principle in Balinese social dynamics can perhaps be clarified by examining the relation of the individual to his enclosed houseyard (*pekarangan*). J. Kersten, forcibly struck by the visual contribution of houseyard walls, paused to fancy their dematerialization:

> Were there no dividing walls (*scheideingmuren*), then the entire village-area would afford nothing to see, other than little clay constructions with grassroofs, sheltered among coconut palms and fruit trees. These long lines with their countless fine extensions bestow order and harmony of the picture of the *desa* (1947: 29).

The Balinese houseyard is the individual's protected place – often in precolonial times his fortified place – which contains his most intimate temple and its shrine to the houseyard origins. Here are buried the afterbirths (*ari-ari*) of each child, symbolic younger siblings and protector of their womb companion's first months of life. The yard is the scene of the cosmological signposts of an individual's lifetime: from one's own *ari-ari* burial; to the commemoration of numerological cycles at the third month, sixth month, and every six months thereafter; to the keepsaking of the dust left from teeth-filing. Only after death are the individual's corporeal remains relinquished to the public sector, consigned to the graveyard and partially entrusted to the ceremonial responsibilities of his non-kin hamlet associates.

The lack of explicitly horizontal bonds within the yard is apparent from Balinese domestic life-crisis ceremonies. There is little sense of community or of the more precise communitas, a concept articulated by V. Turner and associated with rites of transition:

> . . . insofar as it refers to a directly personal egalitarian relationship, 'gemeinschaft' connotes 'communitas,' as, for example, where Tönnies considers friendship to express a kind of gemeinschaft or 'community of feeling' that is tied to neither blood nor locality.
>
> . . . liminality, the optimal setting of communitas relations, and communitas, a spontaneously generated relationship between leveled and equal total and individuated human beings, stripped of structural attributes, together constitute what one might call anti-structure (1973: 216).

In distinct contrast to any such liminal communitas, Balinese initiation rites merely usher actors across the auspicious multiples of their cycles of days and months, in ceremonies that are very similar for the two sexes. There is no specifically male initiation. Specifically female rites – simple seclusion – reflect Hindu concepts of the dangers of menstrual blood to the order of society. But periodic seclusion does not reconstitute the woman as individual; it merely isolates her when impure. Balinese transition rites in life and after death never obliterate, even momentarily and for a cohort of comrades in passage, the actors' social structural attributes. Rather it is precisely such attributes that the ceremonies celebrate. In short, the affective bonds even among agnates within the same houseyard are expressed less as a community of total and individuated human beings than as structured vertical relations of differentiated actors to the houseyard temple.[8]

For these rice growers organized into *subaks*, the yard is not the production unit. It is rather the foremost domestic unit, and almost everything domestic in Bali is ceremonialized. Essentially, kinsmen comprising a yard consume rice from the same storage bin and pursue daily routines together; practically all their other interests might diverge. Even the holy water required for certain rites that obliges everyone to maintain a subordinate relationship with a Brahmana *pedanda* might be fetched from different priests by members of the same yard. Culturally, the agnates, spouses, and adopted children of a houseyard are solidary because they are of the same space.

Certainly a Balinese individual has more interests in common with the agnates of his own houseyard than with unrelated persons. But the cross-cutting modes of affiliation we reviewed above, which constitute a sort of definition by default of the

Balinese person, are far from obliterated in the houseyard. The Balinese individual participates in matrixes of potentially conflicting role sets that rival sociology's view of modernity. In times past the fellow sitting beside someone on his *banjar* council was potentially an enemy in war, in the not unlikely event of a royal dynastic coup. Or currently the relative of a corpse one is burying today is tomorrow's political opponent. Or in a drought the *subak* of one's brother and co-resident might be caught diverting irrigation water from one's own canals. Thus cross-cutting loyalties even penetrate the yard. The walled-in houseyard is at best only a relative locus of *esprit de corps* within the matrixes of obligations.

The same life-crisis ceremonies that bind individuals vertically to a houseyard temple insure that they can vacate that yard without totally sacrificing the affective identity that ties them to it. *Pesimpingan* shrines guarantee as much. At any one time houseyard walls mark the sociological boundaries of a group. But as the site of life-crisis markers, the yard also expresses the religious identity of its members. If the members of one yard divide and relocate, any ties that remain are mediated through their mutual vertical-past relations to a common yard. In general, if group A produces two offshoot groups – B and C – the latter two can manifest strong solidarity only via the houseyard temple of group A. And the houseyard as a cultural unit remains intact, even though its membership might change or completely turn over.

The ritual limits of urbanization

Since Indonesian independence Bali has been adjusting to an exploding population and a burgeoning national bureaucracy which together can produce severe dislocation. How these developments reconfirm the ritual significance of the houseyard can be illustrated by a special new neighborhood in Tabanan town.

Taman Sari is an area inhabited by about fifty families, many of whose fathers are urbane professionals. Their houseyards occupy terraced rows of newly drained paddy, precious productive land engulfed by the expanding town. The area is thought of vaguely as a neighborhood (Ind. *rukun tetangga*). In 1970 it was designated a governmental *banjar* to become the sixteenth bureaucratic unit in Tabanan town, complete with its own administrator (*klian*) and divided into three complexes with a messenger to advise of deaths and deliver official letters. Residents assist each other on a basis of voluntary cooperation – helping if a house burns, witnessing birth anniversary festivities, and so on. But nothing conclusive can be effected here concerning matters of *adat*. Marriages, burials, and cremations must be carried out in affiliation with residents' customary *banjars* of origin. Either the proper expert is fetched to witness the ceremony, or, if kinship relations are still good, the ceremony is performed back in the houseyard of origin.

On the other hand, each houseyard in Taman Sari has a shrine which both commemorates its origin as an inhabited space and serves as the focus of daily ceremonial life. Thus each yard is religiously significant in spite of the fact it is not welded into a customary hamlet. To live in a yard only affiliated to a *banjar adat* through the intermediary of another yard is viewed as an unstable circumstance, eventually to be rectified by the creation of a *banjar adat* in Taman Sari. Yet it is not certain that even then all residents would join the new customary council (*krama*). Nevertheless, it is the religious identity of a yard which enables an ambivalent social situation like Taman Sari to arise at all.

Other developments in Tabanan – also characteristic of Singaraja, Den Pasar, and a few other commercial and administrative centers – suggest some particular qualities of Balinese towns. Tabanan is, we recall, according to the *adat* mode merely a *desa* supported by thirteen *banjars* and partly supported (that is, either its death temple or its origin temple) by a few other customary associations. It is an extreme case of stultified *desa*-dynamics – a village-area that forgot to divide. Around 17,000 people (over 1,000 heads of families) support this single three-temple-cluster. Although there are plans to subdivide the governmental area of Tabanan town into more manageable administrative units, there is no movement to divide it into smaller three-temple-cluster *adat* congregations.

A standard model of urban change might detect here built-in implications of rationalization: (1) the more families to support a temple-cluster, the less cost per capita; and (2) the more crowded houseyards to prepare offerings, the less time-consuming ceremonial tasks for any individual, especially since only one representative from a kitchen (*kuren*) need attend many actual temple ceremonies. Thus, a soaring population plus diminishing ceremonial responsibilities could have worked together to yield surplus manpower for the nonagricultural occupations proliferating under Dutch and subsequently Indonesian bureaucracy. A classic urban/rural dichotomy should have arisen with a town as opposed to a folk ethos. Such in fact is the official Indonesian administrative view, promulgated by the office of the Tabanan chief district officer. Government charts show four zones marked by diminishing progressivity: the town, the fringes of the town, traditional *desas*, and isolated *desas*, usually in the mountains. Progress is viewed in terms of education and orientation to the Indonesian nation as opposed to local religious traditionalism.

However, this theoretical net of a Jakarta-oriented officialdom lets important facts slip through. For example, Tabanan town contains in its heart *banjar*-Malkangin composed of traditionally separatist Pandes, who never proceed beyond grammar school. On the other hand the long, sloping northbound road displays afternoon streams of high schoolers, academicians, and bureaucrats cycling to their upland homes. Moreover, locales such as Pangkong Prabu and Sangolan – within a few minutes' walking distance of Tabanan's assorted secondary schools – still display teknonymous terms of address (a custom considered rustic by superior-castes in court towns), and they esteem Pan as a high respect title above ordinary Nang, rather than I Gde above ordinary Pan. On the other hand a distant village like Tangguntiti reveals more townlike terminological usages and an array of civil servants, in part because of its important elevated Sudra group. These facts demonstrate that progressive influences are felt not by neighbors, but by people who share the same ancestors, real or fictive. This is true even if an individual's kinsmen stay in the country when he comes to town, for his basic identity remains at the location of his ancestral source. There is a persistent positive value on remote origins. It is the continued propitiation of the source (*Kawitan*) that belies the governmental office's concentric circles of diminishing progressivity around an urban core.

Many current bureaucrats tapped into the educational system and post-traditional service professions when the Dutch were conferring preferential treatment on elite Balinese. Today a civil servant employed far from his customary hamlet often fulfills his *adat* obligations by paying a fee to cover the inevitable neglect of his duties, although some *banjars* are more conservative, and generally no exemptions from witnessing cremations are permitted. In this case a man maintains only one set of *adat* affiliations. In a later chapter we shall see that the surest way to perpetuate home ties is to belong to a strong ancestor group that can protect a man's local rights even in his absence, since such groups are less dependent on a *banjar* organization for carrying out domestic rituals.

A more extreme strain on *adat* ties arises when a highly successful bureaucrat receives town housing. He might affiliate with the *banjar adat* there, perhaps an association of perfectly traditional houseyards surrounding a set of shiny, modern bungalows. He could participate in its ceremonial responsibilities (*suka-duka*), but his own *adat* rites still occur in his *banjar* and houseyard of origin. This situation, which we glimpsed in a preliminary form in Taman Sari, is today designated a double-*banjar* membership. A cluster of motives explains this deflection of time, energy, and resources to a remote houseyard source: (1) an underlying belief that ancestors are linked to a sacred point of origin; (2) maintenance of local rights in houseland owned by the *banjar* (and as of recent land reform, maintenance of rights to own agricultural land in one's original subdistrict); (3) care for the elders, sometimes together with supporting an endogamous country wife as well as a second outsider spouse in town; (4) provisions for courtlike leisurely pastimes amidst gardens and aviaries, and eventual retirement; and (5) perhaps most importantly, maintaining good familial and *banjar* relations that will insure a final resting spot and proper ceremonies after death in keeping with one's locally defined rank. The last point is an articulate Balinese concern of utmost intensity. Old folks whose successful sons are living far off in town with their immediate families recount how the sons have to follow their work, how they come home often with little presents, and 'besides after retirement they will return here and die and be buried and cremated . . . , and that's what's important.'

Part of the distinctive shape of Balinese urbanization and so-called modernization stems from the potency of *desa* origins. In this respect Bali contrasts vividly with parts of neighboring Java, where 'townsmen, particularly the pegawai [civil servants] and merchants, rarely have houses in villages' (H. Geertz 1963: 42). A Balinese urbanite, even a religiously skeptical technocrat, remains tied to his original yard, much in the same way that an entire ancestor-group partakes of the nature of its legendary locale. Finally, urbanization patterns in Bali must be assessed in light of traditional social dynamics. The intrinsic thrust of houseyards as corporate spaces becomes evident when members grow aware of their capacity to approximate courtly images and ideals. The thriving yard is crowded, with ample fieldhands to supply its rice bin, with specialist elders to oversee its religious life, and with plentiful candidate spouses and droves of children. A failing yard taxes its available hands; a prosperous yard can thinly disperse all labor and busy work, and it boasts leaders in ritual and often political affairs. Physically the well formed yard is orderly – paved in river stones, graced with songbirds, animated by performing arts, and landscaped with plants useful as medicine and required in ceremonies. Pervaded by a languid tranquility, it conveys a sense of shelter, and relationships within, properly hierarchical, reinforce this sense. The scene most evocative of the feeling-tone of a successful houseyard is the profoundly respected female elder who sits and dotingly plaits innumerable palm fronds into offerings for the gods and ancestors.

Moreover such a yard, and especially a cluster of yards with a mutual origin point, would doubtless come to feel superior to ordinary yards highly dependent on *banjar* and *desa* organizations for various services and needs. The ascendant yard might begin to activate wider kinship and marriage networks and concomitant temple affiliations, sometimes entailing relations with other locales. Such activities might in turn produce internal factions, as ambitious members of the group sought privileged bureaucratic positions or tried to gain particular temple custodianships. Of crucial importance would be the group's marriages, especially if it tended to assume the proportions and the self-image of an ancestral *dadia*.

6. The meaning of marriage and descent

> The possibility that cousin-marriage has acted for long ages as a counteracting influence against variation opens out the way to curious reflection. The variational tendency, on the one hand, is connected biologically with out-breeding, and psychologically with romance; herein is progress. Nature, so careful of the type, is assisted by the conservatism of man, his solidarity even, to keep the balance. Perhaps the race owes more to family-alliances than it wots of.
>
> (Crawley 1907: 63).

> Marriage in descent theory tends to be the negative result of the application of the incest taboos. In the alliance view, it is brought about by the positive value (resulting from the system) attached to exchange. The utility of alliance theory is generally to be found in the analysis of closed systems, i.e., systems that can be conceptually limited to an ordered universe of linked categories.
>
> (Buchler and Selby 1968: 130).

Social dynamics in Bali draw on the cultural argument surrounding marriage. Values and rules supported by symbols and customary institutions, insure that marriage remains a potential predicament, an inherent dilemma. In this section we abstract a scheme of Balinese marriage-types which cuts across and helps define different caste-statuses. The scheme relates most directly to modern Bali, but it encompasses variations of classical (pre-1906) and colonial (1906–48) times as well.

Each type of marriage reveals overriding pros and cons – in actuality unresolvable, therefore socially viable, culturally significant, nonmechanical, human. We first summarize the ethnography of marriage values, both positive standards and negative restrictions, and then suggest a symbol which epitomizes this system of action and its potential conflicts. We later explore complementary terminologies, esoteric marriage lore, and literary episodes from the related native-logic system. Thus, two areas concern us: (1) the system of beliefs, expressive symbols, and value orientations often deemed culture (Parsons and Shils 1962: 21) and in particular that part of Balinese culture which pertains to marriage, as it is often abstracted for cross-cultural comparisons (cf. Lévi-Strauss, 1969); (2) structuralist codes in conventionalized native imagery which relate to the values that underpin social action without merely replicating them. Cultural interpretation of ideas and actions involved in social and psychological needs and structuralist decipherment of imagery from native classifications are found to be more complementary than at odds.

Our approach draws on so-called alliance theory (Dumont 1968; Buchler and Selby 1968: Chs. 5, 6), in that we ask how exchanged women (or self-consciously not exchanged women who find spouses within the family) do or do not distinguish and interrelate categories of groups. However, Bali lacks any closed-system representation – such as Dravidian terms within its caste-statuses, or a small set of original exogamous clans, or any similar 'ordered universe of linked categories' – that would suggest alliance theory is suitable for Balinese marriage (cf. second opening epigraph). Furthermore, the island displays one custom – patrilateral-parallel-cousin marriage (FBD, FFBSD . . .) – which, judging from the alliance school's 'blind spot against parallel cousin marriage' (Das 1973: 44), might discourage applying alliance concepts at all.[1] It is, however, fruitful to plot the social and semantic uses of the marriage bond here, if only to rethink this basic assumption in one variety of alliance theory:

> There are two kinds of marriage. The first results from the whims of two persons acting as private individuals; the second is a systematically organized affair which forms part of a series of contractual obligations between two social groups (Leach 1961: 56).

In Bali this twofold scheme collapses, because organized, contractual marriages can occur between two actors (for example, a man's son and his brother's daughter) who, for kinship purposes other than the marriage, belong to the same social group. In other words, if two members of the same group marry, they are treated ritually as if they come from different groups. This type of marriage is not between different existent social units; rather, the marriage alone represents those involved as two distinct groups. Our aim is to explain this practice and to suggest why the marriage typology which opposes private-individual to intergroup-contractual is inadequate.

Alliance theory can advance our understanding of Balinese marriage but it cannot exhaust the subject, because marriage options reveal the conflictive forms of drama. Individuals, groups, and, it is believed, ancestors have distinct and often opposed interests; this insures recurring predicaments. Finally, marriage here is less a matter of connecting individuals or groups than of sustaining a social, individual, and cosmic hierarchy. Enmeshed in his ritualized, sometimes optional organizational modes, 'the individual Balinese is forever picking his way, like a tight-rope walker, afraid at any moment lest he make some mis-step' (Bateson 1949: 46). In marriage such potential missteps are many, and the effort here as in other social and ritual domains is 'to maximise something which we may call stability' (1949: 50), provided we appreciate the complexity of its components.

Primary positive standards

> Sire nor son nor loving brother rules the wedded woman's state,
> With her lord she falls or rises, with her consort courts her fate.

Car and steed and gilded palace, vain are these to woman's life,
Dearer is her husband's shadow to the loved and loving wife!

Happier than in father's mansions in the woods will Sita rove,
Waste no thought on home or kindred, nestling in her husband's love!

And where in the lake of lotus tuneful ducks their plumage lave,
Let me with my loving Rama skim the cool translucent wave!

(Sita's Song to Rama
Romesh C. Dutt, trans., 1910)

The Balinese case supports Wilder's remark that in kinship studies 'the illusion of exclusive typecases needs replacing by some looser arrangement of combinatory possibilities, as proposed long ago by Lowie' (1973: 130). Two typecase illusions about Balinese marriage recur in the Dutch and English record. Belo (1936) emphasizes the preferred union of FDB or FFBSD; this classic article failed to influence much of the subsequent literature which was concerned with general theories of patriparallel-cousin-marriage systems (e.g., Khuri 1970).[2] Korn (1932) and many others singled out ritualized marriage by capture as the particularly commoner trait.[3] While both patriparallel-cousin marriage norms and mock capture rites are important in Bali, each must be understood as part of a set of options, including: (1) individualized unions supported by literate and folk traditions of romantic love, (2) alliances across groups commensurate with political and economic opportunities, (3) temple group endogamy (including patriparallel-cousin unions and less genealogically precise unions) reflecting beliefs in ancestral demands to demonstrate ascendant status. A given type of marriage cannot properly be said to characterize a particular social status because alternative marriages are themselves devices for asserting status. The interrelations of this cultural triad of marriage values and the social 'registers' of each type can be diagrammed to illustrate the essential alliance issue: the significance of the marriage bond beyond facilitating simple cohesion.[4] This produces a scheme of the cultural components of marriage (Figure 1, p. 122).

Type A: capture

Marriage by capture (*ngerorod*) does not necessarily interrelate different houseyards. Mock capture – true capture is now illegal – is the favored idiom of elopement. Two Balinese individuals may just elope, or they may elope with the fanfare of a capture. A clandestine elopement which is subsequently recognized by the husband's house and hamlet is the ordinary Balinese marriage pattern. (On the rituals of legitimation see Covarrubias 1937: 146–8). By discarding their daughter, the girl's family precludes extended affinal relations, or her family might later recognize the marriage and effectively prearrange it *ex post facto* in order to convert the elopement of individuals into an alliance of groups with mutual invitations to life-crisis rituals. If not, when combined with the woman's lack of property and her ceremonial incorporation into her husband's ancestor-group, elopement minimizes the

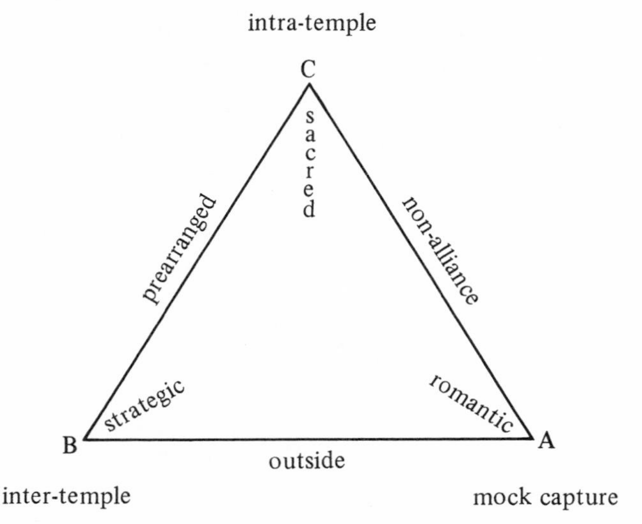

Figure 1. Types of positive marriage standards

Social registers

A Mock capture (individual elopement)
 1 Unacknowledged (daughter thrown away)
 2 Acknowledged (can yield type-B alliance)
B Interancestor temple group
 1 Hypergamous implications (*wargi*)
 2 Egalitarian implications (*beraya*)
C Intraancestor temple group
 1 Loosely reckoned by same generation
 2 Genealogically reckoned by cousin degrees

sociological ramifications of an affinal bond. A houseyard whose daughters have all been captured and whose sons have all captured discarded outsiders, remains unallianced. Its relatively simple organization works to its disadvantage in public affairs of status.

Ngerorod represents 'complex' marriages by individual preference which are not defined by marriage class or classificatory genealogical position.[5] This complex field sets Bali's other marriage types into figured relief. Individual unions are implicitly advocated in rituals of capture; they are not merely the neutral absence of a more distinct type of marriage. This prevents our viewing Balinese marriage preferences exclusively as rules for interrelating groups or categories, even though some preferences do indeed refer to specific genealogical positions and social categories. In Leach's terms, marriage by capture involves 'persons acting as private individuals.' But they do so according to cultural guidelines, gratifying inducements in competition with other inducements that oblige individuals to act as members of groups or as representatives of categories. Informants explain capture marriage as love (Ind.

cinta) winning out. They endeavor to construe all marriages as love matches, even unions of cousins. Marriage by mock capture, however, most clearly acknowledges in a ritual act the love ethos so important to persons approaching marriage. A rich lore outlines the dangers for the personalities involved if love is denied. Stories describe brides who, when married against their will, run amuck at their weddings, grow demented, and produce deformed offspring. When asked about their life histories, informants frequently stress the romance of their adventure of capture: those whose marriages were prearranged sometimes regret missing the excitement of capture. Native views about individual choice and the romantic attraction of distinct personalities and their importance in personal, social, and cosmic stability are most vividly expressed in the Panji and Malat tales found throughout Bali.[6]

One complication in elopement concerns varying customs of bride-purchase payment, here summarized by Belo:

> It is generally said of Bali that marriage is by abduction, the husband subsequently making a payment to the bride's father . . . It is true that this custom is widespread . . . There is much evidence to show that the form of arranged marriage . . . planned to link the households of relatives and friends, and without monetary compensation, is the older and more characteristic procedure. In fact, the old men of Sayan [village] say that in their generation (before the Dutch occupation), girls were often stolen from one village by the young men of an enemy village, but that, instead of the husband's making a payment to the bride's father, the father would make a payment to the young man so that the girl should be returned to her village and the marriage dissolved. To have one's daughter marry in a hostile village was to lose sight of her completely. They say that if the match is suitable the father asks no payment, and only if he were angry would he require compensation of the bridegroom (1936: 26).

Evidently, even precolonial matters of bride-purchase were circumstantial. In general, the purchase money reimbursed the woman's group for its loss of an attendant to the household gods (Korn 1932). Practices involving widows and divorced women suggest that payment was not the complement of a positive exchange but the retribution for a total loss. Currently, in areas where overlords have lost their influence, whether any bride-purchase is paid depends on the parties involved and on pressures brought to bear by various organizations – hamlet, *desa*, or even irrigation society, if antagonism is rife. But the important point is that capture can occur without compensation and sometimes sustains relations of hostility, thus converting individual captures into more social affairs.

Furthermore, under certain conditions another important social implication obtains. In a region marked by intense status drive among commoner ancestor-groups, C. Geertz related the elaborate rites of capture, the fanfare of elopement, to hypergamy:

> Thus, whenever a [patrilineally defined] title-group [i.e., named temple group] exogamous marriage takes place, the group from which the woman comes must at least profess to regard it as a mis-caste alliance, for to do otherwise would be to admit officially to a lower status under the hypergamy rule. As a result, almost all

title-group exogamous marriages are, in form at any rate, marriages by capture, in which the group from which the woman is ostensibly 'stolen' puts up the great show of outrage . . . (1967: 225).

However, in regions lacking both the intense local status competition and the hamlet endogamy provisions reported by Geertz, marriages occur without hypergamous overtones. The groom's house can also oppose the marriage. In such cases the ritual capture format is addressed not to the bride's kinsmen, but to the bride herself. Another familiar high-caste pattern is polygyny, where a man's lower ranking wives may be captured with mock adventure.

In short, one cannot explain Balinese marriage by capture as a means of negating hypergamous implications. It is rather a custom which for sociological purposes neutralizes a woman. Local status competition among near equal ancestor-groups can imbue outmarriage with hypergamous implications which produce negative social bonds of outrage and avoidance, which are in turn perhaps perpetuated by reactionary captures. Elsewhere any manifest outrage simply pertains to the loss of a daughter who might have made a marriage more advantageous to her kinsmen. As long reported, Balinese practice hypergamy rather than hypogamy. If the marriage bond implies differential rank, then wife-receivers are higher. (However, options of ancestor-group endogamy alter the nature of hypergamy in the Balinese context. A woman received is a woman somewhat debased, since she is given rather than kept by her own group; thus wife-providers can argue that they have given an inferior woman. Any advantage of giving a daughter in marriage to a superior yard is counterweighed by the option of displaying ancestor-group strength by endogamy.)[7] Especially in progressive areas, elopement between members of two commoner houseyards neither lowers wife-providers nor elevates receivers. We can thus conclude that the direction of flow in outmarriages is not the stuff and substance of Balinese status. But if members of two groups of unequal status marry, the direction (hypergamy) must reconfirm the existing hierarchy.

In summary, elopement as it is ritually celebrated in romantic capture is often explained primarily with reference to the individual personalities involved. On the other hand, this affinal bond can potentially be construed as an expression of relations between groups.

Type B: alliance

Marriage between ancestor-groups is similar to marriage by capture in that it involves an outsider woman, but it is different in that it is ritually prearranged (*meminang*) between two sets of yards, not necessarily related. The series of visits (*piangan*) by the male's kinsmen to his intended's house usually entails: (1) exchanging customary gifts, (2) reserving the intended, (3) stipulating the personal effects she will bring along, (4) deciding her future status title in her new houseyard, (5) deciding whether her family will provide a dowry to elevate her standing, and (6) stating who will witness the actual public marriage ceremony (similar to the ceremony performed after a capture) which foreshadows the strength of the alliance.

Perpetuated alliances traditionally arose from an initial capture marriage, often more real than mock. For example, the successful capture of a commoner by a lord could initiate a permanent wife-providing (*wargi*) role for her group.[8] A variation in outmarriage alliances is the egalitarian or brotherly bond (*beraya*) in which a land dowry affirms the equal status of the bride. A prestigious ancestor-group receives women from lower groups as same-status wives (*padmi*), who are nearer the rank of endogamous wives than ordinary subordinate outsider wives (*penawing*). Here women flow only one way, but as near equals designated by a special honorific; yet the provider/receiver formula remains a covert hypergamy. To sidestep hypergamous implications, providers assert that they are giving their women, rather than having them taken, and forbid the ceremony of marriage merely to the husband's sword (*kris*). Yet the receivers might stress the hypergamous aspect to a third alliance-partner. Such two-faced social postures facilitate shifts in the prestige hierarchy that have occurred throughout Tabanan and neighboring districts since 1965. Groups begin to claim higher status, signaled by new dowry-backed affiliations with superior ancestor groups, and they cancel egalitarian alliance bonds with their old *beraya*, now deemed inferior.

The strongest indication of egalitarian relations is a counterflow of women, which cancels marriage as a status code. Such a counterflow is illustrated in Figure 2.

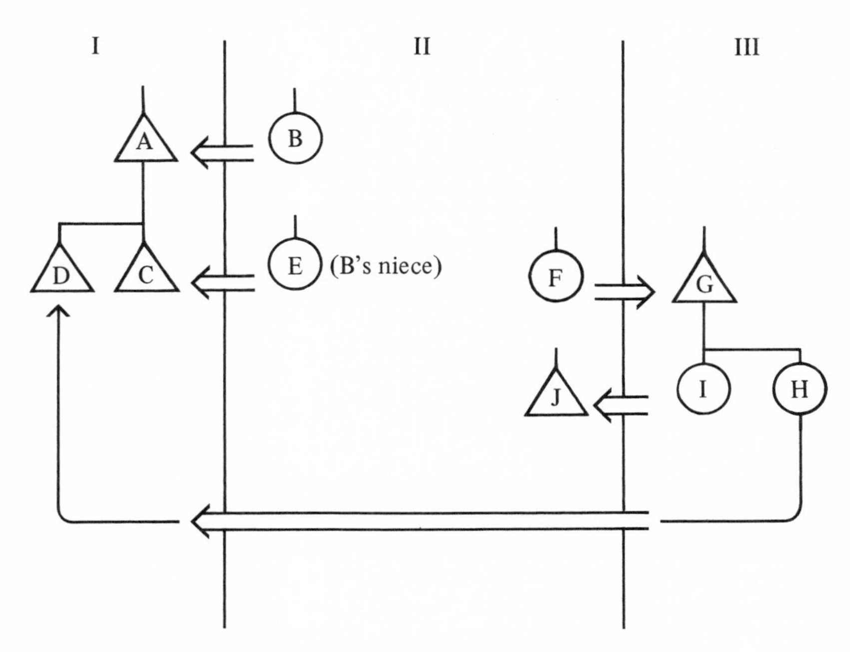

Figure 2. Egalitarian alliances of three ancestor groups – 1972

Note the exchange of women between Groups II and III. Although group I has always received women, it is not automatically the highest. Groups I and II use reciprocal generational terms, and Group II women marry into Group I as equals.[9] Group II explains its repeated loss of women by a rajalike decree by its past leader that Group I could receive them. (Its persistent provider role is explained by citing the rule against a daughter marrying back to the place of her mother, to be discussed later.) By such cultural devices, egalitarian alliances are sustained. These multiple marriage connections are called *mekilit* – 'like a knotted thread.' This possible two-way flow of women, which some informants characterize as a modern development, again illustrates the secondary nature of hypergamous principles in Bali.

It should not be inferred from the diagram that egalitarian ties across groups are always smooth and harmonious. An offshoot of Group I, for example, living several kilometers to the north claims descent from Arya Batin Jero, an important noble line in the northern district Buleleng. Although the Dutch refused to recognize them as such during the colonial period, members of this group today still claim the elevated title Gusti informally. This policy divides them from Group I itself, which settles for the lower title Gde to facilitate strong relations with Group II, their *banjar* associates and very influential backdoor neighbors.

We shall later return to such matters of titles and status. Here it is important to emphasize that every *beraya* relationship has a complex history, and informants can state clearly both their advantages and their drawbacks. This fact can be illustrated by the recollections of a man from Group II above who had taken his wife from Group III:

> If there had not already been *beraya* feelings between my house and my wife's, I would never have been able to go around there to court her. People generally feel ashamed, reticent (*sengan*) to set foot in this Pasek courtyard [elevated Sudra administrators] unless for an important practical need. When I first began courting, my wife's 'father' told my father that if my father's uncle had not once sheltered him in public office, I would have been chased from there in rough fashion!
>
> Now, if I'm traveling around Bali and come to a place like Busung Biu without any money, I will quickly be received as if I were a *pedanda* priest, when the village leader learns who my wife is [an offshoot of her group traditionally provides leaders in Busung Biu]. That's what counts in Bali: tracing you back to your group to see what you are. If you make a good outside marriage it is called 'broadening the houseyard' (*melingahin nata*), so that you have a lot of *beraya*. My marriage was broadening indeed!

In summary, alliances between groups produce networks of cooperation in which power, title, and wealth are calculated by the parties concerned. A group insures its daughter's participation in ancestral ceremonies, since *berayas* extend invitations to each others' rites. Thus, prearranged marriage with outsiders, while not the ultimate means (that is, endogamy) a group has to preserve its own women, avoids the loss of them altogether, with the accessory advantage of an often useful perpetual alliance.

Type C: endogamy

Intratemple marriage or ancestor-group endogamy is complicated by the two major kinds of temple congregations mentioned previously: (1) the three-temple-clusters of village-areas (*desas*) which consist of three religious sites (origin temple, council-house temple, death temple) for contacting the deities influencing the surrounding territory; (2) ancestor temples where reputed descendants of an original founder contact ancestral spirits. At their most distinct, ancestor-temple congregations consist of actual agnatic descendants (yard owners) of a founder, together with outsider wives and endogamous wives. But often such congregations are composed of only reputed descendants of a founder; many of the yards supporting the temple have been redefined by mystical pronouncements, sometimes in light of pragmatic needs of temple maintenance. Finally, as the Dutch literature stresses, the distinction between the two types can blur. Ancestor temples might develop into village-area temples with superior core congregations descended from original settlers.

But in general, temple Type-2 has an explicit ancestral component in its definition; Type-1 does not. Accordingly, at one extreme, Balinese social organization reveals little ancestor ideology. Individual houseyards, which are seldom deeper than three generations, propitiate deities in village-area temples; as the houseyards grow, they simply replicate their own membership or divide. Against this extreme appears the option of monumentalizing an ancestral source in a separate temple. The assorted houseyards that support a public ancestor temple may all be contiguous and fall within the same customary hamlet. Or they may all be affiliated with the same village-area temple cluster but lie in several customary hamlets. Or they may include far flung houseyards whose residents supposedly abandoned their original locale. We saw in Chapter 4 that while inhabitants of simple houseyards have only their village-area temples for revering deities, a bonafide ancestor-group boasts specific idealized forebears.[10] Since an ancestor temple requires a sufficiently populous group to maintain it, its very existence implies a pool of potential spouses who are also temple mates. In short, the group's ceremonial activities and often its youths' marriage needs can be satisfied in great part by persons counted as descendants of the same ancestors.

There is a range of implications for Balinese endogamy. A titled ancestor-group might supplement its endogamous tendencies with restrictions against marrying out of the hamlet, effectively localizing the endogamous group (cf. Geertz 1967; Geertz and Geertz 1975). But these secondary endogamous provisions are optional, and they are rejected by groups seeking to establish a wider temple network, partly through translocal marriages construed as endogamous unions within a diffused ancestor-group organization. Under traditional conditions of local hostilities and status competition, to marry outside one's temple group often meant to marry a ritual stranger or an enemy and inevitably to marry an unequal; this was effected by capture. The only certain source of near equal brides was one's own ancestor-group.[11]

An ancestor temple focuses a group's religious needs inward and articulates a practical social organization that complements values on inmarriage. Ancestral descent ideology favors endogamous wives; ancestor-temple ritual elaborates ceremonies whose proper observance requires women descended from the ancestors honored. Factious classificatory brothers are reunited if one marries the other's actual sister. Our first social register of endogamy refers to this general preference for marrying a generational peer within an ancestor-temple group, with no importance attached to precise genealogical degrees. Moreover, however near the relation, for the purposes of the prearrangement, ceremonies can be conducted and the bride fetched just as with unrelated spouses. An intratemple marriage parallels an intertemple marriage, but the social units involved are houseyards claiming the same ancestry. As a social strategy, the endogamous preference does not specify marriage with a particular patricousin category, whether first cousin (*misan*), second cousin (*mindon*) or more distant relation, but merely with an age-grade comrade. Balinese endogamy implies two primary guidelines: (1) marry a generational peer; (2) marry in your ancestor temple. Often members of an ancestor-group describe their unions as one houseyard or section of houseyards marrying another. The actual genealogical relations between spouses can be very complicated because of past endogamous marriages. When a new endogamous union is to occur, a primary consideration is whether the individuals are generational peers; never is an elder generational female allowed to wed a younger generational male, and the opposite is tolerated but regarded as inauspicious. Any overarching concern with actual degrees of cousins relates to traditions of caste-status; this is the complicating factor in ancestor-group endogamy, sometimes called 'family marriage' (Ind. *kawin keluarga*).

Thus preferences for patriparallel-cousin marriage here cannot properly be regarded as the mere inverse of cross-cousin-type marriage rules. They do not define the limits of preferable marriages; nothing about patriparallel-cousin marriage values precludes cross-cousin marriages or other possible unions (cf. Patai 1965: 334). Moreover, an articulate concern with relative degrees of patricousins is not merely a functional means to 'cement' seditious groups. As H. and C. Geertz argue (1975), endogamous marriages can help recement Balinese ancestor-groups. But a more important point for us is that any such functional advantage would accrue to the vague value on marrying inside a temple, without the parties bothering carefully to distinguish collateral degrees. Mere functional cohesion cannot explain the Balinese interest in the first/second cousin distinction (*misan/mindon*) which we shall consider later. Moreover, while an endogamous union reconnects male collaterals by a 'sister-wife' link, the union can as easily aggravate factions and even permanently splinter a group. It is as dubious functionally to explain parallel-cousin marriage as intragroup cement as it is to explain cross-cousin marriage as intergroup cement (cf. Boon and Schneider 1974). Nor can the Balinese case be identified with certain controversial explanations of some Middle Eastern systems. Balinese marriage offers no sure advantages in consolidating property that might conceivably apply in societies in which daughters inherit land or are necessarily dowered (cf. Murphy and

Kasdan, 1959). Nor are the contents of family role relationships harmonized by marrying patriparallel cousins (cf. Khuri 1970); role harmony is more likely to result from marrying outside, which produces a rightly inferior wife and avoids any complicated affinal relations at all.

Balinese justify any endogamous union by saying that it keeps daughters paying homage to their own ancestors; outsider wives are often lax in these female domestic-ceremonial duties.[12] (It should also be noted that if a male fails to family marry, in these days of rare polygyny he is conceivably depriving a temple mate of her chance to remain in the group, as his own sister might in turn be deprived.) There is a status component in this preference for women from one's own group. Kersten summarizes this component in the Brahmana ideology of *warnas* and subcastes:

> The main cause of this further division [into subcastes] is the influence exercised by the rank and caste of the mother on that of the child. The children by a main wife (*hoofdvrow*) stand higher than those by an extra wife (*bijvrow*); higher too are the children by a mother of the same caste than those by a mother of lower caste (1947: 102).

But the same idea extends to Balinese marriage in general. Basically, spouses from inside rank higher than spouses from outside, and they produce higher ranking sons. This is true even for the masses of Sudras; here caste ideology is less clear because sundry titled groups attached to local origin points dispute their rank. Korn summarizes the endogamous preference of incorporated Sudra ancestor-groups as follows:

> In general the Sudra statuses give preference (*voorkeur*) to marriages between people who are *tunggal dadia* and *tunggal paibon* [worshipping the same gods – *van één godsvereering*] and if the daughters do not comply, they may never more return home to eat and to pray (1932: 471).

For a given ancestor-temple group, the highest permissible wife is one from that group. For traditional rulers and nobles classing themselves as Satria or Wesia, a woman from a house of similar status approximates an endogamous wife, since the members of a given caste-status (*arya*) within a kingdom are thought to descend from the same ancestor. Likewise any Brahmana woman could be construed as an insider wife by another Brahmana group, but Brahmanas are also split into subcastes – most emphasized by the highest one – as explained by projecting a legendary history of primal differential marriage into the past: the arch Brahmana produced the several Brahmana subcastes (accounts differ) by fathering descendants by several wives of different castes. (See Chapters 7, 8.) Often an endogamous woman is designated by a higher title than an outsider. The value on endogamous wives is expressed by naming part of an ancestor temple *paibuan* from the Balinese root for 'mother.' Moreover, ambitious sons, who are themselves often offspring of patriparallel-cousin wives, might take multiple spouses including such a cousin. Elevated wives bear children with higher titles; the actual portion of the name indexing rank varies with locality, general caste standing, and so forth. These values complicate Balinese descent. Ruling lines practiced primogenitural succession to office. Rajas themselves were in principle succeeded by first-born sons of their same-status wife (*padmi*). But a first-born son of a lower wife (*penawing*) might challenge the claims of a later born son by a same-status wife for other privileges. In everything from succession to inheritance to leadership in political and religious affairs, principles of insider/outsider mother plus birth order of offspring make any lineal descent principle misleading. Indigenous religious views of marriage say it must strengthen descent (*turunan*), so to fulfill the duty (dharma) to the enshrined ancestors who are in a line with the gods. As we shall see, the way to gain this strength of descent is by 'family marriage.'

In summary, Balinese marriage types (Figure 1) form a ranked triad. The difference between Type-C and Type-A marriage is a contrast in the status of offspring, whether implicit or explicit, and it is always explicit where high-caste patterns prevail. Type-C marriage is superior to Type-A. Optimally, Type-B marriage reaps the advantages of both – same status plus individual preference – while achieving a useful perpetuated alliance. Thus, judging from these values on different marriage types, marriage in Bali is not preeminently, as alliance theory would insist, a means of achieving a regularized connection between a closed set of social groups, as in matrilateral-cross-cousin marriage systems, or a means of articulating positive rules to define and rank a closed set of social categories, such as wife-givers superior or inferior to wife-takers. Nor at the opposite extreme can marriage be understood to result from 'the whims of two persons acting as private individuals' (Leach 1961: 56). Balinese marriage expresses status at each level of society by opposing relative endogamy to exogamy. When joined with values of romantic love, this in/out marriage system produces individual capture. When joined with values on hypergamy, it produces the general caste scheme that divides Bali into Brahmana, Satria, Wesia, and Sudra. But at the level of interaction within and between ancestor-groups of all castes, the hypergamous provisions are subject to many exceptions, and the crux of marriage concerns falls back on the status implications not of giving versus receiving daughters, but of keeping versus losing them. Neither a personal whim nor a social expression of on-going exchange, marriage here achieves hierarchy.

Secondary negative restrictions

Many Balinese texts list varieties of incest and near incest (*gamia*). For example, real sibling-sibling marriage and real sibling-parent marriages are taboo. Marriage between the senior-female generation and the junior-male generation is prohibited, as is marriage between higher caste females and lower caste males; marriage between the senior-male generation and the junior-female generation is possible but discouraged. Client-guru marriage is also characterized as incestuous.[13] If we consider incestuous unions and intergenerational endogamous ones, especially aunt-nephew, as a core of prohibitions that underlies the three positive marriage types, there remain secondary prohibitions which can influence marriage decisions and thus shed light on the positive standards already reviewed.

Restriction I. One strategical marriage prohibition implements a status relation between two groups to the advantage of both. This is possible because of the range of indexes of rank: title, caste, temple type, legends, and so on. For example, in a newly settled area a temple group claiming noble or even Brahmana status might deem a lower (Sudra) group as *unmarriageable*. Such a rule also implicitly elevates the lower group by distinguishing it from ordinary, potential wife-providers to the superior group. Institutionalized as unsuitable spouses, the elevated Sudra group can cultivate specialized service or ritual bonds with the superior group. The lower group might even explain its relation to the higher group as that of junior to elder 'brothers,' who are prohibited from exchanging sisters, as will be discussed later. In short, prohibiting an ordinarily acceptable hypergamous union helps to actualize a full range of status distinctions in a given locality: high-caste group, privileged-Sudra-ancestor group, both set off against commoners in general.[14]

Restriction II. Mention of the possible codification of higher and lower groups as brotherlike brings us to provisos that restrict marriage options in light of prior unions. The general principle is that a woman may not marry back to the place of origin of either her sister or her mother; this can be brought to bear on group endogamous marriages as well as outside marriages. First there is a prohibition on sister exchange between terminological brothers. Or, two 'brothers' may not arrange an exchange of daughters as spouses for their sons. This restriction qualifies patri-parallel-cousin-marriage preferences, since not every such cousin is a permissible spouse. Moreover, the restriction guarantees that within an endogamous group, the flow of women of one generation between two collateral lines will not be reversed. If applied, the restriction supports hypergamous implications even of endogamous unions and thus accentuates rank between collateral lines.[15]

A related restriction applies to subsequent generations. The rule states that a girl may not return to the origin-place of her mother. Or from the male's point of view, the son of one's 'brother-in-law' may not marry one's daughter. This formula extends the one-way flow of women into subsequent generations by banning father's sister's daughter (FZD) marriages. Both rules are secondary devices for programming consistent marriage directions – one within a generation, the other across generations. Groups with ritual experts who invoke these restrictions reveal pockets of actualized hypergamy in their marriages. By the same token providers of wives can cite these rules as an hierarchically neutralized explanation of their alliance position, which is otherwise liable to be construed as inferior. That is, an ancestor group that has provided wives for another group over several generations can argue that this is simply because a girl cannot marry back to her mother's house. At the level of structure these rules establish a short-term unidirectional flow of women. But at the level of actor rationalizations, they allow the inferior party to explain away hypergamous overtones in the marriage relationship. The rules help to explain how the Balinese value system supports ancestor-group endogamy as well as hypergamy between either different groups or divisions of the same group.

Restriction III. As noted earlier, values on the religious auspiciousness of endogamous daughters reflect the structural basis of a system built around outmarriage/family marriage. In general, insiders are superior to outsiders. This logic can be reapplied within an ancestor-group to differentiate varieties of cousin unions. The restriction in question views first-cousin (*misan*) marriage as less desirable in a practical sense than a second-cousin (*mindon*) marriage. Somewhat paradoxically, it idealizes first-cousin marriage as the most sacred union and its offspring as superior to those of a second-cousin marriage. First-cousin marriage is valued over second-cousin marriage in a sacred (dangerous) sense; therefore, a second-cousin union is preferred over a first-cousin union when the latter is reserved for special groups or individuals.

This complex of secondary restrictions on the preference for first-cousin unions has been repeatedly documented. A patriparallel-first-cousin marriage is considered sacred and dangerous (*panas*). Korn cites these traditions:

> The rest of the Balinese people is accordingly divided. Following one part of society it is best to marry a *misan*, the other half disapproves such a marriage unless one is of royal blood, since it is not altogether lucky. Marriages with *mindons* were generally recommended, with *ming tigas* [the children of *mindons*] again were disapproved, but could be solemnized following a special offering . . . (1932: 472).

Likewise, Bateson and Mead remark about the mountain area in which they worked:

> Parents endeavor (usually without success, except in the high-caste families) to make their children marry cousins. In the plains villages, the preferred marriage is with the father's brother's child, but in Bayung Gde [village] this marriage is *regarded as incestuous* and the preferred marriage is with a patrilineal second cousin of own generation (1942: 257, my italics).

Moreover, Belo alludes to a possible negative evaluation of cousin marriage (1960: 34). Esoteric manuscripts discuss these aspects of cousin marriage; current jingles proclaim the first cousin, especially on the male side (*misan pihak perusa*), dangerous to marry. The popular tendency opposes patriparallel second-cousin marriage to first-cousin marriage as a relatively safer union. It is said first-cousin unions can produce marital discord, afflicted offspring, and the same pernicious psychological consequences noted earlier when individual love is denied.

There are two possible speculative explanations for this optional preference for second-cousin marriage. One is the conceivable strategical advantage as a counter to persistent ancestor-group factionalism. In Bali, any such group is a fragile union because variably ranked sons have different responsibilities in maintaining costly ancestral shrines, and population growth exerts pressure on lands and paddy. Second-cousin marriages can reforge the collateral lines of the group precisely where sedition is most likely. Moreover, a populous ancestor-group would contain enough second cousins to permit some individual choice.

But a second, and I think preferable, speculation returns to the logic of relationship mentioned earlier. If all goes well, first-cousin marriage – the nearest union that is not incestuous – confirms the sanctity of the parties involved and is thought to please the ancestors. It blends the ancestral qualities of father and mother alike in an ascendant collateral line. Yet this auspicious union is risky for the persons involved, who should be of exceptional merit to attempt it. Especially in groups which follow high-caste traditions, if the eldest son marries his first cousin, they produce superior offspring of the highest line who are titled accordingly. Eldest sons in particular might even practice patriparallel-cousin polygyny (cf. Belo 1936) which, if fruitful, concentrates ancestral power (*sakti*) and manpower in the most prestigious genealogical space.

Thus, wherever optional rules against first-cousin marriage are applied to an entire level of society within a given locality, we can assume that the social segment in question is regarded as insufficiently elevated to sustain such a sacred match. Moreover, *ad hoc* rules in a particular ancestor-group apply the same principle, not to the group as a whole but to different individuals depending on their ritual and religious qualities. In this light, second-cousin marriage becomes an advantageous compromise not only in strategical but also in religious terms. It is not as incestuous, nor as godlike – both approximately the same thing. Therefore, it is less dangerous for the mortals contracting it than first-cousin unions. In short, patriparallel-second-cousin (*mindon*) marriage reduces the individual, social, and cultural drawbacks of a patriparallel-first-cousin marriage while retaining many of its advantages. *Mindon* marriage permits a range of choice and often avoids parental enforcement between the few qualified first cousins. It can strengthen endoalliances between collateral lines, and it combines in descendants ancestral worth through both the mother and father without overdoing it. In other words, experts in high-caste esoterica who place extra weight on the advantages of second-cousin marriage thereby free first-cousin marriage to represent a more sacred-dangerous union suitably only for relatively higher, more godlike sublines or individuals of a given group or for superior strata of the whole society. Sociological restrictions on the marriage norms thus harmonize with Bali's hierarchical cosmology and correlate with native views of the inadequacy of ordinary personalities to cope with a marriage so charged with religious implications. The primary significance of patriparallel-cousin marriage preferences is status differentiation.

The options in action and symbols

Just how a Balinese actor approaches his culture's marriage predicament depends on his or her ritual-status ambitions or group interests. Values on individual love support the institution of marriage by capture, sociologically costly because the woman is lost for purposes of alliance. Ritual responses of outrage allow the captured woman's group to deny any hypergamous implications. Romantic marriage by mock capture, so frequent in present-day Bali, runs contrary both to sacred ancestral interests and to political alliances. But even opponents of a given elopement agree that individual will commands respect and that denying love might jeopardize both the religious well-being and the political advancement of the ancestor group anyway. In contrast, prearranged outmarriage reaps practical alliance benefits; yet it runs two risks – displeasing the ancestors for not keeping a daughter and causing the storied psychological repercussions of enforced marriage. The marriage sacred to the godly ancestors, yet potentially dangerous for the mortal descendants involved and instrumental as an alliance only to the extent the group in question is threatened by internal sedition, is 'family marriage.'

Psychological ordeal

To appreciate the real psychological conflicts implied in this scheme, consider the following 1972 case study of individual-romance versus enforced-family marriage. The case involves a high school senior girl from an elevated Sudra ancestor-group and a male age peer from one of the largest Brahmana groups in the district. Only the girl's elder brother's endogamous wife knew of her well requited love. This woman had long facilitated the couple's rendezvous in her houseyard; a romantic at heart and an incurable gossip, she supported their marriage plans to the end. The girl's parents adamantly opposed what might have been a desirable hypergamous union. Disregarding the rather ephemeral honor of placing a daughter in a Brahmana group, they chose instead to insure permanent contact with her by means of an ancestor-pleasing family marriage. She was betrothed to a thirty-two year old 'uncle' (FFBS) and, lest she elope with the Brahmana, was packed off to Jakarta to await the wedding day in the uncle's company. The family thus hoped to stimulate her increased affection for this professionally promising relative. As reports of the daughter's ceaseless tears filtered back to Bali, the parents of the couple – both sets were in favor of the family marriage – deliberated over how to categorize the delicate situation. The fact that she was living away from home with her future spouse normally would suggest marriage by capture. But the enforced elopement had never been officially announced to the girl's parents, since intraancestor group mock-abduction is proscribed. The ever present danger of a counter capture by her high-caste true love precluded their allowing the couple home in time for the pre-arrangement visitations between the two ancestral divisions. A week before the projected wedding date, the failure to make the formal announcement was already raising many eyebrows. The elders were sore pressed to opt for one of two undesirable poses in order to save face. Was it capture, meaning that when the couple returned, the girl would proceed directly to the boy's house, making this appear to outsiders, and ancestors, an unprecedented rift in the group's internal affairs? Or would the girl go to her own subhouse to await the ceremony, thereby casting an illicit glow on the Jakarta episode? The parents adopted the latter pose as the lesser evil. Following an almost comically accelerated series of prearrangement meetings, the more elaborate two-stage rite with a Brahmana priest and expensive offerings was performed. The bride herself, fortunately upstaged by the complexities of the ceremony, remained outwardly composed; all knowledgeable parties had wondered if she would. Thus, this standard Balinese wedding was barely marred by its anxious undercurrents. However, in an unheard of gesture for a nearby, healthy relative, the gossip, the initial sponsor of the love match with the Brahmana, refused to attend.

As this case illustrates, there is no single advantageous way for a group to deploy all its women; pros and cons characterize any type of union considered. Family marriage insures the maintenance of ancestral purity values. Prearranged outmarriage fulfills the more properly alliance ambitions of a yard, and marriage by capture admits of individual wills and psychological needs. An ascendant group implements a range of marriages, hoping that even its endogamous unions and outside alliances will be love matches as well and will not have to be forced. And as we saw, various optional restrictions temper the effects of these positive standards and inject a note of status between groups or collaterals.

But the restriction on first-cousin marriage – the optional preference for second-patriparallel-cousin marriage – best represents the thrust of this system to maximize a combination of interests: ancestral purity (cultural), collateral alliance (socio-strategical), and personal will (psychological). In family marriage the cultural value on inmarriage is weighed against practical benefits, for the collateral lines and the individuals, of marrying a little less in (that is, marrying a second cousin or any generation peer rather than first cousins). In marriage by capture the cultural outrage over such extreme outmarriage is subsequently reconsidered against the practical benefits, for the group, of cultivating relations after all. The Balinese marriage predicament revolves around the tension between the values on marrying-too-in and marrying-too-out, and this tension most clearly appears as preferences for second-patricousin marriage. Thus, in typing Bali with a particular marriage, better second-patriparallel cousin marriage than polygyny, or marriage by capture, or child marriage, or general patriparallel-cousin marriage. The latter earmark is inadequate because the most characteristic form of the preference – first-patriparallel-cousin – is in some instances prohibited, and there is no belief that this is the single preferable union; alliance opportunities and individual choice are always to be considered.

Second-patriparallel-cousin marriage symbolizes more features of the system. Yet, it is perhaps preferable to stress the aim of successful groups to marry both in and out in assorted ways. Even typing Balinese marriage under the refined rubric of second-patriparallel cousin implies a system built on formal principles of genealogy; whereas cousin options are pragmatically applied and are perhaps most preferred when an expanding group has subdivided. Moreover, 'family marriage' itself is sociologically ambiguous. Family marriage automatically means a first- or second-patriparallel cousin union to a small unextended houseyard. To an incorporated ancestor group, it suggests more broadly any ancestor-temple-endogamous union. At the higher caste levels, in which legends and pan-Bali temple networks connect distant groups, family marriage implies broad caste endogamy, since a caste is theoretically an ancestor-group and its women therefore of relatively equal rank. Thus, for individuals in a simple agnatic commoner yard, patricousin marriage is culturally analogous to the prescribed sacred subcaste-endogamous regulations of the most preeminent Brahmana.

Balinese are ambivalent about close endogamy at every level it is envisioned. Later we shall see that 'endogamy' occurs between twin siblings (divinely) and brother and sister (mythically), as well as between first cousins (ideally, but dangerously), second cousins (practically, but compromisingly), and more distant kin, only limited by the extension of the ancestor group as incorporated. And just as marrying too near risks the chaos of delirium or affliction if the parties are inadequate, so mythological forms of inmarriage risk social and cosmic chaos if conditions are not ritually perfect. Moreover, in temple-group endogamy the subgroups involved – the 'brothers' – are portrayed ritually as affines. Thus endogamy is two-faced. To see it simply as a way vaguely to solidify a group by having kinsmen wed, would be to miss much of its significance. Endogamy organizes a temple group by momentarily stressing its implicit divisions into affines and by propagating superior descendants related to two divisions.[16] Ancestor-temple endogamy achieves a facsimile of the whole society and cosmos – a hierarchical totality – within the confines of a single ancestor-group.

Structuralist terms and twins

Many nomenclatures and rules in Bali interrelate social and cosmological strata. Balinese rank everything real and imaginary: (a) offspring (by titled birth-order, interrelated through the repetition in cycles of four); (b) women (by endogamous versus outsider, and also by caste rank below the husband); (c) brothers (by mother's rank in addition to birth order); (d) generations (by teknonymous terms); (e) bilateral kinsmen (by generational terms); (f) individual persons (by beliefs in the four siblinglike components of the human being); (g) pan-society (by caste-status), and so forth.[17] All these terms and concepts establish distinct generationlike strata. And marriage inevitably connects not just individuals, or simple groups, but the cultural strata that individuals and groups partly represent.

An important example of such cultural strata in Bali is the use of so-called teknonymous terms, whose generational aspect I would emphasize even more than recent studies (cf. H. and C. Geertz 1964; C. Geertz 1966: 23–8). Pan Madeg, for example, translates as 'Father of Madeg,' and Madeg's father is called this after the child's birth. But invoking teknonyms as traditionally understood in anthropology creates several problems. First, it misleadingly implies a contrasting set with other naming practices, such as necronyms (named after a deceased person) and autonyms (personal names) (cf. Boon and Schneider 1974). The difficulty perhaps characterizes not just Balinese teknonymy but the very concept of teknonymy when defined as a parent named for his child. Analytic confusion results because the name of the child can last as the child's name only until the child becomes a parent, since he will in turn be named for his child. Teknonyms can never be the simple logical inverse of necronyms or autonyms, or for that matter, of patronyms or matronyms, since these all name persons once and for all, whereas teknonyms necessitate a name change during the full life-cycle. This mandatory future shift in name is the crux of the symbolic power of so-called teknonyms; it is especially apparent in Bali where 'father of' in turn shifts to 'grandfather of'.

In Bali Pan Madeg does not necessarily connect a parent with his individual child, since the father can receive this name even if Madeg is stillborn or dies soon after birth. Moreover, only the first-born child has a personal name identical with his parent's generational name. It would be as accurate to say that the first child is named after his parents' new-found parenthood. That such Balinese terms do not connect the adult with an individual child is clear from certain high-caste options:

> Teknonymy occurs systematically among most casteless people and in a modified form, among high castes, where the appropriate caste term for 'father' or 'mother' is substituted for the personal name without, however, including the name of the child, as is done among casteless people (Bateson and Mead 1942: 259).

Balinese teknonyms are better construed essentially as generation-nyms, and not as codes of parent-named-for-individual-child which only secondarily function to demarcate age sets. The principle behind the nomenclature is not to name parents for children, but to signify a parental generation as having produced a child. Finally, Pan is not merely an isolated parental-generation label; for it implicitly contrasts with alternate names, such as lower Nang or upper Gde which replace it to designate inferior and superior parental-generations among Sudra groups.

Just as teknonyms, kin terms themselves may be considered a stratificational grain in Balinese culture. Terminological mothers are not marriageable; this is a hard, fixed grain. 'Fathers' are not eligible spouses either, but this grain is easier to lie against, because the female would at least be marrying someone of an older generation and thus in a proper relation of homage to the man. Incest qualifications forbid marrying real parents and stipulate that the only *beli* (elder kinsmen of same generation) a girl could marry is her first, second, or more distant cousin. Thus, generational terms accentuate any generational mix-up in marriage. The most contentious actual family marriages are those involving two generations; it is even a matter of concern when a couple from the same generation through the fathers is bigenerational through the mothers, one of whom would have made a family marriage across generations. The terminological grain of marriage is that an 'elder brother' (*beli*) marries his younger family generation-peer (*adi*), unless she is his womb sibling (*kandung*) or half sibling (*tiri*); and that 'mothers' do not wed juniors and 'fathers' hesitate to do so. Moreover, with the potential for extensive group endogamy, bilateral generational terms emphasize the only relations that are kept straight in the confusion produced, at least analytically, by any-direction family marriage. What must be preserved are the respect lines between juniors and seniors, one kind of inferior and superior.

In sum, the nomenclatures support our view that the broader marriage principle is generational and ideological, and the refining principles are biological and strategical. The system can be summarized as follows' (1) When possible, marry within a stratum (generation within a group; caste, or subcaste within the whole society). If not, a superior male weds inferior females, according to respect lines. Thus antihypogamy at the caste level is the same rule (at a different locus) as antiaunt-nephew marriage within a concrete ancestor group. (2) Do not marry too close (for example, true siblings, or sometimes first cousin, or in particular FZD), for incest, or sister exchange, or the exchange of women between alternating generations of two groups threatens the process of creating social networks.

This then is a conceptual world which reiterates generationlike strata at every level and vehemently prohibits both sibling incest and contracts between classificatory siblings which would perpetually satisfy their marriage needs by sister exchange. In such a world it is not surprising that phenomena of twin births have taken on rich dramatic and structuralist significance. The variable meaning of births of twins is a classic topic of Balinese ethnography. Belo (1935) suggested that twins of different sex are used to emphasize caste differences, since their birth is auspicious for high castes and catastrophic for low. Moreover, my own data on same-sex twins, corroborated in the colonial ethnography, suggests that the numerical as well as the sex aspect of twin births is important in Balinese conceptions.[18] Any twins are seen as a meaningful contradiction of the natural fact of birth order – one order per birth. Different-sex twins are doubly complex because the normative stratification of the sexes, male over female, might also be contradicted. Indeed, twin brother-sister incest is relatively less contradictory than twin sister-brother incest, because at least the elder twin is male, as befits his inherent superiority. Given incest, an upper-male-lower-female incest is less contradictory than the reverse. This correlates in actual practice with the guarded acceptability of an uncle-niece marriage versus a strictly tabooed aunt-nephew union, although any intergenerational family marriage contradicts the primary same-generation marriage norm.

Briefly, it is incestuous for opposite-sex twins to occupy a womb; but the higher the status, the less abominable the incest, since for the gods incest is proper. It appears from the persistent Balinese interest in twins that native theorists have reasoned that superior mortals, while still inferior to gods, can approximate divine patterns of incest through cousin marriage. In their eyes one of the recurring proofs of this godly capacity would be that mortals bear opposite-sex twins. With its qualified patriparallel-cousin-marriage norms, the system values incest, mythically advisable in the maharaja's line:

The effort to keep lower castes (*onderkasten*) pure (*rein*) was indeed not foreign to the development of the legend that the Dewa Agung was duty-bound to wed his full sister, so that the royal blood should pass unmixed on to his follower (*opdat het vorstelijk bloed onvermengd op zijn opvolger zoude overgaan*) (Korn 1932: 471).

This value is expressed in ideas about twin births. The ideal ancestral progenitors are, twinlike, a unified male and his consort.[19] In Balinese cosmology the gods marry in the most preeminent fashion: a husband-wife consort = brother-sister of the nearest kind, boy-girl twins. The legendary maharaja can practice brother-sister incest. But well formed ancestor groups actually practice nothing closer than first-cousin unions, and according to some provisos, as seen earlier, only the best brothers among them risk even this. Thus, cousin marriage appears to be a compromise between incest and outmarriage. Patriparallel-cousin spouses are the most nearly incestuous approximation to the sacred Hindu consort motif that actual ancestor-groups dare. An eldest son and his cousin consort maximize in their offspring the ancestral power (*sakti*) of their group as commemorated in its temple.

Balinese ancestor-group endogamy appears to be a series of flirtations with sibling incest. 'Mother'-son and at least real father-daughter unions are excluded from consideration by the principle of distinct, ranked generations; 'brother-sister' or same-generation incest is the ambivalent problem area, highlighted by the concern with twins. As a sacred *lontar* stipulates:

> And so to be born with a wife is to be born as a god, and the twin boy if he marries his twin may have only that one wife, like a god (cited in Belo 1935: 519).

Further stipulations endow this incestuous spouse with sociological attributes by requiring she be reared at a distance from her consort; then,

> When they have reached the marriageable age, they are brought together and married one to another. It is hoped that if the legend comes true and the boy becomes king the wife will *bring him power over the far-away land where she was reared*, and all the land between (Belo 1935: 510, my emphasis).

Thus, by means of a single symbolic woman – a geographically distanced, beloved twin-sister spouse – the triadic Balinese marriage system is here fancied as a whole. It is not going too far to say that this ultimate consort symbolizes the unattainable unification of the diverse marriage preferences of our original diagram (Figure 1): endogamous, relatively incestuous, wives (Type C), wives of prearranged advantageous alliances (Type B), and individually desired wives adventurously fetched from outside (Type A).

This ideological scheme places ultimate value on the marriage of twins who first receive social attributes through separation (that is, each represents a different 'kingdom') and then are reunited. The same idea turns up in the Panji cycle of Javanese court literature which has flourished in Bali for centuries. As if echoing the concept of auspiciousness/disaster of twin births, Panji tales describe the sociocosmic disorder that prevails until lovers who resemble each other to the point of twinship are united and join their two distant kingdoms in fruitful alliance. In some versions, an ostensibly ideal first-cousin marriage (*memisanan*) is first shown to be inadequate, relative to the final union of Panji, prince of Koripan and his preordained mate – he the sun, she the moon, both the complementary twin offspring of the gods. (See Chapter 9.)

The cultural argument

There is greater similarity from this point of view between the morganatic marriage of a king and the incestuous marriage of a subject than there is between the incestuous marriage of a king and the incestuous marriage of a subject, for a morganatic marriage fails to produce an expected alliance between social groups just as does the subject's incestuous marriage (Fortune 1932).

To evoke Bali's marriage system we have highlighted symbols at the cultural level of the individual (love), the social (prearrangement ceremonies, patricousin distance), and the ideological (incest), always with two themes in mind. First, any system of action must allow for individual-personality variations through cultural values which do not coincide with sociostrategical ends or even ultimate religious meaning. Much alliance theory has typologized societies in terms of positive marriage prescriptions that imply holistic social classifications; but the theory has neglected the room made for individual preferences at odds with positive alliance categories. The point is often made that individual preference is not a 'social fact' and remains outside the systematic basis of the society. But, as the Balinese case suggests, the value of individual love is itself a social fact. In Bali, native ideas of personality needs are critical in appreciating how marriage preferences are implemented and how deviation from such preferences is tolerated. Bali as a social system of patrilateral-parallel-cousin marriage cannot be analyzed apart from Bali as a social system of individual romantic marriage. Balinese culture itself takes into account individual wills out of line with alliance or religious values. The dramatic conflicts necessarily engendered are rarely a simple matter of deviant personalities thwarting a patently oppressive social system. (In the previous case study, for example, the girl who resisted family marriage had both hypergamy and the respect for individual love on her side.) Rather, the culture provides the individual adventurer, the sociostrategical group, and the ancestral religion each a means of arguing its case, so to speak, in accordance with the ideals of all three.

The second theme has been that cultural interpretation of action systems can be complemented by structuralist codification of conventional, recurring rituals, legends, and native formulations. A structuralist ratio of the homologous structure between the mythological and sociological planes of our study would be:

twin marriage : sibling marriage : : first-cousin marriage : second-cousin marriage

However, if we refer this ratio back to the symbols of social action, a more adequate characterization of Balinese marriage appears: (1) a really near relation, especially a patrikinswoman, is, just before marriage, ritually handled as if unrelated and contractual; and (2) a really unrelated woman is upon marriage religiously defined into the same ancestral group as her husband. The ritual of prearrangement contracts suggest that father's-brother's-daughter marriage is not conceived of as an endogamy at all. Patriparallel-cousin preferences are rather elementary structurelike provisions that assure getting spouses from near kin; they might imply a one-way hypergamous relation, or they might imply egalitarian returns of women, but this is not mapped by kinterms. The preferences close in the range of the ideal 'alliance society' and tentatively pose a self-sustaining unit in which alliance partners are descendants of the same ancestors.

The essential dramatic tension is that someone really close, through descent or adoption, must be treated in prearrangement rituals as if distant; and someone ostensibly distant – at the most extreme, a lover clandestinely abducted from an enemy village-area – is finally admitted into the ancestor-group. The most culturally significant marriages in Bali balance two factors: either an insider is desired as much as a distant, inaccessible lover; or an outsider takes an active role in ancestor ritual as only a true kinswoman would be expected to. The ideal spouse embodies both adventurous distance-strangeness and sheltered nearness-kinship. The ideological symbol of this ideal spouse is the twin sister who has been separated from her brother-husband until reunion upon marriage, as implied in the Panji tales. Sociological symbols of these ideal spouses are found in real cousins ritually approached as outsiders who produce elevated sons; and, at the other extreme, in abducted outsiders who, through their devotion to ancestral tasks, are eventually buried, cremated, and rendered homage as true descendants.

Second-patriparallel-cousin marriage best represents this dramatic tension. The tension is most vivid for individuals in ascendant groups that: (1) seek advantageous hypergamous or egalitarian alliances; (2) desire to conserve daughters to attest the sanctity and self-sufficiency of their ancestors' descendants; and (3) yet never forget individual love and the dangers of thwarting it. Culturally, every wedding in Bali participates in the symbology of marriage as the reuniting of an only superficially divided whole. The sociological way of achieving the true union is sacrosanct patriparallel-cousin marriage, or if not, at least marriage between status equals. The individual, mystic way of achieving an exemplary union is love; the ideological way is sibling incest. And cosmologically the love linking two personalities in this world is equated with the incest linking the male/female components of divinity. What is love to romantic individuals is incest to the gods, and cousin spouses fall in between.

What we have been viewing as a guaranteed predicament in marriage options can as easily be projected as a theory of descent. This is precisely the achievement of Brahmana ideology in Bali. The well formed Balinese houseyard or cluster of houseyards should strengthen descent by practicing endogamy. This ideal receives thorough elaboration in the self-image of the Brahmana caste. 'Nowadays the Brahmanas still hold high the caste ideal,' attests Kersten (1947: 102). Yet Hooykaas paraphrases the following legend current among specialist elevated Sudra exorcist priests (*sengguhu*):

All was well in Bali providing the King consulted brahmana, bodha, and bhujangga (*sengguhu*) . . . But whereas both bodha and bhujangga practiced continence, the brahmana had three wives and the king even nine. This set the world in stir and commotion, caused anarchy and chaos (C. Hooykaas 1964a: 273).

The conflicting ideals of superior rank yet multiple wives lend the Brahmana category its generative complexity. Thus, the role of marriage levels in converting a *warna* category into what Dutch ethnographers called 'differentiated subcastes' (*verschillende onderkasten*) is clarified in texts on the Brahmana legendary trek. Kersten encapsulates the variable versions to suggest the general thrust of Brahmana legends:

Brahmana know of five subcastes (*onderkasten*) only, and this condition was related back to their legendary progenitor (*stamvader*) Batara Dwi Jendra [Wau Rauh], famous in Balinese history under the sobriquet: the new-come priest.

He came with his family from Blambangan, the kingdom on Java's east point and landed in Jembrana, Bali's southwest coast. After a very adventurous and wonderful trek he came across the Dewa Agung, whose palace was then still in Gelgel, near Klungkung.

Now, this priest had five wives, which is a little peculiar, since Brahmana priests are only permitted to have four – one from each caste.

From these five marriages of the progenitor there came into existence the five subcastes. His first wife, a Brahmana, gave life to the highest division, the Brahmana-Kamenuh. From the second, a Satria-wife, sprang forth the Manuaba. The third, also a Satria, had already been married, but before she had met with her first husband, he died; out of this wife came forth the Brahmana Keniten. His fourth spouse was a Wesia and the last a Sudra. Out of her stemmed the Brahmana Kayu Sunya.

Kamenuh are strongly represented in the north and extraordinarily proud of their standing. Very unwilling are they for their daughters to marry-out to caste associates (*kastegenooten*) of lower groups, whereby the marriage possibilities of these women are indeed limited (1947: 105–6).

Thus, traditional Brahmana typology concerns the origin not of castes, whose existence was assumed, but of subcastes – actually Brahmana ranks based on the status of different wives. The model is intrinsically debatable: the status of the fifth wife, the relative ranks of the two classes produced by Satria-wife forebears. The descendants of the Wesia-wife marriage may be designated Brahmana Mas, and the claims by the descendants of the Sudra-wife to be true Brahmana are sometimes denied. Friederich (1849: 104–5), for example, reports the view that Brahmana Gelgel comprises the second subcaste as descended from a Satria wife and Manuaba represents the third as descended from a Satria widow. Moreover, Brahmana Kayu Sunya are considered descendants of a slave, which renders their claims to Brahmana status problematic. Yet the principle behind the variant schemes is clearly and simply the rank of the wife.

Covarrubias, then, is misleading when he generalizes:

Balinese Brahmana all claim descent from the mythical Wau Rauh, the highest priest of Majapahit, who in coming to Bali took wives from the various castes. His descendants established themselves at various places in Bali and founded the Brahmanic clans we find today, from the purer Kamenuh, to the Keniten, Gelgel, Nauba, Mas, Kayusunia, Andapan, and so forth (1937: 294–5).

This talk of clans confuses two distinct principles. Kamenuh and Keniten are the 'subcastes' of Dutch ethnography based on the ideology of the origins of Brahmana types. Gelgel Brahmanas likewise fall into one of these ranked types, but they also are localized by their ancestral temple and perhaps distinguished by certain special duties, such as providing religious mentors for the raja's line. If so distinguished, a particular local Brahmana group might come to epitomize its subcaste, or to conceive of itself as an independent subcaste with its own temple.[20]

Brahmana traditions also provide a model for role differentiation in the houseyard. A proper Brahmana *gria* contains its religious specialist (*pedanda*) who often weds an equal wife. This *istri pedanda* assists him in ceremonial tasks and in caring for esoteric texts; she is his consort in representing the religious nature of the *gria*. Some *grias* produce an excess of women whose high rank inhibits finding a suitable spouse. As their fecundity wanes, these Brahmana elder virgins (*detua*) perform special ceremonial services for the gods. An Archipelago-Sanskrit *stava* recited daily by Brahmana priests of the Siwa sect expresses the interrelation of the essence of the descent group, its specialist priests, and the universal forces of Brahma:

> Brahma is the manifestation of the Brahman,
> Brahma is a manifestation of Siva, heroic;
> He is known as Siva or the Eternal Siva,
> the Base of Siva's world.
>
> Brahma is the Ruler of creatures in this world,
> known as the Lord of the Twice Born, the Diffuser of splendor.
> He is Siva Who possesses wisdom of all realities,
> perfect in yoga, manifested in the world.
>
> The Diffuser of splendor, Siva's abode,
> His words are perfect sacred formulas;
> He is present in the gods, a Master of yoga,
> (He is) Brahma, Visnu and Mahesvara.
>
> Worship of Siva, yoga of Holy Water,
> is the base of the whole world;
> it destroys all obstacles;
> it renders powerless all diseases.
>
> (He is) the First, the Lord of the Twice Born, Siva,
> He is Brahma, standing in front;
> embodied in all the gods,
> the God Who is both Sun and Moon.

> He is the God, the Ruler of yoga and yogins;
> the real essence of the Brahmanical lineage;
> existing as the Representative of the Brahman,
> and as a God more supreme than the gods.
>
> He has the guru as His form,
> He is the honourable Guru; the God Guru, the first Guru.
> He is the Eternal Siva, of great courage,
> the Base of all gods.
>
> (Goudriaan and Hooykaas 1971: 99).

In brief, the ideology, legends, and ritual practices of the Brahmana caste highlight the ideals of superior ancestor-groups, merely elaborations of ordinary houseyards: (1) married-in women; (2) a sacred forebear whose nature is remanifested in the religious officiant plus consort; (3) ranks of descendants correlated to the mother's status; and (4) a localized temple which elevates its members above ordinary *banjar* and *desa* affairs. As a prototypical descent-group the Brahmana case is exemplary, and inferior groups can conform to diminished versions of its ideals. By now we can appreciate that to discuss marriage is to broach the issue of caste.

7. Caste in retroflexion

> It was surprising to discover the extent to which the question of rank obsesses so simple and democratic a people as the Balinese.
>
> Covarrubias 1937: 46

A central problem in Balinese studies can be expressed most effectively as a challenge to cross-cultural analysis: '. . . what is a *dadia* [ancestor-group]? Is it a lineage? a caste? a cult? a faction?' (H. and C. Geertz 1975: 157). In the following chapters we will argue that the proper response to this half-rhetorical question is 'all of the above'; in documenting this reponse we find in addition that a translocal ancestor-group can even assume the dimensions, if not the impact, of a political party.

Generalizations about Balinese status and caste are notoriously difficult.[1] Covarrubias and others confused the island's local traditions of democracy with egalitarianism. Yet, while a Balinese agriculturalist is willing to give an equal vote to an inferior, there is no implication of an equal share of anything else, least of all ritual purity, social esteem, or sacred merit. Caste in Bali is, to define it most simply, the historical projection over the whole island of a migration legend plus a marriage scheme. Literate traditions record that each caste (*warna*) is descended from a founding Javanese ancestor initially ranked by his function in society – priest, king, or warrior-administrator. High-caste ancestors are sanctified as perpetuators of these founders. Each *warna* is internally differentiated into ranks based both on the birth position of the ancestral sons who established the regnant collateral lines and on the different caste-statuses of a given ancestor's multiple wives who produced his descendants. Bali's three upper *warna* categories – Brahmana, Satria, Wesia – are conceptualized as such expanded ancestor-groups that have organized into temple networks interrelated by an ideology of hierarchy. Often in high-caste accounts, Sudras are ignored; they are merely 'the rest.'

This idealization is deceptively simple; because if such a migration and descent legend can be projected once, it can be projected again. In fact, Bali, like other societies with either caste or exogamous clan ideologies, harbors beliefs in composite origins of its population.

Cautionary notes

In his study of *adatrecht*, V.E. Korn suggests the tangled and inconsistent colonial data on caste:

> Contributions concerning Balinese castes are countless . . . Lekkerkerker Sr. can make no sense out of the division into Sudras; Goris remarks that it is uncertain in Java and Bali who the Wesias were (1932: 136).

He notes the confusions among Balinese themselves, and then obfuscates matters further with a note of totally conjectural history:

> Not only for Western writers, but also for some Balinese rulers themselves, caste was an inextricable problem, for the sense of the particular significance of Balinese caste had been forgotten [!], and they tried to clarify it by using Hindu law books (Korn 1932: 136).

Thus, when Dutch thinkers joined forces with their Balinese counterparts, matters became hopeless:

> Following Liefrinck and Van Eck Brahmanas were designated as *utamaning utama*, 'the choice of the choice' (*het puikje der puiken*), with which term the raja of Tabanan was also intended. Following I Njoman Sraba under *utamaning utama* was understood the priests and rajas, under *utama* the unconsecrated Brahmanas (Liefrinck and Van Eck maintain it was Satrias), under *madija* the Satrias (Liefrinck and Van Eck say the Wesias) and under *nista* the Wesia and Sudras (Korn 1932: 140).

Colonialist assumptions

Meanwhile, Dutch policies had been rigidifying a system which had actually been fluid. Korn described part of the difficulty:

> It is certain that as long as Western writers had been concerned with the caste system, they had designated the I Gustis as Wesias.
>
> The classification assumed by the European administration appeared hardly satisfactory. Actually the division of the population is *currently of more significance* than in kingdom times. The government administration brought greater freedom of movement [into clerical and service jobs], and Western education made the younger generation more cut off from its elders (p. 139; emphasis added).

The less supple Western political ideas about societies, based on corvee labor (*heerendienst-politiek*) 'sharpened the separation between people belonging to the noble castes and the Sudras' (Korn 1932: 139). Dutch administrators were worried by what they perceived as an increasing incidence of attempted hypergamous unions. In precolonial times, hypergamous marriage (*wargi*) of lower women into privileged houseyards was a standard means of creating social ties across caste divisions. Moreover overlords sometimes allowed outstanding lower ranked houseyards to receive a superior woman in marriage. Within a theoretical *warna*, which inevitably was spread across localities, there had most likely been continually shifting claims and ascriptions of rank in light of current marriage possibilities. But Dutch officials tended to construe any flexibility as a sign of the imminent collapse of the traditional system; and they attempted to forestay this collapse by reifying *warna* divisions:

> Whence the innumerable reorganizations even in the first years of our appearance in South Bali. With respect to caste practices . . . insofar as possible they were confined to the theoretical four-caste-system (*vierkastenstelsel*), thus necessitating apportioning the people of the in-between-castes (*tusschenkasten*) among the four chief groups; the awkward divisions of the Satrias and the Wesias were placed under the immediately following lower castes. This rearrangement was effected with the help of priests and district leaders, who appeared all too ready to construe the notion of Sudra as broadly as possible. This classification was especially required with an eye on statute labor and marriage rights. The caste nobility always had a different and lighter service obligation than the Sudras (Korn 1932: 174–5).

Moreover, the Dutch feared that the presence of their administration placed new strains on Balinese life; one way to help mitigate these strains was a policy against so-called mixed marriage (cf. Lekkerkerker 1926: 328–32). This was an understandable position. The fresh social possibilities produced by the new colonial contexts of school and office life in the Dutch administered towns no doubt provoked an upsurge in native concern over caste-status. Individuals who fell in love would try to establish a suitable rank in keeping with the preferences of the colonial courts. And these caste disputes would reverberate in the groups from which the couple originated. The mistake came in assuming that such shuffling and rearrangement was exclusively a product of Dutch presence. Traditional expansion of courtly influence would have produced similar results, although perhaps not to the same degree. But rather than enforcing a mechanical policy against any and all mixed matches, the rajas had sagely reserved the final say as to which marriages were allowable. In contrast, colonial courts viewed any intensification of caste fluidity as a breakdown.

Here as elsewhere, to protect Bali-Hindu life and customs, the Dutch adopted an archaeological outlook. Colonial policies on marriage echoed the provisions on temples: if a temple appeared older than fifty years, it was classed as a monument, and 'the owners could make no modification whatever without the prior authorization of the archaeological service' (Kat Angelino 1932: 408). But a changeless Balinese temple is not a Balinese temple at all; and the analogous point holds for marriage and caste, as current developments, when seen against the precolonial and colonial backdrop, confirm.

Exportability?

A second cautionary note concerns the inevitable distortions, noted earlier, which occur when Hindu spectacles are used to perceive Balinese stratification. Most

Balinese are Southeast Asian wet-rice agriculturalists; there is a striking homogeneity in their subsistence activities, and high- and low-caste patterns are close variations. Caste in Bali does not immediately suggest that famous South Asian 'acceptance of the existence of multiple cultures' (Srinivas 1969: 14). But at a more general level Bali can indeed be compared and contrasted with India. Consider, for example, L. Dumont's discussion of a summary of the major aspects of the South Asian caste system:

Let us take Bouglé's [definition] and say that the caste system divides the whole society into a large number of hereditary groups, distinguished from one another and connected together by three characteristics: *separation* in matters of marriage and contact, whether direct or indirect (food); *division* of labor, each group having, in theory or by tradition, a profession from which their members can depart only within certain limits; and finally *hierarchy*, which ranks the groups as relatively superior or inferior to one another (1970a: 21).

Bali clearly qualifies as a caste society only under the third aspect. We saw that Bali has no equivalent to exogamous clans at variance with the concept of lineage or ancestor-group. In India, great complexity can arise from the play of exogamy/endogamy; for example:

. . . the exogamous clan, and not the lineages of which the clan is composed, is the unit of exogamy (Dumont 1970: 297).

In practice, one often marries not throughout the whole range of the unit of endogamy, but often into a part of it, often a territorial part . . . (p. 113).

In marked contrast to this pattern, Bali reveals no fixed social unit within which marriage is forbidden, apart from parents and siblings at the practical level of incest restrictions. According to Blunt's definitions, a caste in Bali could only be an ancestor-group: 'A caste is an endogamous group, or collection of endogamous groups, bearing a common name (Dumont 1970a: 280).' In Bali the second component of caste, division of labor, is restricted to the concept of *warnas* and rights to temple duties. Brahmanas alone become *pedanda* priests; Sudras are rightful agriculturalists, and each needs the other to remain itself. Moreover, from the royal court's viewpoint, specialized groups exchange the requisite ritual and artisan functions of the kingdom. But there is no true South Asian *jajmani* system of complementary rights and obligations in every type of pure/polluted service, although a superior caste cannot consume the temple offerings of an inferior caste.

But under Bouglé's hierarchy, Bali clearly qualifies as a caste society. Moreover, the island is true to the South Asian model in terms of the status/power distinction that is most apparent in its Brahmanical ideology. Bali thus bears on a recent dispute in South Asian studies:

Is it then possible to provide the word caste with an analytical definition? Dumont does so (1970: 269): ' . . . caste exists only where this characteristic [disjunction between status and power] is present and we would like to classify under another heading all societies, even those constituted of permanent and closed status groups, which do not possess it.' As a key to the nature of Indian society this criterion could not be bettered, but it does not provide a category for a taxonomy of social systems . . . , for Dumont finds that this criterion is missing in fact outside India: Swat and even Ceylon (p. 273) are excluded, for caste proved 'non-exportable' (Pitt-Rivers 1971: 250–1).

Without in the least suggesting that Balinese caste is identical with South Asian caste, we can note that this characteristic – the radical disjunction between status and power somehow tied in with ideally closed status groups – was exported to Indonesia. Or perhaps the Indic notion merely complemented a pattern that was already present in Indonesia and reached into the stratified societies of the Pacific.

Finally, it must be recalled that Balinese social hierarchy is at base a religious concept of ritual purity, not intrinsically related to other social props. Thus, commoner ancestor-groups can be richer, more powerful, more artistic, and more educated than higher ranking groups; yet they remain inferior in the ritual and etiquette expressions, most prominent in temple ceremonies and death rites, that are the primary index of caste standing.

The productive gaps of hindsight

Disparate legends of the history of Bali legitimate the island's system of hierarchy. Houseyards that aspire to high rank often record a version of their own history to be read on festive occasions in the ancestor temple; and each variant reconstrues the larger issues in the history of contacts with Java. Many Dutch experts tried to distill from these textual sources (*presasti*), particularly from the *Usana Java* and the *Usana Bali*, an accurate record of the fourteenth through the nineteenth centuries of Java-Bali relationships. But the source materials resist this effort; moreover, gaps and contradictions in the legendary history insure flexibility in the relative ranks of current houses and yards. Theoretically, a true history would be advantageous only to the highest Brahmana and Satria houses of the island – that ultimate brahmindom-baronage coalition, the royal line of Klungkung and its priests. An obscure history or histories offers occasional advantages to nearly everyone, including both the range of Gustis, which encompass much of the Wesia and/or debatably Satria houses, and the high-ranking Sudra groups such as Pasek.

The macrolegend

A handy starting point for penetrating Balinese hierarchy is Kersten's condensation of the Dutch colonial summary of native histories of Balinese caste synthesized from the courtly chronicles of both Bali and Java:

At the time of the arrival [1343] of Gaja Mada on Bali, the indigenous society still presented that old autochthonous character of self-governing village communities (*zichzelfbesturende desa-gemeenschappen*). The arrival of this general and administrator from Majapahit brought to Bali a new element in its political organization: despotic princely power, and . . . the feudal system, namely the smaller district administrators, dependent on the central ruler but with a great deal of independence in their own territories, the so-called apanage-lords.

As soon as a despotic power was formed over the formerly independent village republics and village associations, the need was felt to give over more remote lands to subordinate administrators. These are in the Hindu-history of the rajas, the kings. Over them stands the maharaja, the great-king, the *oppervorst*: in Bali the Dewa Agung of Klungkung.

Besides this the old Balinese chiefs must also have pledged their loyalty to the Dewa Agung and have been confirmed in their office. Thus there developed in this old democratic land a strongly executed feudal system with many small lords, vassals (*leenmannen*) of the new Hindu-prince.

But this new order was not able to be carried through everywhere the same; it was strongest around Klungkung, in the south and east of its lands, the actual feudal territory. It was much weaker in Buleleng and the mountains . . . here the *desa* better preserved its own administration and autonomy; its village administrators did not become functionaries to the prince as in the south . . .

In the course of time the bond weakened between the smaller kings and the central King of Klungkung. He was the first among peers. The kings of the larger lands strengthened their power, the lesser lords became dependent on them, and finally Bali was divided into nine kingdoms, *negaras*: Klungkung, Bangli, Gianyar, Karangasem, Badung, Mengwi, Tabanan in the south, and Buleleng and Jembrana in the north.

In place of the former feudal dependence there now arose an association based on inter-kingdom law (*volkenrechtelijk bondgenootschap*) of autonomous Kingdoms (Korn). Bali became a confederation.

In connection with the transformation of Balinese society there gradually developed caste.

Majapahit never knew strong, systematic caste divisions. They were acquainted with Brahmana priests and the reigning king with his numerous close and distant kinsmen. The elements for forming castes were already present, but the process apparently could not be completed before the arrival of Mohammedan influence. In Bali the expansion of caste was indeed carried out. As the Hindu-Javanese influence had penetrated the entire island, a considerable time after Gaja Mada's campaign, the caste idea began to carry through. The priests who had followed the nobility from Majapahit to Bali – bearers of the Hindu thought – undoubtedly played a great part in this, but so did the Hindu literature and the striving of the rajas after a society organized along Hindu lines. The priests, with the descendants of the prior Buddhist missionaries, form the first caste, the Brahmanas. The raja of Klungkung and his plentiful descendants belong to the second caste, the Satrias. To the third caste the Wesias, were assigned both descendants of the Majapahit nobility who accompanied Gaja Mada, as well as the old indigenous chiefs who had a role to play in the new kingdom administration. The Wesia caste is thus the status of the kingdom administrators and *stadholders*.

The splitting of the nobility into Satrias and Wesias first occurred later on. But when toward the latter sixteenth century Dutchmen arrived in Bali, the three-way division had already been executed.

Furthermore, Balinese tradition itself carries the new order back to the conquest of 1343. The stadholder from Majapahit who remained behind after Gaja Mada went home, was said to be named Sri Krisna Kepakisan, the progenitor of Balinese Satrias. His successors took on the title of [first Dalem, then] Dewa Agung and built their palace in [Gelgel and then] Klungkung. Sri Krisna Kepakisan brought along the great ones of his kingdom – namely the 'aryas' . . . relatives of the raja of Majapahit, and the progenitors of Balinese royal and noble lineages (Kersten 1947: 99–101).

Kersten's summary reveals the useful vagaries in this retrospect. The source of the lesser lords remains obscure, as does the role of non-Hindu chiefly ranks (*volkstanden*) in the extension across Bali of the idea of 'kingship, with all its cultural consequences' (Stutterheim 1935: 7). From the start this process would have been complicated by two tendencies: any powerful group would seek to establish a tie with an origin-point significant in the Majapahit migration legend; parties already enjoying such ties would often tend to reject new claimants.[2]

Native sociological theories, also variable, accompany these legends. One general scheme considers the Dewa-Agung and his closest descendants as Satrias, and his descendants by lower caste wives as lower Satrias (all of these have Dewa in their title). The descendants of the imported subordinate overlords, regardless of when they migrated, are the Wesias (all have Gusti in their titles). Everyone else is a Sudra, except, of course, the Brahmanas who descend from the archpriest Wau Rauh and from early Buddhist immigrant sages. Yet even this rarified scheme provokes contention: if the rank of wives differentiates Satria offspring, what about Wesias? Is a lower Satria (Dewa) superior to an upper Wesia (Gusti)? The status of women becomes critical, again reflecting a standard Southeast Asian dimension of Balinese courtly concerns:

In any polygamous [polygynous] society such as Thailand, there are an overwhelming number of princes. To gain order in this extensive royal family, some sort of personal ranking had to be developed. Since many of the princes had the same father, position of the mother became of paramount importance (Epstein 1973: 374).

But in Bali the same paramount concern can be traced throughout the commoner social strata as well.

Finally, there is even room for indigenous argument over the very dawn of Brahmana and Satria penetration into Bali; this issue fuels current claims to superior status in the form of newly discovered descent or direct mystical contact with pre-Majapahit nobility. Credible archaeological evidence indeed reveals that Mataram Java controlled Bali in the eighth century and was later succeeded by the Balinese Varmadevas in the tenth century:

The dynasty of the Varmadevas reigned for at least two centuries. In the beginning the kings restricted themselves exclusively to Bali, but later they came again into closer contact with Java, but this time not in the sense of dependence. A daughter of a Javanese king . . . wedded a Balinese prince of the Varmadeva dynasty, whose residence, as shown by archaeological finds, lay in the district of the present villages Pejeng and Bedulu. A strongly renewed Javanization (and, simultaneously, a more intensive Hinduization) resulted from this marriage, and one must believe that this is the period in which various Tantric rites came into vogue in Bali . . .

By this marriage of the Javanese princess with the Balinese king, a prince was born, the famous Erlangga. Through his own intermarriage later he became king of Java, where, in his turn, he disseminated Balinese influences (Stutterheim 1935: 14–15).

The important point for us is that Balinese literati aware of these facts can put them to use in their current status affairs. Moreover, there are Bali Aga groups who consider themselves, not pejoratively as remote un-Hinduized rustics, but positively as descendants of the legendary hero, Kewo Yiwo, an indigenous Balinese giant who let himself be killed by Gaja Mada (cf. De Zoete and Spies 1939: 296).[3]

In spite of such complications involving pre-Majapahit or non-Hindu ascendant status, the predominant historicized legend traces Balinese questions of rank only to 1343 A.D. and makes perfectly clear only the supreme ideological rank of Brahmanas as a division of society and the relative ascendancy of the Dewa Agung as preeminent overlord. Everything else remains contestable; while the contest is never finally decided, its rules can be clarified, especially if we focus on one kingdom and the reapplication of caste principles in ever narrower contexts.

Microcomplexities

One fundamental problem in retrospect is the Wesia (*warna*) or Gusti (title) issue. On the one side the rank of Gusti bears on the Satria question and on the other side it concerns the Sudra:

Abdullah called the Wesias 'the family [*geslacht*: family, lineage, race] of the rajas (*vorsten*) who rule in the island of Bali,' which van Hoëvell considers a great error, since there were many Wesia rajas, 'for all that in Bali Satrias are the only royal caste.'

Abdullah called all Gustis Wesia . . . and [concluded] that in number the Wesias predominated.

In five of the eight kingdoms Gustis always reigned. Van Hoëvell had probably heard of the above-mentioned idea that various Gustis were Javanese Satrias. Van Hoëvell always considers Satria the caste out of which the rulers ought to come and the one which also supplied the maharaja (*oppervorst*), Dewa Agung of Klungkung. Perhaps he knew as well of the tradition mentioned in Friederich, by which the rest of the rajas were also originally Satrias who, however, were ages ago demoted by the Dewa Agung.

If we provisionally pursue the current view concerning the caste divisions, this makes the Satrias descendants of the above named dalem Krisna Kepakisan. Satrias are small in number, yet remain highly respected, at least if they belong to the higher portion of their caste; their lower portion is of less account than the highest portion of the Wesia caste. It is obvious that wherever Wesia rajas were in power they were considered no less than Satrias, and wherever Satrias ruled, the people of the third [Wesia] caste were lumped together with the Sudras (Korn 1932: 145–6).

Korn also relates the theory that Wesias were all descendants of Javanese Wesias; he then explains:

These have as title Gusti, and if they possess no governmental power Gusi or 'Si, which latter title indicates that they have come to stand close to the distinguished Sudras, the so-called *prebali* and *kula wisuda*, favored or empowered Sudras, under whom the people of standing – Bendesas, Paseks, etc. – were classed (Korn 1932: 138).

Korn implies but does not specify an indigenous dialectic between a theory of caste based on idealized descent and a view which relates rank to the type of official duties apportioned to an individual's elevated, localized group.

Dutch observers looked for a simple answer to 'Who were the Wesias.' Yet Gusti is perhaps best thought of as essentially relational, with no substantive meaning if isolated. A Gusti appears Satrialike to his inferiors and is regarded as almost Sudra-like by his betters. The raja of Tabanan for example, is something of a Satria to his subjects and a Wesia to the Dewa Agung. This relational quality is characteristic of any Balinese rank, but it emerges most clearly from the ambiguities of Gusti status.

Evidence that Gusti-Wesia is partly a strategic and polemical status ascription appears as early as 1820, when in his account of Balinese religion, John Crawfurd relates:

The princes of this [Karangasem] family, but they alone, of the sovereigns of Bali and Lombok, are of the Wesia or mercantile class; the rest uniformly of the Satria tribe (1820: 143).

While it is not surprising to find Karangasem's royal line labeled Wesia, it is remarkable that Karangasem is so relegated while the other royal lines of Bali are deemed Satria. We can contrast Korn's summary (1932: 147) which considers Wesias to be subdivided into macrolineages, each descended from a Javanese *arya* installed as apanage lord by the Dewa Agung. Korn's divisions include Arya Kencheng (the name of the ruling houses of both Tabanan and Badung) which makes it Wesia. Crawfurd's information can only be properly evaluated by inspecting his source – the royal house of Buleleng. Buleleng's chronicle (*babad*), drawn up just before the Dutch takeover, provides the needed background. The predominant royal house of Buleleng had been usurped for several generations by Karangasem; but the Karangasem rulers were finally forced to abandon overlordship outside of Karangasem proper (see Worseley 1972). Crawfurd's account doubtlessly reflects the effects of the newly reinstated Buleleng royal house to disparage its past conquerors, even if it meant momentarily elevating (to Satria) other houses in order to emphasize the decidedly inferior rank of Karangasem. Endless obfuscations were generated by such strategies in the corresponding traditional Hindu-Javanese efforts to legitimate authority over and against rival claimants (cf. Schrieke 1957).

The other *triwangsas* of Tabanan Kingdom were the Brahmana houses. Any Brahmana line had theoretically migrated from the east and could be traced to *grias* there which were classified into one of the legendary subcastes. The preeminent Brahmanas of the realm came from Gria Pasekan, the Brahmana line allianced with the raja himself (his *bagawanta*) and source of the priest who conducted royal ceremonies. This Brahmana line of subcaste Geniten was given to Arya Kencheng by the earlier Dewa Agung of Gelgel because its house of origin was Gria Kamasan in Klungkung. There was a second *gria* that provided religious experts, a lower Brahmana Emas-type houseyard which had been elevated to an official capacity after its priest miraculously cured a member of the royalty of leprosy (cf. Korn 1922); the patient's skin was buried in a temple in Sanosari to commemorate the event. Thus, Tabanan kingdom contained Brahmanas distinguished both by legendary subcaste and by official function in the state administration. However, what houseyards were Brahmana was relatively indisputable (but cf. Chapter 8).

Manipulations of caste-status in Bali rely on the fact that royal and noble houses and commoner ancestor-groups alike can be ranked by the same principles that distinguish Brahmana, Satria, Wesia and Sudra *warnas*. As in Brahmana ideology, each *warna* level tends to be construed as the descendants of a sacred forebear stratified according to birth order and mothers' ranks. Yet no mechanical scheme ensues, because of the opposed tendency for groups to inch their rank upwards. Within a kingdom the scheme becomes fragmentary and refractory; contrary to the macrolegend, caste in action is more prismatic than taxonomic.

In Tabanan one current retrospect advocated by ambitious groups considers the kingdom to contain six traditional Satria-level macrohouses, each descended from a Javanese *arya*. The ranks are symbolized in the tiers (*meru*) that can crown an ancestral shrine: any odd number from one to eleven, depending on rank. These six collateral *aryas* included one (Arya Damar) which eventually returned to Java, various *aryas* whose power has relatively eclipsed, and the *arya* of the Tabanan raja (Arya Kencheng). It is acknowledged that the arch forebear of Arya Kepakisan, Sri Krisna Kepakisan (not one of the six brothers), was the descendant of a Brahmana, and an angel, whose rank was lowered upon receiving temporal power. This point clinches the right of Arya Kepakisan and the house of the Dewa Agung to be regarded highest among peers. But in other respects the Tabanan version stresses the competitiveness in power and accomplishments of these ruling houses, depicting how during the conquest of Bali each *arya* arrived from a different direction and assumed control of a particular region – Arya Kencheng winning Tabanan and Badung. Other *aryas*, which in their more eastern home districts claim direct descent from Sri Krisna Kepakisan by lower wives or concubines, figure minimally in the Satria scheme that legitimates the Tabanan raja's authority.[4]

Thus in the narrowed perspective of Tabanan, Arya Kencheng, at least in its upper portion, is no longer problematic. It is virtually Satria; its head is the Chokorda, raja of the kingdom, its pinnacle of status and final arbitrator in all matters of rank, since the Dewa Agung had granted Arya Kencheng authority in protocol over his subjects. As we saw above, there were two main types of titles for Balinese royal houses – the Dewas who included the Dewa Agung and other rulers of kingdoms (for example, Gianyar) claiming direct descent from him, and the Gustis who reputedly descended from other Javanese *aryas*. The Tabanan Chokorda was, and is, a Gusti Ngurah; this house together with the Badung royal line constituted Arya Kencheng. According to classical ideals, there should be no Arya Kencheng group outside of these two kingdoms. From Tabanan's viewpoint the sovereigns of Karangasem and the areas they have sometimes controlled (including Buleleng, Jembrana, Mengwi, and Lombok) were all lower than Tabanan's royal line – mere Gusti rather than Gusti Ngurah. Ideally then, the Chokorda's subjects should include no Dewa, not even a lowered Dewa who could argue his descent back to a higher rank than Chokorda.[5] Rather the highest title, Brahmana excluded, of the kingdom should be Chokorda, which distinguished the raja among the stock of Arya Kencheng collateral lines titled as I Gusti Ngurah. This same arrangement could be repeated within a narrower context: the Chokorda could grant to a lesser house authority in matters of rank below I Gusti Ngurah as far as its subjects were concerned.

In the *puri* of Tabanan, a raja begat sons with the title I Gusti Ngurah Alit ('small') or I Gusti Ngurah Gde ('large') by *padmi* wives, simply I Gusti Ngurahs by *penawing* wives, and by concubines in and around the *puri* a host of Astras, a name meaning acknowledged bastard. Theoretically and broadly speaking, the various rights of these filial ranks were clear: sons by *padmi* wives either succeeded as raja or were domiciled in separate, sometimes eventually insurgent, palaces when their sibling did so; sons of *penawing* wives received lesser offices, residences and lands; and Astra sons were favored according to their ability or the raja's affection for their mothers. But in actual fact, competition among sons of different classes over the different rights was the basis of much warfaring courtly intrigue in precolonial Bali, as military might and mystical evidence alike were mustered to level claims against actual birthright. The Balinese situation no doubt paralleled that of pre-Mohammedan Java:

> We have, then, noted that the jealousy of the princes in matters regarding succession was inherent in the structure of the early Javanese royal house; that time and again ambitious pretenders, the progeny of concubines, could and did disturb the regular course of succession . . . ; that where there were no descendants of the crown princess a prince consort chose as successors his own sons by a wife of lower rank rather than the scions of other branches of the family more closely related to the founder of the house . . . (Schrieke 1957: 24).

But today, since the ruling authority has been transferred to the Indonesian nation, the interesting question in Tabanan district becomes what transpires below the I Gusti Ngurah level, as various groups assert titles and claim prerogatives.

Relentless peripheries

As Tabanan kingdom was culturally peripheral to the sphere of the Dewa Agung yet sought to rival it in every respect short of pure religious esteem, so this peripheral kingdom generates its own peripheries, and so on. In modern Bali the repeating peripheries of kingdoms still outrun any effort to arrive, even analytically, at their limits.

According to the native theory of idealized descent, precolonial Tabanan had only one source of per Gusti: the royal line of Arya Kencheng.[6] This fact is reflected in current upper caste titles. I Gusti Ngurah is the title of a raja before he assumes office and of his brothers and his brothers' sons. A son by an Arya Kencheng mother bears the honorific Gde or Alit as well: a son by a lower woman does not. These I Gusti Ngurah titles are most concentrated around the vicinity of Tabanan town, the court center. However, a more pragmatic theory of power and rank competes with this ideal descent status, or at least complements it. If over time the subjects, bestowed on a Gusti Ngurah house by the raja, ceased to support the rites in its high-caste courtyard *(puri)*, the house forfeited the Ngurah honorific and descended to I Gusti. Or if a raja's kinsman were dispatched with his family and entourage to administer subjects in a borderland area, he could be demoted to reign there as an I Gusti.

These principles persist today in both the ritual codes of status and spheres of informal influence that remain strong even where the actual authority of the royal families has been replaced by governmental functionaries. In the mountains of Tabanan, for example, there resides an I Gusti branch of the house of Subamia, the traditional defense specialists for Tabanan's royalty, which received land as a prize for military service. In this distant Gusti house, the rank of sons worked, and works, as follows: if a Gusti married a commoner woman, she assumed the honorific Mekel and begat sons who were likewise Gusti. But if these Gusti sons, offspring of a commoner female, likewise married commoners, their sons were not Gusti, but Gusi – which can be construed as commoner. The rule is this: if one's father has married below Gusti, one must marry a Gusti to have one's children remain Gusti. In this remote area then, the Satria-Wesia problem fades into Sudra standing, and mother's rank is the critical factor.

This same rule is attested in upland Marga, where a Gusti line can become a Gusi (called 'Si) and in the process lose certain inheritance rights. Thus, one feature – mother's rank – could have different cultural and practical consequences in different parts of the kingdom: near the courtly sphere Gusti were expected to remain such; in remote areas their descendants could drop out of the category, yet they maintained the Gusi or 'Si tag to imply past, not quite forgotten, status claims. This is the view, at least, of current town dwellers. Thus, even in the ideal elitist retrospect, which views Arya Kencheng as the sole authentic source of Gustis, the caste system is fluid. Through marriage with different ranking women, there is potential for a Satria/Wesia and in turn a Wesia/Satria contrast within the category of Tabanan Gusti-Gusi.[7]

This ideal picture of pan-Balinese caste is complicated by the supposed later arrival of other elevated lines from Java. In a parallel fashion, as we saw in Chapter 4, ruling houses imported specialists from more central areas to help in administering the periphery. Such groups might be established as minor overlords with subjects in still more peripheral areas, or be installed as the source group of certain temple officials, or be assigned specific duties such as royal builders, palace doctors, or espionage and military experts. The strategical importance of border regions explains why higher houses and their cultural attributes were often situated in remote locales; within a kingdom the higher courtly statuses would be concentrated both at the sacred center and in peripheral areas between zones of influence of competing royal and noble lines. Some rulers granted as prerogatives the right to wed women from a lower royal house. In Tabanan, however, rewards were generally in the form of land grants or the bestowal of subjects. Any imported Gusti group might continue to propitiate the ancestors of its place of origin, even in another kingdom. Evidence of its origin lay in its title and its rights to pay homage at the distant ancestral temple. Within Tabanan an imported group's elevated status had to be confirmed by the raja who granted it both subjects and the right to maintain a high temple.

Thus, many different shadings of intrakingdom status can still be glimpsed in the way current citizens of Tabanan explain how things were, in order to justify or complain about their present situations. Moreover, the same shadings distinguish every literary version of caste history. One brief manuscript, for example, views all royal houses of Tabanan as descendants of an original Javanese *patih* brought over by Gaja Mada: Arya Kencheng.[8] A legend relates that Arya Kencheng committed a misdemeanor against the Dewa Agung of Dalem Gelgel and made a sacred return trek to Majapahit for repurification. Upon the homecoming to Bali, it was discovered his sister had married low (to the ruler of the subkingdom of Kapal). The hypogamous marriage is construed as punishment for Arya Kencheng's crime and explains its demotion. The story relates the establishment of the royal palace in the mountainous region of Buahan, a subsequent shift seaward, and finally the sacred founding and settling of the area now known as Tabanan town. Thus is portrayed the gradual opening of Tabanan kingdom and the transformation of a minor uplands overlord of Buahan into the sovereign of one of the broadest kingdoms of the Balinese plains. Each time the palace was moved, the abandoned court center was left with Arya Kencheng descendants in their old royal style houseyards. The raja would settle kinsmen in strategic places as he expanded his influence. These lines were titled I Gusti Ngurah or I Gusti, depending both on whether they descended from high- or low-caste wives or concubines, and on their merit and office. For example, a raja's son by a low wife could succeed as Chokorda if there were no suitable son by a same-caste *padmi*. Theoretically the only other Gustis in the kingdom were imported and enfranchised by the raja in keeping with their origin-determined status. These lines could belong to Arya Kencheng if they came from Badung, whose royal line was Tabanan's collateral. Or the lines might be of a different *arya*, such as Arya 'Blog from the neighboring subkingdom of Kaba-kaba. Finally, the nature of Balinese warfare and political expansion meant that as the Chokorda enlarged his sphere of influence, the kingdom would extend around Satria-Wesia lines without physically importing them. The victorious raja would then either acknowledge their subordinate lordship over certain subjects or deny it. But the major guiding principle of the model for caste remained: just as the Dewa Agung was the supreme source of status attributes that had been bestowed on notable subordinates – such as Arya Kencheng – so the Chokorda bestowed relative jurisdiction in status on his own notable subordinates, and the same procedure occurs again and again, toward the ever receding peripheries of Hinduized time and place.

Summary scheme

The continued importance of the classical retrospect lies in the various idioms it embodies to codify caste-status: *arya*, *warna*, personal titles, group titles, temple height, and so forth. *Arya* is the idealized legendary-historical aspect of Balinese *triwangsas*, which views high castes as descendants of heroic Javanese immigrants. *Arya* is a concept currently (1972) of increasing interest even to commoner lines engaged in status mobility. *Warna* is the Hindu theoretical component which assigns each of the three twice-born categories a social function: priest, king, warrior-administrator (agriculture is displaced to Sudras). An analogous idea appears at lower levels of society in which distinct commoner groups possess religious functions or specific temple duties. The *warna* code is complicated by two points of indigenous contention: (1) whether failure to maintain the social function can decrease rank, and (2) the role of the mother's status and birth order in maintaining the rank of offspring within each *warna*.

We must also recall that in the ideal Balinese scheme each *warna* is not only a state-function group, but also a more or less distinct temple group or network. In Balinese ideology a warna *is* a temple network. Brahmanas are ideally a single *warna*-caste. The native view that sees Dalem title-bearers alone as Satria also contrues the second *warna* as a single macrodescent group. Or Satrias might include six other categories descended from the six *aryas* who immigrated after Sri Krisna Kepakisan. (Some accounts call these six 'brothers,' thus making the Satria *warna* into two ranked macrogroups.) Or these latter brothers might be considered Wesias. Such complications mean that an *arya* can be considered to be composed of different *warnas*, and might even cover the entire range of Satria-Wesias-Sudra. All these considerations point to the notion of *arya* or descent group with an ancestral founder as more basic than caste, but the ancestral (*kawitan*) aspect of descent is in turn more basic than the quasihistoric *arya* element. Even high-caste Bali is not composed of *warnas* which contain subcastes; it is composed of ancestor-temple networks, internally ranked according to distance from the founding line and the status of the mother (endogamous-superior versus outside-inferior).

Returning to our opening theme, we might even say that *warna* is the epic view of caste, which posits fixed orders and emphasizes the stable Brahmana-Satria relation that divides and joins status and power. *Arya* then emerges as the romance view of caste, which envisions heroic champions who reestablish a proper hierarchy after the inevitable degeneration over time of the balance between factors of birth, control over subjects, and the requisite ritual purity of overlords and priests. Finally, personal titles for members of *triwangsa* (for example, I Gusti) or of high Sudra groups (for example, I Gde) are the Balinese acknowledgment of participation by a person in a particular rank. On the other hand, group titles (for example, Pesaji) are devices for referring to a line as localized by an ancestor temple, always said to issue from a more sacred, prior temple, that ideally forms part of a pan-Bali ancestor-group. To cite a summary example: Pesaji is the name of a group of titular I Gustis (disputed by some) of an *arya* of Wesia *warna* from Buleleng kingdom, but now localized in a Tabanan village-area, and therefore demoted. Pesaji is a social unit partaking of an ancestral essence (*kawitan*), and that essence is registered in migratory legend (*arya*), in caste (Wesia *warna*), in personal honorifics (I Gusti), and in the temple established in the group's more recently adopted locality. This same complexity can characterize Sudras as well.

Augmented Sudra

Until now we have avoided the vital issue of Sudra caste. One of the nagging difficulties both with Balinese *triwangsas*' own view of their origins and with the Dutch emphasis on pre-1343 democratic *gemeenschaps* as the foundation of indigenous social organization is the sense of hierarchy among the Balinese masses. Reports on supposedly non-Hinduized villages (for example, Korn 1933) describe the organization according to classes. Moreover, many commoners could appear in a high-caste guise. Thus Kersten has to note almost apologetically:

> Only the people of Hindu castes and sometimes also those of commoner classes (*volksstanden*) such as Pasek and Pande who live scattered through the Sudras, stand outside the religious community of the *desa*. They have other gods and origins, where they annually return to carry out the *odalan* (1947: 46).

It was often suggested that these Sudra *volksstanden* developed from the original village-area chiefs who were allowed to retain their office by victorious Hindu overlords:

> In the *Usana Bali* different classes of Sudras are mentioned – viz., Mandesa, Gaduh, Dangka, Batu-Haji, Pasek, Kabayan, Ngukuhin, Talikup; these, however, are not different castes, but are all Sudras, some of whom have been degraded to this caste from that of the Wesias, and still maintain, in a political sense, a higher position than the common Sudras (Friederich 1849: 102).

Clarity

Regardless of their origin, such groups could achieve great importance in the precolonial kingdoms. Two Sudra caste-statuses, Sengguhu and Pande, are relatively distinct because they were invested with exclusive functions indispensable to the Hindu realm. Just as a raja required an allied Brahmana house to provide Hindu priests and legists, so he needed a Sengguhu group to provide exorcists, a Pande Besi to act as ironsmiths, and perhaps a Pande Emas for goldsmiths. Various traditions explain the status and knowledge of Sengguhus and assert their superiority over Pandes (cf. Hooykaas 1964a). In colonial Tabanan some Sengguhu leaders tried unsuccessfully to be recognized as legitimate Brahmanas by the courts. Today Sengguhus are considered along with Brahmanas the least alloyed category of society in Bali. Pandes share something of the same reputation; they tend more to marry among themselves and, like the Sengguhus, they have their own holy men (*Empu* for Pande, *Sang Gde* for Sengguhu). As noted by Hooykaas (1964a: 272): 'There is no genealogical group in Bali which has such marked places of worship of their deified forefather in the ancestor-sanctuary Besakih on Gunung Agung as the very group of smiths' (cf. Goris 1960c). Pande endogamy was sometimes complemented by prohibiting Pande women to marry non-Pandes. It is still said, for example, that in Buleleng no one would want to wed a Pande Emas and that a child who did so would be thrown away. A popular lore sustains the reputation of Pande Emas women as risky spouses, and Buleleng is considered most fanatical on this point by Tabananers. Also, Brahmana men were not permitted to wed Pande Emas women. These traditions reflect the sacred-dangerous status of Pande metal workers, although legends differ on whether Pandes are indigenous Balinese or immigrants from Java.

Of more immediate interest are the Pasek and Bendesa statuses of Sudras. These are complicated by the fact that their social functions overlap with those of the Wesia houses. Kersten acknowledges as much and summarizes the Dutch sources that speculate how earlier slippage must have occurred between the old-time nobility and the *triwangsa*:

It is certain that many people from the old nobility were gradually taken up into the rank of Wesias, and thus incorporated by the *triwangsa* – a process that to this day has not yet been arrested. The respect of the old families was at this time completely surpassed by the might and luster of the Hindu-castes.

Plentiful lontars that were kept in their ancestral temples testify to the elevated descent of the Paseks, Sengguhus and Pandes. The origin of these families was referred back to great figures out of Bali's past, even to the highest Hindu-godheads . . . They feel themselves elevated far above the ordinary Sudras (Kersten 1947: 118–19).

In his midnineteenth-century account, Friederich reported a contrary explanation of Pasek origins which sounds more like a current self-aggrandizing Pasek view:

Pasek are also Wesias who have been degraded to Sudras, and still retain a certain superiority of rank above the rest of the populace (1849: 142).

Kersten goes on to list important offices held by Pasek and Bendesa lines:

Their task in old Bali was desa administration, in which side by side a Pasek and a Bendesa each had his share. In old-fashioned villages this arrangement has remained, but in the southern feudal area has largely been lost. The Pasek is in the desas of Buleleng the master of the origins temple; the Bendesa exercises authority over the 'village temple' [*pura desa*?] and public worship (1947: 119).

This view of the general role of Pasek and Bendesas contrasts with the situation in Tabanan kingdom. It is possible that Tabanan's population was sparse until the opening up of various areas by so-called Arya Kencheng. Thus the issue of previously organized villages and indigenous chiefly-lines may be less relevant in this part of Bali. Regardless, one current formula depicts the role of the Pasek in classical Tabanan as central. There are manuscripts prescribing Paseks as aids to the raja; failure to use Pasek functionaries would jeopardize the realm. Pasek groups furnished two types of officials: (1) *perbekels*, the agents who carried information from the royal court down, and (2) the leaders of the village-area temple clusters to oversee local *adat* administration. The main sources were the two supreme Pasek groups of the kingdom: Pasek Tangguntiti and Pasek Wanogiri. Both of these were considered offshoots of the Pasek ancestral temple in Gelgel, the cultural navel of Bali. Each of these groups in turn dispatched representatives to distant territories to head up important village-areas. Today even a non-Pasek will attest that the Tabanan raja's strength stemmed from the Arya Kencheng-Pasek coalition. A Pasek lineage in an area devoid of *triwangsas* could relate to its inferiors much as a Gusti would.

The place of Bendesa as a Sudra category is less clear in current Tabanan. Some informants consider Bendesa merely the name of the offices Paseks were, and usually still are, qualified to fill. Bendesa is here construed as the title most befitting senior lines of a Pasek group, since seniors are considered to be naturally qualified office holders. Other informants understand these labels as two distinct statuses, with the superior Paseks enjoying a more elaborate temple network. Those who consider Bendesa the office title reserved for elder Pasek lines tend to view *kebayan* (the custodianship of important temples) in the same way. Yet Kebayan can also be regarded as a separate type of ancestor-group. In fact Tabanan contains a Kebayan group with a localized ancestral temple near the kingdom's sacred mountain, which provides *pemangkus* for royal temples. The important point is that these two native interpretations are not exactly conflicting. According to the general caste scheme, a Kebayan branch could have differentiated out of Pasek in olden days. There might well have been a Kebayan-type, once-Pasek line that became institutionalized as simply Kebayan in a particular locality, while individual *kebayan* functionaries continued to be appointed from groups still considered Pasek. These variations in interpreting Bendesa and Kebayan social categories again hinge on the crucial Balinese structural ambiguity of whether the group's status is a product of official religio-political duties or of ideal descent as memorialized in a local ancestor temple.

Controversiality

The relatively clear-cut ideology of the upper branches of Tabanan Paseks contrasts with the island's plethora of title groups of ambiguous and continually disputatious rank. To understand this complexity in title groups, one must look both beyond the Pasek and across kingdoms. In 1972 a list of title groups from a local area in Klungkung district (C. Geertz 1967: 222) was checked against the ready knowledge of two sorts of Balinese experts from widely separate locales: (1) a Tabanan civil servant (familiar with traditional, esoteric manuscripts) who had experienced far ranging contacts with title groups throughout Bali, especially in Tabanan, Badung, Gianyar, Karangasem, and Buleleng. His knowledge was limited, however, insofar as it was Tabanan-oriented, for Tabanan is relatively poor in title groups. (Compared to eastern kingdoms it seems to have experienced fewer wars and thus reveals fewer groups degraded by defeat; Friederich concurs: 'Tabanan does not engage in many wars' – 1849: 125.) (2) a Brahmana *pedanda* from Bangli district, whose knowledge is based largely on *lontars* such as *Benchangah Prelinteh*, an esoteric treatise on the origins of title groups, including some commoner ones. Bangli was one of the two or three most conservative kingdoms. Here many demoted title-groups attributed their lost superiority to the legendary revolt against the Dewa Agung when he was still Dalem Gelgel, or even to revolts against forced labor during Dutch administration. Kersten condenses the renowned prototype of such rebellions as follows:

> The consideration [of the Paseks and Bendesas] in Hindu-times rested partially on the fact that the raja often took his lower wives from the gentry (*volksadel*). Many of these became *punggawas* and *perbekels* and were put on a par with the immigrants from Majapahit. In light of their influence on the population, they were considered as 'the bond which entwined and held together the kingdom.' Yet they would be readily ousted from their functions, and their dissatisfaction over this was expressed through a rebellion in Klungkung, where under the leadership of the chief administrator they expelled the Dewa Agung and came into great power. A Pasek was chief administrator for the new maharaja, but his glory was short lived; the Dewa Agung reestablished his family and four hundred Pasek families fled to Gianyar, whereby as well their influence in the central kingdom was to a great extent lost (1947: 119).

Many parties view subsequent Balinese history as an effort to reforge affiliations among the groups which were thus degraded, fragmented, and dispersed.

We shall call the first informant 'T' for Tabanan and the second 'B' for Brahmana of Bangli in describing their responses to a sample from the list:

Pande Tosan. T says there are many of these but he is unsure of their nature. B relates they are obviously smiths (Pande) specializing in the manufacture of agricultural tools.

Pulsari. T says that according to one chronicle they are Gusti because descendants of Dalem Gelgel. But now they are considered Pasek. Perhaps this is because they and the Warga Pasek (see below) descend from Brahmana ancestors. Pulosaris suffered defeat in the war against Gelgel, he says. B concurs.

Bagus. (Listed as a *triwangsa* group recently demoted to Sudra by their *banjar* because of a sexual scandal.) T considers this a variant title for a demoted line of Arya Kepakisan, Bali's highest Satria status; he deems the sexual scandal story improbable. B differs and proclaims Bagus an independent title-group of Brahmana descent.

Tianyar. T never heard of it. B explains a twofold significance. It is the name of a locale in Karangasem inhabited principally by Pasek and sacred to them. However, in Bangli there is a group of Dewa personal title-bearers known as Tianyar; Dewa Tianyar is a true *arya*, he says.

Tangkaban. B says this is a *triwangsa* group (*per Agung*) in Bangli.

Manikan. T says that in Tabanan there are none of these, but it is a type of commoner house in Badung with its source in Den Pasar.

Sangging. T says this is not a title-group term, but the professional designation of painters, carvers, and so on. B adds that it is the name of the office of Pasek Pulasari.

Tegeh. This term alone is unfamiliar, but T explains that Tegeh Kori in Tabanan was an Arya Kencheng line which warred with its collateral and was demoted. Now there is no Tegeh Kori member who today bears the title I Gusti Ngurah; they are all plain Gusti. Its ancestral temple is in Gianyar, where the line migrated following its defeat. B relates that Tegeh Kori is the line of the exraja of Badung before Arya Kencheng took over; Tegeh Kori descended to commoner status after the war with Kencheng, but previously was of the same *arya*.

Pring. T knows this only as a *desa* name. B says this title group exists in Bangli and tells its story: the line descends from a legitimate child of the early maharaja Dalem Gelgel who, because of misconduct was demoted to become Arya Den Charik (still noble). There was another crime and another demotion, this time to commoner. The line, however, persisted in employing the title Dewa Gde Pring, but was never acknowledged as such by subjects.

Selain. Unknown to T, this title is corrected to Selahin by B, who explains it is a Pasek Sanak Pitu line institutionalized as official assistants to Kebayan lines.

Badeg. B clarifies this group as a Pasek line originating in Mengwi, and perhaps

Karangasem, which was scattered when, in light of its extraordinarily bold elder, the raja feared that it might attract too many followers and one day lead a revolt.

Bondem. T and B correct this to Bandem. T has met this title group in Karangasem and Tabanan, and in fact his brother-in-law in a Tabanan town *banjar* is so categorized. T is unsure if it is higher or lower than Pasek, but knows that the Bandem line in Tabanan moved from a *desa* of that name in Karangasem during kingdom times. His brother-in-law has recently been well received there on a return trek. T assumes Bandem was a commoner line elevated by the raja (*kawi suda*) whose members, if they migrated without their office, would not be entitled to high rank. B adds that Bandem are Pasek, but not of the Pasek Sanak Pitu variety, and there is a sacred text of their origins.

So it goes through the title groups. In spite of his unusually broad experience, the Tabanan informant was a stranger to additional titles (for example, Maspada, Bendul) and considered others only *desa* names (for example, Kedisan, Sawan). In contrast, the Brahmana, whether he was familiar with them or not, felt obliged to demonstrate appropriate expertise concerning each title; this is frequently the case with *pedanda* priests who must live up to a burdensome reputation for learnedness.

Contrasting the perceptions of distant title groups of a progressivist Tabananer expert with those of a traditionalist Bangli Brahmana priest is not a means of obtaining final answers as to the basis of legitimacy in order conclusively to grade these groups. Moreover many of the above interpretations might be quite different in Klungkung itself. But juxtaposing the different views can suggest the rich interplay of claims and counterclaims of superior status in Bali. This on-going polemic – a sociological exegesis founded on principles of sacred origins, birth order, legitimacy, ideal descent, actual duties, scandal and migration, and more – is the trademark of Hindu-Balinese social life, while actualized corporate groups are only exceptionally (see Chapter 4) one of its products. The principles of the cultural polemic are the key to the dimensions of 'romance' in Bali, which must be thoroughly appreciated if we are to understand Balinese versions of new programs launched by the Indonesian nation as well as endogenous social change.

8. Situational hierarchy

In social life there is, of course, no traditional diametrically opposed to modern – hence the power of culture. Societies resist clean slates. In progressively Indonesian Tabanan, for example, a now powerless raja is still occasionally borne aloft to the paddy fields of his voting subjects to beckon rain during drought or to turn back the rats during plague. Nor are such seemingly archaic spectacles mere nostalgic echoes of a silenced royal epic. Balinese culture can adapt to new conditions because its rules and values allow for and in fact thrive on native argument, and the bounds of the social units to which the rules and values apply are themselves adjustable. Such principles of the social romance belie any facile dichotomy of Balinese history and experience into commoner/noble, town/rural, or traditional/progressive. Built into religion and culture are persistent expectations that the lowborn will regenerate the heights of supreme values, that relative rustics will from time to time accede to the privileged arena of courtly lifestyle, and that new epochs will surely remanifest the same dimensions as the old. The tenacity of such expectations is nowhere more evident than in the latest chapters of the legendary history of castes.

Gusti anew

The vexed issue of Gusti rank revolves around two traditional bases for claiming or ascribing caste-status: (1) Is *warna* rank a function of offices held and subjects bestowed? (2) Or is *warna* a product of descent from an *arya* as recorded in literary chronicles (*babad*)? Where the two strains of native theory are blended, idealized descent takes on the subcaste dimensions we found in Brahmana ideology.

Achieved status

The different levels of Tabanan Gusti titles traced above are sometimes reified by native exegetes as follows: (1) Gusti Ngurah (including the apical Chokorda); (2) Gusti (from lower mothers); and (3) fallen or demoted ex-Gusti with no twice-born title who often, however, display lore revealing their ultimate relation to Arya

Kencheng. Following many *lontar* manuscripts, to qualify as legitimately Satria a group must display three attributes: holy men (*rsi*), plentiful subjects, and pervasive influence. This quasi-achievement theory of caste is advanced to oppose views that emphasize descent. Brahmana experts are sometimes accused of suppressing the achievement theory, for example by concealing texts that stipulate a criminal Brahmana must be lowered in caste.

Tabanan district overlords in particular are remembered for demoting under-achievers. This policy resulted in a proliferation of groups known as Bulu Pada – a joking Indonesian term shortened from *bulu ramput pada kaki*, ('head hairs on feet') which implies an inversion of rank. Bulu Pada designates a Gusti who, although still able to pay homage in an Arya Kencheng ancestral temple, possesses no official function, house property, or other visible index of his hypothetical status. This division of Tabanan's Gustis echoes more formal divisions in the superior Arya Kepakisan of Klungkung. Tabanan informants outline three levels in Arya Kepakisan: (1) the Ida I Dewa (including the ultimate Dewa Agung); (2) demoted Dewas known as Pungakan; and (3) a potentially commoner level known as Sang in the east, Gagus in Tabanan, and Bagus in Buleleng. The divisions relate to Hindu legal notions whereby criminal groups descend in caste but retain their *arya*. Friederich mentions Pungakan (along with Dessak and Pradewa) as 'names of Satrias who have much Sudra blood in their veins' (1849: 110). Current rival interpretations consider the Pungakan level less a fallen Satria than a separate group descended from a Brahmana; this makes each level a different *arya*. (It should be stressed that most Balinese conceptualize caste in terms of temple affiliations, personal titles, and manifest prerogatives. Only literati bother over *arya* labels as outlined in the *Usana Bali* and other texts.) Informants admit that the analogy between the levels of Tabanan Gustis and Klungkung Dewas is imperfect. Gusti levels are expressed in Gusti Ngurah versus Gusti versus absence of title; while Dewas have terms for their lower levels plus secondary status qualifications, such as descent from a lesser Brahmana. In contrast the Gustis and Bulu Padas of Tabanan can claim superiority only through connections to Arya Kencheng.

These native interpretations across kingdoms of the Satria-Wesia-Sudra dimension facilitate current mobility in title caste. For example, Tabanan district has experienced a proliferation of Dewa groups. In precolonial Tabanan only one Dewa line, brought from the east to serve as court medical sages, was officially recognized. It was presumably the sole exception to the rule that a Gusti-Ngurah raja should possess no Dewa subjects whose title implied superiority. Any other Dewa groups that migrated to Tabanan were received as demoted Gagus (level three). In keeping with their rigidification of the caste system, the Dutch colonial courts considered Gagus as ordinary Sudras and enforced no punishment if a Gagus woman married a commoner. But today Gagus groups can activate Dewa titles and temple shrines in their Tabanan residences. Such mobility is possible, informants comment, because now there is no law against it.

In the village-area of Soka, for example, many supposedly Gagus residents have been contacting eastern Dewa groups at their ancestral temples on *odalan* day to confirm their status. Informants explain that sometimes an eastern Dewa receives a Tabanan Gagus and allows him to pay homage, for a price, while not truly believing his claims inwardly. However, the eastern Dewa risks displeasing purist members of his own group, who might eventually even refuse to demonstrate ritual familial contamination (*sebel*) upon his death. It would be easier for an ambitious Gagus houseyard to verify its superior status by receiving recognition from the old legitimate Dewas in Tabanan. But this authentic Arya Kepakisan group is chary with such favors; its members could well refuse to eat from the same plate (*saling charik*) of the aspirant during the ancestor-temple ceremony.

Typically, then, an ambitious Gagus returns from his sally eastward with fresh evidence of Dewa standing, such as witnesses to the ceremonial commensality and/or a reworked genealogy. Informants recall that after the Dutch were ousted and before political party activity intensified, many impoverished Satria-Wesia lines in Klungkung and Gianyar discreetly sent scouts to other districts to contact status seekers. Genealogies (*silsilah*) were then prepared in the form of sacred *prasasti* manuscripts; the palm leaves were stored in a smutty hearth for aging and later sold to the appropriate commoners when they journeyed east seeking an elevated source. Many elevations are necessarily unofficial, especially if a kinsman belongs to the civil service, the military, or some other organization with records of his group's prior title. But unofficially the superior rank can be expressed in the prerogatives of burial and cremation, if the elevated group can convince a Brahmana *pedanda*, required to perform the higher ceremony, of its legitimacy. Today in Bali priests hesitate to dispute their followers' claims, since a devoted body of clients rather than a powerful raja is often a main source of livelihood. Within a set of houseyards the wealthier family heads sometimes spearhead upward mobility, and they oblige their lower, less presumptuous kin to affirm the claims. However a strong *banjar* or even *desa* might impede such actions by its members.

Resistance

Balinese positively disposed toward these Gusti developments favor the chance for undifferentiated localities to sprout *triwangsas* whose elevated lifestyles, they feel, can benefit everyone. Yet what appears in remote, local contexts as a reenactment of the basic hierarchical impulse that achieved Hindu-Bali, appears in more sophisticated, long stratified, courtly towns as belated petty ambition, superficial status play. Accordingly, a status seeker from a remote area might allude to his caste affairs with embarrassment in town, where residents hope to preserve their own exclusivity. A few progressive citizens who espouse the traditional achievement view of worth and rank consider such issues merely a matter of social graces and politeness. In schools oriented to the Indonesian nation, children are taught that if one is clever and skillful, one deserves to be addressed as a Satria. One 'liberated' Tabanan

Sudra explains his views this way: If he bumps into the I Gusti of the royal line (Arya Kencheng) of subkingdom Krambitan, he will ask: '*Ke dja, 'tu*?' (Where to, [Ra] tu?) This is because he knows this Satria age peer personally. But an individual who received his livelihood from the Satria would call him not simply by the honorific Ratu, but by the more highly honorific Ratu Ngurah. He goes on to say that if he met a lower Gusti Ngurah or Gusti, he might be less fastidious and call him not Ratu but simply Anak Agung (the general *triwangsa* designation in Tabanan), depending on his actual importance. As for certain other Gustis, while some people address them as elevated Ratus, he would never do so, but would use Anak Agung or perhaps even Gusti. This Sudra proclaims such niceties unimportant, but he calls his own first-born and fifth-born sons by the privileged birth-order title Putu!

Thus as Gagus becomes Dewa or Bulu Pada becomes Gusti, the traditional argument of what constitutes legitimacy of caste-status is revived. Gusti mobility often requires contacts across districts; mobile houseyards profit both from the demise of an overlord's power to control the prestige hierarchy among his subjects and from ambiguities in the scheme of caste. But it is those would-be Gusti houseyards with no traditional basis of legitimacy that are disparaged as the newest of the *baru*. They must go overboard in professing respect to a genuine Gusti line in order to receive token reciprocal honorifics. Their detractors point out comical contradictions in their status expressions. Some call themselves Gusti yet employ commoner biers in their cremation ceremonies. Gossipy stories dwell on the problems that often ensue, for example: Gusti Si Doman luckily had already gained a higher honorific before landing a job; but there is a brother Gde Anon (laughter) who, if he followed suit, would have to sacrifice his salary, since there is no Gusti Anon on his office rolls (much laughter). Detractors add that in olden days any nouveau Gustis could have been killed for such presumptions. In contrast they praise those worthy citizens of Tabanan who have authentic ties to superior eastern groups, but who rest content with commoner status designations in their adopted district. Accordingly any new Gustis advance their claims guardedly. They might require of their immediate neighbors Gusti titles of address, while not pressing the point with affines.

Or, as we saw in Chapter 6, the contrary is also possible. Consider, for example, the case of an elevated Sudra youth who ran away with a girl whose family had been aspiring to the title of Gusti. The suitable official was engaged by the boy's parents to inform her family. The official and the boy's representatives were obliged to wait at the girl's house because her father was still working his paddy. He later walked in, muddy from his labors, and assembled his brothers in their ceremonial pavilion. The official verified what his symbolic lamp foretold: their daughter had out of love voluntarily run away with her intended, taking such and such jewelry, watch, and clothing; the marriage would take place on date X, and would they attend? The formula question was answered with the negative formula response. Thus the daughter was for all purposes thrown away by her mud-covered nouveau-Gusti father, whose kinsmen had two short generations earlier given a woman to this very suitor's grandfather, before they began hoisting their title. Such is the way with many once brotherly (*beraya*) relations across temple groups in contemporary Bali.

The list of tactics in social mobility is long and varied. Three examples particularly scorned by self-appointed purists were the following: (1) A supposedly fallen Satria in the district general assembly took the name of Subamia – Tabanan's traditional Gusti military experts. His opponents decried this obvious effort to dazzle the eyes of voters. That this was a matter of simple political expediency became clear when the true Subamia group refused to admit him to its ancestral temple. (2) Many teachers employed far from their home districts refer in passing to their *aryas* while still using commoner names. (3) In some Tabanan *banjars*, several houseyards have adopted the Gusti label *jero*; they have even posted name plates on their gates, while their spatial dimensions and single portals proclaim to all knowledgeable parties their commoner status.

Opponents of these tactics admit that if a friend so indulges himself, they go ahead and call him Anak Agung, without employing the whole gamut of Balinese honorific speech, just to keep on good terms and 'so they will still be able to borrow what he has that they need.' They cite sacred texts to affirm that genuine Satrias or Wesias who are impoverished or have no official function corresponding to their rank would never seek such recognition. Yet the purists themselves reveal something of a double standard, since they disparage even those new Gustis who display traditional evidence of forgotten status to back up any recent occupational strides. In this case the opponents of renewed Gustis appear to feel the achievement criterion of rank applied once, but they deny the theory's relevance to the contemporary new rich. Many current ambitious groups can use the same theory to justify their own reaffirmations of timeless rank in light of their renewed prosperity. None of this disputation is a simple product of modernization or nationalization; rather it is implicit in the basic traditional theories of Balinese caste and status.

Status pride and group effort

Opponents of emerging Gustis disparage the protocular acknowledgment they wrest from their newly perceived inferiors. Yet the opposition overlooks, and perhaps intentionally, the potential sociological importance of redefined rank. New Gustis attain more than empty expressions of obsequiousness; they achieve a means of relating to a translocal temple-network and its affiliates, imputed kinsmen, as well as the respect of the inferiors who acknowledge them. Being a Gusti enables one to attend the temples of an *arya*. Usually this advantage affords few practical benefits; but without such a network built on status claims, no concerted group effort is even conceivable. In schism-prone Balinese social organization, group cooperation is kindled only by the spark of status pride. For over three decades of Dutch administration, this spark was extinguished at levels of society below the entrenched ruling houses. In Chapter 4 we encountered a group which profited from the Dutch policy by strengthening its internal organization, while relaxing translocal temple connections.

The clearest case of actual economic advantages, one envied by many non-Gusti Tabananers, concerns a temple network centered in a village-area that straddled the old Tabanan-Mengwi border and consequently was a center of courtly standards of social organization. The several Gusti groups here have organized themselves as cloth dealers, complete with trade stations and retail outlets stretching between Den Pasar and Java. While the six Gusti houses involved compete among themselves for ultimate status honorifics, for the purposes of the cloth business their cooperation is exemplary. Each family that runs an outpost maintains an ancestor-temple shrine, and economic obligations follow the general lines of temple-network ritual observances. The material wealth of these Gustis and their complete liberation from field labor has grown legendary. Moreover, status competition among the six Gusti houses has intensified. In the early 1960s one of the group's leaders, also the head of the *desa*, wrote the governor of Bali to request official recognition of his house as part of Arya Kencheng, the royal line of Tabanan and Badung. As evidence of this rank he cited a testimony from a house in Karangasem district, reputedly Arya Kencheng. The subsequent rejection of his request was based on the principle that the Karangasem group could not qualify as Arya Kencheng, since this status is legitimate only in Tabanan and Badung. Regardless, his claim merited the attention of the island's top officialdom because of the conspicuous business success of these Gustis. Unlike the several cases of entrepreneurial activity reported among traditional twice-born Balinese in the 1950s (cf. C. Geertz 1963), these Gustis have continued to expand; they appear to have been most successful in harnessing practical organization to increasing status pride. (Another case of this pattern, this time among Sudras, will be discussed later.) Even one example of Gusti prosperity has caused many denigrators to take pause.

There is another reason to pay particular attention to emergent Gustis: they often receive the enthusiastic acknowledgment of the lowest commoners around them. Indeed, Bali reveals that general paradox of hierarchical systems: the most ardently antiegalitarian actors are often the lowest in the hierarchy. In areas distinguished by few high-caste attributes, there is evidence of quick popular support for newly detected Gustis. And wherever a full range of status distinctions already exists, it is the lowest strata who insist on careful distinctions among the divisions of the upper strata. Thus, for example, Badung district contains a village-area with two different lines of I Gusti Ngurahs, and only the superior one merits the honorific 'Anak Agung.' Both lines contain members who hold government jobs in Den Pasar; in this most cosmopolitan urban setting of Bali the lower Gusti Ngurah presents himself as Anak Agung to new acquaintances. Yet if someone inquired after him as Anak Agung in his own *desa*, no commoner would profess to know him under such a title. There is general consensus as to the relative rank of these lines, and in any village ceremony graced by the attendance of both, Sudras meticulously distinguish the higher from the lower by style of food container, speech, and the range of honorifics.

The lowest commoners in Bali's hierarchy still tend to support classic distinctions among their betters, and they quickly recognize the legitimacy of new Gustis, often hoping themselves to move up a notch in their reciprocal honorifics. Such pervasive procaste sentiments are enough to suggest that Balinese commoners are far from alienated. But perhaps the clearest evidence of the hold of hierarchy on the lower ranks of society is the peculiarly Balinese turn taken by the growth of the Communist party (PKI) in the early 1960s. One remote area studied in 1972 had been a center of PKI organization until the party collapsed during the GESTAPU reaction in 1965. During its rapid growth in Bali the PKI rallied followers around the issue of land reform by denouncing high-caste feudal proprietors and demanding that they should surrender their excessive paddy holdings to the masses. At the same time, however, PKI officials in this remote center, all of them kinsmen from the traditional Gusti houseyards that had been established here to guard a mountainous frontier of old Tabanan kingdom, consolidated their local influence by reemphasizing the traditional ties between these subjects and their resident Gustis. As the power of PKI increased, these officials accentuated their caste privileges, while providing their followers with new roads, better market areas, and increased prosperity. When PKI collapsed and these officials disappeared, other anti-PKI family members who had emigrated during the early 1960s returned home. One of them had converted to Christianity, and he assumed authority in the now leaderless Gusti houseyards so recently under the sway of PKI. He managed to convert the old pro-PKI Gusti group effort into a new pro-Christian one, or at least one which tolerates missionizing in the region. Yet again, it is the sense of caste distinctions that persists and that has lent a semblance of continuity to the different ideological thrusts of these reemergent Gusti overlords – sometimes 'atheist' (the Bali-Hindu epithet for PKI), sometimes Christian, but always hierarchical.

In Bali today, the most effective way to consolidate a following for a group effort remains renewal of status ties. The ranked exchange of benefits implied by the concept hierarchy has yet to be eliminated by a realpolitik of outright coercion.

The party of the popular elite

Pasek is a Balinese term for groups with traditional rights to local administrative offices. The Pasek-people (Warga Pasék) today refers to an entire organization of elevated Sudra ancestor-groups which, like high castes, trace their origins to the Javanese Majapahit epoch or before. The fourteenth-century vanquishers of Bali reportedly brought with them Pasek experts in war, local government, and religion to serve as village-area officials. Pasek traditions relate that the founding hero of Hindu-Bali, Gaja Mada, originally licensed Brahmana leaders to oversee the island's local administration, but they proved incompetent and were replaced with the

Pasek. These Pasek eventually came to employ the personal title I Gde; their purified ceremonial specialists bore the honorific Empu; and like the high castes, they never used teknonymous-looking systems of naming as did 'indigenous Balinese.'[1]

This ideology, which enables members of the Warga Pasek figuratively to assert 'I am Brahmana,' does not characterize all groups called Pasek. There are, for example, Pasek Kayu Selem who classify their descent by plant categories. But true Warga Pasek traditions correlate with a set of sacred shrines called Chatur Paryangan, devoted to several legendary brothers who bore the once-Brahmana honorific Empu. In 1972 a Pasek religious expert enumerated the sacred landmarks: One shrine in the heart of classical Hindu-Bali (Gelgel) commemorates Empu Gana who had no descendants. Another shrine in Karangasem (East Bali) is dedicated to Empu Kuturan who possibly begat one daughter who remained in Java. (Pasek literati are currently researching these matters, in particular a Javanese shrine traced to Erlangga's tenth-century reign and dedicated to Empu Berada, thought to be the progenitor of Brahmana and Satria; thus Pasek literati refer to a pre-Majapahit era to legitimate their status.) A third shrine at the Balinese state temple Besakih is for Empu Sumeru, who also bore no descendants. Finally, a fourth shrine in Bali commemorates Empu Gde Jaya who begat the seven descendants, who in turn presumably generated the whole current population of Balinese Warga Pasek. A sacred genealogy traces the progeny of these seven to a contemporary assortment of local Pasek ancestor-groups.

Thus, like Satria, Pasek believe they are descended from Brahmana stock; but they never gained authority to rule, only to administer locally. They currently comprise the island's largest category of elevated commoners and enjoy a popular reputation for cleverness in governmental and military matters, suggested by envious remarks such as: 'If you're a village leader, you've got to be Pasek! They're smart all right; why Sukarno was of Pasek blood by his mother.'

Campaign methods

Recent efforts to revitalize ideas of a special Pasek social role have sometimes been denigrated by non-Pasek as 'smelling of politics' (Ind. *berbau politik*). Even before the elections of 1955, there were rumors of bickering between Pasek and ordinary Bendesa groups, who provide heads of village areas, over their relative ranks. But the movement to unify the true descendants of the seven Pasek ancestors gained momentum after 1965, during the confusion produced by the anticommunist reaction. Before the elections of 1971, leaders tried to secure a Pasek seat in a district assembly by arguing that the district's Pasek population was its largest constituency. Their effort failed, possibly because of worries by the Nationalist party (PNI) over any potential split in its ranks. Informants say that before the GESTAPU the Pasek included many communists, but after it they were largely PNI. By 1971, many were joining the functional groups (GOLKAR) created by Suharto's administration to replace ideological parties. Several districtwide meetings of Pasek groups were planned in different regions, with all-Bali Pasek conventions in 1969 and 1970. Then in 1971 a Pasek leader tried to enlist the support of a respected Pasek elder to help form a stronger district branch in Gianyar. In 1972 some observers felt the elder's visible reluctance foreshadowed the waning of the Pasek movement under Indonesia's new COLKAR antiparty political system.

Regardless, the fact that the movement can consolidate a popular representational base while employing an idiom of exclusivist caste principles to authenticate its membership is suggestive of the, persistently disowned, flexibility in Balinese social status, religion, and politics. This apparent paradox of hierarchical populism can be penetrated by considering the fundamental Balinese premise that most troubles arise from neglecting, or worst of all forgetting, the ancestors. Typically several brothers suffering some misfortune – illness, crop failure – will seek the advice of a magician-healer (*balian*). The latter often diagnoses a failure to propitiate the ancestors and recommends they go in quest of their true origins. He might even specify a particular Pasek temple worth visiting on its festival day, to determine if it is the proper ancestral source. Brahmana priests, knowledgeable in the legends of forgotten Pasek status after the collapse of Gelgel, are often enlisted to search manuscripts for clues illuminating true origins. If the elders in the Pasek temple receive them, the brothers make a payment – perhaps a bit of gold and three meters of white cloth – and they become Pasek, although not necessarily acknowledged as such back home. Unlike Gusti status, any commoner might aspire to be recognized as Pasek in perfect confidence that he merits this embellished standing.

A doubtless exaggerated report on the scope of rediscovery of Pasek origins appears in the organization's magazine, *Warta Duta Warga*, whose contents, in Indonesian and Balinese, include traditional Hindu texts, articles on Bali-Hindu philosophy, a printout of the chronicle collected from palm-leaf manuscripts which legitimizes Pasek authority, and information on the proper construction and dedication of Pasek houseyard temples. Each issue also contains a section of progressive compilation of Pasek ancestor temples (*ring pura-pura paibon, panti, dadia*) – with every temple's location, information on its founding, and names of its religious custodian, chief elder, and chairman of its council. Finally, the number of family heads who support the temple is noted, a figure ranging between ten and two thousand per temple. By temple sixty-three the Pasek movement already tabulated as members around 5 percent of the family heads in Bali. Judging from the potential redefinition of old temples and statuses, no end was in sight.[2]

Differences in local social organization affect the feasibility of converting to Pasek status. If an area has several established Pasek ancestor-groups, the process can be restricted, since a group that admits aspirants is apt to be downgraded by its rivals. On the other hand, there are economic advantages to augmenting the family heads who finance a temple's ceremonies and repairs. One possible compromise can allow for a continued aura of exclusivity while meeting practical financial needs: local expansion is restricted but geographically distant members can be affiliated.

The latter, although not part of the death-contamination (*sebel*) group, contribute maintenance costs. In conservative regions traditional overlords may retain a voice in authenticating memberships of any caste-status, as may a strong village-area or hamlet organization. Thus, the Pasek movement has the greatest potential for sweeping local effects in areas characterized by few antecedent distinctions in caste-status.

Each case is particular. For example, in Sangolan village-area near Tabanan town sixty family heads support the Pasek ancestral temple in neighboring Pangkong Prabhu, ten more than a few years ago. According to informants, after family illnesses the new supporters 'remembered they were Pasek descendants, and now they are well received in Pangkong Prabhu.' Sangolan also boasts its own ancestor temple for the twelve Bendesa-type family heads who provide a leader of Sangolan desa. The local upper crust thus contains both the Pasek group and the Bendesa group which does not, yet, consider itself Pasek. These two groups claim sole rights to a minor honorific (Pan) rather than the ordinary peasant appellation (Nanang) – a privilege articulated several years ago by a Pasek who was the area's only salaried civil servant. Paseks and Bendesas vie over who merits the more prestigious spot in the graveyard and similar matters.

Of particular interest here is the story that in olden days Sangolan was split into three divisions by the raja, each apportioned to a different specialist who provided ritual holy water. Two divisions were the clients (*sisia*) of Brahmana Siwa *pedandas*; the third, however, became clients of the holy man in Pangkong Prabhu, a mystic in charge of the Pasek ancestor temple. This situation is susceptible of two different interpretations. Either the Sangolan clients were construed as kinsmen of these Pasek, since a Pasek holy man (*empu*) sanctifies water only for his own kinsmen. Or the royal house considered the Pasek holy man as equivalent to a Brahmana priest and thus one who can maintain non-kin clientele. Regardless, it is a telling sign of current social dynamics that the Sangolan-Pangkong Prabhu relationship, retrospectively coded as a guru-client bond, is today coded in terms of kinship relations of an interlocal Pasek ancestor-group.

Participation in a Pasek temple, which is theoretically part of a network of locales sacred to an enormous group descended from a single Javanese *empu*, involves an area in the higher Hindu strain of Balinese culture. By becoming Pasek, commoners accumulate more ancestral spirits to watch over their interests, spirits enhanced through commemoration in texts. If enough houseyards agree on their status and discover which Pasek temple they issued from, they can in turn construct an ancestor temple, the members of which might tend then to marry within the temple congregation. (Some observers contend that Pasek-type houseyards may build an ancestor temple with fewer members than other kinds of commoners, since they have automatic links with Pasek in other areas.) The new congregation, whose core group manifests mutual religious contamination, represents an additional source-point in the expanding Pasek network. A new Pasek gains the practical benefits of potentially influential associates. But he also assumes financial obligations to support additional temple ceremonies; sometimes brothers are divided over whether they should assert Pasek status.

Opponents and prospects

Unsurprisingly, opponents of the Pasek movement challenge its legitimacy. They insist that Sengguhu and Pande ancestor-groups, which provide specialists in exorcist rites and in metal work, contain no false members: there are no 'new Sengguhus.' It is argued that earlier the raja alone could recognize a new Pasek. Even the Dutch are said to have allowed only authentic Paseks to be *desa* officials. Opponents scoff at the obvious profiteering when outsiders are admitted to ancestral festivals. 'Seventy-five percent of Bali seems to be Pasek,' they joke. They deride political jockeying by officials who allow the rededication of a temple as a Pasek shrine. Such events in Tabanan may attract a district chief official, the district leader of the national ministry of religion, and an officer from Parisada, an organization for rationalizing Bali-Hindu now that it is officially recognized by Jakarta (see Chapter 9). Opponents deny that these affairs constitute, as their participants insist, a valid continuation of tradition, in which the then-district-chief (the raja) and his functionaries supervised such dedication ceremonies.

Even when the authenticity of a new or refurbished Pasek temple is unquestionable, any obviously opportunistic political overtones provoke cynicism. Consider the case of an important civil servant from the primary source of Pasek officials in old Tabanan kingdom. He recently acquired a government house in the capital where he now keeps his first wife (a Sundanese) and their children; back home a second wife, his patricousin, looks after the old folks. A new dwelling requires a new house-temple, and on the propitious day a *pemangku* and a group of elders were trucked forty-odd miles, from the ancestral source, to conduct the dedication ceremony. They sat cross-legged upon grass mats crowded onto the front stoop. The guests, a cosmopolitan array of officials, sat inside in aluminum folding chairs, smoking Kansas brand cigarettes, and drinking beer and palm wine to the recorded tune of 'Two Lonely Flowers Surround my Heart with Tears,' waiting to consume the traditional ceremonial feast being prepared back in the kitchen. Outside were the skeletal elders from the sacred source. Inside was the corpulent power contingent which included – and this is what mattered – the head of Badung district, himself a Pasek who came to witness the dedication of a bureaucratic bungalow to the ancestors he shares with this up-and-coming member of his constituency. Afterwards, non-Paseks who had witnessed all this scoffed well into the night.

Membership in a Pasek ancestor-group allows an individual greater flexibility in forwarding a career by enabling him to delegate *banjar* and *subak* responsibilities to kinsmen who can also represent his religious interests back home. Yet there are differences of opinion among Pasek and non-Pasek alike concerning the ultimate goals of their movement. The organization seeks unity, a familial feeling among both old and newly rediscovered Pasek. Some hope to convert this solidarity into a means of controlling a vote bloc at various levels of government. Others seek merely to coordinate Pasek control within the Balinese bureaucracy. After independence, it is explained, Pasek individuals were fragmented and their lines grew even more obscure. Now, since they number many government employees, Pasek leaders hope to increase bureaucratic efficiency, to control access to white-collar positions, and thus to endow the traditional category of Pasek with pragmatic advantages. A Pasek pedigree is one of the surest ways to win a salaried position in contemporary Bali.

Thus we find both in the upper echelons and at the grassroots a combination of aims and motives. The Pasek movement is on the one hand a cultural endeavor to unify all true Paseks as naturally endowed administrators, to revitalize what in Java would be called a *priyayi* sector. But it is equally an opportunistic political maneuver to consolidate a bureaucratic in-group and to build an effective vote bloc as (prior to 1971, at least) an alternative to the Nationalist party. Moreover, the movement capitalizes on both the yogic-mystic proclivities of leaders and the enlivened sense of ritual obligations of their followers, whether real or imputed kinsmen. The combined political, social, and religious aspects of the Pasek phenomenon – this modern lateralization of a prestigious Sudra caste-status – are neatly subsumed in an informant's traditionalistic commentary:

> The Warga Pasek are looking for their source, for family connections. They are seeking their deified ancestors (*kawitan*). Now the *lontar Jatua Sarasmuscaya* disproves the *kawitan* theory; it says there is only one *kawitan* (God – Ind. *Tuhan*), which has broken up because of the various social functions. But people still search for their own kind, in order to eat with them, yes, in order to have someone to eat with.

Caste in parturition

Antosari is a government-designated area in western Tabanan district. Progressive and commercial, it straddles the Dutch-built road between Java and the Balinese capital Den Pasar. Around four-hundred heads of families inhabit the vicinity, which contains twelve hamlet councils whose members are distributed into four customary village-areas and fragments of other village-areas. In recent years some eighty households have transmigrated to Sulawesi; they represent a welcome success in the government's long-faltering transmigration program. (Sulawesi's advantages are, in contrast to Sumatra, hilly terrain and enough water to support a traditional Balinese irrigation system.) During 1971–1972 the national transmigration office sponsored return trips to Bali for the most enthusiastic migrants, and the Antosari contingent persuaded another score to join them in Sulawesi. Among those convinced were many members of prospering Pasek groups. Although a transmigrant might sell his paddy to kinsmen, he is required to contribute enough land to cover his share of costs for cremating any ancestors not yet exhumed.

Determining origins

West of Antosari stretches a region first opened by the Dutch in 1913. Precolonial Antosari lay beyond the subkingdom of Krambitan, under the Tabanan raja's collateral, which marked the western extreme of courtly society. Judging from present-day ranks, even due east there were no Satria-Wesia houses and only a few Brahmana *grias*. The only glimmer of Hindu hierarchy in old Antosari emanated from an ambiguous group reputedly descended from a forebear exiled from Tabanan's noble neighborhood. There is an elaborate legend about the group's founding hero: how his shameful exile was transformed into a legendary trek; how by white magic this mystic sage foiled the raja's men, achieved miracles, and finally settled beside a river on haunted ground normally uninhabitable. His descendants still live there and use this legend to explain how the house of an exiled Gusti came eventually to bear the Brahmana label *gria*. They say the founder's healing powers won him the devotion of the simple surrounding folk. By these devices, it appears, a courtly caste configuration slipped into commoner Antosari behind the raja's back, and a controversially Brahmana house emerged, complete with providers of holy water for loyal supporters and its own graveyard for exclusive cremation ceremonies. In the colonial period the group's holy men sought official recognition as Brahmana *pedandas* by the courts, but they were refused. Today, however, even officially legitimate priests agree that the remarkable feature of the riverside house is its capacity to attract and maintain outsider *sisias*.

Although two kilometers away, this group participates in Antosari's northeast hamlet, also the source of many transmigrants and populated largely by Pasek, at least recently. Elaborations of Antosari's local ranks currently concern four local Pasek branches: (1) Pasek Gelgel; (2) Pasek Tangguntiti; (3) Pasek Toh Jiwa; and (4) Pasek Antosari. The first two groups trace their origins to the traditional Pasek source-points named in their titles. The Pasek Toh Jiwa claim to stem from a group in a subkingdom bordering on Tabanan. Finally, Pasek Antosari is a laughable title to some, since Antosari is obviously not a traditional Pasek source. This admittedly new group first felt it originated from Toh Jiwa and then leaned toward either Emas (a Pasek source in Gianyar district) or Gelgel. Its members are still examining chronicles, but they now frequent the festivals at Emas. Whether they are Gelgel or Toh Jiwa might appear a moot point, since the latter themselves arose from Gelgel before migrating, and they still have shrines in the Pasek Gelgel temple. But the issue is potentially vital for discerning the relative rank of Pasek Antosaris among Paseks. One other Sudra group of Pande title (traditional smiths) has its own minor temple, an offshoot of a larger one in a neighboring subkingdom. There are as yet no Pasek temples, not even a partially independent *pura pemaksan* (which is actually the highest level temple that could be built here, since the only legitimate larger Pasek *panti* temples in Tabanan district are still considered to be in Tangguntiti and Wanogiri.) Thus, apart from the previously mentioned *sisia-guru* bonds, Pasek classification represents the apical Bali-Hindu pattern of Antosari. Finally, certain Pasek leaders claim their group's women are forbidden to marry into the anomalous Brahmana house – another instance of restricting hypergamy so to elevate a specialized Sudra line as superior to ordinary wife-providers.

Antosari arrives

In spite of their still obscure origins, the Pasek groups have been busily correlating their status claims with specific functionary rights. For now Pasek superiority is expressed less by corroborating distinctive religious origins and more by apportioning rights to temple duties and protocular forms. The Pasek Tangguntiti families do not yet share in the division of offices. Although theoretically their status claims are most easily verified, they have not confirmed them with written texts; they do, however, claim the privilege of using burial and cremation towers. Based on the eastern Balinese archetype of hierarchy, the Pasek Gelgel should merit the highest biers and the highest honorifics since the eastern Pasek Gelgel are considered descendants of the eldest brother in the legendary chronicles. But the Pasek Gelgel of Antosari have yet to assert these privileges.

As might be expected Pasek Antosari (Emas) is the least protocol-minded group; in light of its subordinate position, it has more to gain by stressing the exclusive tasks outlined in Pasek traditions. Its members claim special official rolls at a nearby temple sacred to the general population of Tabanan district. The fifteen Pasek Antosari family-heads organize and oversee the festivals here, and they are responsible for all-night watches when the gods descend. It is not forbidden for other Paseks to assist but this group is in charge; they are already educating a successor for the current priest-custodian (*pemangku*). The Pasek Gelgel and Pasek Toh Jiwa reserve the right to supply *pemangkus* for Antosari's *desa* temple-cluster, in which special duties in preparing offerings are reserved for the Pande group as well. People in Antosari realize that their own practices fall short of Bali's exemplary East, where the prescribed group must fill its special offices, even if none of its members desires to. If this unlikely situation arose in Antosari, the position would simply revert to another group.

Antosari thus demonstrates caste-statuses in parturition, born of the consolidation and redefinition of temple groups articulated by the Pasek ideology. We can speculate that competition over ritual protocol will gradually increase, especially in the ultimate sphere of Balinese religion: differential funeral privileges. As neighbors argue their ranks, there is little danger of exhausting the supply of offices which express status, since new temples can always be erected. For example, sixty northern households recently broke away from the Antosari village-area to build a separate origins-temple where, a religious expert divined, a long-forgotten temple once stood. The new temple will provide more meticulously differentiated duties for the ranks of Paseks.

The emergence of a debatable hierarchy of exclusive temple functions, all of which must be confirmed by certain government officials, has been accelerated by the area's commercial prosperity. Moreover, one can connect the recent success of the transmigration program here with the intensification of Pasek traditions. Antosari presents an exception to the general stereotype, as pervasive inside Bali as outside, that no Balinese could bear to abandon his island. But the apparent exception actually reflects the hope of Pasek enthusiasts to extend their distinctive ancestor-groups to new locales. Transmigrants to Sulawesi more willingly leave their kinsmen and local customary obligations and privileges, knowing that their family and collaterals constitute a thriving temple-network. While establishing a productive Balinese *subak*-system in a strange territory, they can rest assured that 'the people they eat with' will tend to their ritual interests in Antosari – this sacred source that remains available if the absentees wish to return there, physically or spiritually.

Thus, ancestor ideology in Antosari today plays a role similar to the one it played in fourteenth-century Java when, as legend has it, the advent of Bali's first Hindu-Java temple brought civilization to the rustic Bali Aga. Pasek enthusiasts openly espouse the view that, just as the generals of Gaja Mada once bestowed on Bali Majapahit standards of court and temple, so now have Pasek groups conveyed to lowly Sulawesi new congregations who trace their superior origins to Antosari. From Java to Bali and from Bali to Sulawesi, the traditional process of Hinduization continues, however altered its scale or diminished its courtly aura.

Principles of recrudescence

The growth of the Balinese gentry appears to have been largely endogenous (C. Geertz 1963: 101n).

We have patched together Dutch colonial views of caste, native literary accounts, retrospects by reflective Balinese, and current regional and local developments to suggest the criteria that continue to set off upper from lower in Balinese experience. Little detailed information has been given about Bali's dazzling surface of status expressions, the varied language levels to express refined *politesse* (cf. Kersten 1948: 7–14), ranks of housestyles and shrines, death and cremation privileges, and the related ritual paraphernalia: heights and ingredients of offerings, rights to use banyan leaves, which variety of chicken feathers one merits from the rich classification of plumages, and so on. While nothing in the natural or social surroundings escapes the imprint of hierarchy, we have stressed the social and cultural criteria of status because, even as some of their more flamboyant expressions become unpracticable, the criteria themselves still play a great, and perhaps even an increasing, role in Bali today.

Social mobility and neutrality

The view held by some outsiders and Balinese alike that caste is eclipsing is based mainly on the diminishing opportunities, and in some circles the diminishing will, to dwell on its expression. In Tabanan town this view is occasionally propounded by a supercillious Gusti or Gusti Ngurah. The classical system has vanished, they say; Satria and Brahmana alike are no longer respected by the people, except perhaps in Karangasem. Independence killed caste, they insist; one need only sample the high government office-holders: the head of Tabanan's general assembly is a Brahmana, but his assistant is a Sudra. The district leader (Bupati) and his secretary are Satria (-Wesias) but this is not always the case: after independence the first Bupati was the raja, then a Sudra took over, then a Brahmana, and now a Satria. Relative percentages aside, we should note that in true Satria-Wesia fashion, no mention is made of whether a preponderance of the Sudra in high positions might be Pasek. From a noble vantage such niceties in Sudra rank merit little concern. These grandees also overlook other values of ordinary commoners. But as a more sensitive informant noted, to a Tabanan paddy worker nothing on earth could sound more prestigious than 'Chokorda I Gusti Ngurah Gde – Angotta DPR Pusat,' which means, approximately, 'His Most Highly Revered Royal Highness, Member of the National General Assembly.'

Any surface indications that caste concerns are diminishing can be countered by other indications that they are reviving. Whereas of old, Arya Kencheng remained above and beyond customary hamlet affairs, today the royal houseyard members associate with a *banjar adat* for reciprocal burial and cremation tasks. Moreover low-slung, sometimes-functioning electric wires indeed block towering cremation biers from Tabanan's graveyard; thus caste is dead. Yet that caste survives is evident from the failure after independence to level Bali's personal titles by having everyone address each other with reciprocal Indonesian *bapak*. In time, people reverted to a ranked usage; and while they were at it, many did not simply resume their past titles but moved up a notch: Nang became Pan, and I became Gde. As political parties proliferated and their activity flourished during the 1950s and early 1960s, interest in caste apparently receded. But with the downturn in party politics since 1965, the resultant ideological vacuum has been filled by a resurgence of caste concerns, at least below the Satria ranks esconced in their *puris*.

When the traditional Balinese state apparatus, altered and propped-up during the colonial administration, finally collapsed during the Japanese occupation and Indonesian revolution, Balinese hierarchy persisted. As we have seen, after the fall of South Bali during 1906–8, the Dutch unwittingly undermined the state system by redefining the nature of relations between subjects and overlords and by territorializing the organization of the kingdoms. The old system of vertical allegiances expressed in ceremony, warfare services, and taxation in kind was reconstrued as a feudalistic social control based on land holdings. Colonial administrators applied the *warna* scheme to categorize Balinese society, and of course the royal houses they recognized supported this policy. Yet since the final undoing in 1965 of post-colonial elitist preferences and policies (perpetuated by Sukarno's regime which identified with and favored Bali's courtly sector when granting licenses and providing stimulus for economic development), Balinese commoners have continued to vie for enhanced caste-status, even without the actual example of powerful royal houses before their eyes.

The mobility of the 1970s looks vastly different from the precolonial period, only if one assumes that traditional caste divisions were rigid. Judging from that assumption, the demise of the state system would have released around 90 percent of the population – the outsider Sudra masses – into unauthorized and unprecedented status competition. Yet, as we have stressed throughout this account, colonial tallies of the *triwangsa* as clear-cut Brahmana, Satria, and Wesia sectors inevitably relied on royalist sources. Consequently, informal caste censuses never revealed as much about Bali as they were presumed to. The figure obtained for *triwangsa*, around 6 to 10 percent, overlooked the shiftable boundaries of Wesia or Gusti ranks and the whole matter of elevated Sudra houses. The very assumption that caste memberships in Bali can be tabulated reinforced the tendency to view caste as a foreign intrusion coercively imposed on victimized communal farmers rather than an integral paradigm of prestige for all levels of Balinese society.

Colonial observers felt that the obscurities of Balinese caste arose from natives applying an imported Hindu legal and mythic code to old-fashioned *adat* practices. Moreover, we have documented the traditional contradictions between native theories of *warna* as achievement and *warna* as descent. The resurgence of Gusti expansion and the fresh articulation of Pasek-Sudra status suggest that Balinese caste inevitably entails contradictions and recurring mobility. Legendary, geographic mobility is part and parcel of the Balinese idea of caste, and social mobility does not deny hierarchy but vitalizes it.

Current developments suggest another aspect of Balinese caste which recalls M. Singer's demonstration that in modernizing India the persistence of caste practices requires 'a *compartmentalization* of two spheres of conduct and belief that would otherwise collide' (1972: 321). Similarly in Bali, colonial and postcolonial schools, banks, businesses, civil service offices, transportation services, and a few factories have given rise to strategies which neutralize expressions of status differences in contexts in which they impede necessary interaction. Yet current Balinese compartmentalization of caste-status recalls also that caste never dictated all relationships in every context; there are clear precedents for neutralization of relative ranks. In the performance of Balinese musical arts, for example, ritual caste-separation is put in abeyance. Musical performances in Bali contrast completely with Indic *jajmani* practices which restrict all ritual and practical skills to specific ranked social divisions:

Even in the thirties the informality of the [Balinese caste] system was evident in the organization of the gamelon, where musicians from all four [*warna*] classes could be found united in the occupation of making music (McPhee 1966: 13).

In a discussion of stratification in musical arts, D. Nash rightly singles out the 'Balinese scene where, despite considerable social stratification, musical cleavages have not developed' (1968: 776). Musicianship is just one instance of the general contrast between Bali and South Asia where, according to Hocart, every occupation is a priesthood, and 'castes are merely families to whom various offices in the ritual are assigned by heredity' (1950: 20). Moreover, Hocart continues:

> In the words '[a barber] is like a priest on the cremation ground' we have the key to the whole [caste] problem. [In Ceylon] the barber and the washerman, like the drummers, are not so much technicians as priests of a low grade, performing rites which the high-caste priest will not touch (1950: 20).

Bali never developed this differentiation and exclusivistic distribution of all ritual tasks because of two diametrically opposed dimensions in its social life. First, on the one hand, its arts are wide open, universalistic; the sundry fashions of entertaining gods and ancestors during temple festivals are performed according to interest and ability. Second, and in contrast, many ritual duties are not parceled among specialist groups because they are reserved for near kinsmen. Balinese are in-focused not only in marriage preferences, but in rites of corpse handling as well – not only endogamous but 'endofunereal.' In the distinctly Indonesian fixations of their culture, Balinese ritualize-in. There is no barberlike 'priest of the graveyard,' since it would be unthinkable to relinquish a family corpse to an outsider. Actual Balinese priests (*sengguhus*) associated with netherly forces style themselves after Brahmana *pedandas* to propitiate dark divinities. The rituals of these exorcist priests are sublimated and have nothing to do with tangible human corpses. Moreover, a Brahmana priest who officiates at a corpse preparation specifically does not handle the body; rather, insulated by his ritual purity, he sprinkles the holy water that converts it into a fully regaled princely figure.

The underlying neutrality of Balinese caste-status is most conspicuous in the organization of wet-rice agriculture. Paddy ownership was never a simple function of caste. Brahmana houses and sometimes specialized Sudra houses could escape agricultural responsibilities, but only so long as a royal sponsor maintained enough loyal subjects to insure a surplus for providing them with food. High-titled persons would, of course, disdain actual labor in the fields, and sharecropping to this day occurs widely. Rajas, the spiritual embodiment of the water, tried to benefit from surplus production and from the loose ends of the socioeconomic system: for example, they often amassed lands of heirless descendants and brought widows to their court. But newly opened wet-rice land has always been the property of the *subak* members who convert it into productive paddy (Liefrinck 1969: 4 ff). In principle a raja was answerable to the *subak* as was a commoner landowner. Overlordship did not pertain directly to agricultural production. The *subak* system, although sometimes improved through royal administration, was still controlled collectively (and is today) by the mutually interested, yet competing, local-level *subak* societies protecting their rights to water. The collapse of the state system has barely affected the design and effectiveness of the subsistence system. Above this local subsistence organization, antagonistic upper houses vied not for land but for subjects, just as current political movements vie for adherents.

A similar insulation of subsistence needs from status expressions obtains at the domestic level as well. While sons may be ranked according to both birth-order titles and mother's status, they are little differentiated by actual inheritance of agricultural property. In fact, birth-order titles insure that the prestige of sons can be graded more finely than mere wealth would allow. Thus the ideology of the Brahmana-Satria coalition in the affairs of the precolonial state expresses the same principle as the terminological ranking of sons over and above any differentiation by inheritance alone: the components of prestige versus power and wealth are distinct.

Cultural contradictions and *warna*

Finally, to appreciate the broader significance of status codes and the *warna* scheme in Balinese culture, we must stress again the relational quality of expressions of rank and caste. This quality is most conspicuous in simpler coding devices, such as birth-order terms used to rank offspring in cycles of four or five. Typically, Wayan is a birth-order term that positively labels the first purely positional stratum of offspring. It heads up the sequence 'Wayan, Made, Nyoman, Ktut' used as titles for the first four children and every four thereafter. But Wayan has a relational aspect as well: it designates lower commoner lines in contrast to the alternate 'Putu' of upper lines, likewise set in a sequence with Made (or Kadek), Nyoman (or Komang) and Ktut. The Wayan/Putu contrast serves as a diacritical to articulate different ranks of Balinese society at the domestic level.

But such diacritical aspects of cultural concerns do not always simply distinguish other spheres of social experience. Cultural diacriticals can also articulate conceptions of altogether different realms of existence. The ultimate significance of cultural ideas and codes is not to mesh perfectly with and to positively inform the sense of reality of social actors (that is, not to serve merely as a functionalist charter), but to achieve a sufficient balance between credibility and otherliness to render them worth thinking about or with at all. Cultural forms do not only define and infuse the known or subconsciously sensed; they posit the unknown, both the tabooed and the exemplary, that serves as backdrop to the known. Culture not only clarifies the ideal, it evokes the other.

These general points are critical, I think, in appreciating the place of the *warna* scheme in Balinese culture, especially as *warna* principles help legitimate the ranking of titled ancestor-groups. Consider, for example, the following functionalist comment about Indic *warna*, in light of the situational and relational qualities we have found in Balinese caste:

Thus the position of castes in the hierarchy as it actually exists is liable to change, whereas in the *varna* model the position of each *varna* is fixed for all time. It is really a matter for wonder that in spite of the distortions of the reality implicit in the *varna* model, it has continued to survive (Srinivas 1969: 4).

From our position it would be more cause for wonder if, given no distortions in the model, anyone, whether indigene or outsider, had ever been interested in South Asian *varna* at all. The functionalist outlook is inappropriate here because the value of any such scheme is the plausible paradox it establishes; ideals are supposed to distort. In the case of Bali, titles are particularly noteworthy for failing to correlate directly with anything:

The title system establishes an authoritative allocation of cultural prestige that is acknowledged and maintained in terms of the symbols of propriety and politesse, no matter how well or poorly it happens to fit with the realities of power, wealth, or character (Geertz 1967: 223).

Part of this authoritativeness in Bali stems from the *warna* scheme itself. Balinese titles and caste-statuses are more adequately viewed not as a risible ambition blind to the exigencies of reality, but as a native theory of prestige, senseless if it merely mirrors the pragmatics of individual interests in areas of economics or political power. D.F. Pocock has warned in another context against a pragmatic framework that would lead analyzers to credit people with 'an immense capacity for self-deception' (1967: 304). Accordingly, we should no more expect Balinese titles to be refuted by mere everyday reality than we should presume ideas of *karma-phala* and *samsara*, found especially in Brahmana circles (cf. *Upadeca* 1968), must crumble if wicked men are found to be happy. Nothing would be more absurd than a *karma-samsara* belief complex in a society in which each actor already possessed his cosmically just reward. Mythlike, any such theory's power lies in the feasible contradictions it accentuates. Distorted ranks are conferred at every level of Balinese society – *warna*, subcaste, houseyard (by mother's rank) and kitchen (by birth order). These expressions mutually reinforce each other and point to the ultimate cosmic-prestige hierarchy hitched to an antithesis of mundane social tasks as described in learned manuscripts. Titles help establish the cultural problem of pragmatically earned versus divinely endowed status. If the titles simply offered a redundant index of political power, they would ring hollow. It is the guaranteed lag in the hoped-for congruence of prestige and power that animates social life. Except for the theoretical, but nonexistent, acme of all status codes – a wealthy, powerful, first-born (of a patricousin mother) Brahmana-Kamenuh *pedanda* – every Balinese has self-interested reason to suspect that something is culturally out of gear – that his title is too low and another's is too high. Balinese titles, like Hindu *warna*-categories, perpetuate a contradiction that would not be there unless they were.

As *warna* is fundamentally problematic, so it is with many Balinese cultural concerns: the ambivalent value of patriparallel-cousin spouses, the worth of mother's descent, the kinship relations coded by varieties of temples in sacred space. These matters are what W.B. Gallie calls 'essentially contestable' (1968). Such fundamental arguments are far from the first thing one can know about a culture; as we have seen in our historical review, they are perhaps nearer the last. Moreover, from a certain viewpoint these concerns are epiphenomenal, in that, for the more immediate needs of social cohesion, Bali could conceivably degenerate into simple, agnatic paddy owners, capturing outsider, unallianced brides for houseyards unadorned by temple complexes and unenriched by their religious significance. Indeed, Bali might have lately been expected so to degenerate under conditions of nationalization. Instead, recurrent movements rise and fall to reformulate and shift the locus of hierarchy but never, yet, to dismantle it. The continued dynamics of Balinese caste are thus suggestive of the ordering power of beliefs and values, and it is perhaps justifiable to deem these dynamics 'romance.'

9. Images in action

Drama, like music, is an ensemble performance for an audience, and music and dance are most likely to flourish in a society with a strong consciousness of itself as a society, like Elizabethan England.

(Frye 1957: 249)

Literature and society converge in at least two important ways: actually in the tendency of many societies to style themselves according to literary ideals often borrowed from other places and times, and analytically in the occasional congruence between theories of social interpretation and schools of literary criticism.[1] That Balinese social forms are very much in touch with literary and dramatic images is indisputable, but an interpretative framework for understanding this intersection of the social and the imaginative has proved elusive. The best we can do is to hazard a few tentative suggestions concerning the social and ritual basis of Balinese literature and the literary and dramatic basis of society. But first we must briefly review a sociologically inadequate appreciation of the artistic quality of Balinese life.

The long swan song

I went there half-unwillingly, for I expected a complete 'bali-hoo,' picturesque and faked to a Hollywood standard; I left wholly unwillingly, convinced that I had seen the nearest approach to Utopia that I am ever likely to see (Gorer 1936: 42).

During the 1920s–1930s an assortment of European and American observers came to Bali to explore its expressive genres and personality types (cf. Belo 1970: Introduction). Some long-term residents felt they were witnessing the swan song of an abnormally artistic civilization and historical archaism:

Until the Dutch conquest in 1906, which brought in its train of schools, hospitals, taxation, Boy Scout clubs, and tourists, a medieval world had survived intact (McPhee 1970: 293).

This supposedly new secularization of the deeply religious Balinese was assumed to be the death knoll of their performing arts:

Under Dutch rule the island was at last consolidated, and divided into eight districts, each under the guided administration of some former regional ruler. A deep cultural change now began to take place. One by one the leading palaces relinquished their traditional formality and display. Court theaters were discontinued and gamelans sold to neighboring villages or given as payment for what were once feudal services. A few lesser nobles continued to keep their gamelans and maintain dancers, but in the thirties all court gamelans had become the property of village music clubs or reposed in government-run pawnshops (McPhee 1966: 5).

These Western devotees of Bali included painters, choreographers, and musicologists as well as anthropologists. They were actually witnessing more of a rejuvenation of arts and performances, partly in response to new tourist markets in the 1920s, which out of an inertia typical of Balinese enterprises continued into the Depression years. Fearing the Balinese way of life was moribund, they settled in to appreciate and document what remained of its psyche and muse. In general the contingent outside of colonial officialdom paid little attention to the copious Dutch material on Balinese history and society (Covarrubias 1937 and the earlier studies of J. Belo are notable exceptions). They appreciated in the island's arts and interior life an 'interwoven contrast between the serene and the turbulent' (Bateson 1973: 255), a quality which they sought either to evoke, imitate, record, publicize, or sometimes to explain.

Even the best ethnographic works of this period (De Zoete and Spies 1939; Bateson and Mead 1942) are marred by a hasty reliance on anecdotes shared among the resident enthusiasts. For example, few observers failed to echo comments like these:

When two strangers are brought together, it is necessary before they can converse with any freedom, that their relative caste positions be stated . . . When each knows the caste of the other, each will then know what etiquette and what linguistic forms he should adopt, and conversation can then proceed. Lacking such orientation, a Balinese is tongue-tied (Bateson 1949: 44).

It is not surprising that Bateson here chose a psychosomatic metaphor, in light of the then ascendant culture and personality school of cross-cultural studies. But such a 'tongue-tied Balinese' is most probably merely deciding which level of linguistic honorifics is suitable in the present context, not suffering, as was often implied, psychic breakdown out of social disorientation. Moreover, few accounts fail to retell the story of the Balinese youth who takes his first long-distance motor trip and upon disembarking falls ill muttering obsessively 'Where is Mountainward?' Anyone, even a non-Balinese, first experiencing the island's hilly and curvacious byroads and employing a Malayo-Polynesian locative would likely have reacted much the same way. But this case of car sickness plus linguistic idiom was taken to illustrate something special in the psychology and sociospatial orientation of these strange island inhabitants, whose culture was billed as 'less like our own than any other which has yet been recorded' (Bateson and Mead 1942: xvi).

Such comments suggest not the social romance of Bali but the kind of subjective romanticization which infused the impressions of many casual visitors between the wars. Out of 176 pages of plates in the famous album on Bali by Kraus and With (1922), twenty-six pages revealed nude bathers; consequently the Art Deco reading world came to see for itself. Perhaps the most effusive champion of the island's threatened joys was Grace Thompson Seton, who in her book *Poison Arrows: A Strange Journey with an Opium Dreamer through Annom, Cambodia, Siam, and the Lotus Isle of Bali* (1940) published a poem on Bali as 'A Vignette of Happy People:'

> Oh lovely Isle, oh verdant pearl!
> Set in the brow of farthest Ind.
> Your wet rice fields in mirrors swirl
> Upon the breast of vale and hill.
>
> Your treasures are straight bodies, lithe
> With ivory grace in dance or play;
> And temples where rich carvings write
> Of Nagas, scrolled with Hindu gods.
>
> Show us how love with rhythmic fire,
> In full-lipped ease from Nature's lore,
> Weaves magic spell on quivering lyre.
> Give us your wreath of tropic joy!

Seton's rival is G. Gorer who, describing Bali as 'the only happy large community I have seen in my life' (1936: 102), enlists the aid of William James, mysticism, and his own mescaline experience. Gorer's sometimes insightful study concludes with hints to Gatsby-epoch 'Trippers' (p. 236–7).

Even after the waning of Bohemianism, long-term observers of Bali in more serious times sometimes succumbed to the island's charms. Jef Last, for example, in his perceptive study of *Bali in de Kentering* (Bali at the Turning Tide) salutes the islanders' secretive love of life, notwithstanding his subsequent report:

> [I] heard President Sukarno speaking in the Wisjnu theatre in Den Pasar. He made a passionate plea to the youth of Bali to put an end to this [post Japanese-occupation, anti-Dutch] unrest. 'You want to be heroes of the revolution,' he said, 'but where in your Ramayana or Mahabharata . . . do you have heroes who with their daggars murder in the dark, and when have Krishna or Ardjuna ever revenged themselves on women and children?' (Last 1950: 7).

Last's work is a valuable and complex view of Bali under stress; and to be fair, the earlier aficionados of Bali, who would admit of no demerits in the island's ways, also conveyed a part-truth. Balinese existence is easily romanticized because many social forms and actions appear to be closely controlled variations of each other, not just within the arts but between the arts and daily life. The intricately coiffured maiden trussed in silk who bears meticulous offerings to her temple is but an aesthetic refinement on the ragged tradeswoman who portages burdensome wares to her market stall. The maiden's male counterpart performs at temples a sacred obligation which contrasts to her ritual duties in the same way his field labor contrasts to her domestic chores: men bear divine or mundane paraphernalia on their shoulders; women use their heads. Or a mighty Balinese Brunhilda, a frequent somatic type missing in Kraus and With's album, striding beneath a precariously balanced twenty-foot banana tree trunk glances at a passing bus with the very eye movement prescribed for the fragile dancers of the ubiquitous *legong*. Bali's lavishly integrated visual and kinesthetic qualities continue to stimulate countless such descriptions, even worse ones, in increasingly commercial effusions. Balinese sensitivity to life's ecological advantages and limits, which is restated continually in rites and ceremonies and arts and crafts, partly explains its persistent appeal to outsiders, Westerners and Indonesians alike, who likewise continually fear its demise.

One aim of the present study is to rescue this important swan-song theme of Bali from mere sentimental romanticizing and to restore the theme to its proper place as part of the sociologically crucial qualities of romance pervasive in Balinese culture. Bali inevitably suggests a tragicomic demise, a falling away from a purer golden age. And part of this aura arises from the situation of dramatic images in and around social processes, images which provide on-going commentary on the processes themselves. To understand this relationship requires a bit of background in the prominent role of courtly literature in everyday Balinese life at least since the decline of Majapahit Java.

To mix our metaphors, fourteenth-century Java provided a Gargantuan program of symbols for orchestrating the interrelation of religion, subsistence, power, status, and daily routines of a neighboring demographic and geographic Lilliput.[2] In old Java the political stakes were empires, in Bali (until 1906–8) merely hillsides, but the game was apparently no less intense. So drastically to reduce the manpower and resources that convinced the Javanese aristocracy of the breadth and import of its authority perhaps automatically produced a 'romance,' with views as to the religious significance of social forms qualified, lightened, and concentrated. Perhaps this historical process accounts in part for that Balinese self-consciousness, not a decadence so much as a vaudevillian sense of playing cultural forms to the hilt; philologists notice it too:

> ... [in Bali] a rapidly growing population, confined to the same geographical boundaries, and for lack of industry restricted to the same occupations, creative and artistic, seems to have found an outlet in the manu-facturing (in the forgotten literal sense of the word) of gradually more and more complicated offerings, so that at the outset one is far from sure whether it will be possible to find, let alone easy to find, the original religious substratum which has become inextricably mixed with a lush development of aesthetic, even at times lighthearted, elements (Hooykaas 1973a).

In Bali the impact of courtly performances was enhanced by extending active roles throughout the population. It is impossible today to know exactly how remote Majapahit royalty remained from the Javanese masses, but it is bound to have been more removed than its Balinese counterpart. Over time most Balinese no doubt experienced a sense of gradual elevation, of increased participation in prestigious forms that remained foreign to the rustic, noncremating Bali Aga, who came to symbolize, if not actually fully to remain, non-Hindu. The courtly arts in particular – gamelan, dance, drama – were not restricted according to birth, literacy, or wealth. One of the ultimate exemplars of refined etiquette and manners was the gifted dancer, and in Bali nearly everyone could dance, or try to.

Accordingly, Balinese continue even today to prefer performed literature, whether in oral recitation (singing) or dramatic (danced) stagings. Performers specialize in scenic episodes from the Javanized-Indic cycles that flourished after the fourteenth century. In other thematically related tales protagonists display more properly Balinese attributes, yet they share the general contours of counterparts from the *Ramayana* and the *Mahabharata*. Such literary episodes – whether chanted, or represented in shadow puppet plays, or performed in operatic dances – are appropriate at certain points in rites of marriage, tooth-filing, and cremation, or at times of serious divine malevolence indicated by disease, crime, severe weather conditions, or freakish births or accidents. Literature and drama are often used programmatically and allegorically. Explicit equations are made between these tales of divine forces and either the actual transitions experienced by parties in a rite or the hardships leading to a community's self-exorcism through a performance of the famous Rangda witch dance from the *Chalonarang* or the less well known Tektekan.

The three-ring-circus quality of such literary and ritual performances can be glimpsed in J. Hooykaas' description of the daylight *wayang lemah*, especially during marriage ceremonies:

> The *wayang lemah* performance is obviously intended for the gods as the place in which it is given indicates. The puppets are first laid against the white thread stretched between two freshly cut *dapdap* branches, and it is between these two branches that the puppets are manipulated during the actual performance, at the conclusion of which the white thread is broken by the *dalang* [puppeteer].
>
> This feature of the two *dapdap* branches linked by a thread that is later broken occurs also in the marriage ceremony . . .
>
> . . . the marriage ritual can be divided into two phases. The first phase, which I would define as an *adat* marriage ceremony, is conducted by a *pemangku* even when a *pedanda* is also present to prepare the holy water and to present the offerings to the gods.
>
> The *adat* phase is generally regarded as a *palukutan*, a lustration ceremony removing all impurity. In the villages it is only after the completion of this *adat* phase that the ritual bath of the bridal pair takes place. Following this the bride and bridegroom dress in their nuptial attire so that they might do homage to the gods.
>
> During the bridal procession the white thread joining the two *dapdap* branches is broken by an old woman who walks in front. It is my opinion that the *adat* phase of the marriage ceremony is more ancient than the ceremony of preparation of holy water in the temple by a Brahman priest. I imagine that when this 'Hindu-Javanese' elaboration was added to the lustration ritual, the practice was also adopted of presenting to the gods a performance of the similarly Hindu Javanese puppet show, while the concluding act of the original ritual, the breaking of the thread between

the *dapdap* branches, an ancient and essential element of the lustration ritual, was retained.

The inseparable association of the performance of the *wayang lemah* with the simultaneous preparation of holy water by a *pedanda* is quite obvious when the actual ritual is observed. The tinkle of the *pedanda*'s bell is scarcely audible above the hoarse shouting of the *dalang* and the music of the four instruments played as an accompaniment (J. Hooykaas 1961: 24–5).

Whether or not the *adat* phase is historically precedent, for us the important point is that in both its form and optional episodes, the *wayang* performance alludes to the transition ritual in progress. Now, Balinese literary expressions range far and wide: from mythic formulations appended to magic spots and events, to homey folktales full of stale jokes and foul language, to manuals for achieving religious liberation, to the chronicles of leadership we sampled earlier, to the beloved tales and romances derived from the Hindu epics. But even texts containing internal elements of suspense and integral plot structures are generally performed ritualistically. That is, they serve as ingredients in larger active classifications of society and cosmos at the required points on the calendar.

For over a century the labor of translation has proceeded and important catalogs and classifications of Balinese literature and the music and dances to which some of it can be set have been produced.[3] Yet, genuinely context-sensitive readings of most of these materials have barely begun. We have already sensed what a rich field for cross-cultural interpretation awaits here, when we detected some of the in-built conflicts and dilemmas of *babad* chronicles as they attempt to relate cosmology, power, and topography. For example, geographically the uncourtly, noncremating so-called Bali Aga must be relegated to the remote mountains, yet cosmologically the mountains are the divine source and assurance of Hindu power and authority. Hence *babad* chronicles often explain how royal scions were involved with remote commoners, as the accounts reconstrue what must have been hesitant infiltrations over impossible terrain into a brave sweep of divine influence across the forested hinterland.

In a sense, then, *babad* chronicles are a genre in closest conformity to principles of epic as an expression of foregone legitimacy. Moreover, as R. Friederich first appreciated, many of the most imaginative texts of Bali are virtually books of courtiers:

The *Ramayana* and the *Parvas* are to the Balinese a sort of pattern for princes. The *adat* of the princes, and of the second and third castes, is contained in these works, holy to them, whilst the Vedas and other secret writings furnish the rules for the Brahmans. The princes and the chiefs of Bali are to regulate their lives in accordance with the Epic writings, and as long as they do so peace and quietness shall prevail and increase in the country (Friederich 1849: 17).

But a complementary element of Balinese literature does not merely affirm and elaborate upper caste precepts and comportments; it articulates distinct sources and means of upheaval and subsequent rejuvenation. This literature does not simply mirror the self-satisfied court but provides leverage for countering it. In short, literary ideals in Bali can embrace social dynamics, thus contrasting with certain interpretations of India where, it has been claimed,

> the reigning ideal principle is that of social immutability while the ruling actual principle is that of social competition among those close to each other in rank (Mandelbaum 1970 II: 430).

Any easy dichotomy between ideal immutability and actual competition is untenable in Bali, and the role of its literature and drama in society is one of the reasons why.

Literary vehicles of Wisnu

> [In Balinese drama] it is as though every Pamino were accompanied by a Papageno, every King Henry by a Falstaff. The parallel with *The Magic Flute* is the nearer (Gorer 1936: 65).

A socially efficacious literature inevitably presents something of a paradox. Its images and scenes must reflect and underscore the options and possibilities (and not, of course, the statistical actualities) provided for in social action. Yet the literature must also contain codes and formulae sufficiently rarified to remain internally consistent apart from any specific mitigating context. Any essentialist approach to literature – whether psychologistic, phenomenological, or existentialist – celebrates the first side of this paradox. Any structuralist approach celebrates the second side, and a fully semiotic approach must embrace both sides. If not for such structuralist-type abstractable formulae, especially important at the sociological ligaments where groups or statuses distinguish and stereotype themselves vis-a-vis each other, there could be no processes like Hinduization and little communication across cultures. Literary tropes and semantic codes must be both context-laden and, to borrow a term from our preceding discussion of caste, exportable.

Love and order

The continuing relevance of Balinese literature to social life, as images of both integration and differentiation, is apparent in the role played by tales of romantic love in the system of marriage options detailed in Chapter 6. As a preliminary, let us briefly recall the three types of marriage, each supported by religious, pragmatic, and sometimes literary values: (1) Marriage preferences between so-called patrilateral-parallel cousins: the children of brothers or the grandchildren of brothers and members of the same potential ancestor-group. Balinese traditions cite the religious and status advantages of these ancestor-pleasing unions yet warn the ritually impure against attempting them; only the godlike should try it. (2) Prearranged alliances between different families or ancestor-groups, often with strategic dowering and careful assessments of the relative caste-statuses. Alliances range from modern egalitarian unions to the traditional hypergamous unions in which inferior wives receive titles higher than their original families'. (3) The celebrated Balinese individual marriages by mock capture that often totally estrange the wife's original family. Men who marry by capture and remain monogamous forego the religious or social advantages of cousin or prearranged marriage. Yet their unions are supported by beliefs that denying individual love can produce serious magical consequences, such as deformity, insanity, and so on. The couple may have to withstand ancestor-group hostility but they derive gratification from traditions of romantic love highlighted in the ritual escapade of mock capture, which echo themes of Panji-type tales such as *Bagus Umbara* (cf. Hooykaas 1968). Kersten notes the view of colonial scholars concerning these romantic ideals, when he says:

It has indeed been surmised that the numerous love adventures of gods and heroes in the Hindu literature have stimulated the fantasy of the Balinese to this romantic form [of capture marriage, Dutch *vluchthuwelijk*] (1947: 80).

A famous love story in Bali is the Jaya Prana legend concerning star-crossed lovers whose individual happiness conflicts with the social hierarchy. The tale enjoyed a post-World War II revitalization with complex ramifications throughout the island (Franken 1960), after which its hero assumed the proportions of a combined nationalistic and specifically Balinese folk deity identified with the arch Brahmana Wau Rauh (Puthta 1954). Since then it has become a classic of pan-Bali cultural identity; its Indonesian printout is a mainstay of the literary repertoire in public schools. One of the highlights of current year-end student trips is a stop at the enshrined cremation sites of Jaya Prana and his lover. C. Hooykaas discusses the legend as an example of the death-without-guilt theme and of the death-letter index-motif in his appealing translation used below (1958a: 1–22). But more to our purposes are possible interpretations which point up traditional Balinese sensitivity to the difficulties romantic love faces in a society pervasively stratified, particularly in matters of marriage. Here is the skeletal plot: Raja rewards talented, loyal subject with choice of kingdom's beauties; subject weds chosen one; raja is smitten by bride; raja has subject murdered; widow commits suicide; raja and entourage follow suit; the lovers join in heaven. Although Jaya Prana and his deathmate Layon Sari are the heroes, the raja is not precisely a villain; for their fates, it can be argued, are dictated by the social context. That we are distinctly within the province of romantic love is clear from the first encounter of the ideal couple:

And then there came one from the south
adorned with a costly scarf;
her hair, but lightly-tied, yet showed
the tail that fell upon her neck;
a slender waist, her body straight,
small pointed breasts
the peer of ivory coconuts.

Just like an image made of gold,
I Layon Sari was she called.
I Jaya Prana nearly swooned
beholding such a wondrous girl;
they said she was Bandesa's child,
come from the east,
and lived in Banjaran Sekar. (pp. 40–1)

Layon Sari, then, is daughter of a Bendesa, a local administrator-title for high-ranking Sudra groups. But who was Jaya Prana – merely a commoner orphan whose Sudra parents and siblings had died of plague (p. 35); the raja owed even so extraordinarily able and comely a waif no more than shelter. We know at once that Layon Sari's father disapproved the match, because Jaya Prana is referred to in a common fashion as a palace servant when they meet, whereupon the Bendesa 'took fright' but concealed his true feelings (pp. 44–5). Then enter the central antagonists, the village headmen, and counselors to the ruler. It is they who must witness incommensurate favors showered on Jaya Prana; they who 'sweating toiled to make a house of quality' (p. 52) for a servant normally their inferior. Layon Sari's father is most conspicuously caught in conflicting status patterns: first, in his relation with Jaya Prana whom he now addresses honorifically as Dewa Gusti (p. 65); second, with his own daughter, as he faces the plight of any father whose daughter marries higher than her own kin (p. 68). The village headmen, approximate peers of the father, advance Jaya Prana's downfall. Earlier they lay the foundation, when beseeching the raja:

But this boon do we crave from you,
if comes a foe
that you make us your champions. (p. 58)

Accordingly, the newly enamored king begins to anticipate Layon Sari's widowhood:

Then spoke the Anak Agung thus:
to all the headmen who were there,
'My uncles! Give me your advice,
tell me the course I should now take,

Jaya Prana to bind by spell
that he may die
by use of guile or by a ruse.
To make it so upon his death
that I Njoman may come to court.

If I should fail to get her here
Layon Sari, Queen of my heart,
in truth I shall depart this life,
in sorrow die . . . (pp. 72–3)

And the headmen concoct the murder plot. But the literary legend is no mere melodrama of fiend and hero; indeed, the headmen weep in grief (p. 88) at the portentous death they necessarily orchestrate. It is rather a tragedy of individual love in a society whose status patterns fall out of balance. That this is the crux of the trouble is made explicit in the raja's death-notice to Jaya Prana:

> Lack of respect, your only fault,
> you dared to vie with me, your Lord,
> and Layon Sari took to wife;
> her will I take unto myself;
> it is not fitting she be yours. (p. 85)

But it is by now no more fitting that she be the raja's; for she is a widow. Just as at the story's beginning the ruler acted excessively by making a court-sheltered orphan a peer, he now acts excessively by trying to make a court-sheltered widow his wife. Lustful 'madness seizes Anak Agung' (p. 96) as he even urges her to forego mourning her husband's death (p. 98) and begs the widow marry him 'without delay' (p. 100). Thus the kingdom falters as status distinctions and *adat* regulations lapse into disarray. By suicide Layon Sari joins Jaya Prana. The raja commits a final excess against her remains:

> Lifting her he stroked and kissed her
> though now a corpse, strong his desire. (p. 103)

The chaotic climax is achieved as the palace society runs amuck and the raja finally kills himself in ignominy. The only order that remains is the now perfect love of the heavenly couple, and the memory of what it might have been in a society stratified solely by love itself, when

> I Layon Sari homage paid
> devotedly
> to Jaya Prana her beloved. (p. 77)

The possible significance of the popular Jaya Prana revitalization which centered on cremating newly discovered remains of the folk hero has been discussed by Franken and Swellengrebel (1960), especially the later efforts to discover a *lontar* proclaiming him of high princely birth and to equate him with the arch Brahmana. Both efforts were, I think, ways of carrying the legend itself to a more perfect conclusion by proclaiming Jaya Prana Layon Sari's superior in the first place, thus surrounding any contradiction between the social order and the couple's love. The common factor linking the competing views of Jaya Prana as Brahmana or Jaya Prana as lord is that either interpretation converts this into a clearly proper marriage, in line with the social strata. But the broader point is this: Jaya Prana is not revolutionary literature. First, as even our rapid internal analysis of Hooykaas' translation revealed, it is inaccurate to deem Jaya Prana a melodrama of discontent about (in Hooykaas' words) 'the innocent victim of his feudal lord's jealousy.' This imposes a modern sentimental view on a literary genre as much concerned with preserving caste-defined social roles as with depicting a champion who ignores and momentarily escapes them. Jaya Prana's personal innocence is less important to the tale than his social excess, and the lord, as a lord, was justified in his jealousy; he finally only overstepped his proper royal license when he committed religious crimes against a corpse.

Another inaccurate view of *Jaya Prana* is to suppose with W.F. Wertheim that the poem 'gives a vivid expression to hidden discontent with the imposed caste order of Balinese society' (1956: 354) – a view which gained currency in the early post-Independence years. Anticaste sentiments here are not hidden at all. The sentiments are both overt and articulate, but they are less anticaste than countercaste. They allow for individual exceptions that lead not to an overthrow of hierarchy and privilege but merely to its episodic relocation and cyclic relegitimation. To infer any revolutionary qualities is to misread Balinese experience according to the old colonial stereotype that traditionally only the upper crust worried over rank. The courtly conflicts and ideals expressed in the Jaya Prana story are, however, not caste-specific; they relate equally to the dilemmas of a backward and lowly Nanang making a prearranged or capture marriage if some of his kinsmen begin to consider themselves Bapa who should wed only other Bapas and perhaps even near relatives. Today Sudras and per Agung alike can respond to the story in the sentimental sense that implies self-identification.

It is unnecessary to proclaim one literary text or brand of literature either a celebration of the status quo or a highly insulated, heavily camouflaged, revolutionary proclamation against it. Rather, we might take a tip from B. Anderson's (1972) portrayal of the role of *pesantren* ideals in Javanese society and the role of Javanese society in *pesantren* ideals. In *Java in a Time of Revolution* the traditional *santri* lifestyle – which stresses sexual abstinence, fraternal solidarity, selfless devotion, nomadic wanderings, and supernatural contact – is designated a 'counter-institution.' The *pesantren* ideals are enmeshed in classical literature; for example, they underlie a central conflict in the Arjuna-Durna story. The ideals are strengthened during retreats of specialized, isolated interest groups where they are consolidated, applied and refined, occasionally 'flowing out into society' where they gain periodic popular support (Anderson 1972: 9).

In Bali, literature itself acts as a storehouse of ideals and images, based on implicit conflicts. But literature is not a passive reserve; rather it provides exemplary texts to inform action, and it allows ordinary actors and groups to read high-caste dimensions into their experience. The Jaya Prana story might have been revitalized out of nationalist ardor and pent-up frustration in 1949, but the reason for its continued popularity into the 1970s hinges more, one suspects, on its role in vitalizing social options. There is no simple sociological, economic, or political advantage that obliges Balinese to worry about patriparallel cousins or hypergamous provisions. The institution of capture marriage can get around these possibilities by ignoring them. But when conditions force or permit, Balinese accelerate formation of quasi-corporate interlocal ancestor-groups. When this happens, the kind of marriage contracted and the various pros and cons partly illuminated, although never decided, by Jaya Prana become very important.

Thus, many Balinese literary genres – including portions of *babad* chronicles, Panji tales, and Balinese versions of the Hindu epics – support part of a counter-caste world view in Bali. Such literature finds positive significance in the periodic disintegration of courtly authority, in initially improper marriage, and in the upset of status divisions. The literature we have been considering is better seen as an active commentary on current Balinese social possibilities than as a distorted vestige of a perishing or even vanished system. Could this view help resolve the long-standing debate on the significance of Panji?

Panji recycled

Balinese dance is perhaps best known for the *legong*, in which drama is latent while animated bodies display a 'whole orchestra of movement' as they dart 'face to face, back to back, dipping, curving, shuffling, now poised on one leg, now on the other, continually sinking to the ground and rising in an endless undulation, with infinite indirections in their progress' (de Zoete and Spies 1939: 223). Yet other varieties of dramatic dance pertain more directly to society:

> There broods over Balinese dance an ancestral shade; every dance-form, one is often told, is ultimately derived from Gambuh; all dance-technique originates in its movements, all scales and melodies from its peculiar *gamelan* . . . there will come a moment, during a temple feast or a cremation, of which latter Gambuh is a recognized accessory, when one will become aware of a strange wailing of flutes and *rebab*, the clash of cymbals and clamor of strident voices rising above the gay contention of several gamelans and the tinkle of the *pedanda*'s bell . . . There is no doubt that Gambuh is old-fashioned. It has resisted all development, while the other sung drama, Arja, with which it shares one entire cycle of themes, has been much more pliable. Gambuh neither develops sentimental situations nor admits women to the male parts, nor gives scope for improvised comic interludes which the Balinese adore; and except in short passages between the king's traditional body-servants, whose speech has no heroic stilts to walk on, the language is fourteenth-century Javanese (rather like playing to a modern English audience in Chaucerian English).
>
> But for us it has interest if for no other reason than that it mirrors the costumes, language, and gesture of the great courts of east Java during the fourteenth century, when they were at the height of their splendour and of their influence on Bali . . . (de Zoete and Spies 1939: 134–5).

The cycle of themes shared by Gambuh and Raja are the Balinese Malat versions of Javanese Panji tales relating 'the intricate love adventures of a mythical prince with many mystifying impersonations' (de Zoete and Spies 1939: 135n). Friederich noted the parallels between the corpus of Panji tales and the *Ramayana* as a repertoire for performances:

> The Malat contains the history of the celebrated hero Panji who had his adventures on Bali also. The work is as voluminous as the Ramayana; it is, however, not written in the Kawi measure or language but in Kidung, which means the newer Java-Balinese measure. The subjects contained in it are exhibited to the public in the

Gambuh (dramatic performances by men, who speak themselves). The same is the case with the Ramayana (1849: 33–4).

Such Balinese literary texts serve as scripts for staged performances with choruses of paraphrasing between various archaic, refined dialects and the more accessible ordinary Balinese. (The newer dramatic forms introduce Indonesian as well.) Moreover, written versions of Malat-Panji tales are not in Old Javanese (Kawi), but predominantly in Middle Javanese or what S.O. Robson has called 'modern Kawi' (1972: 325), which was the dominant courtly idiom during the Majapahit era. Selections from Malat-Panji are apt to be sung and paraphrased at any meeting of reading clubs (*sekaha babasan*) and at many transition ceremonies, such as a child's third *otonan*, at weddings, or at rites after death (*Pitrayadna*). Robson has alluded to the cavalier native exegesis of the ritual use of such texts:

Before cremation, the bones of the deceased are exhumed. As a number of people will be cremated on the same afternoon, three days beforehand the bones are exhumed by various parties scattered across the graveyard. While watching one of these parties, I noted that at the depth of about a metre they had reached the skeleton. While digging proceeded and the bones were extracted one by one and deposited on the side of palm-leaf matting, one man stood over the grave holding a branch of the dapdap tree and a string of cash, while another sang *kidung*. I was told that the *kidung* was Malat, and that the aim was simply to comfort the deceased at being roused (1972: 319).

The history of the diffusion of these romances remains unclear, as illustrated by remarks such as these:

. . . the Panji theme is found not only in Java and Bali, but also in Sumatra and the Malay Peninsula, in Borneo, Celebes, and Lombok, not to mention Cambodia, Thailand, and Burma on the mainland (Robson 1972: 15).

It does not belong to the category of imported themes, whether Ramayana, Mahabharata or any other; that is to say it is Javanese in form and inspiration (Robson 1972: 11).

Moreover, even the distinction within Java-Bali between *kakawin* and *kidung* is not perfectly crisp. For example, in a discussion and translation of an Old Javanese poem with Balinese illustrations which explains the origin of the vow of the Night of Siwa, we find a *kakawin* that seems to be straining toward the later motifs of the *kidung*:

But in other respects this *kakawin* is not at all typical of the genre. The hero is a hunter, a man of extremely low caste. His name, Lubdhaka, is not in fact a proper name in Sanskrit, but a word for 'hunter'. In our text his lowly social status is constantly underlined . . . The descriptions of his domestic life, his conversations with his wife, and so on, touching in their humanity, are very unusual for Old Javanese literature. Similarly the description of his illness and death are unique in their portrayal of the everyday life of the ordinary man (Teeuw, *et al.* 1968: 32).

These features that are remarkable in Old Javanese *kakawin* became more commonplace in later *kidung* during the development of Panji episodes, again suggesting in Bali the transition from aloof aristocratic epic to vernacularized and popularized, although never vulgarized, romance.

J.J. Ras has recently recalled the famous protostructuralist studies of Panji by W.H. Rassers (1922, 1960) which conclude that in Java 'a certain connubial arrangement obtained, which permitted certain marriages whilst prohibiting others. This would mean that the Panji myth is here putting us on the track of a primitive exogamous social organisation' (Ras 1973: 424). The Panji myth persists in Bali along with intense interest in the thematically related episodes in the *Mahabharata* and *Ramayana*. But in Bali, and for that matter in Java, I find no need to posit some sort of *Ur*-moiety or primordial dual organization to explain the myths. Rather, every prearranged marriage in fact establishes contradictions similar to those that motivate both the Panji tales and the South Asian epics. In the event of a marriage between the children of brothers the relations between the collateral divisions of the supposedly whole ancestor-group take on the same tensions that characterize those between two different groups newly allied by a marriage. In Bali the *Ur*, so to speak, recurs.[4] Thus protostructure bows to social action.

To be more specific, let us consider what S.O. Robson calls 'the lowest common denominator of the Panji theme:'

> . . . there are two kingdoms, Kuripan and Daha . . . of which the former is the senior. The prince of Kuripan is betrothed to the princess of Daha but, before they can marry, a complicating factor . . . intervenes. . . . When the problems have been solved by the prince, in disguise and using an alias, then he can finally reveal himself and claim the princess. Through their marriage the world returns to its former settled state (1971: 12).

Panji's romantic adventures, and the problem of whether the two kingdoms (read 'groups' or sometimes 'collateral divisions') can coexist in spite of implied status differences, are themes that characterize Bali's marriage system as much today as in the legendary times of its literature.

Balinese marriage rites dramatize Panji tales which celebrate and articulate marriage options in a more integral fashion than the fragmentary twin-birth beliefs and legends we discussed earlier. If, for example, we compare certain Gambuh episodes to more sentimental Arja versions, we find that the latter invent ways retrospectively to prove the status propriety of Panji's union in marriage with his beloved. For example, in one Gambuh tale:

> Nusapati, who had long been in love with the princess of Daha, now spent his time in searching for her. Night fell as he was passing through the forest of Tratebang; he lit a fire in order to see the way and by mistake set fire to the forest. The king sent out his people to discover who had done it, and they brought Nusapati before him. There was a duel in which the King of Tratebang was killed by Nusapati. As the duel took place on Mount Merasim, Nusapati changed his name to Panji Malat Rasmin. He became King of Tratebang, but still could not find his beloved.
>
> The King of Gegeland, while he was in the mountains, was attacked by one of his nobles, while another noble attacked the king's palace in the city. Panji, who

went to his assistance, routed both the nobles and was adopted by the king out of gratitude (de Zoete and Spies 1939: 286–7).

But in the Arja story of Pakang Raras which reworks this Gambuh tale, a miraculous sign proves our hero to have been a man of high birth. This is romance:

When he was told that he must go at once with the *patih* to Blambangan, Pakang Raras knew that he was going to be put out of the way and asked leave to go and change his clothes for the journey. In his own room he wrote a hasty letter to the princess, in which he said: 'Little sister, I am Mantri Koripan. Forgive me for not telling you. I am taking leave of you now, for I must die' . . . And on the way to Blambangan, he said to the *patih*: 'You may as well kill me at once, *patih*. I know that I must die because I dared to make love to the princess. But listen! If my blood smells sour you will know I was of low caste. But if it smells sweet, that will be proof that I was of royal blood.' So the patih stabbed him then and there, and his blood smelt very fragrant.

Weeping bitterly [the princess] set off into the forest to look for him and after long searching she found his body, and would have killed herself upon it, had not Siwa taken pity on her sorrow and brought Pakang Raras to life again.

They returned radiant and rejoicing to the palace, and Pakang Raras, wearing his royal dress, went straight to the king, who at once recognized him as Mantri Koripan and gave his consent to the marriage, which was celebrated amid universal rejoicings (de Zoete and Spies 1939: 312).

This is approximately the same field of concerns we witnessed in Jaya Prana, and it reflects on Balinese marriage values in a way that recalls the complex problems and benefits described in the famous hypergamous alliance between Kosala men and Videha daughters that sets off the *Ramayana*.

Rassers emphasized certain Indic components of Panji tales, 'such as the *sayembara*, the contests of prowess between the gallant suitors of a noble young lady in order to decide who is to win her as his bride (reminding us of the Indian *swayamwara*)' (Ras 1973: 426). Yet whereas South Asian *swayamwara* traditions appear to legitimate 'individual' marriage choice as an ultimate social ideal (cf. Boon and Schneider 1974: 812), Panji episodes are concerned with converting an individual choice into something as preordained as if it were dictated by firm rules of kinship or even twinship. We can better understand this aspect of Panji thanks to Robson's (1971) welcome translation of the Panji romance *Wangbang Wideya*. Recall again that 'the gist of the Panji story is the motif of the young prince of Koripan being separated from his beloved, to be united with her only after a long search full of adventures and struggles with enemies and rivals' (Ras 1973: 419). Foremost a song-drama of love, *Wangbang Wideya* expands this gist into a complex work of poetry expressing exemplary characters and actions, with more intricate shadings and nuances than simple black and white epics of victorious good. As in the Jaya Prana legend, there is no patently evil antagonist:

The king of Lasem is . . . our nearest approach to a villain, but he is in fact not a villain at all. He is a pathetic figure, who arouses our pity. This man is . . . prey to a morbid or excessive desire for women; this moves him to want the princess as well. Having failed in a first attempt to get her, he launched a large-scale expedition against Daha in order to capture her. But fate has decreed against him, and he leaves for the battle in the teeth of ill omens. This provides us with a famous passage of Javanese literature. So he finds death on the battlefield, the ideal of the true warrior. Our author's depiction of the king of Lasem is not exaggerated or vengeful, but delicate and convincing. He is, of course, important in that he provides the cause for Panji's first real success, as a result of which he is *adopted as son of the king of Daha* and morally wins the upper hand over the princess's husband (Robson 1971: 27; emphasis added).

But in addition to its value as literature per se or as quasihistorical material, *Wangbang Wideya* implies a sociologic through its repeated tokens of foreshadowings that the prince of Koripan and the princess of Daha, who through adoption finally become siblings, were from the start made for each other. Without at all wishing to reduce this poem to a set of cryptic signals, we can appreciate an additional level of significance by tracing a few of them.

Wangbang Wideya begins with a theoretically ideal, for such elevated personages, first-cousin marriage (*memisanan*) by Panji:

The princess of Singharasi was also taken as a wife by Raden Makaradwaja; they were first cousins, she being the daughter of the king of Singhasari; she was very beautiful, *vying with the full moon* of the month of Kartika. Her name was Dyah Kesawati, and she possessed a refined nature and gentle, as well as being clever and virtuous (Robson 1971: 59; emphasis added).

Could there be a more perfect match? Later we learn that the 'moon' she vies with is Panji's ultimate consort. Because Panji had failed to wed the princess of Daha, here called Raden Wanastrasari, 'the whole land seemed sick' (p. 61). Then Wanastrasari's father explicitly dreams she is the moon. Wanastrasari is betrothed by her father to Singhamatra, who, however, 'realized that he was not her equal, as they were not alike in appearance or in virtue either' (p. 68). Much later when Panji himself catches Wanastrasari's eye, not only is it 'as if honey were mingling with sugar' (p. 87), but the servants see how they 'formed a perfect pair' (p. 89). Later still Panji is seen 'wearing the same clothing as the princess; he seemed to be acting as if he belonged with her' (p. 97). In fact through every art of visual description the poem insists:

She belongs with Panji like a god and a goddess – what a pity they are not equal by birth (p. 103).

We have already reviewed a few of the devices in Panji traditions that convert an inferior lover into an equal spouse. But our point here is that Panji episodes reflect a mythic system which compares sun-moon to identical appearance to ideal couples to twins. In traditional Javanese literature similar appearance generally implies similar status.[5] And in the codes of Indonesian and Malayan romance, complementary sun-moon imagery and identical appearance both imply the complementary and identical status at birth symbolized by twins. This is clear in the Malay Panji story *Hikayat Cekel Wanengpati*, the first manuscript treated by Rassers:

In heaven the god Naya-kusuma has two children, twins, one of each sex, by the nymph Nila Utama . . . *The children are like the sun and moon.* They grow up separately, but when they meet one day they immediately fall so deeply in love with each other as to become inseparable. Since a marriage is of course out of the question the father decides that they must incarnate themselves on earth (Ras 1973: 416; emphasis added).

Mythologically, such is the source of ideal spouses which join two factions. Our point is this: why force the conclusion that Panji tales refer to a lost pantribal organization? With great insight Rassers argued that 'reduced to their oldest core, Raden Inu and Chandra Kirana are the twin brother and sister who descended from heaven to become the ancestors . . . '; but he insisted as well, ' . . . the ancestors of the two phratries of the original tribe' (Ras 1973: 434). Could not such supposed archphratries have always been merely two sides of a political marriage, both of them hoping that this union might achieve the impossible? Indeed, Panji standards reinforce both twin-lore and positive marriage rules which suggest that the ideal union connects separated halves, two near relatives, two different factions, and two romantic lovers simultaneously. Impossible! But marriage rites back up this scheme by converting any outsider into a candidate ancestor upon marriage and by programming romantic fetching into the ceremonies even between patriparallel cousins. Panji tales join marriage rites in enhancing the actual components of a given marriage; they push each of the faulty options toward the holistic ideal which surpasses even actualizable cousin marriages.

In sum, this literature which engages social action also houses structuralist oppositions somewhat divorceable from their context. But these oppositions are not an obscure index of an ancient, actual dual-organization of the tribe that once was Java, but a persistent dualistic predilection accentuated whenever two parties wed. Earlier we saw that beliefs about twins relate to a panoply of Balinese marriage values and norms – to potential psychological duress in spouse selection, to strategies of elevating group status, and to a hierarchical cosmos in which nearly incestuous relations are seen as a risky assurance of sacred-dangerous superior descent. Panji can be seen in part as a literary expression of similar concerns. Panji romances are in some senses 'serial myths' (cf. Lévi-Strauss 1971; Boon 1972) which piece together into a story fragments of mythic codes involving twin and solar imagery and cosmic classifications of both real and imaginary divisions of society. But it is at least conceivable that here the courtly romance was imported integrally (after 1343?) and was gradually stretched toward existing classifications in Balinese practice and legend, thus reversing the order suggested by Lévi-Strauss [1971: Ch. 3] in his own series – first, mythic *bricoleur*, then serial myth, then novel (*roman*). If we do construe the archantipodal kingdoms of Panji tales as more accurately the temporarily antipodal parties arranging any marriage, it can be argued that in Bali today the romance of Panji, at least in its 'lowest common denominator,' lives! The presumed archaism is a continual current event.

Society's sakti

The story of the prince of Koripan/Janggala and the princess of Daha/Kediri, who are united in marriage after a series of complications, is typically a wedding-story. This is also illustrated very clearly in the Hikayat Cekel Wanengpati where the adventures of Raden Inu and Chandra Kirana are enacted on the stage during the solemn celebration of their own marriage. By the identification of the prince of Koripan with Wisnu and that of the princess of Daha with Dewi Sri the story gains an extra dimension and becomes an allegorical representation of the union of the god Wisnu with the Goddess Sri, repeated or re-enacted on earth in this royal marriage (Ras 1973: 438).

There is no more hazardous scholarly pursuit than essaying Hindu-Balinese glosses for the Sanskritic divinities and concepts that pervade its religious imagery. As Soebadio has cautioned:

. . . We do not know yet which Indian traditions have in fact influenced Indonesia and in what form, for it is not at all certain that the sects which were recognized by Goris [1920] have indeed reached Indonesia in precisely the forms suggested, or that they are to be considered the only traditions for that matter (1971: 8).

Yet much evidence supports our hunch that Wisnu is the god of Bali's social romance and that his preferred vehicle is an ascendant, expanding ancestor-group. Friederich rightly stressed Bali's lack of a proper Wisnu 'sect,' observing that here Wisnu has 'nowhere been the chief object of worship' (1849: 40). However he later adds:

Wisnu is nevertheless an important personage to the Balinese; in his various incarnations he is the hero of most of the Kawi works; it might be said that *Siwa is the high and invisible, Wisnu the incarnate god*, who has acquired infinite fame by his deeds on earth, and whose conduct serves as an example for all the actions of princes and people (Friederich 1849: 45; original italics).

The development of Panji themes followed the rise in eleventh-twelfth century Java of such 'Wisnuism,' whose worldly deity required *audiences* to regard his manifestations in literary *spectacles*, while Brahmana-Siwa priests assumed the duty of reciting vedic mantras while the *worshipers* engaged in *rituals*. At this time doubtless euhemeristic dramas became a preferred mode of expression in the courts. By the time the courts reached Bali, they could leave to each Brahmana *pedanda* his concern with cosmic harmony and ritual balance, while they celebrated temporal adventures and expansion of influence in popular theatrical romances. In the eleventh- and twelfth-centuries Java (perhaps)

saw the advent of the Panji story. This was a period in which Wisnuism, 'the religion of the Mahabharata and Ramayana epics,' was the most prominent religion in Java. Characteristic of the Panji story is the identification of Panji and Chandra Kirana with Wisnu and Sri respectively. In the *wayang purwa lakons* we find a similar identification of Kresna and Rukmini or of Rama and Dewi Sinta with Wisnu and Sri (Ras 1973: 442).

While Ras is here concerned to demonstrate a pre-Hinduistic basis of the Panji-Wisnu themes, we wish instead to correlate the Panji-Wisnu complex of ideals and values with the alternative outlook on society and that optional set of social possibilities emphasized throughout this study. Wisnu serves as something of a counter-divine to the Brahmana-Siwaic status quo.

It is difficult not to conjecture about what happened when Wisnuism entered fourteenth-century Bali with fresh literary and religious programs to be interrelated with what might have been prior usages of patriparallel-cousin marriage, abduction, and so on. We shall probably never excavate the dynamics of this historical process, but eventually the complex of Panji themes, some aspects of twin beliefs, cousin-marriage provisions, fervent trance, and dramatic episodes from South Asian epics came to constitute a sort of artillery of status principles, which we are now calling Wisnuism, that at times could oppose Brahmana-Siwaic ones. The latter principles involve closed castes, vedic rituals, priestly meditation, and kingly authority and religious purity. Wisnuvaic principles stress ancestor-groups, magical champions, and princely challenge and political prowess.

Thus rulers themselves are somewhat ambiguous. The rising prince is Wisnuvaic; the arrived king is Siwaic. One cannot simply parcel out a deity to a caste (that is, Brahmana-Siwa, Satria-Wisnu, and so on) or a deity to what G. Dumézil calls in Indo-European traditions the three 'functions' – sovereignty, force, and fecundity.[6] Rather in Bali Siwaism sees regular devolution and destruction in a stable hierarchy, and Wisnuism sees persistence of hierarchy as a dynamic romance. Wisnuism insists on infusions of new religious and status energies from the periphery; Siwaism construes any such change as a camouflaged continuity.

Of course, the Siwaic perspective was for centuries most accessible to outsiders: literally, since emissaries generally talked to Brahmana priests, but logically as well, since a rigidified view of supposedly archaic religion and society confirmed Western prejudices. Moreover, the colonial administration avoided the Wisnuvaic outlook partly implied in *babad* chronicles to accentuate the alternative Siwa-Brahmana view of society as strictly distinct castes interrelated to affect and reflect cosmic harmony. In this view optimal marriages are conceived of as within the same reified, concrete caste or subcaste or between lower women and upper men. In the competing outlook, optimal marriages are construed as being between near kin categories of a theoretical descent-line, and any caste-status differences are subject to mystical qualifications, as ancestral atrributes are rediscovered by subsequent generations.

Wisnu/Siwa is the nearest native Balinese concept to that very Indo-European distinction we are calling romance/epic. Wisnuism is authority on its episodic upward push, challenging for the moment social divisions and statuses. Siwaism is authority locked in, sacralized by the priestly support which is bypassed by the Wisnuvaic forces seeking magical contact directly with the gods and ancestors. In a word Wisnu is *sakti* engaged in the world, and a well formed ancestor-group is the social form required to actualize it. While Lekkerkerker (1921: 159) echoed the familiar Indic sense of *sakti* as 'energy, female principle, consort (*energie*, *vrouwelijk beginsel*, *gemalin*),' J. Gonda in his remarkable *Sanskrit in Indonesia* provides a gloss more appropriate for Bali:

> In Bali Siva as Batara Guru is thought to reside on the highest mountain of the island. Brahma and Visnu are only Siva's *saktis* (Skt. *sakti* . . . 'the energy or active power of a deity represented as a divine person') – the same term has spread over a large area in the sense of 'supranormal power, magico-religious potency' . . . The possession of this power involves invulnerability, invisibleness and similar properties. In Malay romantic narratives based on Hindu sources *sakti* is represented as a divine power to compass extra-ordinary events; the gods are told to combat by such exploits of *sakti*. Even in modern times warriors and prophetic figures have been considered *sekti*, *sakti* (Gonda 1973: 223).[7]

Just as there are ideal personality types and astrological-cosmological arrangements, evoked in romances, to receive and betoken this intrusion of divine *sakti*, so there is an ideal social form to contain it, a sort of sociological avatar: the ascendant ancestor-group, marrying-in its own consorts and spreading its descendants over sacred spaces to fulfill ancestral instructions to its leading elders. As a group's affairs prosper and its members expand into or join a temple network, they are able to review their own history and importance according to literary romances that become increasingly interesting to their ritual specialists and are more frequently employed in the group's ever elaborating rituals, particularly in marriage and death.

As we have seen, ascendant Balinese groups or political parties can be perfectly aware of building a semiindependent microhierarchy to express their emergent (Wisnuvaic) *sakti*. In fact the currency of this social romance is, if anything, greater since the demise of classical kingdoms and the colonial conservatism that replaced them – a conservatism partly perpetuated by Sukarno, whose administration was in its own way Siwaic, resisting the *sakti* forces of Balinese society.

Ritual contraries of Bali-Hindu

> There have been so many thousands of human tongues, there still are, because there have been . . . so many distinct groups intent on keeping from one another the inherited, singular springs of their identity, and engaged in creating their own semantic worlds, their 'alternities' (Steiner 1975: 232).

A cross-cultural reading of a social romance must appreciate not simply what the romance is about but equally what it is against. Every romance harbors not just an alter-image of epic, but implicit allusions to antiromance. Similarly, a culture should not be interpreted holistically simply as different levels of integral reaffirmations of a few guiding principles, but also as partial entrenchments against other ways of life the culture itself stereotypes antithetically.

The most proximate 'other' – a rejected 'alternity' – that lends Bali-Hindu religion and society a feeling of integrity, notwithstanding variation, is, of course, Islam. Indeed, if courtly Hindu texts and ideals embody certain positive, flexible standards for most Balinese, Islamic rites provide negative images against which Balinese sense they themselves stand in starkest contrast. This very much neglected aspect of Balinese traditions can be approached here only tentatively and tangentially. To suggest the posture of Bali versus Islam, we shall critically review a standard macrohistorical model of Islamization in the Indonesian archipelago. This general model tends to view the advent of Islam as an epiclike, in fact, nearly sagalike thrust; it not only sidesteps historical evidence of local complexities and conflicts but omits altogether the ritual components of Islam which are most critical in Bali's on-going reaction against its religious neighbors.[8] Finally, after suggesting that the negative stereotypes that reinforce the 'romance' of Bali occur most vividly at the ritual, rather than doctrinal, level, we end by speculating that ritual practices may in fact provide clearer indices of current religious changes in Bali and perhaps throughout Indonesia.

Islamization rejected

The predominant metaphor for the Islamization of Indonesia has been recalled by Van Nieuwenhuijze in a recent summary of 'the general picture of the spread of Islam so far as we know it:'

> This is often said to resemble an *oil stain*: gradual yet effective. Many, too, have praised its peaceful nature. Again so far as we know, the acceptance of Islamic doctrine has been a gradual process, partly thanks to the practice of conversion prior to indoctrination. The accent has not been on critical rethinking of tenets and positions as much as on the quiet absorption of those elements of creed and practice which at a given time must have appeared compatible with the ongoing life style, including any persistent elements of earlier religious, philosophical, and legal patterns. If the basic currents of this procedure can be described as syncretic, they appear as typically Indonesian rather than strictly Islamic ones. Conversely, this may help to explain the fact that one of the signal characteristics of Indonesian Islam is a continual struggle for purity (1973: 133; emphasis added).

According to this view, the gradual saturation of Islam into Indonesian life and institutions was facilitated by a peculiar interplay between mystic and rationalist variants of Islamic traditions. Speculative histories of the initial penetration of Islam see a personal mysticism as the advance wedge that rent the Hindu-Buddhist-animistic fabric of religious life, especially in Java, starting from the coastal trade enclaves, penetrating the courts, and diffusing downward. Again, Van Nieuwenhuijze:

> In the first centuries of the conversion of Indonesian life to Islam, converts were attracted by the mysticism of Islam rather than by any other aspects of its doctrine.
>
> Mysticism gradually gave way, making room for orthodox dogmatism (1958: 39, 43).

B. Schrieke concurs:

The mysticism characteristic of Islam during the period of religious transition made conversion . . . less objectionable (1957: 237).

Islam, as a consequence of the mystic elements which had infiltrated it, was highly adaptable (1957: 309).

The simultaneously mystical and anti-European reactionary impulses of early Javanese Islam is a major theme of H. Benda's *The Crescent and the Rising Sun*:

Javanese Islam was, indeed, for long of greater political than religious significance. Even though it provided a sense of unity and identity, at the outset at least it did not bring about radical changes in religious and social life on Java.

Partly this may have been due to the fact that Islam reached Indonesia not from its Middle Eastern heartland, but from India, and that this Islam, filtered through the religious experience of India, and studded with mysticism, had found the ground well prepared in Hinduized Java. It was, indeed, Sufism, or Islamic mysticism, rather than Islamic orthodoxy, which for a long time held sway in Java and in parts of Sumatra (1958: 12).

Moreover, according to Benda, 'although rivalries and dynastic wars among converted Islamic rulers had not infrequently given the Portuguese and the Dutch an opportunity or a pretext for interfering in Indonesian political affairs' (p. 11), it still facilitated the formation of identity across the diverse islands and regions of Indonesian *adat*.

For all its 'impurities' and compromises with pre-Islamic practices, Islam came to serve Indonesians as a rallying point of identity, to symbolize separateness from, and opposition to, foreign, Christian overlords (p. 13).

It was apparently in opposition to foreign powers that the rationalist, bureaucratic apparatus of Islamic traditions was adopted by the courts, as the ever mystical leaders replaced their old Hindu-Buddhist Brahmana literati with *ulama* who articulated Islamic principles of legitimacy and served as counselors, judges, and religious experts.

In other words, Indonesian courts did not necessarily become Muslim courts; in spite of conversion, they remained centers of a priyayi civilization. Again, though Islamic law became the accepted judicial norm, primarily in matrimonial matters, it could not supersede the prevailing customary *adat* in other domains (p. 14).

Yet reaction eventually set in, marked by a sort of love-hate relation between the vestiges of the Hindu-Buddhist power structure and the upholders of Islamic tenets and precepts, as each tried to cope with the changing Dutch administrative policies. For the sake of brevity, we must mistreat Benda's careful account by collapsing the several centuries he reviews into a semitelegraphic report. The Mataram dynasty – newly converted to Islam but the perpetuator of centrist, interior concepts of Javanese statehood – began to fear the Muslim zealots and to repress the *ulama*. There developed a polarization between the aristocratic *priyayi* values and the *santri* values of the *ulama*. The *santri* outlook eventually divided into the secular, legal administrative network focused on the mosque versus the Koranic purism now championed by the *ulamas* themselves. The gravitation of the rationalist-mosque interests toward the aristocratic-*priyayi* burgeoning civil service intensified as the *ulama* sector grew more ardent and, applying its exposure to Mecca and firsthand experience of Mideastern orthodoxy during the nineteenth century, organized separatist schools and retreats which often took on mystic overtones.

Even this gross simplification of a complex historical process suggests that by the latter nineteenth century any distinctly Islamic-mystic components in Javanese religion were to be found among those Muslims most opposed to the old *priyayi* sector of society, the very sector that during Islam's initial penetration apparently had been won over by Sufi mysticism alone. Nevertheless, in the latter nineteenth century the give-and-take between mystic rebels and orthodox bureaucrats – the latter including both *priyayi* civil servants and Islamic legists and educators – remained crucial in Javanese religion. Sartono has clarified this persistent dynamic in peasant revolts and rural religious revitalization:

> The religious elite, either *hadji* (Mecca pilgrim), *kjai* or *guru* (religious teachers), became a major factor in the development of traditional social movements. This elite was in fact a major symbol of the traditional order and enjoyed a high social standing amongst the rural population. At the village level it frequently assumed political leadership. Popular belief in their supernatural attributes and magical capacities allowed the religious leaders to exercise charismatic power, and by means of such religious institutions as the *pesantren* (village religious school), and the *tarekat* (mystical brotherhood), and by means also of their personal following, they could often control the village communities to a considerable degree. The absolute obedience to his *guru* required of the *murid* (disciple) established a group solidarity which could cut across the limits imposed by kinship ties and local loyalties (Sartono 1973: 7).

B. Anderson (1972) and others have traced this recurrent pattern of social and religious change into twentieth-century Indonesia: sometime mystic rebels and their bands of ardent youths retreat as all varieties of Islam, including orthodoxy, begin to eclipse. These enthusiasts later emerge from their entrenchments, and with renewed purist vigor they fuel a re-Islamization of local village life that ends up, however, looking more like rational Islamic administration than the extremist *pesantren* brotherhoods that helped Islam weather the storm.

Finally, throughout the nineteenth century repeated contacts with Mecca helped reformists oppose both mysticism and what they perceived as a hopelessly diluted, compromising rationalism. The result of all these tendencies is today's polymorphic Indonesian Islam, 'now occult and emotional, now crabbed and scholastic, now dogmatic and puritan' (Geertz 1968: 43).

This instant historical replay of mysticism, rationalism, and reformism is worth attempting for two reasons: (1) to suggest the complexities of such religious trends, which are particularly important if we are able to relate the trends to extra-Islamic traditions; and (2) to argue that this entire approach to the history of Islam leaves something important out of the picture. There is certainly profound historical importance to the well documented hostility yet mutual need of mystical and rational strains of Javanese religion. Islamic seers and Islamic bureaucrats and the specialized institutions of each have probably, over the centuries, never liked needing each other. Yet there is a difficulty in projecting this mystical/rational mutual reliance back to the days of early so-called conversions and in presenting the advance of Islam exclusively as a coupling of an odd theological paradox with a political and economic strategy. The first attractions of Hindu-Buddhist rulers to Islamic mysticism do recall the:

> odd paradox that Sufism, whose major premiss is the absolute distinction between God and man, should arrive at a conception of mystical experience that seems to be identical with that of the monistic Hindus who start from the totally contrary premiss that man is in some sense God (Zaehner 1969: 14).

And doubtless the onslaught of European powers hastened the routinization of companion rational organizations, more suitable than the old Hindu-Buddhist repeating structural microcosms, for consolidating a nearly pan-Indonesian identity to help thwart the challenge of foreign traders and armies.

But difficulties arise when scholars of early Islam view its spread exclusively in terms of this ready mystic appeal which then grew responsive to 'the commercial-political power games being played throughout the archipelago, with first the Portuguese and then the Dutch as major participants' (Nieuwenhuijze 1973: 145). This theory of Islamization tends to reduce religious change to economic strategies of power and, I think, to overlook possible conflicts experienced by ordinary parties confronting Islamic practice. If Islam were merely an assortment of abstract precepts concerning either mystic sources of knowledge, or rational methods of law enforcement, or reformed insistence on the reliability of the Koranic word, then Islam might indeed have gradually stained Java and Sumatra and elsewhere, seeping in wherever intellectuals and court officials, or local charismatic sages, or ardent reformers could demonstrate to peasants the advantages of the mosque, or of the *pesantren*, or of the book. But all these variants of Islam also require an alteration in world view, a shift in outlooks on the individual's progress through life, and in beliefs of what the present generation requires of its successors. That is to say, Islam is a ritual system as well, an emotive patterning of the life process in society. And it is as a ritual system that Islam had to challenge wherever it spread – and one here thinks primarily of Java – rival systems that pervaded the lives of its intended converts.

Below the level of commercial-political power or the preferences of rulers and scribes, what happened when local *adat* practices and Islamic legal principles could not be so neatly compartmentalized from each other as many historians of Indonesian religion assume? What happened when the often overlooked ritualism of Islam came into conflict with local customary rites, thus making impossible that easy syncretism generally suggested in broad historical overviews? Or to ask a question we can answer, what happens when, for example, Islamic advocacy of circumcision rites encounters Hindu-Buddhism and its totally contrasting ceremonies of life's transitions? This question points to the negative side of dramatic images in Balinese life. Balinese ritual incorporates images of Indic royalty, but these images grow all the more intense where they confront the most insistently non-Bali-Hindu, in particular Islam.

Circumcision against syncretism

Islamic Indonesians circumcise their sons; Bali-Hindu Indonesians do not. This is the nearest thing in Indonesia we find to a sense of radical disjunction between Hindu and Muslim communities. The presence or absence of circumcision is an intense religious index, not merely a pedantic flourish of tiresome purists. Perhaps only the ardent Javanese Muslim steadfastly rejects pork; but even the most syncretist Muslim must circumcise his sons. In neighboring Sumatra apparently indigenous Indonesian practices have been recorded that range from noncircumcision to male and female incision, to male circumcision (Loeb 1972). But to judge from Bali, we must assume that at least the heavily court-influenced areas of Majapahit Java were noncircumcisors. Of course, even Islamic circumcision rites vary greatly throughout Indonesia. Circumcision among intensely reformed groups, such as the one we will observe, ultimately suggests hazy traditions in which 'Mohammed is said, like other prophets, to have been born *sine praeputio*' (Ency. of Religion & Ethics, III: 678). A prophetlike individual ordeal demonstrates that the male, anywhere between the ages of six and the late teens, has mastered his will and courage enough to enter the community of the faithful.

Javanese *abangan* circumcision ceremonies require less severe individual isolation. It is suggestive that C. Geertz (1960: 51–3) compares the Javanese boy entering circumcision to the Javanese girl entering marriage, rather than the girl entering ritual isolation at the onset of menstruation. In Java circumcision entails shadow-play performances, gamelan orchestra accompaniment, and elaborate offerings prepared by females; and it is the mother who supports the often queasy initiate. If circumcision were precisely Koranic, one might call Javanese variants yet another instance of that 'tension between the spell of Majapahit and the pull of the Koran' (C. Geertz 1968: 40) that has prevailed since the Mataram revival of Hindu-Javanese arts and values after the early coastal victories of Islam. But circumcision, never mentioned in the Koran, is not precisely part of its articulate moralism; it is rather a pre-Islamic Middle Eastern practice that remained central to the proselytizing zeal of Muslims. To borrow a theme from the works of James Peacock (1968, n.d.), we might see Javanese circumcision as the prototype for the individualistic ordeal and struggle (Ind. *perjuangan*) that in reformist circles is elaborated into the life-long quest for male solidarity and release from female-familial shackles. For reformed Javanese Muslims, circumcision is doubtless an important signpost along the road to becoming a *haji*; elsewhere circumcision ceremonies are skewed toward the traditional complementary antithesis of Hindu-Buddhist/*abangan* Javanese rites and classifications familiar in traditions of the clown, the transvestite, and the cosmological balance of the shadow play.

Perhaps Hindu-Javanese originally did not circumcise, were early converted by protoreformists to circumcision, and only gradually stepped the rites back to readmit the older Hindu-Buddhist outlook on transition. Or perhaps they originally circumcised and in *abangan* society never adopted reformed Islamic rites. Or perhaps they were noncircumcisors and could only accept so un-Java-Hindu a practice if they softened this linear, goal-oriented struggle by surrounding it with the more gentle mesh of Hindu-Buddhist *priyayi* schemes. We cannot be sure. But here, for the sake of illustrating the importance of ritualism for any plausible theory of Islamization in Indonesia, we need only consider Bali-Hindu's abhorrence of any circumcision, especially reformist circumcision.

Migrant Buginese from Sulawesi are traditionally Islamic purists, and the Bugis whose forebears entered South Bali after Dutch occupation during 1906–8 are no exception. In Tabanan town a gregarious assortment of Buginese tradesmen lives in the Islamic quarter known as *Kampong Jawa*. In a house whose extended family contains twenty-six children, on a cold morning in June, 1972, three boys around six years old were to be circumcised. At the last circumcision in the neighborhood one of these boys had told his father he was 'ready.' By the time funds were available and the date selected, two of the boy's peers had elected to join him. Early morning is preferable, the father explained, because cold retards the flow of blood. The men and neighborhood dignitaries assembled in the courtyard; women and children clustered inside (I was invited to photograph). At 6:15 a.m. the surgeon arrived, and the initiates were ushered into a room lighted by the dawning sun, with a plastic-covered operating table, a shelf of instruments, medicine and cleansing agents, a tape recorder playing Arabic songs, and a lone calendar on the otherwise blank whitewashed walls. There simply could be nothing less Balinese: a painful initiation rite in an imageless, flowerless, smokeless, holy-waterless cell.

Each boy was held down by three or four men, including the conspicuously proud father. From eight to ten men mulled about, plus one vagrant tot in an orange dress who kept running up to inspect the initiates. The other women and girls watched from behind a partition. The first boy suffered most acutely; although the foreskin was stretched and clamped and partly anesthetized, the cuts provoked uncontrolled screams. 'Too much blood with this one,' the operator murmured in Indonesian. With much comforting, laughter, and prattle by all around, he quickly finished cutting, applied an antiseptic and bandage, and attached a protective brace to keep the boy's formal *sarong* from irritating the wound. The second initiate fared better, the last was exemplary. The latter's father, swelling with pride, related his son's stoic endurance and unflinching control even during the anaesthesia injection to the boy's similar courage at the dentist's office. Finally, all three were perched in their mosque attire on linen-covered pillows to await the communal feast later in the day.

Before recounting the Balinese reaction to this aspect of Islam, it should be noted that southwest Bali is well known for the cooperation that prevails among Muslims and Bali-Hindus, especially when both share the same wet-rice irrigation apparatus. In fact, 'religious obligations are fulfilled by each group according to the requirements of its faith, though in case a Bali-Hindu has a Muslim sharecropper a half share is expected to be provided for the Balinese [irrigation temple] ritual' (Grader 1960a: 286). Intermarriages between Bali-Hindus and Muslims are often taken in stride, especially when the woman is Muslim. Lately there have been conscientious efforts to hold complementary Islamic prewedding ceremonies for the families of women who are marrying into a Balinese ancestor-group.

Moreover, the very Buginese group under inspection harbors a Balinese spouse whose original group enjoys friendly relations with the whole Islamic sector of Tabanan. This makes the reaction of this woman's Balinese kinsman all the more remarkable, when he heard that his affines had allowed an outsider to witness their circumcisions. Disgust clouded his eyes as he struck out against those very friends who a moment before had been commended for their honesty and reliability. At the mention of circumcision the Balinese dike of tolerance collapsed; the outpouring in Indonesian went something like this:

What are they doing that here for? That's the trouble with Muslims, too fanatical. They're not like Christians who adapt to prevailing conditions. Now you take the Muslim rule against applying water to a dog bite; you have to use dirt instead. That might make sense in desert Arabia, but it's contrary to medicine here. These Muslims are more Arab than Arabia. They won't translate the Koran. Worst of all they won't eat meat, even chicken, unless it is slaughtered by another Muslim. They won't hang around with Balinese. If you invite Muslims to your house, you have to get an Islamic food preparer to come too; if you don't, they will only eat the rice. Also, if a Balinese man marries a Muslim he is liable to get ensnared by duties to support his wife's family as well (Ind. *mimikul keluarga isteri*). Chinese here like to marry Balinese, but they rarely marry a Muslim; their differences are too great.

Balinese informants could not even bring themselves to discuss circumcision per se; at the thought of it they were disgusted to the same degree Buginese are disdainful of Balinese for not practicing it. Conversely, in death rites it is Muslims who abhor Balinese corpse preparation and later cremation and Balinese who disdain the Muslim community for refusing such responsibilities.

Balinese reaction to circumcision is heightened by the contrast they sense with their own ceremonies for initiating males, and females, into full social being. Bali's nearest equivalent to circumcision occurs when an infant has survived three months of the permutational calendar. At this auspicious moment the child is outfitted as a divine god-king, sometimes renamed, and, if money permits, surrounded with the colorful attributes of the Hindu cosmology in a way that is likely to be repeated only for his marriage, if he marries well in a prearranged alliance favorable to his ancestor group, and for his death and eventual cremation. (Nowadays the later puberty ceremony of tooth-filing can be postponed until just before marriage or even put off indefinitely; but the demonlike canines must be filed before homage can be paid to the corpse at its burial or cremation.) Thus, at the age of three months a Balinese becomes whole and suffers no extreme transition for the rest of his existence, unless he becomes a ritual specialist (*mewinten*). The three month life-progress ceremonies for a first-born Brahmana boy described here are merely the fullest elaboration of the transition in principle experienced by every Balinese.

The three-month ceremony occurs in the household temple; to honor the infant is to honor the ancestors he perpetuates. As in every Balinese ritual for divinities, as opposed to demons, the essential ingredients are smoke, flowers, and holy water. The infant is outfitted to reflect the dimensions of the cosmic scheme and surrounded by the ultimate expressions of the unity/diversity of the universe. And he is placed next to the *dalang* and the now shadowless puppets of a daytime performance of the *wayang* known as *wayang lemah*. In fact the infant himself is a now shadowless puppet of the *wayang*, a human miniature of the cosmic mountain *kayon*, the eye of the storm of antagonistic yet complementary categories of life and society.

Every reflective Balinese who pauses to consider the surrounding Islamic circumcision in Java and Lombok, and in western and northern Bali and in the Muslim quarters of various towns, must implicitly contrast it to this sort of Balinese transition ceremony. It would, of course, be wrong to assume that current Balinese antipathy to such Islamic practices accurately reflects earlier encounters of Islam and Hindu-Buddhism in Java. Islamic circumcision would not necessarily have been the total anathema even to noncircumcising earlier Javanese who, unlike current Balinese, had not spent five centuries shoring up their traditions against Islam itself. But to assume the other extreme – that historically the imposition of different life-crisis rites should have totally avoided such conflicts – is implausible as well. (Today with a little speculation, one can surmise that for several centuries Balinese transition rituals have been elaborated in half-aware counterdistinction to Muslim ones, as the sole enclave of thriving Hindu-Buddhism has grown increasingly entrenched.)

We know that a Balinese can adjust his marriage and irrigation obligations to get along with Muslims; and as we shall see, Sufism and Bali-Hindu mysticism are somehow compatible. But whether a Balinese could stand by on a cold morning as a specialist removed his son's foreskin is another matter. Circumcision seems to be one of those things that religions take pains to institutionalize, about which it is particularly difficult to be syncretic. Religions tend to solidify their adherents and to set themselves against opponents by means of what K. Burke (1965) calls 'hortatory negativity,' the thou-shalt-nots that imply a thou-shalt. Often this characterizes the level of domestic rituals in which actors can sense conflicts that epic-minded historians tend to gloss over.[9]

Religious changing

The intense division of Bali-Hindu from *orang* Islam is not manifested in subsistence techniques in which cooperation is exemplary, or in marriage in which adjustments are increasing, but in life-crisis rites. This example points to problems in the general idealized retrospect of the smooth penetration of the Crescent, with its cutting edge of mysticism, into non-Islamic regions. The problem of emotion-laden rites of passage advocated by Islam – below its ethereal mystics and back home after its legal institutions and educational centers and mosques have emptied for the day – is important in current religious dynamics as well.

What might be called religious dislocation in Indonesia intensified after 1965 during the prolonged anticommunist reaction. These developments are most easily described in negative terms. There were mass efforts in Java, Bali, and Sumatra to escape into an acceptable religious pigeonhole – Christian, Bali-Hindu, or *Kebatinan* (mystic) – in order not to appear a communist (atheist) when the massacres were taking place. Of course, this worked to the advantage of the religiously affiliated political parties. But to describe the subsequent situation as a general direction in Indonesian and especially Javanese religion, including Islam, is more difficult.

In a paper on religious change in post-Gestapu Indonesia, C. Geertz (1972b) enumerates several trends involving mystical interests and practices. Formal *kebatinan* movements are the main example, but a tendency toward Sufi thinking in Islam is noted as well. From what we saw earlier, it could be argued that a turning back to mysticism and bureaucratic rationalism – the two are hardly mutually exclusive in Indonesian history – is the traditional way of guaranteeing Islam's appeal within the context of Javanism which stresses rituals, arts, and ancestor worship.[10]

Geertz also provides glimpses of conversions in East Java from Islamic to Bali-Hindu. These are often described by enthusiasts as returns to properly mystical concerns. But this native view of conversions to Bali-Hindu in Java conceals a paradox. The organization which proselytizes for Balinese religion outside of Bali is Parisada, an agency for the rationalization and codification of Bali-Hindu doctrines, officially recognized in the new Indonesian political system of functional groups (GOLKAR). According to many, by no means impartial, Balinese informants, any swing in Bali toward Parisada-type Bali-Hindu organization is a swing away from mystical concerns. On the other hand it is as yet difficult to determine precisely what the adoption of Parisada-organized Bali-Hinduism means to communities in East Java. In the East Javanese context, even a rationalized Balinese religion might appear mystical, at least relative to the Islam that preceded it. But in Bali itself, one finds rational administration of religion pulling one way and ancestor-oriented, mystically inclined religious practitioners pulling another.[11]

There is, in short, a rational/mystical dichotomy cutting across all the developments we have mentioned. Kebatinan movements have their intellectualist/curative dichotomy, the first involving scholastic geomancy, the second stressing the efficacy of folk potions. Islam has its bureaucratic-educational/Sufism dichotomy. And Bali-Hindu has its Parisada/ancestor-worship dichotomy. The dichotomies make it hazardous to generalize about the nature of Indonesian religious change as any unitary process such as rationalization. But perhaps by attending to the ritual aspects of such developments we can suggest touchstones of change more suited to the particular qualities of Indonesian religious dynamics.

Consider again recent trends in Bali-Hinduism, beginning with rationalization and the fledgling native suspicions that rituals are irrelevant to certain aims or even in competition with other areas of life – suspicions most characteristic of the Parisada organization. The only possible effect of this rationalism when it is implemented in, for example, East Java, is a more 'mystical' social organization, centering on ancestor worship and increasing temple ceremonialism. Moreover, any eastern Javanese village that converts to even a rationalized variety of Bali-Hinduism would begin to display a more hierarchical social pattern, if only because the custodians of its new temples will tend to be ranked above the mainstream, and so possibly will the custodians' descendants. Thus what looks like a movement toward rationalism and antiritualism in Bali can in Java appear as a program for mysticism among leaders complemented by increased ritualism among followers. There are similar complexities in current Balinese experiments with rationalism and reformism, especially Parisada, which seem almost to promote countersurges of both mysticism and revitalized ceremonialism. These correlate with the political and caste developments described above. District leaders and partisan politicians throughout the island begin to cultivate a mystical and yogic strain of religious observances; they discover new relations with different temples, and their groups then augment their obligations to support these temple festivals. We might call this an intensification of the *rsi* pattern in Balinese religion and society, wherein traditionally any group can produce a sacred meditating sage who escapes the ritual paraphernalia that pervades Bali but for that very reason increases the ritual responsibilities of the group that has produced him.[12] Such ritualism is the idiom of politics and economics in Bali; in fact it approximates the old Javanese *priyayi* status system of organization, which was the nearest thing to rational bureaucracy in Bali before Parisada. In short, that see-sawing between mysticism and rationalism that has characterized the whole of Islamization in Java continues in current religious developments, even in Bali-Hinduism.

Finally, if a resurgence of Javanese mysticism (Ind. *kebatinan*) has accompanied a greater receptivity in Java for Bali-Hinduism, what about the reverse issue of the impact of Javanese religious concerns on Bali? It is precisely here that concrete, ordinary outlooks on death and circumcision become critical. We probably cannot learn the details of the emotional strains in the early spread of Islam. But by observing current religious differences at the local level preferred by anthropologists, we can improve on a schematic, abstract, and elitist historical theory, necessarily oblivious to the grassroots, in assessing the current and future state of Islam, *keba-*

tinan, and Bali-Hinduism as well. It seems that the kind of religious change covered by terms such as Hinduization and Islamization requires at some point either/or decisions, even in a part of the world famous for syncretism. At least in present-day Bali it would take a personal quantum leap into Islam, even if the result does not look very Islamic from Mecca's vantage, to enable an elder to accept the fact of a new generation of circumcised sons, never to be cremated. Such must have been the case in Java as well. Any sense of conflictual change is hard to recover from the historical record, but there is little basis today for assuming it was altogether lacking.

Even where Balinese religious practices are not in vivid confrontation with Islam, issues of the ritualistic versus rationalistic components of Bali-Hindu are currently much in view. For example, during 1971–2 a scandal reverberating to Jakarta exploded over a seaside shrine that lay in the path of the projected expansion of an important tourist facility. After the area's district leader announced his intention to demolish the temple, resistance spread among local residents and officials in a neighboring district as well. The leader offered a compensatory payment for the temple and its lands and promised to rebuild it nearby. This proposal was rejected, since the space a temple occupies and the productive lands it holds are supposedly inviolable. When the demolition squad was eventually dispatched anyway, its members lost their nerve; the priest who had agreed to sanctify the proceedings (even temple-undedications are religiously dedicated in Bali) reportedly became powerless, and two days later his wife died. To abate the growing protest, the district leader backed down, and the hotel extension was built elsewhere.[13] Thus, this particular temple still stands, but the conflict reflected in the episode persists, especially in areas of rapid tourist development.

The exact contrary to this leader's apparent neglect of sacred shrines arises where an official's conspicuous devotion to temples and ritualism is denigrated by his opponents. One such case concerned a district leader in southwest Bali whose obsessive refurbishing of temples and ceremonies contrasted sharply with his predecessor's programs for improved roads, electricity, and commerce. The successor, previously an active military officer, observed personal ritual and mystical precautions and reconstructed the district market temple and death temple. Most controversially, he reactivated an obscure set of shrines near his headquarters which, although once sacred to the royal house of the kingdom, had been neglected since 1906–8. He laid the groundwork for qualifying the temple for district-government financing, and he offered fuller participation in ceremonies there to political favorites. These measures indirectly enhanced the status of his own ancestral houselands which happen to adjoin the temple. Yet even Chinese merchants were assessed for funds, as if it were a general public shrine. In 1972 the dispute continued; some parties accused the politician of trying to elevate his own group by outfitting at public expense a temple that might eventually be construed in some circles as its ancestral monument.

Although diametrically opposed, both cases reflect the same potential rift between religious, economic, and political affairs. In retrospect at least, these domains appear traditionally to have been amalgamated; any bald conflict between sacred ceremonialism and other concerns was unlikely, since ritual provided the backdrop and often the realization of any political, economic, or otherwise pragmatic measure. Then during 1957–8 C. Geertz (1964) reported a fresh sentiment among some Balinese that rituals might be irrelevant to certain aims or even dysfunctional. This budding attitude of reformism – championed by the urban, elite Parisada organization, many of whose members are Brahmana – can be perceived behind both the attempted desecration of a temple and the criticisms of an official for religious fanaticism, since both reveal a separation of religious action from other kinds.

Glimmers of reformism in Balinese religion raise issues not only of Weberian rationalization, or at least disenchantment, but of Javanization. The specter of the presumably far-reaching effects post-fourteenth-century Islamic reforms had on traditional Javanese religion looms in any consideration of reformist tendencies in neighboring Bali. Balinese reformers themselves expect rapid results in rationalizing their so-called feudal, archaic compatriots. The post-Independence reform movement has in recent years, however, suffered some setbacks. Participation in the unusual temple constructed in the heart of Den Pasar (Pura Agung Jagadnatha) by the Parisada organization has become politicized. Opponents say that only coerced school groups now attend the dogmatic sermons preached there; they recall the heavy-handed, partisan promotion of the original dedication ceremony some years ago and point out that its site was originally a favorite haunt of prostitutes. Parisada did help to win Jakarta's recognition of Bali-Hindu as a legitimate religion and to design the systematic religious education of Bali's masses. But its efforts to normalize the island's complex and variable temple system and to give preference to village-area origin temples as mosquelike corporate confraternities appear to have faltered. At least the widespread renewed emphasis of ancestor-group temples and networks – inevitably detracting from village-area temples – undermines this aim.

If the religious tendencies highlighted by the Parisada organization had reached the proportions of a genuine reformation, then parts of the Pasek movement and other efforts we have described to reinstate the social and political underpinnings of elaborated ancestor-temple ceremonies would constitute something of a counter-reformation – a reenchantment of the world by revitalizing some of the social and political dimensions that were part and parcel of the enchantment in the first place. But such sweeping macrohistorical formulations are too bold to depict Balinese developments, which illustrate reenchantment occurring before disenchantment has made much headway. Bali suggests how Weberian rationalization of religious organization and an intensification of ritualism keyed to a hierarchical cosmology can sometimes coexist or even sustain each other, nor need either necessarily advance by denying the other's legitimacy, provided each find a sphere of action relatively compartmentalized from the other's. Thus, Parisada has attempted to codify an internalized Bali-Hindu doctrine, to ingratiate it in a national bureau of religious affairs, to extend it beyond its confinement in Bali and Lombok, and to relegitimize an urban elite, this time as professors of dogma. Simultaneously the Pasek movement and other resurgent caste tendencies have further propagated rituals of status, thus replicating traditional caste ideals by claiming mystical and ritual expertise for local charismatic figures and influential groups.

If the higher ranks move to rationalize their religious concerns and to alter their role in society, their traditional inferiors tend to assimilate any older patterns almost at the moment they are discarded. While this instant assimilation is obscured by the time the historical record rolls around, it is vivid in ethnography. Consider, for example, that Parisada effort to standardize and limit the role of Brahmana priests, to streamline their exclusive rituals, to dictate their internal character traits by demanding exemplary behavior even in nonritual matters, and to test their achievement in mastering sacred literature, often reinterpreting ancient texts to confirm these new policies. While many Balinese have accepted such reforms of Brahmana priests, they have also continued to support practitioners from lower ranks who still conduct unfettered, unreformed ceremonies. This fact is illustrated by the revival of charismatic Pasek Empus with new temples as ritual settings. The Pasek case is in keeping with the preference for old or newly construed ancestor-groups to cultivate their own ritualists, calling less often on Brahmana *pedandas* or outsider commoner *pemangkus*. It appears, then, that if Brahmana priests ever become a truly routinized religious elite, concerned more with edifying internal character than with ritually juxtaposing the propitious ingredients of the divine universe, this latter task will have proliferated below them.

To conclude, Balinese religion *continues* to change. The changes appear heterogenetic where the ritual duties required by temples are newly considered to conflict with other needs.[14] But elsewhere they are orthogenetic; in large measure Balinese religion and ritual is changing just as it always has. The expansion of temple networks is in general conformity with the precolonial history of the extension of Bali-Hindu ritual centers into new territory. Any wave of reform in Balinese religion generates many eddies of ritualistic revitalization as well. An alternative to speculations by Indonesian reformists and by those fearing them that traditional Bali-Hindu ritualism could be eliminated by a sweeping reform movement is that ritualism will suffer changes in the social strata attending to it. It is at least worth noting that some two decades after a nationalist reform policy for Bali was launched by religious elites, in less elevated spheres – individual resurging ancestor-groups, enhanced commoner temple-networks, and newly enlightened rustic locales – Balinese temple ceremonies continue to facilitate the redefinition of political allegiances under the rubric of caste relations, and to imbue recent trends with the religious aura of the very old and ritually preordained. Moreover, as such orthogenetic events continually enliven fundamental tensions and complexities, the sense of religious integrity intensifies wherever Bali-Hindus who aspire to courtly social and literary forms encounter the concrete rituals that they themselves oppose, whether noncremating Bali Aga or circumcising *orang* Islam. In a way these aspects of religious change both reflect and underlie Bali as a dynamic romance.

Conclusion

The end of romance?

> [Liberation itself] is in the end the same as the holy ash to which the adept's body is reduced after death and cremation.
>
> (Soebadio 1971: 52–3)

By keeping closely attuned to Balinese institutions and imagery – legends and texts, caste ideology, temple networks, marriage preferences, rituals and epithets – and by viewing them against distortions both in the history of Balinese ethnology and in current opinions by inevitably self-interested informants, we have tried to penetrate some of the dynamic resilience of Balinese culture. To surmount oversimplified sociological strateographic schemes such as traditional/modern, or even more complex ones such as Bali Aga/rural Hinduized plains/traditional towns/ cosmopolitan towns, we have concentrated on problematic areas in actions and categories to trace relationships between various domains of Balinese culture now, as in times past, in town and hinterland alike. Certain of these sensitized areas of Balinese experience could be deemed principles of its anthropological romance: (1) Bali's flexible response and strategic adaptation to the Western presence since 1597; (2) the social efficacy of imaginative elders; (3) reconstructing history to legitimate political power in the Bali of both Suharto's and Sukarno's Indonesia, and before; (4) internal differentiation of expanding ancestor-groups; (5) a corpus of ritual that facilitates adaptive responses for expanding a subsistence technology and for maintaining lines of political allegiance across locales; (6) a system of primary marriage norms backed by secondary qualifications which support religious meanings; (7) the possibilities of hypergamy and individual love within a system characterized by endogamy; (8) Brahmana ideology as a model for differentiated marriage and descent concepts; (9) the pervasive issue of mother's rank with different consequences in diverse spheres of society; (10) the legendary history of caste, with its echoes of an idealized Majapahit Java, as an essentially polemical animator of social life and a trademark of Balinese concerns; (11) modern revitalizations of traditional caste issues, which dispute sacred-ancestral-fountainhead versus pragmatic power as theories of status legitimacy; (12) revivals of literary legends and the courtly rites that accompany them; (13) the creative properties of dramatic and religious images, heroes, and stereotypes in Balinese motivations; and (14) the historical complexity of Bali-Hindu's retrenched position in relation to Islamic organizations and rites.

By concentrating on such ethnographic topics and contexts, we have tried to detect systematic interrelations in Balinese categories. For example, we analyzed policies of second-patriparallel-cousin marriage as a means of implementing endogamy at the sociological pressure point of factionalism. This emphasis on second-cousin marriage enables first-patriparallel-cousin marriage to be reserved as a sacred-dangerous union which keys to concepts of incest. Likewise we itemized the varied advantages in provisions which forbid generally acceptable hypergamous marriages between elevated Sudra women and a superior group. Such an optional rule demonstrates the social value of fruitful ambiguity, by which different parties can construe matters each to its own advantage.

It is worth pondering this latter rule one final time in order to appreciate the vital importance of a cultural approach to cross-cultural studies. Again, ordinarily Bali is hypergamous: inferior woman may marry superior males. How, then, do we interpret this special rule prohibiting marriages between elevated Sudra groups and privileged dynasties, such as the anomalous *gria* group of Antosari (Chapter 7) or the royal line of Tabanan? A sociofunctional answer might be that the rule is a device to eliminate any possible suggestion of hypergamy: a hypergamous marriage would underscore the groups' inequality, when it is to the superior group's interests to pamper and compliment the useful Sudra party. But one learns from elders of such Sudra groups that they themselves do not adopt this flattering interpretation. In one case the rule was considered an atonement by a past raja for having impregnated one of the Sudra group's women. These Sudras feel they stand to their superiors as brothers, thus devising an even more flattering interpretation than the previous one. They suggest that any marriages between them would appear slightly incestuous, and in fact one that has occurred is denounced accordingly, although it is tolerated.

The importance of these conflicting views is this: if the rule is seen merely as a device to reject the implications of hypergamy, this would block our perception of its value in asserting fraternity. These two interpretations are culturally different, even though the social structural correlate – nonmarriage between the two groups – is identical. (Note in passing that if marriage were in fact allowed, the two groups would not even then in and of the marriage be hypergamously ranked, since in the logic of Balinese kinship the union could hypothetically be construed as an assertion of their cousin-likeness!) Yet, if one precluded the hypergamy argument simply because one segment of indigenes does not understand matters this way, one would submit to a naive brand of so-called emic analysis which refuses to profit from the reservoir of theoretical possibilities known to anthropological science. Worst of all, such a policy would make the sole source of verification of interpretations the natives themselves (or more exactly one segment of them, or more exactly still one's best informant), which would render the comparativist endeavor of anthropology trivial and its only important research tool polyglot-stenography.

The normative fact of social structure is that the two groups should not marry. That once or twice they have married is a simple empirical fact, interesting mainly to the extent it provokes expressions of conflict over broken rules. The social structural fact defines the relations of groups, or of the categories of groups. But a further cultural fact is that these particular groups should not marry because it would be from one party's viewpoint somewhat incestuous. A cultural study includes social structural rules about categories and groups as well as alternate interpretations of the rules. Here the idea of incest is used to legitimate a rule which might, as the comparativist scholar knows, be explicable as a strategic refusal to allow hypergamy into play – an explanation actually very much in keeping with other aspects of Balinese thought and action. The paramount point thus becomes, as we have seen, this nexus of incest and hypergamous principles and its relationship to ancestor-group endogamy, caste categories, and much more.

The present study has attempted to review and advance the quest of understanding Bali's basic unit of social and cultural process – the optional ancestor-group. Taking a cue from Jane Belo's (1936) important documentation of parallel-cousin marriage frequencies and from H. and C. Geertz's work over two decades later on a specialized locality, we have more or less stood earlier holistic views of Bali on their heads. Only by placing these earlier views in their own historical context and by tracing the complexities of current developments can one assess the inadequacy of a rigid stratigraphic model of Balinese culture. Such a model, however, cannot be merely tossed into the rubbage pile of foreigners' misapprehensions, since it indeed conforms to an aspect – what we have called the epical aspect – of Balinese institutions themselves. Moreover, there are many Balinese, both highest and lowest, who consider caste *warnas* and absolute marriage distinctions to be the essence of Bali. Finally, while some early outside observers glimpsed the collateral sedition of royal houses as well as the flexibility of marriage, as far as they could grasp it, their nineteenth-century successors, building on frameworks provided by early Sanskritists, converted most of what they saw into a form of vestigial archaic absolutism; and the latters' successors in turn formulated policies which helped create a colonial Bali to reflect these distortions.

Januslike, Bali faces the Pacific as well as the Indic. It is neither *warna*, nor divine kingship, nor Archipelago-Sanskrit-Hindu texts, but optional ancestor groupings and the ideology and ritual surrounding them that are keys in Bali to what Lévi-Strauss has called the anthropological 'order of orders:'

> Thus anthropology considers the whole social fabric as a network of different types of orders. The kinship system provides a way to order individuals according to certain rules; social organization is another way of ordering individuals and groups; social stratifications, whether economic or political, provide us with a third type; and all these orders can themselves be ordered by showing the kind of relationships which exist among them, how they interact with one another on both the synchronic and the diachronic levels (1967: 306).

For Bali these synchronic and diachronic relations are vividly illustrated by the special story of Marketside East, and they appear clearly in current political developments, status concerns, and religious changes – all aspects of a cultural argument expounded in variable texts and contexts reverberating over these meticulously irrigated rice lands.

In our exploration of the anthropological order of orders, we have isolated and interrelated ideas and actions which underlie native historicism, subsistence values, social change, kinship and marriage, partisan organization, and religious and ritual activity. These are the values which lend Balinese culture its – no other term will do – style. One can regard these values either as positive valences that shape Balinese experience and infuse much of daily life, or as selected features that articulate 'Bali' out of a hypothetical set of possibilities known to a cross-cultural perspective, thus making the Balinese case comprehensible by implicit contrast. The 'shaping' approach is the favored idiom of American cultural studies; the 'selecting' approach is the idiom of continental structuralist frameworks (cf. Boon 1973b). Neither of these comparativist outlooks has as its object of analysis a thing-itself. Rather both embrace in their fields of investigations concatenations of dislocated forms, symbols, and institutions, realizing that cultures can only be captured when they are caught off-balance.

Some of our findings are more speculative than others, to be improved or refuted by further research and comparison. But any future study will doubtless confirm at least one central conclusion: rules in Bali can sound rigid only because the portions of society to which they pertain are not stable isolates. Part of the role of rules is to define the field of application of action. It is a lesson of cultural anthropology meriting repeated attention that social rules do not always simply interrelate the constituent units of *a priori* bounded groups: they sometimes create the groups; that is, they formulate the relevant social field, in the act of being applied. The fullest sense of this conclusion is that even Bali itself is not a stable isolate. The supposed cultural entity of 'Bali' is in truth an intersection, a nexus, of cross-cultural, interpenetrating systems, at the most extreme of India and Polynesia. When read in terms of its endogamous provisions, Bali is certainly many societies; and in a way it is many cultures as well.

Yet there are to these cultures enduring, almost substantive themes. What is perhaps the major one of these – the place of death in Balinese traditions – is also the topic which best reveals the necessity of a cross-cultural theory that emphasizes the formative value of ideals and images. Beyond death's universal existential impact, the cultural significance of *Balinese* death was first made palpable to this fieldworker in July 1972, when the long bedridden senior-most elder of the group we met in Chapter 4 passed quietly away. His body was placed on a shrouded pallet to be guarded night and day during the forty-eight to seventy-two hours before burial by droves of kinsmen in hubbub, *banjar* mates and special guests, the night watchers fending off sleep with games of chance. This lengthy wake – variable according to caste and to whether a corpse is to be buried or directly cremated, the latter a privilege for only the highest titles – is an old way with the advantage that it allows time for descendants living at a distance to return home for the funeral. On the nearest auspicious day the corpse was washed and costumed, honored by the generations of descendants (*mapegat*), borne to the graveyard, and buried – a sequence of rites of enormous importance. In the closest thing to fervor, short of trance, to be seen in Balinese ceremony, the corpse is first pawed, handled, and cleansed by a clutch of descendants through both its sons and endogamous daughters, and then decked out like a god-king. This is the first stage of symbolically elevating the mortal to the rank of the divine. There follows the elaborate *mapegat* in which children, grandchildren and great grandchildren, agnatic and family-uterine alike, render him his initial godlike homage. Then occurs that, to me, scintillating trademark of Balinese rites and processions: the send-off, always the same, in which the sacred burden is thrust upon a crowd of shoulders in a portable, crepe-papered version of the future shrine in brick and stone where the deceased's spirit will make visitations, after his corporeal remains have been exhumed and further spiritualized through cremation and perhaps ultimately elevated in the ceremony of *mukur*. Arriving at the cemetery, each family member tosses a bit of soil into the open grave, the crowd disperses to seek a shaded vantage, and the coffin and its contents are lowered in, face down (to facilitate assuming an homage-giving position, they reason) as the mandatory gongs clang on. The ceremonial detail and ritual precautions persist in the death rites of this progressive citizenry, even when other life-crisis formats have been attenuated. But from our story's point of view the significance of this elaborate next-to-the (or next-to-the-next-to-the . . .) last rite of a senior elder is that for about fifteen minutes the heavy truck and military traffic on the main road from Bali's Indonesian provincial capitol, through Tabanan, to Java's busy port of Surabaya is blocked by a cortege of some five-hundred people – at the moment one group, whose ancestors, according to their own story, arose out of Klungkung, the foremost kingdom and culture cradle of precolonial Bali.

It is corporeal death that this society's cultural forms are most fervently about. If any complex of values could be said to cement the diverse strata, factions, and times of Balinese culture, it is the premises around which death and cremation rites occur.[1] Balinese themselves consider cremation the major index of their own Hinduization as contrasted to the culturally stunted Bali Aga or the renegade Bali-Islam. The island's ritual and artistic expressions are like a vast historical and ethnographic musing, not on abstract 'death' versus 'life,' or on any theological program of life-after-death, but on the concrete inevitability of the eventual rigor mortis of now dancing physiques. The ultimate dilemma of Balinese life and thought would appear to be the ineluctable conversion of provisionally pulsating, organic human motion into skeletal stillness; and the aim of corpse preparation, cremation, and its after-rites is to deny or at least to retard this finality.

Even the obscure principles of the social structure of local life achieve near transparency at the time of special mass cremations. For then each *banjar* council house becomes not a civic hall whose functions overlap confusingly with those of *desa*, *subak*, and central government, but a *tugu* shrine contributing to the ultimate mass cremation process. If viewed as sets of specialized task forces to assure proper dispensation of deceased torsos, the Balinese social landscape reads nearly like an open book. Yet these task forces serve primarily as each other's audience. And perhaps the most revealing cross-cultural perspective on Balinese islanders is that they are a people who ideally marry-in (second- or first-patriparallel cousin), who bury-in and cremate-in (in the sense of confining the handling of corpses to family members), and in the few instances where religious transmigration ideas have taken hold (for example, same-sex twin beliefs and the hazy equation of great-grandfather with great-grandson) who reincarnate-in.[2] In Bali, transmigration of souls could never become a Hindu scheme ordering and interrelating the entire diversity of the cosmos from bestial to divine. It could only become an additional means to insist on the basic social principle of romance – the optional self-sufficiency of elevatable, flexible ancestor-groupings.

If tourism or nationalism or political events ever overwhelm Bali as Mohammedism was once considered to have overwhelmed Hindu-Java, the cultural transformation should register most vividly in the island's death and cremation rituals. Yet whatever the future of Bali, it will not be simply a matter of a sprawling national bureaucracy entangling a pristine indigenous flower or of insensitive tourists trammeling a naive native paradise. That Bali is more complex and sophisticated than such fears would admit is evidenced in its traditional potential to self-destruct, as when temporarily ascendant southern rajas partially sold each other out to the Dutch before the courtly suicides of 1906–8. The impression lingers that if the island's culture ever succumbs, its death will take the form not of a quiet burial but of one last and total cremation, a final romance of burning pyres and caste-specific sarcophagi that symbolize the splendid hierarchy of always vulnerable, inward-turning groups in search of sacred ancestral sources plus the religious distinctions, economic wherewithal, and political prowess necessary to maintain and interrelate them – a resilient hierarchy that has found singularly intensive expression in some million acres of heavily gullied, tropically vegetated, volcanic ash.

Notes

Introduction: Beyond epic

1 Northrop Frye has thoroughly elaborated epic and romance as genres or modes of literature, for example:

> In every age the ruling social or intellectual class tends to project its ideals in some form of romance, where the virtuous heroes and beautiful heroines represent the ideals, and the villains the threats to their ascendency . . . Yet there is a genuinely 'proletarian' element in romance too which is never satisfied with its various incarnations . . . The perennially childlike quality of romance is marked by its extraordinarily persistent nostalgia, its search for some kind of imaginative golden age in time or space . . . The complete form of the romance is clearly the successful quest, and such a completed form has three main stages: the stage of the perilous journey and the preliminary minor adventures; the crucial struggle, usually some kind of battle in which either the hero or his foe, or both, must die; and the exaltation of the hero. Thus the romance expresses more clearly the passage from struggle through a point of ritual death to a recognition scene that we discovered in comedy . . . *The central form of romance is dialectical*: everything is focussed on a conflict between the hero [champion would be better] and his enemy . . . The conflict however, takes place in, or at any rate primarily concerns, our world, which is in the middle, and which is characterized by the cyclical movement of nature. (1957: 186–7; emphasis added).

Actually Frye is here blending romance with epic, in order to contrast them to classical myth that deals with the suprahuman ways of the gods. Later he notes that 'the social affinities of the romance, with its grave idealizing of heroism and purity, are with the aristocracy . . . It revived in the period we call Romantic as part of the Romantic tendency to archaic feudalism and a cult of the hero, or idealized libido' (p. 306).

2 However, if Balinese society was never feudal, its culture might still be deemed chivalric or perhaps troubadorial (cf. Mead 1939)!

1. Bali-tje

1 Throughout this section we employ three volumes (7, 25, and 32) of a twentieth-century edition by the Linschoten Vereeniging of the sixteenth-century accounts: G.P. Rouffaer and J.W. Ijzerman, ed., *De Eerste Schipvaart der Nederlanders naar Oost-Indie onder Cornelis de Houtman, 1595–1597*; I *D'eerste Boeck* *van Willem Lodewycksz.* (1915); II *De Oudste Journalen der Reis* (1925); III *Verdere Bescheiden Betreffende de Reis* (1929). The modern commentators referred to later are Rouffaer and Ijzerman, who annotate this edition; the English map is reproduced in Vol. II, pp. 89, 202.

A fourth volume compiled by J.C. Mollema (*De Eerste Schipvaart* . . . , Linschoten Vereeniging, 1935) consolidates a chronological account (*relaas*) with more details of the relations among the Dutchmen. Here we read, for example, a speculation as to the (previously mentioned) obscure motives of those who remained in Bali: 'It is not completely out of the question that the velvet eyes and comely figures of the Balinese maidens made an impression on the two youths' (p. 341).

2 Such 'Demillean' restaging of initial contacts is one of the most tenacious rhetorical devices in the romantic imagery of ethnological literature. It reminds one of the sort of routinized, recurring metaphors called *topoi* by E.R. Curtius in *European Literature and the Latin Middle Ages* (1953: Ch. V). Anthropology's counterpart to *topoi* such as 'the world upside down' or 'boy as old man' (*puer senilis*) is 'captain greets king' or more recently, 'collectivity welcomes fieldworker.' The *topos* remains very much with us, as evidenced by a recent television broadcast of a film made of Margaret Mead's return to one of her Pacific islands for a generation-later restudy. Ms. Mead is rowed up in a boat and the jubilant natives run out *en masse* to welcome her (evidently, collectively awaited) return. We are not told how she was concealed while the *other* crew got the beach camera into position.

3 'Zy zijn Heydenen aenbiddende tghene haer des morghens eerst int gomoet comt' (1915: 197). A similar *topos* appears as early as the writings of Marco Polo (cf. Benda and Larkin 1967: 13).

4 Some of these reasons can be glimpsed in Pieter Geyl's succinct account of the political and religious complexities in the late sixteenth-century Netherlands. Unlike their successors, the voyagers who first confronted Balinese ritual and hierarchy lacked a firm, dogmatic Calvinist base from which to react against Indonesian 'idolatries' and 'profanations.' Geyl describes the slow 'Protestantization' from the top down and the tenacity of local Catholic officialdom; for example: 'In 1593 a [Reformed] commission appointed by the States of Utrecht . . . made a tour of the province, questioning the newly installed ministers as well as the former priests. Their report gives a vivid picture of the motley and sometimes extraordinary conditions prevailing. In the large majority of villages the old priests were still functioning . . . Several priests refused to submit, and continued to distribute "the popish sacrament" at Easter, or at least showed a suspicious reluctance to marry their "housekeeper" . . . so, at this moment, were the Reformed Synods in all the seven provinces to which the Union had been reduced admonishing States assemblies and town governments to deal more severely with "superstitions, idolatries, abuses and profanations" ' (1964: 39–40).

5 Rouffaer and Ijzerman, Vol. I (1915), pp. 196, 202; plates 40, 41, 42. The composite version discussed below is from L. Hulsius, ed., *Eerste Shiffart an die Orientalische Indien, so die Hollandisch Schiff, im Martio 1585 aussgefahren, und in Augusto 1597 wiederkommen, verzicht* . . . (Nuremberg, 1598, first edition), (Frankfurt am Main, 1625, fifth edition). The plate in question appears on page 54 of Volume I of the 1606 edition.

6 We might note that German book editors, always enthusiastic illustrators, were here doing with the new literature of discovery (incipient ethnology) what they had done a century earlier with popular handbooks on philosophy and morals;

> . . . the ubiquitous books of emblems and devices presented the Renaissance reader with verbal pictures of an exemplary moral nature. Initially these were

> intended to consist only of words; the first emblem writer, Andrea Alciate, defined an emblem as a pictorial epigram, a verbal image, and the first edition of his famous *Emblemata* (1531) was not designed to include illustrations. The pictures were added by Alciate's German publisher, and though they were a logical enough development of the original idea, they remained very much an addition: the pictorial part of the emblem is a function of the verbal part, and to interpret the picture correctly, one must know how to read it.
> S. Orgel and R. Strong (1973: 3).

It is perhaps best to think of seventeenth-century pictures, such as Hulsius', as cross-cultural blazons, with a suitable one to adorn each of the world's worthy cultures. For Elizabethan-Jacobean stereotypes and *topoi* on 'East Indies' worship, color (tawny, sunburnt, swarthy), and so forth, see Cawley (1938: 154 ff).

7 While this review cannot possibly cover all relevant sources, we should at least note the 1633 report by Hendrik Brouwer which is 'the oldest report on Bali and the Balinese drawn up in the name of a Governor-General that has come down to us concerning the Hindu-culture and the death ritual on this island' (Hallema 1932). Covarrubias (1937: 377) cites a remarkable cremation description from this 1633 mission to gain Bali's help in combatting the Sultan of Mataram.

The period of Anglo-Dutch rivalry is very complicated. For a sense of the compounded misunderstandings between different Governor-Generals and other Western officials and their Balinese counterparts, the reader should consult the references in the text. A subsequent famous episode in the history of Balinese-Western commercial relations centers on the trading post established by the Danish adventurer Mads Lange in south Bali that flourished from 1839 to 1856; a recent English description of the 'white raja's' enterprises is Hanna (1971c). The third major episode of European economic interests in Bali – after Raffles and later Lange – comes with the actual military conquests, first of northern Bali in 1846, then of southern Bali during 1906–8. One manageable English chronicle of these events is Hanna (1971b). On the whole series of encounters during the takeover of northern Bali, see Deklerk (1938: 319–27); see also Tate (1971: 309–11). That Bali played no role in the plans of Governor-General Daendels (Raffles' predecessor) for a *colonie impériale* worthy of receiving Napoléon le Grand is clear from the account of French policies in the Indies in Collet (1910). As we see later, Raffles virtually rediscovered Bali.

The topic of Bali under conditions of revolution and warfare deserves an entire separate study; critical sources would include Last (1950), Weitzel (1859), Vlijmen (1975), Pendit (1954) and its accompanying album.

8 I am analyzing this early description of the state apparatus to prepare for later discussions of land and water rights at the local level and to appreciate the basis of Dutch colonial stereotypes of Balinese society. The Balinese state per se is discussed in a forthcoming work by C. Geertz (n.d.), with extensive documentation of Dutch source materials and a portrait of precolonial rice production, trade, state ritual, and so forth.

Not surprisingly, it was Van den Broek's sensational evocation of the plight of 'Joe-Bali' that took hold back home, especially during the Liberal period. On his expedition see Kemp (1890).

9 In his forthcoming work on *negara* Geertz (n.d.) offers an interpretation of the religio-political ideal, where the iconography of the supreme raja is sustained in ritual by Brahmana literati and in action by a momentarily effective administrative apparatus. As Geertz suggests, the ideal was probably only imperfectly, if ever, actualized. We can surmise the state symbology flourished especially during periods

of enhanced royal income, resulting from the support provided by different external parties – sometimes Chinese, sometimes (perhaps) Buginese, sometimes Dutch. Geertz captures the Java-derived courtly epic of Bali (and its complex context) when it worked.

10 The lasting achievement of these nineteenth-century scholars has been saluted and confirmed by C. Hooykaas and his many colleagues in Balinese philology. These works cannot simply be relegated to the past history of conceptions of Bali; they remain vital source materials for the discussion of current internal images of Balinese society and will be employed further later.

11 On this use of neoclassical versus romantic as holistic outlooks and attitudes, see especially Abrams (1971). The standards of generalization that Van Eck required for his description of the cockfight are one of the only cross-cultural theories I know to have received visual form. A decontextualized cockfight in fact appears in the famous grouping of statues by Malvina Hoffman in the Chicago Field Museum called 'Malay Archipelago Types Watching a Cockfight' with onlookers representing a man from Madura, a woman from Bali, a boy from Java, and another man from Borneo.

12 The history and problems of missionary work on Bali are too complex to treat adequately in this study. Summary work in Dutch includes Swellengrebel (1948) and Kersten (1947). There are on-going Catholic and Protestant (especially Pentecostal) efforts on the island. Another important nineteenth-century source is J. Jacobs (1883), crucial for any medical anthropology of Bali; see also Goris (1937).

2. Balipedia

1 We have focussed here on the local organization of *subaks* as Liefrinck did. In Chapter 5 we shall return to the rituals surrounding irrigation and their relation to cosmology and ecological variation.

2 Actually the twice-born idea in Bali is attenuated, and the upper castes are better designated three-peoples (*triwangsa*). According to Friederich, for example, 'the Brahman-band (*upavita*) belongs in India to the three upper castes, which are . . . 'born twice' (the second time through adopting this band). In that country it is of different kinds, according to three different castes. In Bali it is found only among the [Brahmana] *pedandas*, and then only if they are in full dress. But Satrias and Wesias, and even Sudras, who have obtained permission from the pedandas, also wear a protective band, a sort of amulet in ward . . . ; they only wear it, however, in time of war' (1849: 77).

3. Baliology

1 'It might indeed be doubted whether the arrangement of Balinese social life will ever be able to be totally clarified.'

2 Strangely, in spite of Bateson's eye for mythic redefinition and the interpretation of old-fashioned and Hindu, in his study of Bayung Gde with Margaret Mead (1942), they largely ignored Korn's data (1932: 228) on the upland area's contacts with the courts.

3 Achievements in archaeology and epigraphy are well represented by the two volumes of *Bali Studies* . . . (1960, 1969).

4 This typical case comes from *Awig-awig* (1972), a Balinese publication aimed at standardizing the variable contents of *desa* constitutions. The same concern with not giving more than one's share – and with ceremonializing the precautions to this end – characterizes irrigation organization as well. As Liefrinck notes: 'The generosity of the [*subak*] members was not left to chance, for it is laid down which foods, and how much of each must be contributed' (1969: 16).

For a very interesting account of the expressive forms for decision making and balancing interests in a group of *banjar* meetings, see Hobart (1975). His study reports on intensive fieldwork in a faction-ridden area near Bali's culture cradle. Orators in the meetings embody a kind of divine equilibrium, and their orations reveal a distinctly courtly quality: 'Emphasis is placed on calmness and refinement in public discussion and is evident in the quiet voices used and the self-abasing posture with eyes slightly downcast and hands on lap which are the ideal, and usually the practice' (Hobart 1975: 77–8). This refined style is less typical of *banjar* organizations in the areas the present study emphasizes. Moreover, in Tabanan and adjoining districts the 'limited catchment area' for recruiting personnel, said by Hobart (p. 68) to be 'effectively coterminous with the settlement' is expanded by means of interlocal temple associations.

An interesting study would be to compare the formal idiom of elaborately circumspect orators to the abrasive accusations often played out in rituals of trance by other specialist performers.

5 The anthropological faith in the privileged nature of information resulting from a fieldwork experience demands thorough study in its own right. Although precision is hardly one of ethnography's merits, the faith persists, and ethnographers tend after the fact to read into their fieldwork incontrovertible results. Yet, especially now that few colonial offices remain to shelter the roving anthropologist, fieldwork is a messy business, seldom successfully performed with the well filed fingernails of philologists. We first stumble awkwardly into hopelessly unfamiliar surroundings and throw together some temporarily bearable way of life to maximize information input as many hours of each day as we can endure. Then later, by carefully delineating what we feel we have gotten to know, what improvements we claim to make over our forerunners!

4. Bali now

1 Such chronicles also bear many similarities to the narratives comprising what James Fox has called the 'common form of historiography throughout the Malayo-Polynesian world' (1971). When viewed across these narrative materials many of the diverse societies of the Lesser Sundas appear culturally much closer than the old ideas of *kulturkreisen* would have allowed.

2 For a discussion of Tabanan town with emphasis on the post-Independence business and commercial life, see C. Geertz (1963: 17 ff). Post-war endeavors in local agricultural reform and cooperation throughout Tabanan district are described in Grader (1950–1).

Again, all personal names in the present study are pseudonymous.

3 On the GESTAPU see, for example, Arnold C. Brackman, *The Communist Collapse in Indonesia* (New York: W.W. Norton, 1969). On the 'academic debate' over whether the army or the PKI initiated the September 30 movement, see Stephen Sloan, *A Study in Political Violence: the Indonesian Experience* (Chicago: Rand McNally), 50 ff, and the sources he cites. Firsthand impressions up the subsequent massacres in Bali are described in John Hughes, *Indonesian Upheaval* (New

York, David McKay), 173–83, and Horace Sutton, 'Indonesia's Night of Terror,' *Saturday Review*, (Feb. 4, 1967), 25–31.

4 One way to obtain a more adequate sense of the very complicated nature of GOLKAR organization, and of the apparent rationales behind the program as it unfolded prior to the 1971 general elections, is to peruse *Indonesian Current Affairs Translation Service*. For items on the 'functional groups,' their relation to the armed services and so on, see the January–June, 1971 issue, pp. 17–22, 87–9, 161–3, 240–6, 315 ff, 379–82.

Marketside East's candidates represented three organizations under the GOLKAR banner: KOKARMENDAGRI, the old civil servants' lobby which was converted into a campaign machine, and two similar organizations in other governmental spheres, SOKSI and MKGR; on these aspects of the functional groups, see R. William Liddle (1972, 1973); see also Nishihara (1972).

5 See most recently P.J. Worsley, *Babad Buleleng* (1972) and the sources of Balinese royal chronicle (*babad*) literature he cites; we treat these sources more fully in Part II.

6 Later we shall address the issue of types of Balinese temples. I am alluding here to the ancestor temples called *dadia* by C. Geertz (1967). Some *dadia* (or *panti*) temples are clearly supported by a genealogical kingroup, as is the case in Marketside East. Others are ideationally a kingroup but questionably actually so. Some local so-called village-area temples were reported by the Dutch as originally ancestral *dadia* to which new unrelated residents accrued, converting them into locality origin temples (*pura puseh*). In Tabanan district certain types of *dadia* temple congregations (e.g. Pasek) are less tightly knit than those reported by Geertz or than Marketside East.

The principles for zig-zagging a line of authority in Balinese ancestor-groups recall Malay patterns in transmitting magical skills. As K. Endicott has summarized: 'The Malays consider three things in evaluating magicians: *tuntut* [instruction and practices such as prayers and fasting], . . . *pesaka* (the fact of hereditary transmission) and *baka* (that which is inherited). The hereditary factors seem to weigh more heavily than *tuntut* as such, though, if it is spontaneous, *tuntut* has the value of indicating heredity. Most respect and confidence is granted to the hereditary magician who has had a revelation . . . Revelation can skip one or several generations of hereditary magicians, and, if this is the case, the person skipped can combine his heredity with instruction. The slight deficiency in prestige for such a person is probably due to a belief that *ilmu* [magical science] transmitted directly from the ancestors is more valuable (perhaps more "pure") than that obtained through fallible human transmission' (1970: 17–18).

Finally the dynamic tension between perpetuating and founding a social grouping perhaps characterizes so-called conical clan social systems associated with Polynesia. Indeed Bali could almost be tagged as 'conical clans' (Sahlins 1973) with preferred endogamy and elaborated into a pan-Balinese *warna* scheme.

5. The social matrix in place

1 Many cosmological interpretations are reviewed in Covarrubias (1937) and Swellengrebel (1960). Recent Indonesian language summaries of the Hindu significance of temples appear in Upadeca (1968) and Ardana (1971). A sample of the vast Dutch colonial work on temples is translated into English in *Bali, Studies* (1960, 1969); see also Hooykaas (1964c); Swellengrebel (1948); and Goris (1960b;

1969a, b). There has, however, been little work on local status and political implications of temples and temple networks or on the recent political uses of temples.

2 A recent intellectualist codification of this formula relating *kayangan tiga* temple type to deity manifestation is contained in Ardana (1971: 14, 23) from which I take these Indonesian equivalent terms for the Hindu tripartite deity. On the great traditional scheme see also Goris (1960a, b).

3 On the *golgol* tenure system in Java, see C. Geertz (1965: 22); H. Geertz (1963: 87) reviews the Batak case, where 'the lineage which first claimed all the land in a certain region for its own continues to receive the respect of the members of all groups arriving later.' For further comparative data on the rights of original settlers, see Koentjaraningrat (1967: 398–9). In a discussion of Bali's old/new village pattern Bakker still considers that the new plains social organization arose when princely administration systems diminished original settlers' rights to land (1936: 596). Of course, first settler rights can be nostalgically evoked by current inhabitants, but their authenticity is often questionable. Consider, for example, Sangolan, an isolated *banjar* that is also a complete *desa adat* which independently supports a three-temple-cluster, geographically proximate but culturally distant from Tabanan town and long denigrated there for its rusticity. Current inhabitants of Sangolan tell how formerly there was also a single *subak* composed of entirely locally owned irrigated plots. Hard times, they say, eventually forced many of them to sell out to strangers.

4 Swellengrebel (1960: 56) mentions as well the possibility that in new settlements an ancestor temple (*pura dadia*) might develop into the origin temple (*pura puseh*) of the new desa (cf. Grader 1960b). The speculative social history which sees *pura dadias* as preliminary *pura pusehs* tallies with the emphasis on first settler rights in earlier studies.

5 The sacred spatial aspect of individual identity appears clearly in the *ngulapin* ritual used when someone dies whose corpse is unavailable for burial. If, for example, a Tabananer succumbs in Jakarta and must be buried there, his soul may be fetched home if his family carries proper offerings to Tabanan's western border (toward Jakarta). With geographic mobility increasing, there is much current discussion of *ngulapin*. One case involved a women who left her husband and children when he took a second wife. She was received back home by her family of birth but was denied renewed membership in her original *banjar* (abandoned when she married away). She soon died and was buried by her immediate family of origin, *banjar*-less, in an ill-defined section of the Tabanan graveyard. Subsequently her estranged husband decided to 'fetch' her by returning portions of her gravesite to the corpse's rightful resting place. Observers presumed he did this partly out of pressure from his children by the deceased and partly because she had, after all, become a candidate ancestor to his yard upon her marriage. It will later be this yard's duty to cremate her.

6 On this aspect of India, I learned much from a paper read by R.S. Khare at the Institute for Advanced Study, Princeton, 1975.

7 As James Fox (n.d.) has stressed and demonstrated, much work must be done to fill in the continuum between the standard theoretical poles of Indonesian subsistence represented by irrigation versus swidden. This is true even in the heartland of Indonesia's wet-rice belt.

8 One partial exception is the *guru-murid* rite of consecrating a new Brahmana *pedanda* priest, involving exemplary death/rebirth symbolism and a temporary obliteration of rank (see Korn 1960). This rite is, however, restricted to a fraction of one percent of the population, sort of a communitas in its purest and most

exclusive form between the supreme dyad in the society. There is no popular monasticism and little sectarian activity in Bali. Another seeming exception is the cockfight, described by Geertz (1972) something as a burst of liminality; but it hardly levels the actors, except for the few seconds the claws are flying; rather in Geertz' interpretation, it reaffirms principles of status differences. Teeth-filings are said to have once been surrounded by initiation-type rites, but these have eclipsed even in remoter areas. Moreover, traditionally both men and women undergo this operation and often individually. Korn (1932: 470) relates a female tooth-filing to the onset of menstruation, and sees it as a means of proclaiming a woman nubile. Vroklage (1937: 192) concurs and further deems it basically a matter of cosmetics (*schoonheidsmiddel*). One other Balinese phenomenon that might be approached as anti-structure is Nyepi, the yearly purge of evil spirits from *desa* territories; but this would merit close analysis, and it could equally be considered ritual inversion.

Belo (1949: 13) attests to Hinduized Bali's traditional 'absence of particularly marked puberty rites, initiation ceremonies and the like' in contrast to the rest of Southeast Asia. Since independence, however, popular education has introduced the communitas-based initiation rites of age-groups moving into secondary school.

6. The meaning of marriage and descent

1 There is good reason to apply an alliance framework in areas incompatible with its preassumptions, to help gauge its generality as a theory apart from its internal consistency as a doctrine. If the monograph (1975) by H. and C. Geertz on optional local 'corporate group' formation in traditional Bali is a study in how this case strains against 'descent theory,' this chapter hopes to suggest how Bali strains against alliance-theory premises about marriage, even as it is clarified by them.

2 The standard outlook in general surveys can be illustrated by Linton: '[Arabian nomads] were one of the few groups in the world in which marriage with a father's brother's daughter was not only permitted but preferred' (1955: 287). Even Patai's specialized study (1965), while criticizing Murphy and Kasdan (1959) for their too narrow claims of the range of patriparallel-cousin marriage, makes no mention of Bali, although it is described in the Human Relations Area Files he uses in a way which would qualify it under his 'endogamous unilineal descent groups.'

Actual rates of first- or second-patriparallel-cousin marriages in Bali can be very high. In one ancestor group of over 500 members it was 48 percent. H. and C. Geertz (1975) and Belo (1936) suggest parallel figures.

3 Other marriage traits singled out are child betrothal, hypergamy, Hawaiian generational kinterms, ban on widow remarriage, *suttee* or otherwise the levirate. Many are cited in Korn (1932: 472 ff).

4 We are emphasizing Balinese marriage as it persists where manipulation by overlords of their subjects' marriage rights has diminished. Such social engineering could be extreme; for example: 'In Badung the rajas had specified that the *kula wisuda* [a specially privileged Sudra group] and the *wargi* [inferior wife providers to the royal house] might marry each other, while [ordinary] Sudras who captured daughters from these groups were banished or punished by levying an increased compensation price (*bruidschat*)' (Korn 1932: 471). But the overlord patterns are themselves variations on the current system of marriage options.

5 I loosely adopt the terms 'complex' and 'elementary' from Lévi-Strauss (1969); other terms are possible. It is worth recalling the basic reason for Lévi-Strauss' interest in cross-cousins: '. . . in an exogamous system [cross-cousins] are the first

collaterals with whom marriage is possible' (1969: 98). As should become clear, in ancestor-group-endogamous Bali we find this same impulse (which Lévi-Strauss sees as the foundation of elementary-type systems) to define as preferable mates the nearest relatives not absolutely excluded by definitions of incest. Yet, in Bali, incest prohibitions vary with rank (at least ideally), and thus so do preferences.

Unlike Tikopia (Firth 1936: 539), Balinese capture marriages cannot be explained as a neutralization of political overtones in marriage, since they are not restricted to ruling groups.

6 While considering the love ideal, one should not overlook other motives behind a capture. In one case, for example, a sonless father wanted a 'borrowed son' (*sentana*) to marry his daughter so his line would continue, and her lover was the father's choice as well. But the lover's group forbade its men to marry out 'as women,' which implies inferiority. Thus, the lover had to capture his bride against her group's will. However, the romantic element provided the couple subsequent gratification.

7 This high regard in Bali for in-married women compromises (without totally eliminating) hypergamous principles in upward mobility, of the sort described for India by Srinivas: 'The giving of girls in marriage to boys from a higher caste or higher section of the same caste added to the prestige of the wife-giving lineage and caste. In some cases it also enabled the lower group to claim, eventually, equality with the higher group' (1969: 30).

8 A contrary practice, and a prime example of overlord interference in marriage, was the habit of some rajas to give women from a select noble house to commoners who performed an outstanding service. This move could be interpreted either as the raja nullifying the ordinary rules of hypergamy or as proof of the commoners' rights to a higher rank. The commoners would likely adopt the latter view.

Prearranged marriages (*mapadik* or *meminang*) confused those Dutch colonial schemes which radically distinguished the Hindu 'wave' of Balinese plains culture from the supposedly casteless hill peoples (Bali Aga). As Covarrubias summarized this trait which resisted appropriate distribution: 'Mapadik marriage is in general the old-fashioned, respectable way for the feudal aristocracy to marry and perhaps originated with them. Although, curiously enough, it is still prevalent among the Bali Aga of the mountains' (1937: 150).

9 This repeating, one-way, nonhierarchical marriage practice is noteworthy, if only because it is one of the few Balinese data which would, if overgeneralized, make Bali's Hawaiianlike kinship terms 'make sense.' It 'motivates,' as only 100 percent family marriage otherwise might, bilateral generational terms, since theoretically anyone your 'mother' marries is your 'father' along with his brothers, and his sisters are 'mothers,' and their children older or younger 'siblings', and so forth. Such practices are the more likely the more *beraya* feeling exists, and most likely of all if reasserted every generation. In other words if the proverbial fieldworker dropped in and happened to get these two houses' four generations of marriage as his inadequate sample, he would have a mechanical social structural explanation of Bali's terminology.

10 There can be two statuses of affiliation to an ancestor temple: (1) the geographically proximate core who regularly pay homage there and share the death contagion (*sebel*) of any deceased member; (2) the sometimes far-flung associates who give financial aid and occasionally attend festivals but do not suffer contagion. Ancestor groups are least likely to remain aloof from village-area death rituals. Traditionally only the highest nobles or royalty were independent of village-area death temples with exclusive rights to burial in a separate graveyard or to immediate cremation.

11 Informants also cite the advantage of marrying within one's own village-area which enables even out-married daughters to attend some ceremonies with original kin. Whether village-area congregations are consistently a reference point for selecting spouses is difficult to know. There are conceivable advantages to marriage within one's village-area, or one's irrigation society membership, or one's market network. But wherever there is an ancestor temple, the value on endogamy is clear.

12 This same distrust of outsiders appears when a son-in-law is adopted as heir (*sentana*) by a sonless man. Belo cites the priorities for choosing a *sentana*: 'take the family nearest on the male side, and if there is none, only then can he be taken from the female side' (1936: 21). The 'female side' may or may not be members of the ancestor group. Thus, the priorities run: agnate, matrifiliatively reckoned (of an in-married mother) temple-group male, outsider affine, and only in a pinch, or if a houseyard is unconcerned about its ideal descent, an unrelated outsider. Likewise, if a childless man adopts a daughter with the hopes of attracting a *sentana* for her, he looks for a patriniece. Adoption is a vast topic in itself; a thorough colonial study is Hunger (1934).

13 Some of the complex and variable prohibitions involving step relatives and in-laws are found in Korn (1932: 472). We should note as well that intercaste hypergamous provisions traditionally allowed for certain exceptions; for example, a Satria (princely) house threatened with extinction could take a Brahmana as wife.

14 This optional policy of forbidding marriage does not of course preclude the contrary and more conventional strategy of poor upper caste houses seeking lower wives who bring large dowries from inferior but wealthier groups. The interesting point about Bali is that given its multiple indexes of rank it can support both strategies.

15 Korn (1932: 151) mentions this restriction (*mekedeng ngad*) just once and then only as part of the origin tale of Balinese *ur*-folk: the first-generation couple sprang from the mind of the Godhead, the second generation was born of their incestuous relations, and the third generation was begotten through the *mekedeng ngad* relations engaged in by the second. Belo (1936: 27) mentions the prohibition under the Indonesian term *malik terbalik* which implies an illicit reversal. She says sister-exchange between matriparallel cousins (as coded by the bilateral, generational kinship terms) is also prohibited. De Brandts Buys consolidates Belo's findings as follows: 'In other words a youth and a maid who are each other's siblings [writing in Dutch, he uses the capitalized German *Geschwister*] must not marry another pair of siblings, if the father of one pair is the father's brother of the other pair or if their mother is the other's mother's sister' (1937: 411).

I checked for both *mekedeng ngad* and the next restriction to be discussed (*ngulihin bengbengan*) among members of different caste-statuses in four kingdoms with positive results.

16 On the related descent pattern of 'sinking status' through time, especially in royal and noble houses, see Geertz and Geertz (1975: Ch. V).

17 C. Geertz (1966) has analyzed the contents of certain titles, especially how some strata are converted into cycles (e.g., fifth birth-order equated with first, fifth generation recreates first). On the four elder sibling spirits (*kanda mpat*), see Hooykaas (1973). Lists of many of the terms that can be argued to be 'kinship terms' in Bali appear in Belo (1939: 14–15) and Geertz and Geertz (1975: Appendix).

18 De Zwann (1919) makes the interesting remark that same-sex twins are considered reincarnations into the family line of its own ancestors, an 'endo-reincarnation' theme recently reiterated by Hooykaas (1973: 23) as a feature of

Balinese religion. Belo documents the indigenous rethinking of the twins issue: twins versus triplets, one placenta versus two, different sex combinations; she also reports several local reversals of the standard formula which make same sex twins more portentous than opposite sex ones (1935: 528). H. Geertz (1959: 31) reports on a case in the 1950s in which political party alliance dictated the position on twin births taken by certain groups.

19 For some of the Hindu and Tantric wedding imagery, especially Siwa-Sakti and Siwa-Uma, in Balinese texts, see J. Hooykaas (1957), who concludes that in the Javanese Middle Ages the religious basis of marriage was the union of Siwa and Uma (p. 135–6).

20 Of course so-called subcaste in Bali has nothing to do with Indian *jati*; but Balinese caste ideology does derive in part from traditions in Indian texts. For example, Manu laws on principle marriage in the same caste and subsidiary marriages (hypergamous) with inferiors; reversals in the relative length of death contagion from *warna* to *warna*; and much more (cf. Dumont 1970a: 126–7, 114, 70, 51). Perhaps most important, as we saw, in certain marriage rites in Bali (just as in India): 'the Hindu finds himself symbolically and temporarily raised from his condition and assimilated to the highest, that of prince or Brahman for a non-Brahman . . . ' (Dumont 1970a: 53). Of course the issue of polygyny among Brahmanas remains vexed for Balinese themselves.

7. Caste in retroflexion

1 In the next chapters, and insofar as possible throughout this study, the concepts of status, rank, caste, and hierarchy are distinguished as follows: Status is the loosest usage and refers to practices and ideas which contrast two social units as more or less worthy, prestigious, sacred, important, and so forth. Rank implies a distilled, pure status criterion which can be projected into a consistent classification – as in Western military rank. Caste implies divisions of society which are distinguished by different kinds of descent thought of in terms of rank and often correlated with particular religious or political roles. Hierarchy suggests a more elaborate ideology which orders the physical and conceptual universe into configurations of rank and caste, especially with regard to life cycles and cosmic cycles as related to deities. The relation of these usages to *warna* and *dadia* should become clear later. Perhaps the most suitable term for Balinese social organization is the awkward hybrid 'caste-status.'

2 Friederich (1849) remains an indispensable source on Balinese perceptions of their own historicist traditions. In particular he suggests how rhetorically loaded the *Usana Bali* must have been: 'The Usana Bali does not tell us by what earthly means this religion was established, and the reason of [sic] this seems to be (1) that, in order to attain its full sanctity, the religion must be introduced by the gods themselves; (2) that it was desirable or necessary to spare the feelings of the conquered people (the original Balinese) by representing them as conquered, not by men, but by gods. The Usana Bali is intended only for the people' (p. 113). He contrasts to this version the *Usana Java*, wherein 'Arya Damar and Patih Gajah Mada were sent from Majapahit in the capacity of generals against the rebellious Bali. Arya Damar conquers the north, while Patih Gajah Mada remains inactive in the south; but, on the approach of Arya Damar, the latter portion also submits to this victorious general. The crossing over of the prince of Majapahit is caused, according to the Usana Java, by the appearance in Bali of a demoniacal king . . . ' (p. 113).

While Friederich attempts to cull from such discrepancies 'what would seem nearest the truth' (p. 114), his extensive account conveys many of the points of persistent dispute that remain at issue today among ambitious groups and their spokesmen.

3 Similarly, in 1972 there were reports from Jembrana district that several houseyards had rediscovered their descent from Balang Tamak, Bali's proverbial trickster (cf. Grader 1969c) and, according to some informants, the only notorious figure ever to be commemorated in temple shrines, which reflects his special non-competitive status.

4 We are here concerned with current opinions of interested Tabananers who have put the caste schemes to their own use. The texts on caste are themselves still continually reworked into differing versions. The philological concept of a definitive, authoritative 'standard' is misleadingly applied to these materials.

5 We should mention certain complications in this gross and disputable division of Balinese royal lines into Dewa and Gusti. Before the storied revolt which forced Sri Krisna Kepakisan's line to move from Gelgel to Klungkung, the line was titled Dalem. Ida I Dewa Agung was a demoted title of Bali's highest raja, which signifies the fall in status brought about by the coup attempted against his house. Also, the Gianyar and Karangasem royal lines are now officially called Anak Agung, which serves in Tabanan as an informal referent by outsiders (commoners) to all insiders (cf. *dalem* [insider] versus *jaba* throughout Bali). Tabanan informants relate that the Gianyar royal line (originally Ida I Dewa) and Karangasem (originally simply I Gusti) were granted the exclusive use of 'Anak Agung' as a title by the Dutch as a reward for their help in winning over South Bali or for subsequent cooperation. This is a Tabanan perspective on Anak Agung. All these titles can be translated by variable multiples of 'royal highness.'

6 A fairly complete account is in (*Babad Tabanan*); variant versions are found scattered throughout Tabanan in manuscripts owned by different parties, each of which inevitably reformulates the scheme to its advantage. Friederich (1849: 125) lists the Tabanan royal line as Arya Damar, a claim which would implicitly elevate it above most other ruling lines in Bali, since Damar appears as the first *arya* brought over by Gaja Mada. Currently however, one *Babad Tabanan* account is that Damar returned to Java, and Tabanan and Badung descend from Arya Kencheng. (Friederich interprets Kencheng as another name for Damar.) I follow informants in designating Tabanan royalty Kencheng; but no formulation by *arya* should be taken too literally.

7 The term Gusti has other meanings as well; for example, it is a positive honorific for a member of a higher Sudra line such as Pasek, when addressed by inferiors. Such complications illustrate again why it is so important in Bali to start with principles rather than with terms.

8 A dittoed Indonesian language version of this story is listed in the bibliography under *Sedjarah Singhat.* Friederich (1849: 127 ff) says much of Buahan, also recorded as the source of the Badung royal lines, which correlates with the view that Tabanan and Badung are collaterals.

8. Situational hierarchy

1 One version of the Warga Pasek traditions is compiled in I Gusti Bagus Sugriwa (1957). Van der Tuuk's 1897 dictionary glossed *pasek* as ' "the name of a class of people said to be descendants of the Dewa Agung" (the King of Klungkung, the suzerain of the other Balinese kings) "by a *sudra* (common) woman; many *paseks* are *mangkus* (guardians of village sanctuaries). They presume to be higher in rank than the *perbalis* and to belong really to the third caste;" ' cited in Theodore C. Th. Pigeaud, *Java in the 14th Century* (1962: 260–1).

2 The journal was issued bimonthly throughout 1971. Later it folded, only temporarily according to some supporters. The Pasek organization also issued a calendar with notes on the festival dates of, from its point of view, important temples; another guide to Pasek privileges in Balinese and Indonesian is *Bisama Pasek*, ed. I.N.S. Atmanadhi (1970). For the thirty Pasek temples whose figures I have, 7,870 family heads are tallied, and for the incomplete list of sixty-three temples as of issue ten, we can guess around 14,000 (out of a total population of over two million or around 250,000 family heads).

9. Images in action

1 An example of the latter type of convergence – in this case between (1) Lévi-Strauss' structuralist theories of preliterate myth and society and (2) nineteenth-century French Symbolist poetics – is developed in Boon (1972).

2 Let me couch in a footnote one last historical analogy to help evoke the stylistic relation between Java and Bali. In a recent study C. Geertz (1976) suggests that there were similarities in social rhetoric between the state processions of fourteenth-century Java and the renowned royal progresses of Elizabethan England. If this is true, then the successors to each might likewise be similar. Consider first the Elizabethan-Jacobean transition. Elizabeth's progresses marshalled the resources of an expanding mercantilism to symbolize the universality and supratemporality of the monarch's nearly divine authority. There was an actual institutional component to the elaborate symbology. Then, during the Jacobean-Carolinian era, such infra-structural expansion diminished; or at least, as parliamentarianism advanced, the economy faltered, and James rejected reformist theatricism, the imagery of mercan-tilism was unhitched from the monarch's star (cf. Yates 1974). Those earlier pro-gresses – as much indices of an expanding trade network and increasing inter-nationalism as icons of an insular Virgin Queen – were converted into the court masques of James I and Charles I. The latter scenic allegories presenting Platonic theories of royal authority (cf. Strong 1974), closed in on themselves; they grew removed from actual politics and economic enterprises, becoming esoteric cults of the privileged few rather than rhetorical strategies for persuading the masses. Masques ended by approximating something between 'an elaborate peripatetic charade' and a 'highly finished dramatic performance' (Summerson 1953: 69). It has been noted that in the previous century other European monarchical symbol-isms for asserting majesty and authority later degenerated into 'almost entirely a substitute for action' (Elliott 1975: 33). At least superficially the masques of Inigo Jones and Ben Jonson have a similar aura. It is not that Jacobean-Carolinian masques bear no relation to social, economic, and political processes, but that they persisted in the elaborate theatrical allegories (earlier used to tie the provinces to Elizabeth's throne) in spite of the diminishing verisimilitude of a symbology that projected into cosmic proportions the authority of the monarch (cf. Yates 1969).

This same sense of obsessive performance pervades Bali, but for quite different reasons. Just as Elizabethan pageantry for consolidating all the shires under the queen withdrew into the small circles of Jacobean-Carolinian elites, so Javanese symbology for integrating Majapahit's diverse domains partially withdrew (whether in the form of actual men or of texts and ideas) to a few fertile slopes next door.

3 The still definitive, remarkably durable work on Balinese dance and drama is de Zoete and Spies (1939). Any study of Balinese written literary traditions must begin with T. Pigeaud's volumes (1968–70); the collection of Balinese manuscripts in both the Kirtya Liefrinck-van der Tuuk in Singaraja and in the Leiden University Library is described in Vol. II (p. 5 ff); on palmleaf diagrams and illustrations, see Vol. III (pp. 39–46).

S. Robson lists one version of reading preferences in Bali: 'Easily the most popular is the *kakawin* Ramayana, followed by Sutasoma, Arjunawiwaha, Bharata-yuddha, and Bhomantaka . . . Ramayana is regarded as the finest from the viewpoint of beauty of language, while Sutasoma is the most significant from a religious point of view. Arjunawiwaha is difficult, largely because of its descriptions of nature . . . (1972: 316). Elsewhere C. Hooykaas explains the special place of the Old Javanese Ramayana in Bali: ' . . . it is considered to be the "*adi-kakawin*", the first and oldest of the "court poems," and consequently more or less the prototype or example for all the later ones (1958: 5). Finally, for a sense of the close link between drama and literature as depicted in a court poem, see Robson (1971: 32–40).

4 Although well formed Balinese ancestor groups have in ways styled themselves on South Asian high castes as depicted in Indic epics current in the island, we still have the problem of Balinese cousin marriage. Consider these observations on India by Karve:

> We find from these [epic] narratives that all the princesses came from kingdoms other than those of the grooms. The only exception to this is that of King Dasharatha, the king of Kosala, marrying a woman called Kausalya (a princess of Kosala). This suggests two different possibilities: (a) That he married his 'sister,' i.e., a woman belonging to his own patri-family. The story in the Buddhist literature about Rama in Dasharatha Jataka seems to take this view. It mentions that Dasharatha married his 'sister.' [This would almost certainly be the Balinese view as well]. (b) That there were two kingdoms of Kosala, a southern kingdom allied to the kingdom of Kashi and a northern one whose capital was Ayodhya. We have seen that the terms 'brother' and 'sister' were also used for the distant paternal relations of one's own generation. In the Mahabharata and Ramayana there is no mention of marriages between actual brothers and sisters or even of near patri-cousins (1965: 42–3).

I think that Balinese group endogamy is styled not after legendary Hindu high-castes, but after Hindu gods.

5 On this point I am grateful for suggestions by Ben Anderson.

6 The challenging studies of Georges Dumézil could occupy scholars of Bali for a long time; here only a few exceedingly preliminary suggestions will be hazarded. C. Littleton summarizes Dumézil's main theme:

> The common Indo-European ideology, derived ultimately from one characteristic of the Proto-Indo-European community, is composed of three fundamental principles: (1) Maintenance of cosmic and juridical order, (2) the exercise of physical prowess, and (3) the promotion of physical well-being. Each of these principles forms the basis for what Dumézil terms a *fonction* or 'function,' that is, a complex whole that includes both the ideological principle itself *and* its numerous manifestations in the several ancient Indo-European social and supernatural systems (in Huagen 1973: xi).

Applying this scheme to Bali's Southeast Asian-Pacific social life might parcel out Balinese concerns something like this: The third function certainly centers on rice and the rituals of agriculture; thus the *subak* rather than a particular caste appropriates Indic symbology in this sphere. The second function has most to do with residence, particularly as elaborated in the spatial lay-out of palaces (*puri*), which thus becomes the exemplary Satria sphere. The first function in Bali is concentrated in the symbology of death, the special province of Brahmana *pedanda* priests. Each *pedanda* is in meditation a living corpse; their cremations and their involvement with Siwa are explicitly connected with 'maintenance of cosmic and juridical order.' Moreover by stressing the vedic properties of Brahmana priests (these totally sublimated sacrificers) rather than the epic properties of the Brahman-baron coalition, our epic/romance contrast could be shifted toward Dumézil's mythic (vedic)/epic framework in his *Mythe et épopee* (1967–71). He attributes to epic (versus mythic) the more dynamic sense that we have reserved for the notion of romance (versus epic).

This latter concern of Dumézil comes out most clearly in his analysis and synthesis of symbols associated with the figure of the warrior:

> As Dumézil sees it, the Indo-European warrior, divine or mortal, played an ambiguous role in the ideology. He was at once integral to the system, forming, as we have seen, the 'second function' thereof, and at the same time something of an outsider, an untrustworthy fellow who might at any time turn against representatives of the other two functions . . . the Indo-European warrior figure typically commits three acts that run counter to the three ideological principles. These include defiance of the sovereign, be he god or mortal (an offense against the first function), cowardice in battle (a sin against the function of which he is the prime representative), and an assault, usually sexual or venal, upon a representative of the third function (Littleton in Haugen 1973: xiii).

We find here just the kind of leverage on hierarchical systems that we have traced in Balinese traditions and institutions and have found most directly expressed in images of Panji and Wisnu.

Finally, we might note the work of D.J. Ward (1968) following in Dumézil's footsteps on divine twins:

> . . . he suggests that the central figures in the Kudrun saga are comparable to those in the Ramayana, that is Rama, Hanuman, and Sita. In both cases a pair of heroes (functionally speaking, a set of twins) search for and eventually rescue an abducted bride (Littleton 1973: 209).

It is certainly provocative to note that the Indo-European ideology Bali draws on tends to portray same-sex twin heroes who are champions for an unrelated ideal spouse. Bali then converts these into opposite-sex twins, one of whom is the very spouse herself. I can think of no more vivid 'watershed' between the symbologies of Indo-Europe and the Pacific.

We cite Dumézil here because he has gone so far in trying to relate social praxis to cosmology, which is precisely our aim in calling expanding ancestor groups 'Wisnuvaic.' Of course, one must proceed with due caution. In *action* Panji can be Wisnu personified, but this in no way contradicts the historical-philological fact that Bali was influenced by Tantrism, and that 'one of the trademarks (*kenmerken*) of Tantrism is the worship of Siwa as god-of-love' and that 'the god-of-love Kamajaya, who is incarnated in Panji, is precisely Siwa' (J. Hooykaas 1957: 123). Elsewhere C. Hooykaas (1958: 65) mentions that the passage in the Old Javanese Ramayana where Waruna proclaims Rama an avatar of Wisnu is a later addition. This would support our view that the hero-champion figure came increasingly to be associated with an active image of Wisnu after the Old Javanese period and during the flowering of Majapahit and its subsequent partial retreat to Bali.

Again, however, all such formulae of divinity and 'function' are relational. Panji can be Siwa-love in one sense and Wisnu-*sakti* in another. If Panji can appear as an 'incarnation of Kama' where Siwa is the 'divine power' (*goddelijke kracht*) behind both (J. Hooykaas 1957: 124), then Panji can also be an incarnation of Wisnu whose divine power is likewise *ultimately* vested in an infinitely more remote Siwa served directly only by Brahmana *pedandas*.

7 In this respect Bali-Hindu *sakti* can perhaps be compared to Malay *kramat* as reviewed and analyzed by Endicott (1970: 92 ff). The ultimate comparativist accomplishment would be to plot the various soul-power terms – *semangat*, *roh*, and so on – against each other across Indonesian and Malay societies.

8 We are not, of course, referring to all individual historians. Drewes (1966), for example, emphasizes complexities and conflict between Javanism and Islam, and many scholars suggest how Indonesia's embrace of Islam was not wavelike at all:

> It is obvious therefore that the process of Islamization far from excludes a new wave of Hinduism; on the contrary, both religions side by side were giving Java new impulses until well into the fifteenth century – just as in South India itself these two religions were active at the same time and, one may surmise, just as in Malacca, even though officially an Islamic sultanate, Hinduism in one form or another was professed at least by the Indian and Javanese colonies there. (Teeuw, *et al* 1969: 23).

But when it comes to explicitly comparativist generalization, this lively sense of conflict and erratic movements in Indonesian religious change is often deadened.

9 In future work I hope to concentrate on another aspect of such 'ethnic boundaries' (Barth 1969), namely that the native sense of disjunction between Islamic and Hinduistic traditions probably increased with the intensification of colonial administration.

10 In a paper predominantly on developments in Islam in Jakarta, A. Samson (1972) reported on the recent expansion of mystic organizations and discusses their range of content and appeal. We find on the one hand the intellectualist *kebatinan* of cosmographic bureaucrats in the highest ranks of Javanese *priyayi* administration, and on the other hand so-called *abangan kebatinan*, curative soothsayers and their followers. According to the organizational schemes of the bureaucrats and their military counterparts, this is all one movement, but it is hard to find a common element in the religious experience of these diverse mystics. Samson concentrates on the Javanese shadow play and traditional courtly ideology as keys to the significance of mysticism, without elaborating the 'untutored version' of rural areas. (It is precisely in ordinary domestic mysticism that issues of ritualism are apt to loom largest.) Elsewhere a secularization and rationalistic modernism characterize an elite Islamic faction which is coping with the reaction against Islam caused by the post-GESTAPU role of ardent Muslims in mass killings. Both kinds of developments in Islam – mystical tendencies and bureaucratic modernism – are trends away from the mosque, but in opposite directions.

11 In his note on modern Bali-Hindu movements, 'phenomena that have been at work for more than fifty years,' Bagus lists these rationalist aims: '1. A trend toward simplifying the costly ceremonies. 2. A spread of knowledge about religion to the common people, based on monotheistic conception of Hinduism. 3. The rising of modern organizations, both political and social, based on religious principles' (n.d.: 5). Important literature by and about Parisada includes *Upadeca* (1968), Punyatmadja (1970) and a history (*Sedjarah Parisada . . .* 1970).

12 We might note the striking contrast between these sociological ramifications of Bali's *rsi* pattern and India's traditions of renunciation, wherein 'a man's right to leave his caste is recognized and he may literally die to his caste in order to conse-

crate himself to that which transcends man, in order to become a *sanyasi*' (Dumont 1970: 12). A Balinese 'renouncer' creates, if anything, more sacred 'busy work' (*karya*) for his kinsmen.

13 Reported in the Indonesian weekly news magazine *Tempo*. issue on 'Changing Bali' (*Bali yang berobah*) May 27, 1972.

14 For a review and explanation of the concepts of heterogenetic and orthogenetic social and cultural change, see M. Singer (1972: Ch. 9).

Conclusion: The end of romance?

1 Balinese death awaits its definitive cross-cultural spokesman. The two most important secondary sources on texts and death and after-death rites are Crucq (1928) and Wirz (1928). Some vivid descriptions of ceremonies and their ingredients appear in Covarrubias (1937: Ch. XI). Yet these efforts remain sociologically superficial and largely insensitive to cultural flexibility.

2 C. Hooykaas has most recently emphasized Balinese implications of rebirth: '. . . typically Balinese is the thought that frequently one is reborn in the circle of the blood relatives. Then the consulting of a *balian* will reveal which grandparent's soul has found its site in the baby asked about' (1973: 23). Also, from *Bagus Umbara* we sense that 'it is a common belief in Bali that the dead are reborn amongst their descendants and that they can often be recognized. The loving father is here shown predicting that his dear daughter will soon become pregnant and that she will bear a male child who will be the vehicle of his own soul' (C. Hooykaas 1968: 35).

Bibliography

Abrams, M.H. 1953. The Mirror and the Lamp: Romantic Theory and the Critical Tradition. London: Oxford University Press.

Adatrechtbundels. 1930. XXXIII.

Anderson, Benedict R. O'G. 1972. Java in a Time of Revolution. Ithaca: Cornell University Press.

Ardana, I Gusti Gde. 1971. Pengertian Pura di Bali. Proyek Pemeliharaan dan Pengembangan Kebudayaan Daerah Bali. Den Pasar.

Astley, Thomas. 1745. A New General Collection of Voyages . . . Vol. I. Published by His Majesty's Authority, London.

Atmanadhi, I.N.S. 1970. Bisama Pasek. Den Pasar: Maha Gotra Sanak Sapta Rsi.

Avé, J.B. 1970. Ethnic Groups in the Republic of Indonesia. *In* Anniversary Contributions to Anthropology. Leiden: E.J. Brill. pp. 95–123.

Awig-awig. 1972. Awig-awig: desa adat di Bali. Den Pasar: Parisada Hindu Dharma.

Babad Tabanan. n.d. Indonesian-Balinese Typescript in Kepustakaan Kesusasteran. Den Pasar: Universitas Udayana.

Bagus, I Gusti Ngurah. n.d. A Short Note on the Modern Hindu Movements in Balinese Society. Den Pasar: Jurusan Antropologi Budaya, Universitas Udayana.

Bakker, J.B. 1936. Structuur en Bevolking van Zuid-Bali. Koloniaal Tijdschrift. XXV: 595–602.

1937. Uitkomsten van een plaatselijk onderzoek gehouden in eenige desas van Zuid-Bali. Koloniaal Tijdschrift. XXVI: 529–48.

Bali, Studies. 1960. Bali, Studies in Life, Thought, Ritual. The Hague: W. van Hoeve.

1969. Bali, Further Studies in Life, Thought, Ritual. The Hague: W. van Hoeve.

Barth, Frederick, ed. 1969. Ethnic Groups and Boundaries. Boston: Little, Brown and Company.

Bastin, John. 1961. Essays on Indonesian and Malayan History. Monographs on Southeast Asian Subjects, No. 2. Singapore: Eastern Universities Press.

Bateson, Gregory. 1937. An Old Temple and a New Myth. Djawa. 17 (5–6): 1–17. (Reprinted in Belo 1970).

1949. Bali: The Value System of a Steady State. *In* Social Structure: Essays Presented to A.R. Radcliffe-Brown, Meyer Fortes, ed. Oxford: Clarendon Press. pp. 35–53.

1973. Style, Grace, and Information in Primitive Art. *In* Primitive Art and Society. Anthony Forge, ed. London: Oxford University Press.

Bateson, Gregory and Margaret Mead. 1942. Balinese Character, a Photographic Analysis. Special Publication, 2. New York: New York Academy of Sciences.

Belo, Jane. 1935. A Study of Customs Pertaining to Twins in Bali. Tijdschrift voor Indische Taal-, Land-, en Volkenkunde. LXXV: 483–549.
1936. A Study of a Balinese Family. American Anthropologist. 38 (1): 12–31.
1949. Bali: Rangda and Barong. Monographs of the American Ethnological Society, 16. Seattle: University of Washington Press.
1953. Bali: Temple Festival. Monographs of the American Ethnological Society, 22. Seattle: University of Washington Press.
1960. Trance in Bali. New York: Columbia University Press.
Belo, Jane, ed. 1970. Traditional Balinese Culture. New York: Columbia University Press.
Benda, Harry J. 1958. The Crescent and the Rising Sun. The Hague: van Hoeve.
Benda, Harry J. and John A. Larkin. 1967. The World of Southeast Asia, Selected Historical Readings. New York: Harper & Row, Publishers.
Berg, C.C. 1929. Kidung Pamancangah, de Geschiedenis van het Rijk van Gelgel, Critisch Uitgegeven, I. Santpoort: Javaansch-Balische Historische Geschriften.
Birkelbach, A. 1973. The Subak Association. The Cornell Modern Indonesia Project. Indonesia. 16: 153–69.
Van Bloemen Waanders. 1859. Aanteekeningen omtrent de Zeden en Gebruiken der Balinezen, inzonderheid die van Boeleleng. Tijdschrift voor Indische Taal-, Land- en Volkenkunde. VIII: 105–279.
Boon, James A. 1970. Lévi-Strauss and Narrative. Man. 5 (4): 702–3.
1972. From Symbolism to Structuralism: Lévi-Strauss in a Literary Tradition. Oxford: Blackwell's; New York: Harper & Row, Publishers.
1973a; Dynastic Dynamics: Caste and Kinship in Bali Now. Unpublished dissertation, University of Chicago.
1973b. Further Operations of 'Culture' in Anthropology' A Synthesis of and for Debate. *In* The Idea of Culture in the Social Sciences. Louis Schneider and Charles Bonjean, eds. Cambridge: Cambridge University Press.
Boon, James A. and David M. Schneider. 1974. Kinship vis-à-vis Myth: Contrasts in Lévi-Strauss' Approaches to Cross-cultural Comparison. American Anthropologist. 76 (4): 799–817.
Brackman, Arnold C. 1969a. Indonesia: The Gestapu affair. New York: American-Asian Educational Exchange.
1969b. The Communist Collapse in Indonesia. New York: W.W. Norton Company, Inc.
Brandts Buys, J.S. 1937. Tijdschriftenoverzicht. Djawa. 17 (5–6): 408–30.
Van den Broek, H.A. 1835. Verslag Nopens het Eiland Bali, de Vorsten, Hunne Geaardheid en Betrekkingen, den Handel, de Culture, de Bevolking, Hare Zeden en Gewoonten, Godsdienst en Andere Bijzonderheden. De Oosterling. Tijdschrift van Oost-Indie, eerste deel: 158–236.
De Bruyn Kops. G.F. 1917. Baliërs. Encyclopaedie van Nederlandsch-Indie, tweede druk, erste deel. The Hague: Martinus Nijhoff.
Buchler, Ira R. and Henry A. Selby. 1968. Kinship and Social Organization. New York: Macmillan, Inc.
Van Buitenen, J.A.B., trans. 1973. The Mahabharata. Volume I. Chicago: The University of Chicago Press.
Burke, Kenneth. 1957. The Philosophy of Literary Form. Revised. New York: Random House, Inc.
1966. Language as Symbolic Action. Berkeley: University of California Press.
Burling, Robbins. 1964. Hill Farms and Padi Fields: Life in Mainland South-East Asia. Englewood Cliffs: Prentice-Hall, Inc.

Cabaton, A. 1911. Java, Sumatra, and the Other Islands of the Dutch East Indies. Bernard Miall, trans. London: T. Fisher Unwin.
Cawley, R.R. 1938. The Voyagers and Elizabethan Drama. Boston: D.C. Heath & Company.
Cohn, Bernard S. 1971. India: The Social Anthropology of a Civilization. Englewood Cliffs: Prentice-Hall, Inc.
Collet, Octave-J. A. 1910. L'Ile de Java sous la domination française. Bruxelles: Librairie Falk Fils.
Covarrubias, Miguel. 1937. Island of Bali. New York: Alfred A. Knopf, Inc.
Crawfurd, John. 1820. On the Existence of the Hindu Religion in the Island of Bali. Asiatick Researches. XIII: 128–70.
1856. A Descriptive Dictionary of the Indian Islands and Adjacent Countries. London: Bradbury and Evans.
Crawley, A.E. 1907. Exogamy and the Mating of Cousins. *In* Anthropological Essays Presented to Edward Burnett Tylor. Oxford: Clarendon Press.
Crucq, K.C. 1928. Bijdrage tot de kennis van het Balisch Doodenritueel. Santpoort.
Curtius, E.R. 1953. European Literature and the Latin Middle Ages. Princeton: Princeton University Press.
Das, Veena. 1973. The Structure of Marriage Preferences: An Account From Pakistani Fiction. Man. 8 (1): 30–45.
Drewes, G.W.J. 1966. The Struggle Between Javanism and Islam as Illustrated by the Serat Dermagandul. Bijdragen tot de Taal-, Land-, en Volkenkunde. 122 (3): 21–365.
Dumézil, Georges. 1966. Mythe et épopée. I. L'Idéologie des trois fonctions. Paris: Gallimard.
1968. Mythe et épopée. II. Types épiques indo-européens. Paris: Gallimard.
1971. Mythe et épopée. III. Un héros, un sorcier, un rois. Paris: Gallimard.
Dumont, Louis. 1968. Marriage Alliance. *In* International Encyclopedia of the Social Sciences. O.L. Sills, ed. New York: The Free Press.
1970a. Homo hierarchicus: An Essay on the Caste System. Mark Sainsbury, trans. Chicago: University of Chicago Press.
1970b. Religion/Politics and History in India. Paris: Mouton.
Dutt, Romesh C., trans. 1910. The Ramayana and the Mahabharata: Condensed into English Verse. New York: E.P. Dutton & Co., Inc.
Van Eck, R. 1879. Schetsen uit het Volksleven (I Hanengevecht). De Indische Gids. pp 102–18.
Elliott, J.H. 1975. Imperial Image Makers (Review of Astraea by Frances Yates). New York Review of Books, XXII (2): 32–4.
Encyclopaedie van Nederlandsch-Indië [Encyclopedia]. 1917. Volume I. The Hague: Martinus Nijhoff.
Encyclopedia of Religion and Ethics. 1908–26. New York: Charles Scribner's Sons.
Endicott, Kirk Michael. 1970. An Analysis of Malay Magic. Oxford: Clarendon Press.
Epstein, Adele G. 1973. Review of Thai Titles and Ranks, by Robert B. Jones (Cornell University Southeast Asia Program Data Paper #81, 1971). Journal of Asian Studies. XXXII (2): 374–6.
Firth, Raymond. 1963. We, the Tikopea. Boston: Beacon Press.
Fortune, Reo F. 1932. Incest. *In* The Encyclopedia of the Social Sciences, vol. 7. New York: Macmillan, Inc. pp. 620–2.
Fox, James J. 1971. A Rotinese Dynastic Genealogy: Structure and Event. *In* The Translation of Culture. T.O. Beidelman, ed. London: Tavistock. pp. 37–78.

n.d. The Clash of Economies. Stanford: Center for Behavioral Studies, (typescript). Revised (Harvard University Press, forthcoming).
Franken. H.J. 1960 [1951]. The Festival of Jayaprana at Kalianget. *In* Bali, Studies. (1960): 235–65.
Frick, Christopher and Christopher Schweitzer. 1700. Voyages to the East Indies. The Seafarers' Library, 1929. London: Cassell.
Friederich, R. 1849. Over de Godsdienst van Bali; and Voorloopig verslag van het Eiland Bali. Revised and published in English, and republished as The Civilization and Culture of Bali. Ernst R. Rost, ed. Calcutta: Susil Gupta, 1959.
Frye, Northrop. 1957. Anatomy of Criticism. Princeton: Princeton University Press.
Gallie, W.B. 1968. Philosophy and the Historical Understanding, second edition. New York: Schocken Books, Inc.
Gardner, Erle Stanley. n.d. Simanis dan Harta Warisan. Herdian Suhardjono, trans. Jakarta: Saka Widya.
Geertz, Clifford. 1959. Form and Variation in Balinese Village Structure. American Anthropologist. 61: 94–108.
1960. The Religion of Java. New York: The Free Press.
1961. Review of Bali, Studies in Life, Thought, and Ritual. Bijdragen tot de Taal-, Land- en Volkenkunde van Nederlandsch Indie. CXVII: 498–502.
1963. Peddlers and Princes – Social Change and Economic Modernization in Two Indonesian Towns. Chicago: The University of Chicago Press.
1964. Internal Conversion in Contemporary Bali. *In* Malayan and Indonesian Studies. J. Bastin and R. Roolvink, ed. Oxford: Clarendon Press. pp. 282–302.
1965. The Social History of an Indonesian Town. Cambridge: The M.I.T. Press.
1966. Person, Time, and Conduct in Bali: An Essay in Cultural Analysis. New Haven: Yale Southeast Asia Studies.
1967. Tihingan, a Balinese Village. *In* Villages in Indonesia. Koentjaraningrat, ed. Ithaca: Cornell University Press.
1968. Islam Observed. New Haven: Yale University Press.
1972a. The Wet and the Dry: Traditional Irrigation in Bali and Morocco. Human Ecology. 1 (1): 23–39.
1972b. Religious Change and Social Order in Soeharto's Indonesia. Asia. 27: 62–84.
1972c. Deep Play: Notes on the Balinese Cockfight. Daedalus. 101 (1): 1–37.
1973. The Interpretation of Cultures. New York: Basic Books, Inc. (Contains 1964, 1966, 1972c).
1975. Centers, Kings, and Charisma. *In* Culture and its Creators. J. Ben-David and T. Clark, eds. (forthcoming).
n.d. Negara, the Theater State in Bali (manuscript).
Geertz, Hildred. 1959. The Balinese Village. *In* Local, Ethnic, and National Loyalties in Village Indonesia. G.W. Skinner, ed. New Haven: Yale University Southeast Asia Studies. pp. 24–33.
1963. Indonesian Cultures and Communities. *In* Indonesia. Ruth T. McVey, ed. New Haven: HRAF Press. pp. 24–96.
1972. Bali. *In* Frank LeBar, ed. Ethnic Groups of Insular Southeast Asia. New Haven: HRAF Press. pp. 60–5.
Geertz, Hildred and Clifford Geertz. 1964. Teknonymy in Bali: Parenthood, Age-grading and Genealogical Amnesia. Journal of the Royal Anthropological Institute. 94 (Part II): 94–108.
1975. Kinship in Bali; Chicago: The University of Chicago Press.
Geyl, Pieter. 1964. History of the Low Countries. New York: St. Martin's Press, Inc.

Goethals, Peter R. 1967. Rarak: a Swidden Village of West Sumbawa. *In* Villages in Indonesia. Koentjaraningrat, ed. Ithaca: Cornell University Press. pp 30–62.

Goldman, Irving. 1970. Ancient Polynesian Society. Chicago: University of Chicago Press.

Gombrich, E.H. 1969. Art and Illusion. Princeton: Princeton University Press.

Gonda, J. 1973. Sanskrit in Indonesia, 2nd edition. New Delhi: International Academy of Indian Culture.

Gorer, Geoffrey. 1936. Bali and Angkor, Or Looking at Life and Death. Boston: Little, Brown and Company.

Goris, R. 1937a. Boekbesprekingen (Review of J. Belo 1936). Djawa. 17 (5–6): 431.

1937b. The Balinese Medical Literature. Djawa. 17 (5–6).

1960a [1935]. The Religious Character of the Village Community. *In* Bali, Studies. pp. 77–100.

1960b [1938]. The Temple System. *In* Bali, Studies. pp. 103–11.

1960c [1929]. The Position of the Blacksmiths. *In* Bali, Studies. pp. 290–9.

1969a [1937]. Pura Besakih, Bali's State Temple. *In* Bali, Further Studies. pp. 75–88.

1969b [1948]. Pura Besakih through the Centuries. *In* Bali, Further Studies. pp. 89–104.

1969c [1939]. The Decennial Festival in the Village of Selat. *In* Bali, Further Studies. pp. 105–30.

Goudriaan, T. and C. Hooykaas. 1971. Stuti and Stava (Bauddha, Saiva and Vaisnava of Balinese Brahman Priests). Verhandelingen der Koninklijke Nederlandse Akademie van Wetenschappen, Afd. Letterkunde 76.

Gouldner, Alvin W. 1973. Romanticism and Classicism: Deep Structures in Social Science. Diogenes. 82: 108–16.

Grader, C.J. 1960a [1939]. Irrigation System in the Region of Jembrana. *In* Bali, Studies. pp. 267–88.

1960b [1949]. The State Temples of Mengwi. *In* Bali, Studies. pp. 155–86.

1960c [1939]. Pemayun Temple of the Banjar of Tegal. *In* Bali, Studies. pp. 187–232.

1969a [1940]. Pura Meduwe Karang at Kubutambahan. *In* Bali, Further Studies. pp. 131–74.

1969b [1939]. Balang Tamak. *In* Bali, Further Studies. pp. 175–88.

1950. De Rukun Tani-beweging in het landschap Tabanan. Indonesie. 4 (5): 392–420.

Hall, D.G.E. 1964. A History of South-east Asia. London: Macmillan Publishers Ltd.

Hallema, A. 1932. Hendrik Brouwer, Gouverneur-Generaal van Nederlandsch Oost-Indie, 1632–1636, en zijn 'Expresse Commissis' naar Bali in 1633. De Indische Gids. 54: 310–28, 399–418.

Handbook of the Netherlands East-Indies. 1924. Buitenzorg, Java: Division of Commerce of the Department of Agriculture, Industry, and Commerce.

Hanna, Willard A. 1971a. American University Fieldstaff Reports. Southeast Asia Series. Bali and the West, I: Early Contacts. XIX (12).

1971b. American University Fieldstaff Reports. Southeast Asia Series. Bali and the West, II: Later Conflicts. XIX (14).

1971c. American University Fieldstaff Reports. Southeast Asia Series. The Mads Lange Factory. XIX (15).

1972a. American University Fieldstaff Reports. Southeast Asia Series. Too Many Balinese XX (1).

1972b. American University Fieldstaff Reports. Southeast Asia Series. Cultural Tourism. XX (2).

1972c. American University Fieldstaff Reports. Southeast Asia Series. Population and Rice. XX (4).

Haugen, Einar, ed. 1973. Gods of the Ancient Northmen, by Georges Dumézil. Introduction by C. Scott Littleton. Berkeley: University of California Press.

Hiltebeitel, Alf. 1974. Dumézil and Indian Studies. The Journal of Asian Studies. XXXIV (1).

Hobart, Mark. 1975. Orators and Patrons: Two Types of Political Leader in Balinese Village Society. *In* Political Language and Oratory in Traditional Society. M. Bloch, ed. London: Academic Press, Inc.

Hocart, A.M. 1950. Caste, A Comparative Study. London: Methuen.

1970. Kings and Councillors. Introduction by Rodney Needham. Chicago: The University of Chicago Press.

Hooykaas, C. 1958a. The Lay of Jaya Prana. London: Luzac.

1958b. The Old-Javanese Ramayana: An Examplary Kakawin as to Form and Content. Verhandelingen der Koninklijke Nederlandse Akademie van Wetenschappen, Afd. Letterkunde. LXV (1). Amsterdam: N.V. Noord-Hollandsche Uitgevers Maatschappij.

1964a. The Balinese Sengguhu-priest, a Shaman, but not a Sufi, a Saiva, and a Vaisnava. *In* Malayan and Indonesian Studies. J. Bastin and R. Roolvink, eds. Oxford: Clarendon Press. pp. 267–81.

1964b. Weda and Sisya, Rsi and Bhujangga in Present-day Bali. Bijdragen tot de Taal-, Land-, en Volkenkunde. 120: 231–44.

1964c. Agama Tirtha: Five Studies in Hindu-Balinese Religion. Verhandelingen der Koninklijke Nederlandse Akademie van Wetenschappen, Afd. Letterkunde. LXX (4).

1966. Surya-Sevana, the Way to God of a Balinese Siva Priest. Verhandelingen der Koninklijke Nederlandse Akademie van Wetenschappen, Afd. Letterkunde. LXXII (3).

1968. Bagus Umbara, Prince of Koripan. London: British Museum.

1973a. Balinese Baudda Brahmins. Verhandelingen der Koninklijke Nederlandse Akademie van Wetenschappen, Afd. Letterkunde. 80.

1973b. Religion in Bali. Institute of Religious Iconography. State University Groningen. Leiden: E.J. Brill.

1974. Cosmogony and Creation in Balinese Tradition. The Hague: M. Nijhoff.

n.d. Hinduism of Bali. The Adyar Library Bulletin.

Hooykaas-van Leeuwen Boomkamp, J.H. 1957. De Godsdienstige Ondergrond van het Praemuslimse Huwelijk op Java en Bali. Indonesie. X/2: 109–36.

1961. The Ritual Purification of a Balinese Temple. Verhandelingen der Koninklijke Nederlandse Akademie van Wetenschappen, Afdeeling Letterkunde. New series. LXVII (4).

Hughes, John. 1967. Indonesian Upheaval. New York: David McKay Co., Inc.

Hulsius, L. ed. 1598, 1625. Eerste Shiffart an die Orientalische Indien, so die Hollandisch Schiff, im Martio 1595 aussgefahren, und in Augusto 1597 wiederkommon, verzicht. First edition (1598) Nuremburg: Hulsius; fifth edition (1625) Frankfurt am Main: Hulsius. Frontispiece from 1606 edition, Vol. I.

Hunger, F.W.F. 1932. Adatdesa's en gouvernementsdesa's in Zuid-Bali. Koloniale Studien. Weltvreden. XVI (ii): 603–16.

1934. Over Eigen en Geadopteerde Kinderen op Zuid-Bali. Koloniaal Tijdschrift. XXIII: 237–66.

1937. Adatuitgaven in Zuid-Bali. Koloniale Studien. XXI: 610–40.

Hurgronje, Snouck. 1924. Verspreide Geschriften IV. Bonn and Leipzig: Kurt Schroeder.

Indonesian Current Affairs Translation Service. 1971. Jakarta.

Jacobs, Julius. 1883. Eenigen Tijd onder de Baliërs. Batavia.

Karve, Irawati. 1965. Kinship Organization in India. Bombay and New York: Asia Publishing House.

Kat Angelino, P. de. 1920. Het Balische Huwelijksrecht. Weltvreden: Koloniale Studien. IV (i): 27–53, 221–48.

1932. Le Problème Colonial, vol. II. E.P. van der Berghe, trans. The Hague: M. Nijhoff.

Kemp, P.H. van der. 1899. Het Verblijf van Commissaris Van den Broek op Bali (18 December 1817–24 Juni 1818). Bijdragen tot der Land-, Taal-, en Volkenkunde. 50: 331–90.

Kennedy, Raymond. 1962. Bibliography of Indonesian Peoples and Cultures. Second Revised Edition. New Haven: Human Relations Area Files Press.

Ker, W.P. 1957. Epic and Romance. New York: Dover Publications, Inc.

Kersten, J. 1948. Balische Grammatica. The Hague: N.V. Uitgeverij W.W. van Hoeve.

1947. Bali. Eidhoven: Uitgevermaatschappij 'De Pilgrim' N.V.

Khuri, Fuad I. 1970. Parallel Cousin Marriage Reconsidered: A Middle Eastern Practice that Nullifies the Effects of Marriage on the Intensity of Family Relationship. Man. 5 (4): 597–618.

De Klerk, E.S. 1938. History of the Netherlands East Indies. Rotterdam.

Koentjaraningrat. 1967a. The Village in Indonesia Today. *In* Villages in Indonesia. Koentjaraningrat, ed. Ithaca: Cornell University Press. pp. 386–405.

1967b. Tjelapar: a Village in South Central Java. *In* Villages in Indonesia. Koentjaraningrat, ed. Ithaca: Cornell University Press. pp. 244–80.

Korn, V.E. 1922. Lepra en Kastenverschil op Bali. De Indische Gids. XLIV (i): 231–5.

1932. Het Adatrecht van Bali. Second Edition. The Hague.

1933 [1960a]. De Dorpsrepubliek Tnganan Pagringsingan. Santpoort. Partial translation in Bali, Studies. (1960): 303–368.

1948. Adat Law. *In* Report of the Scientific Work done in The Netherlands on behalf of the Dutch Overseas Territories during the Period between approximately 1918 and 1943, B.J.O. Schrieke, ed. Werkgemeenschap van Wetenschappelijke Organisaties in Nederland.

1960b [1928]. The Consecration of a Priest. *In* Bali, Studies. pp. 131–54.

Kraus, Gregor and Karl With. 1922. Bali. Hagen i. W., 1921, 2 vols.

Van der Kroef, J. 1963. The Dialectic of Colonial Indonesian History. van der Peet.

Kuhn, Thomas. 1962. The Structure of Scientific Revolutions. Chicago: The University of Chicago Press.

Lach, Donald. F. 1965. Asia in the Making of Europe. Volume I. The Century of Discovery, Books I and II. Chicago: The University of Chicago Press.

Lansing, John S. 1974. Evil in the Morning of the World. Ann Arbor: Michigan Papers on South and Southeast Asia No. 6.

Last, Jef. 1950. Bali in de Kentering. Amsterdam.

Leach. E.R. 1961. Rethinking Anthropology, London School of Economics Monographs on Social Anthropology, 22. London: Athlone.

Lekkerkerker, C. 1921. De Baliërs. *In* De Volken van Nederlandsch Indië in Monographieen. II. J.C. van Eerde. Amsterdam: Uitgevers-Maatschappij 'Elsevier.' (1943).

1926. De Kastenmaatschappij in Britsch-Indie en op Bali. Mensch en Maatschappij. 2: 175–332.

1918. Hindoerecht in Indonesie. Dissertation, University of Leiden. Amsterdam.

Lévi-Strauss, Claude. 1967. Structural Anthropology. New York: Doubleday & Co., Inc.

1969. The Elementary Structures of Kinship. J.H. Bell and J.R. von Sturmer, trans. Rodney Needham, ed. Boston: Beacon Press.

1971. L'Origine des manières de table (Mythologiques III). Paris: Plon.

Liddle, R. William. 1972. The 1971 Indonesian Election: a View from the Village. Asia. 27.

1973. Evolution from Above: National Leadership and Local Development in Indonesia. Journal of Asian Studies. XXXII (2): 287–309.

Liefrinck, F.A. 1927. Bali en Lombok: Geschriften. Amsterdam.

1969 [1886]. Rice Cultivation in Northern Bali. *In* Bali, Further Studies. pp. 3–73.

Linton, Ralph. 1955. The Tree of Culture. New York: Alfred A. Knopf, Inc.

Littleton, C. Scott. 1973. The New Comparative Mythology: An Anthropological Assessment of the Theories of Georges Dumézil, Revised Edition. Berkeley: University of California Press.

Loeb, Edwin M. 1972. Sumatra: Its History and People. Kuala Lumpur: Oxford University Press.

McKean, Philip F. 1971. A Preliminary Analysis of the Inter-action between Balinese and Tourists: The 'Little', 'Great', and 'Modern' Traditions of a Culture. Den Pasar: Museum Bali.

McPhee, Colin. 1966. Music in Bali. New Haven: Yale University Press.

1970 [1948]. Dance in Bali. *In* Belo, Jane, ed. 1970. Traditional Balinese Culture, New York: Columbia University Press.

Mandelbaum, David G. 1970. Society in India. 2 vols. Berkeley: University of California Press.

Masselman, George. 1963. The Cradle of Colonialism. New Haven: Yale University Press.

Mead, Margaret. 1939. The Strolling Players in the Mountains of Bali. Natural History. XLIII: 17–26.

1970. The Art and Technology of Fieldwork. *In* A Handbook of Method in Cultural Anthropology. Raoul Naroll and Ronald Cohen, eds. Garden City: Natural History Press. pp. 246–65.

1974. Review of Tahitians: Mind and Experience in the Society Islands. Robert I. Levy. Chicago. American Anthropologist. 76 (4): 907–9.

Mollema, J.C. ed. 1935. Der Eerste Schipvaart der Nederlanders naar Oost-Indië . . . Linschoten Vereeniging. (Sequel to Rouffaer and Ijzerman 1915, 1955, 1929).

Van Mook, H.J. 1958. Kuta Gde. *In* The Indonesian Town. The Hague: W. van Hoeve.

Murphy, Robert F. and Leonard Kasdan. 1959. The Structure of Parallel Cousin Marriage. American Anthropologist. 61: 17–29.

Nash, Dennison. 1968. The Role of the Composer. *In* Readings in Anthropology, Volume II. Morton H. Fried, ed. New York: Thomas Y. Crowell Company Inc. pp. 746–78.

Nielsen, Aage Krarup. 1928. Leven en Avonturen van een Ostinjevaarder op Bali.

Translated into Dutch by Claudine Bienfait. Amsterdam: Em. Querido's Uitgevers-Maatschij.
Van Nieuwenhuijze, C.A.O. 1958. Aspects of Islam in post-colonial Indonesia. The Hague: W. van Hoeve.
1974. Indonesia. The Legacy of Islam. Joseph Schacht, ed. Oxford: Clarendon Press. pp. 144–56.
Nieuwenkamp, W.O.J. 1906–10. Bali en Lombok. Reisherinneringen en Studies omtrent Land en Volk, Kunst en Kunstnijverheid. 3 vols. Edam.
Nishihara, Masashi. 1972. Golkar and the Indonesian Elections of 1971. Ithaca: Cornell University Modern Indonesia Project, 56.
Nitisastro, Widjojo. 1970. Population Trends in Indonesia. Ithaca: Cornell University Press.
Orgel, Stephen and Roy Strong. 1973. Inigo Jones: The Theatre of the Stuart Court. Berkeley: University of California Press.
Parsons, Talcott and Edward A. Shils, eds. 1962. Toward a General Theory of Action. New York: Harper & Row, Publishers.
Patai, Raphael. 1965. The Structure of Endogamous Unilineal Descent Groups. Southwestern Journal of Anthropology. 21 (4): 325–50.
Peacock, James L. 1968. Rites of Modernization. Chicago: The University of Chicago Press.
1973. Indonesia: An Anthropological Perspective. Pacific Palisades: Goodyear Publishing Co. Inc.
n.d. Clown and Transvestite in Java: Symbolic Inversion and Social History. Forthcoming in Barbara Babcock-Abrahams, ed. Ithaca: Cornell University Press.
Pendit. Nj.S. 1954. Bali Berdjuang. Jajasan Kebaktian Pedjuang. Den Pasar.
Piegeaud, Theodore G.Th. 1968–70. Literature of Java. University of Leiden.
1968. Vol. II. Descriptive Lists of Javanese Manuscripts.
1970. Vol. III. Illustrations and Facsimilies of Manuscripts . . .
Pitt-Rivers, Julian. 1971. On the Word 'Caste.' *In* Translations of Culture. T.O. Beidelman, ed. London: Tavistock. pp. 231–356.
Pocock, David F. 1967. The Anthropology of Time-reckoning. *In* Myth and Cosmos. John Middleton, ed. Garden City: The Natural History Press. pp. 303–14.
Powell, Hickman. 1930. The Last Paradise. New York: Jonathan Cape and Harrison Smith.
Punyatmadja, I.B. Oka. 1970. Pancha Cradha. Den Pasar: Parasada Hindu Dharma Pusat.
Purchas, S. 1625. Hakluytus Posthumous or Purchas His Pilgrimes, Volume 5. 1905 Reprint of 1625 edition. Glasgow: The Hakluyt Society.
Puthra, I Ktut. 1954. Riwayat Djayaprana. Den Pasar.
Raffles, Thomas Stamford. 1817. The History of Java. Two volumes. London: Black, Parbury, and Allen.
Raka, I Gusti Gde. 1955. Monografi Pulau Bali. Jakarta: Bagian Publikasi Pusat Djawatan Pertanian Rakjat.
Ras, J.J. 1973. The Panji Romance and W.H. Rassers' Analysis of its Theme. Bijdragen tot der Land-, Taal- en Volkenkunde. 129 (4): 411–56.
Rassers, W.H. 1922. De Pandji-roman. Dissertation, University of Leiden.
1960. Panji, the Culture Hero: A Structural Study of Religion in Java. The Hague: Martinus Nijhoff.
Ravenholt, Albert. 1973. Man-Land-Productivity Microdynamics in Rural Bali. American University Fieldstaff Reports. Southeast Asia Series. XXXI (4).

Ravenswaay, J.V. 1941. 'Tenged'-begrip op Bali: Baliers laten uitgestrekte stukken grond niet zonder reden onbenut invloeden van aardstralen. Wat de Volksmond zegt. Java-Bode, January 31, 1941. Batavia.
Robson, S.O. 1971. Wangbang Wideya: A Javanese Panji Romance . . . Bibliotheca Indonesica. Koninklijk Instituut voor Taal-, Land- en Volkenkunde 6. The Hague: Martinus Nijhoff.
1972. The Kawi Classics in Bali. Bijdragen tot de Land-, Taal- en Volkenkunde. 128 (2–3): 307–29.
Rouffaer, G.P. 1906. Introduction of Nieuwenkamp (1906–10). Bali en Lombok. Reisherinneringen en Studies omtrent Land en Volk, Kunst en Kunstnijverheid. 2 vols. Edam.
Rouffaer, G.P. and J.W. Ijzerman, eds. 1915. De Eerste Schipvaart der Nederlanders naar Oost-Indië onder Cornelis de Houtman, 1595–1597. Volumes 7, 25, 32. I. D'eerste Boeck van Willem Lodewycksz. Lindschoten Vereeniging.
1925. De Eerste Schipvaart der Nederlanders naar Oost-Indië onder Cornelis de Houtman, 1595–1597. Volumes 7, 25, 32. II. De Oudste Journalen der Reis. Lindschoten Vereeniging.
1929. De Eerste Schipvaart der Nederlanders naar Oost-Indië onder Cornelis de Houtman, 1595–1597. Volumes 7, 25, 32. III. Verdere Bescheiden Betreffende de Reis. Lindschoten Vereeniging.
Sahlins, Marshal. 1963. Poor Man, Rich Man, Big Man, Chief: Political Types in Melanesia and Polynesia. Comparative Studies in Society and History. 5: 285.
1973. Tribesmen. Englewood Cliffs: Prentice-Hall.
Samson, Allen. 1973. Kebatinan and Islam in Indonesia: Genesis of a Conflict. Paper presented at the 25th Annual Meeting of the Association for Asian Studies.
Sarkar, Himansu Bhusan. 1970. Some Contributions of India to the Ancient Civilization of Indonesia and Malaysia. Calcutta: Punthi Pustak.
Sartono, Kartodirjo. 1973. Protest Movements in Rural Java. New York: Oxford University Press.
Schneider, David M. and Raymond T. Smith. 1973. Class Differences and Sex Roles in American Kinship and Family Structure. Englewood Cliffs: Prentice-Hall, Inc.
Schrieke, B. 1955. Indonesian Sociological Studies; Part I. The Hague: W. van Hoeve.
1957. Indonesian Sociological Studies: Selected Writings, Part Two – Ruler and Realm in Early Java. The Hague: W. van Hoeve.
Sedjarah Parisada Hindu Dharma. 1970. Disimpun oleh Sekretarian Parisada Hindu Dharma Pusat. Den Pasar: Balimas.
Sedjarah Singkat Pura Batur Wanasari. n.d. Anonymous Indonesian Typescript obtained from I Gde Ktut Buwana.
Seton, Grace Thompson. 1940. Poison Arrows – A Strange Journey with an Opium Dreamer through Annom, Cambodia, Siam, and the Lotus Isle of Bali. New York: House of Field.
Short Account . . . 1930. Short Account of the Island of Bali, particularly of Bali Baliling. Singapore Chronicle, June, 1930. Reprinted in Notices of the Indian Archipelago and Adjacent Countries. Under the authorship of J.H. Moor. Reprinted 1968. London: Frank Cass.
Singer, Milton. 1972. When a Great Tradition Modernizes: an Anthropological Approach to Indian Civilization. New York: Praeger Publishers, Inc.
Sloan, Stephen. 1971. A Study in Political Violence: The Indonesian Experience. Chicago: Rand McNally & Company.

Soebadio, Haryati, ed. and trans. 1971. Jnanasiddhanta. Bibliotheca Indonesica. The Hague: Martinus Nijhoff.
Srinivas, M.N. 1968. Mobility in the Caste Ssytem. *In* Structure and Change in Indian Society. M. Singer and B. Cohn, eds. Chicago: Aldine Publishing Company.
1969. Social Change in Modern India. Berkeley: University of California Press.
Van Stein Callenfels, P.V. 1947–8. De Rechten der Vorsten op Bali. Indonesië. pp. 193–208.
Steiner, George. 1975. After Babel: Aspects of Language and Translation. London: Oxford University Press.
Strong, Roy. 1973. Splendor at Court: Renaissance Spectacle and the Theater of Power. Boston: Houghton Mifflin Company.
Stutterheim, Willem F. 1935. Indian Influences in Old Balinese Art. London: The India Society.
Sugriwa, I Gusti Bagus. 1957. Babad Pasek dalam Bahasa Indonesia. Den Pasar: Balimas.
Summerson, John N. 1952. Architecture in Britain, 1530 to 1830. New York: Penguin Books.
Sutton, Horace. 1967. Indonesia's Night of Terror. Saturday Review, February 4, 1967. pp. 25–31.
Swellengrebel, J.L. 1948. Kerk en Tempel op Bali. The Hague.
1960. Bali: Some General Information. *In* Bali, Studies. pp. 1–76.
1969 [1948]. Nonconformity in the Balinese Family. *In* Bali, Further Studies. pp. 199–212.
Tarling, Nicholas. 1962. Anglo-Dutch Rivalry in the Malay World, 1780–1924. Cambridge: Cambridge University Press.
Tate, D.J.M. 1971. The Making of Modern South-east Asia. Vol. I. The European Conquest. Kuala Lumpur: Oxford University Press.
Teeuw, A. *et al.*, ed. 1968. Siwaratrikalpa of Mpu Tanakung. Bibliotheca Indonesica 3. The Hague: Martinus Nijhoff.
Tempo. 1972. Tempo, Majalah Berita Mingguan. May 27, 1972. Issue on Bali yang berobah: Bila waktu menjamah Bali. pp. 44–8.
Turner, Victor. 1973. The Center out there: Pilgrim's Goal. History of Religions. 12 (3): 191–230.
Van der Tuuk, H.N. 1897–1912. Kawi-Balineesch-Nederlandsch Woordenboek. Four volumes. Batavia.
Upadeca. 1968. Upadeca: tentang Ajaran-ajaran Agama Hindu. Den Pasar: Parisada Hindu Dharma.
Van Vlijmen, B.R.F. 1875. Bali 1868: Eene Bladzijde der Indische Krijgsgeschiedenis. Amsterdam: J.C. Loman.
Van Vollenhoven. 1918. Het Adatrecht van Nederlandsch-Indië, Vol. I. Leiden.
Vroklage, B.A.G. 1937. Tandvijlfeest op Bali. De Katholieke Missien. 10: 189–192.
Walker, Millidge and Irene Tinker. 1975. Development and Changing Bureaucratic Styles in Indonesia: The Case of the Pamong Praja. Pacific Affairs. 48: 60–73.
Wallace, Anthony F.C. 1961. Culture and Personality. New York: Random House, Inc.
Ward, Donald J. 1968. The Divine Twins: an Indo-European Myth in Germanic Tradition (Folklore Studies: 19). Berkeley: University of California Press.
Warta Dutta Warga. 1971. Numbers 4, 5, 6, 9–10. Den Pasar.
Weitzel. A.W.P. 1859. De Derde Militaire Expeditie naar het Eiland Bali. Gorinchem.

Wertheim, W.F. 1965. The Sociological Approach. *In* An Introduction to Indonesian Historiography. Soedjatmoko, ed. Ithaca: Cornell University Press.
Wilder, W.D. 1973. The Culture of Kinship Studies. Bijdragen tot der Land-, Taal- en Volkenkunde. 129 (1).
Wirz, P. 1927. Der Reisbau aund die Reisbaukulte auf Bali und Lombok. Tijidschrift voor Indische Taal-, Land- en Volkenkunde. LXCII: 217–346.
1928. Der Totenkult auf Bali. Stuttgart.
Worsley, P.J. 1972. Babad Buleleng. Dissertation, University of Leiden. The Hague: Martinus Nijhoff.
Yates, Frances A. 1969. The Theater of the World. Chicago: The University of Chicago Press.
1972. The Rosicrucian Enlightenment. London: Routledge and Kegan Paul.
Zaehner, R.C. 1969. Hindu and Muslim Mysticism. New York: Schocken Books, Inc.
De Zoete, Beryl and Walter Spies. 1939. Dance and Drama in Bali. New York: Harper's Magazine Press.
De Zwann, J.P. Kleiweg. 1919. Denkbeelden der Inlanders van den Indischen Archipel omtrent de Geboorte van Tweelingen. Tijdschrift van het Koninklijk Nederlandsch Aardrijkskundig Genootschap. XXXVI: 145–68.

Index